REVIVAL AFTER THE GREAT WAR

Revival after the Great War
Rebuild, Remember, Repair, Reform

Edited by
Luc Verpoest, Leen Engelen,
Rajesh Heynickx, Jan Schmidt,
Pieter Uyttenhove, and Pieter Verstraete

LEUVEN UNIVERSITY PRESS

Published with the support of the KU Leuven Fund for Fair Open Access, the City of Leuven and LUCA School of Arts

Published in 2020 by Leuven University Press / Presses Universitaires de Louvain / Universitaire Pers Leuven. Minderbroedersstraat 4, B-3000 Leuven (Belgium).
© 2020 Selection and editorial matter: Luc Verpoest, Leen Engelen, Rajesh Heynickx, Jan Schmidt, Pieter Uyttenhove, and Pieter Verstraete
© 2020 Individual chapters: The respective authors

This book is published under a Creative Commons Attribution Non-Commercial Non-Derivative 4.0 International Licence.

The license allows you to share, copy, distribute, and transmit the work for personal and non-commercial use providing author and publisher attribution is clearly stated. Attribution should include the following information:
Luc Verpoest, Leen Engelen, Rajesh Heynickx, Jan Schmidt, Pieter Uyttenhove, and Pieter Verstraete (eds.). *Revival after the Great War: Rebuild, Remember, Repair, Reform.* Leuven, Leuven University Press. (CC BY-NC-ND 4.0)
Further details about Creative Commons licenses are available at http://creativecommons.org/licenses/

ISBN 978 94 6270 250 9 (Paperback)
ISBN 978 94 6166 354 2 (ePDF)
ISBN 978 94 6166 355 9 (ePUB)
https://doi.org/10.11116/9789461663542

D/2020/1869/60
NUR: 648

Layout: Friedemann Vervoort
Cover design: Anton Lecock
Cover illustration: A family posing on the Old Market in Leuven (Belgium) around 1921.
(© City Archive Leuven)

Table of Contents

Acknowledgements

Introduction
Revival After The First World War: Rebuild, Remember, Repair, Reform
Luc Verpoest, Leen Engelen, Rajesh Heynickx, Jan Schmidt, Pieter Uyttenhove & Pieter Verstraete   10

PART ONE — REBUILD   33

Catastrophe and Reconstruction in Western Europe: The Urban Aftermath of the First World War
Pierre Purseigle   36

Reflections on Leuven as Martyred City and the Realignment of Propinquity
Richard Plunz   54

Making Good Farmers by Making Better Farms: Farmstead Architecture and Social Engineering in Belgium After the Great War
Dries Claeys & Yves Segers   64

"C'est la beauté de l'ensemble qu'il faut viser." Notes on Changing Heritage Values of Belgian Post-World War I Reconstruction Townscapes
Maarten Liefooghe   86

Rebuilding, Recovery, Reconceptualization: Modern architecture and the First World War
Volker M. Welter   106

PART TWO — REMEMBER   123

Reclaiming the Ordinary: Civilians Face the Post-war World
Tammy M. Proctor   126

Expressing Grief and Gratitude in an Unsettled Time
Temporary First World War Memorials in Belgium
Leen Engelen & Marjan Sterckx   140

Remembering the War on the British Stage: From Resistance to
Reconstruction
Helen E. M. Brooks 164

A War to Learn From: Commemorative Practices in Belgian Schools
After World War I
Kaat Wils 178

PART THREE — REPAIR 197

High Expectations and Silenced Realities: The Re-education of Belgian
Disabled Soldiers of the Great War, 1914–1921
Pieter Verstraete and Marisa De Picker 200

Back to work: Riccardo Galeazzi's Work for the Mutilated Veterans of
the Great War, Between German Model and Italian Approach
Simonetta Polenghi 218

Competition over Care: The Campaign for a New Medical Campus at
the University of Leuven in the 1920s
Joris Vandendriessche 238

PART FOUR — REFORM 253

An Argentine Witness of the Occupation and Reconstruction of
Belgium: The Writings of Roberto J. Payró (1918-1922)
María Inés Tato 256

The New Post-war Order from the Perspective of the Spanish Struggle
for Regeneration (1918-1923)
Carolina García Sanz 268

The Act of Giving: Political Instability and the Reform(ation) of
Humanitarian Responses to Violence in Portugal in the Aftermath of
the First World War
Ana Paula Pires 282

Reconstruction, Reform and Peace in Europe after the First World War
John Horne 296

Bibliography 317

List of Contributors 347

Acknowledgements

The present publication first wants to warmly welcome its readers, critically inquisitive and eager to learn. They are naturally indispensable for the real life of any book.

This book has been quite a long time in the making. Now that it's here and in your hands, we would like to take a moment to thank some people and institutions who have been of great importance for this project. First, we wish to thank the contributors to this book for sharing their research and insights, for their commitment to this book and for their patience: Helen Brooks, Dries Claeys, Marisa De Picker, Leen Engelen, Carolina Garcia Sanz, John Horne, Maarten Liefooghe, Richard Plunz, Ana Paula Pires, Tammy Proctor, Simonetta Polenghi, Pierre Purseigle, Yves Segers, Marjan Sterckx, Maria Inés Tato, Joris Vandendriessche, Pieter Verstraete, Volker M. Welter and Kaat Wils.

The six members of the editorial board, also authors of the general introduction, Rajesh Heynickx, Leen Engelen, Jan Schmidt, Pieter Uyttenhove, Luc Verpoest and Pieter Verstraete first met as members of the scientific committees of the *Revival. Leuven after 1918* exhibition (Leuven, May-November 2018) and international conference, *Revival After the Great War* (Leuven, May 2018), to which this book is the capstone.

The 2018 Leuven exhibition and international conference were a joint initiative of the then mayor of the City of Leuven, Louis Tobback, in collaboration with the Rectorate of the University of Leuven and the then rector, Rik Torfs. Thanks to both of them for their organizational and financial support and to their successors, rector Luc Sels, vice-rector Bart Raymaekers, and Mayor Mohamed Ridouani for their continued encouragement. Curators of the exhibition were Luc Verpoest (KU Leuven) and Joke Buijs (City of Leuven). Organizational support for the conference was provided by Dominique De Brabanter (Conference and Events Office, KU Leuven) and Lesja Vandensande (coordinator of the project for the City of Leuven).

A book only really comes to life when it is duly published. Many thanks to Leuven University Press for seeing this book to fruition. Thanks to the anonymous reviewers of the book for their just and encouraging comments. Thanks also to Kate Elliott for the language editing, to Aurel Baele for his invaluable help with the bibliography, to Rebecca Gysen and Liesbet Croimans of the Leuven City Archive for providing illustrations and advice, and to all archival institutions and documentation centres worldwide, contacted by the individual authors, for providing illustrations.

This book was published with the generous financial support of the KU Leuven Fund for Fair Open Access, the City of Leuven and LUCA School of Arts.

Luc Verpoest & Leen Engelen,
Principal editors

Rajesh Heynickx, Jan Schmidt, Pieter Uyttenhove & Pieter Verstraete,
Members of the editorial board

No, this much is clear: experience has fallen in value, amid a generation which from 1914 to 1918 had to experience some of the most monstrous events in the history of the world. Perhaps this is less remarkable than it appears. Wasn't it noticed at the time how many people returned from the front in silence? Not richer but poorer in communicable experience? And what poured out from the flood of war books ten years later was anything but the experience that passes from mouth to ear. No, there was nothing remarkable about that. For never has experience been contradicted more thoroughly: strategic experience has been contravened by positional warfare; economic experience, by the inflation; physical experience, by hunger; moral experiences, by the ruling powers. A generation that had gone to school in horse-drawn streetcars now stood in the open air, amid a landscape in which nothing was the same except the clouds and, at its centre, in a force field of destructive torrents and explosions, the tiny, fragile human body.

Walter Benjamin, *Experience and Poverty* (1933).

Introduction
Revival After The First World War: Rebuild, Remember, Repair, Reform

Luc Verpoest, Leen Engelen, Rajesh Heynickx,
Jan Schmidt, Pieter Uyttenhove & Pieter Verstraete

2018 marked the 100th anniversary of Armistice Day, 11 November 1918. Ironically, "the war that would end all wars" turned out to be a war whose end was long anticipated but "that failed to end" nevertheless.[1] For some, the end of the war was already in sight in 1917: the Russian revolution, the American entry into the war, the Brest-Litovsk Treaty (signed in March 1918 between Germany and Russia) had the potential to turn the tide. Nonetheless, new complexities extended the war by another year. While the conflict was still ongoing and the final offensive came into view, reconstruction was prematurely on the agenda. Concrete initiatives, such as the rebuilding of the first of the burned homes in the "martyred city" of Leuven, anticipated large-scale post-war reconstruction initiatives. At the same time the rhetoric of responsibility, sacrifice, gratitude and economic compensation – that would reach its height in Versailles in 1919 – was already a common trope across the media and civil societies.

The Great War brought about a dramatic and comprehensive political, social and economic disruption. In the 1920s soldiers and civilians alike had to recover, rebuild, repair, reform, while keeping and cultivating – almost compulsively – the memory of that great human disaster of the Great War. The official commemoration of war – ceremonies, cemeteries, monuments – prioritised military casualties. Civilians – the millions of family members of millions of killed soldiers and many others not at all involved in war politics… – have been very much forgotten, if not ignored. Only rarely did commemorative events and war memorials in the 1920s pay attention to them. The same is true for war historiographies, still dealing very much with military power and political tactics as a breeding ground for political regimes that fundamentally did not testify to humanising and civilising intentions. The emergence of a cultural history of the Great War since the 1990s –through the work of research centres such as the *Historial de la Grande Guerre* in Péronne (France) and initiatives such as the *International Society for First World War Studies* in 2001 (with the publication of the *First World War Studies* journal since 2010) – explicitly extended "war studies" from the strictly political and military to a global and comparative perspective on the war and its international consequences, thus substantially expanding the scope of research in chronological, geographic and topical terms. The present publication is another testimony to these research reorientations, with "distinctive approaches and perspectives" and "without preconceived chronological, geographical or topical constraints", focusing above all on the recovery of daily life in all its facets against the background of major political, economic and societal transformations.[2]

History: past and present

The First World War set off a war machine that threatened never to stop and eventually never really did. The breakthrough of a brutal militaristic culture, in combination with a radical nationalism and revolutionary violence, remains a crucial legacy of the First World War.[3] The revanchist spirit in countries which had lost the war – or those countries that believed that they did not get their fair share in the peace settlements – and the violence that accompanied the transition from war to peace in many parts of the world were in more than one way accountable for the rise of aggressive dictatorships that eventually led to the Second World War.[4] Yet, historians have stressed the complexity of the relationship between the First and the Second World Wars and pointed rather at the importance of factors such as imperialism and geopolitics.[5]

When assessing the post-war era, one should not overlook the fact that the First World War also occasioned a strong dissemination of international cooperation that favoured a peaceful, tolerant and non-violent attitude, aiming at a humanitarian solution for conflicts in the future. But these new or renewed international movements were also confronted with nationalist and authoritarian ideologies and regimes. It is safe to say that international solidarity regularly came under pressure with the erosion of post-war democratisation processes as a consequence.[6] The war was not just the cause of such disruption; the constant threat of further armed conflicts and military violence across Europe and beyond also continued to hamper society's recovery in the 1920s in a context that remained particularly fragile and uncertain.[7] The economic crisis from 1929 onwards further brought whatever recovery had been achieved to a de facto standstill. An international debt crisis, massive unemployment, impoverishment and aggravated political unrest further fed the ongoing struggle to survive between one crisis and the next and created an ideal breeding ground for another war. In parallel to that, European colonial powers were already confronted, in the 1920s, with worldwide independence movements that finally led to the definitive loss of their "colonial possessions" after the Second World War. Also, the construction of the post-colonial world and the decolonisation of minds and politics can be considered a difficult and still ongoing process to rebuild, remember, repair and reform.[8]

The global political consequences of more than a few issues that emerged during or after the First World War are still palpable today. Nevertheless, the official commemoration of the 100th anniversary of the Armistice – at least in Western Europe[9] – was still predominantly the expression of "a no longer contested friendship between European nations". However, in that friendly atmosphere of commemoration "more delicate issues [were] rarely touched upon", such as the role of the First World War in sustaining European imperialism and colonialism.[10] We could, to cite only one example, refer to the global political consequences of the Sykes-Picot treaty of 1916 and its significance for the making of the modern Middle East after the Second World War, to understand its ultimate impact on the contemporary problems in the region and worldwide, "to understand that at least a few of the issues raised but not solved by the Great War and its immediate aftermath are still with us today".[11]

Rebuild, Remember, Repair, Reform

When considering the ravages wrought by war, material rebuilding or reconstruction is often the first thing that comes to mind. Bricks and mortar are the tangible prerequisites and thus the starting point for a wider process of societal recovery and revival of daily life in all its aspects: housing, healthcare, education, labour and leisure, culture …. We like to think of the post-war era as an era of "reconstruction", as rebuilding is probably the most perceptible result of that process. In the first instance, this notion of reconstruction refers to the rebuilding or reassembling of something demolished or broken – as in a building or a city, but also in relation to the human body (think of reconstructive surgery). Another meaning of the word is of course "to re-create or reimagine (something from the past)", with the aim of gaining an "accurate understanding" of a particular occurrence, event or process: history as (re-)construction, as constructed narrative.[12] This reconstruction is usually based on thorough research of physical evidence and source material, an activity in which those involved in historical research have special interest and skill. So, when we speak of "reconstruction" in relation to the post-war era, we speak not only of buildings, but also of bodies and of narratives, processes, practices and events that can be uncovered by historical research. The editors chose to streamline these issues along thematic lines of action. The already long tradition of "reconstruction history", mainly as part of architectural and urban historiography, is used as a blueprint. Accordingly, next to the topic of "Rebuild" the themes of "Repair", "Remember" and "Reform" are taken as anchor points in this volume. These particular fields of action are all essential to the overall societal recovery after total disruption through war; to its reactivation, reanimation, restoration, *reveil*, renaissance, rehabilitation, revivification, revitalisation, to its… revival.

"Reconstruction architecture" and actual post-war planning and building have been the subject of ample academic research.[13] The latter shows that the war was not only a serious dislocation of industrial society, but was also seen as a challenge and unique opportunity for architects, urban planners and industries. The war functioned as an accelerator for new policies and practices for urban planning.[14] These "new" pathways were often based on principles that had already germinated before the war, but for different reasons had not blossomed. Rebuilding meant creating a solid material infrastructure that would not only allow society's restauration but also stimulate future-orientated social progress and profound modernisation. At the same time, rebuilding was anchored in the present moment and needed to be meaningful for its dramatically dislocated contemporaries. The sight of familiar buildings and cities, and the good and comforting memories they invoked, offered consolation and perspective.

When the armistice was signed, the war did not disappear. It was over but not forgotten. The "past" put a heavy burden on the present and the future.[15] It was felt in almost every daily activity: working, family life, education, leisure activities… Very quickly, a certain kind of "normalcy" had forced itself upon people. But how do you live and rebuild your life with the heavy weight of the war on your shoulders? Commemorative practices in different social and cultural arenas played a massively important role in this. To remember is to recollect, interpret and narrate the past to bring it into the present. Commemoration practices are fixed on the hinges between the past and the present. They are necessitated by the past, shaped through the prisms of the present, and made instrumental for the future. In that respect they strongly resemble the material reconstruction of society. Ever since the publication of seminal works such as Paul Fussell's *The Great War and Modern Memory* (1972) and Jay Winter's *Sites of Memory, sites of Mourning* (1995) memory has been on the agenda of First World War scholars.[16] Recently, stimulated by the development of Memory Studies as a thriving academic field, scholars have started to investigate the ways in which the war has been commemorated, remembered and represented in terms of mediated memory or post-memory.[17] Meanwhile, the first scholarship on memories "a hundred years on" and the centenary commemorations is being published.[18] It has become almost unthinkable to speak about the post-war period without considering remembrance and commemoration, the bulk of which took place while cities were being rebuilt and landscapes healed. Commemoration practices – religious and civil ceremonies, inauguration of monuments, pilgrimages – are not restricted to dedicated moments and activities. They are implicitly or explicitly present in people's daily lives, in educational programmes or leisure and cultural activities. All these experiences and practices have to be studied in order to understand how the war influenced and became constitutive of individual and communal identities thereafter, constructing the past in order to prepare for the future.

The scholarly interest in remembrance and commemoration practices is only one emanation of the increasing attention to the more intangible aspects of post-war reconstruction. In recent years, the daily physical and mental, individual and communal experiences of people attempting to reclaim and reconfigure their daily lives in dramatically changed circumstances have been put on the research agenda.[19] The war had caused human suffering on an unprecedented scale and this continued to affect society significantly for many years after: the loss of a substantial, young and male part of the population; the social care for widows and orphans; the re-integration of servicemen and prisoners of war in the community, the family and the workforce; the challenging care for those suffering mental and physical mutilation, etc. Of the innumerable questions triggered by the return and presence of invalid or traumatised soldiers many had to do with the social. How to reintegrate a mutilated man into the family he left in one piece?

Like architectural reconstruction, the political devastation after the Great War was seen as an opportunity to reinvigorate political and social reform, both in countries directly involved in the war and in those which were not. Many political, economic, social and cultural reforms taking shape in the late nineteenth century were drastically halted in 1914. The war affected ongoing change and reform. At the same time the scale, global repercussions and overall impact of the war stimulated renewal and reform once it was over. Despite a profoundly changed context, many pre-war reforms were also taken on again or revived. The book sheds light on how the dislocation of the war as well as the manifold processes of physical, social, political, economic and cultural reconstruction inspired post-war reform in and beyond the former belligerent countries. On the one hand, political discussion and reform frequently revealed nationalist and revanchist tendencies within the societies of the former belligerents. On the other hand, the war led to initiatives aiming at strong international cooperation. The League of Nations and similar initiatives fostered peaceful, tolerant and non-violent attitudes and advocated humanitarian solutions for future conflicts. Recent studies on humanitarianism and the implementation of such policies after the war show how they were increasingly confronted with authoritarian ideologies and political systems.[20] Radicalisation, political violence, authoritarianism and populism, imperialism and colonialism put serious pressure on post-war democratisation and reform processes and the international peace movement. These processes were initially successful but soon turned out to be dramatically powerless:

"the war that would end all wars [...] but that ultimately failed to end", recalling Robert Gerwarth's conclusion.

In his essay "Experience and Poverty" (1933), the German philosopher Walter Benjamin focused on the condition of loss that marks modernity. An old, authentic mode of inherited experience (*Erfahrung*), passed on from one generation to another through parables and tales, had become fractured by the lived experience (*Erlebnis*) of a contemporary society, one propelled by mass-consumed technology. This entanglement of an eroding *Erfahrung* and a rapidly changing *Erlebnis*, Benjamin argued, had reached its zenith with the war of 1914-1918:

> For never has experience been contradicted more thoroughly: strategic experience has been contravened by positional warfare; economic experience, by the inflation; physical experience, by hunger; moral experiences, by the ruling powers. [...] A generation that had gone to school in horse-drawn streetcars now stood in the open air, amid a landscape in which nothing was the same except the clouds and, at its center, in a force field of destructive torrents and explosions, the tiny, fragile human body.[21]

Benjamin's analysis of the complete disjunction between the authentic, yet fractured and quickly eroding *Erfahrung* of the war and the lived *Erlebnis* can be used to unpack the layered phenomenon of post-war "rebuilding".[22] Rebuilding, then, means to build in such a way that it works effectively in its own time and to dialogue, integrate or even evoke modern impulses in the process. Yet, rebuilding can also stand for an attempt to return to the "good" situation before the war. Here, a restorative mode, a desire to embrace *Erfahrung* set the agenda. This double movement of "looking forward" while (sometimes literally) "building on the past" is not limited to material reconstruction, but can be traced in numerous facets of post-war society. From very large social and political reforms through which societies were coming to terms with themselves and with others to more idiosyncratic reforms on the level of, for instance, individual hospitals or schools dealing with traumatised returned soldiers and their families. In this volume we extend this idea of what it means to rebuild a society to remembrance practices, physical and mental recovery of those involved in the war and larger social and political reforms.

The Book: A Social History Without Borders

While the main focus of this book is the post-war era, roughly the 1920s and 1930s, the date this story of recovery begins is not necessarily Armistice Day in 1918, nor the signing of the Treaty of Versailles in 1919. One could argue that the process of repairing, rebuilding and even remembering in (former) war zones took off almost immediately after the war started: ruins were cleared, the first war hospitals opened, emergency housing was built, and the first houses rebuilt, infrastructure repaired, the first provisional monuments erected. Pre-war reforms in all areas, dramatically stopped in 1914, were taken up again already during the war, as far as the extremely difficult conditions allowed. Nevertheless, it was only after the war – when the military action had stopped and international relations had been sufficiently restored – that reconstruction and overall recovery could develop fully and for the better. Along the same lines, the impact of many of the processes and policies analysed in this book extends far beyond the 1930s and the Second World War.[23] More than by a clearly demarcated timeframe, this book is characterised by its focus on issues of recovery and further development, transcending the usual chronological borders.

Not only did the war itself have a considerable impact far beyond the theatres of military fighting in Europe, but so did the post-war developments. While many of the chapters in this book focus on the former belligerents in Western Europe, attention is also paid to how the war played out in regions that were not (or not to the same extent) or were only indirectly involved in and affected by military actions during the war. What kind of influence did the processes of physical, social, political, economic and cultural reconstruction of the 1920s and 1930s or their perception have beyond the former main belligerents and beyond Europe? Whether we want to study the 1920s and 1930s as a period between two wars in which overcoming the first one seamlessly blended into preparing for the next one or we want to assess the 1920s and 1930s as the decades logically following the 1910s will depend among other things on the geographical focus chosen.[24]

The book explores a variety of developments in society in the 1920s and 1930s worldwide, in relation to the wartime destruction and disruption, and post-war recovery in Europe. "Rebuild", "Remember", "Repair" and "Reform" are the sections of this book, hereafter further introduced as to each theme and as to the articles in each section.

Rebuild

The first section of the book defends the idea that the development of a city or building that had been damaged or destroyed lined up with multiple temporalities, like the transition from "*Erfahrung*" to "*Erlebnis*" described by Benjamin. In the essays collected in this section the topics Benjamin pointed at, "fragile bodies" or "annihilated landscapes", are present, be it sometimes in a more implicit way. Next to that, the epistemological problem Benjamin raised in "Experience and Poverty", namely the post-war disconnection with clear stories, left an imprint here as well. As we now know, historians will, despite their tremendous and highly varied efforts, never succeed in turning the war's massive madness into a unified narrative of what happened and why.[25] Or as the historian Lucian Hölscher sharply remarked: can one ever understand the lives of so many people who went through the rupture of the war? Would it therefore not be better, he wondered, to develop a "hermeneutics of non-understanding", bringing the limits of understanding more sharply into focus?[26] The essays in the Rebuild section present surprising entry points for understanding the material rebuilding of a world "in which nothing was the same, except the clouds".[27]

If the First World War turned villages, towns and cities into battlefields, their damage and rebuilding are only the visible results of the "complex geographies and temporalities" which intertwined local, national and transnational decisions and policies. In his chapter "Catastrophe and Reconstruction in Western Europe: the urban aftermath of the First World War", Pierre Purseigle clarifies how discourses of reconstruction oblige historians to "rethink and redefine national projects and identities". Reconstruction offered an opportunity for an ambitious programme of urban modernisation that he proposes to consider against the background of an all-encompassing narrative of sacrifice and symbols, as well as material and social efforts or political decision making. As there is no single perspective from where this can be written, multiple networks and organisations operating across national boundaries are to be envisaged.

In "Reflections on Leuven as Martyred City and the Realignment of Propinquity", Richard Plunz is looking over the historian's horizon for the boundaries between historiography, historical interpretation and contemporary criticism. Forty years ago, this American urban planner and historian wondered about the architectural and urbanistic meaning of the rebuilding of Belgium's villages and towns after the war. He initiated important research on this, at the time unexplored, topic. Plunz moves from initial interrogations as "why this largest single urban initiative in Europe in the 20th century" was not included "in the canons of 20th century urbanism", to the question whether this reconstruction could be understood as a "modern project". The exercise Plunz is undertaking here is to cross temporal and disciplinary borders and to continue to question, if not to re-question, the meaning of urban reconstruction in a contemporary context. Realignment ideals of propinquity, "as key to encouraging diversity", are today more than relevant in terms of community, space and place. With Sarajevo, Mosul, Aleppo, Eastern Ghouta and Palmyra in mind, the author wonders "if the most profound remembrance can be to acknowledge that urbicide is alive and well". The rupture Walter Benjamin so powerfully disclosed is definitely not just a faint memory.

In "Making Good Farmers by Making Better Farms: Farmstead Architecture and Social Engineering in Belgium after the Great War", Dries Claeys and Yves Segers unfold a microstudy of the Flemish village of Merkem and, by doing so, illuminate how the destruction of thousands of farms in the Belgian countryside near the Western Front paired traditional ideas on architecture with social progress and insights gained from the war experience. In "Rebuilding, Recovery, Reconceptualization: Modern Architecture and the First World War", Volker Welter zooms in on how architects who had served in the trenches reconfigured their ideas on the integration of architecture in landscapes. Welter tells how the modernist architect Richard Neutra (1892-1970) incorporated his battlefield experiences into his plans for the famous 1946 "Kaufmann Desert House" in Palm Springs, California: also in one of the most important examples of international sytle architecture, the trauma of the old continent loomed. Claeys and Segers contend that the reconstruction of farms not only tried to serve a regionalist mindset by absorbing local materials and traditional typologies, but also wanted to create hygienic, sophisticated production plants. A material restoration went hand in hand with economic modernisation. In sharp contrast to Neutra's Kaufmann house where the smooth surface had to please one client, the regeneration of local communities stood central in the reconstruction of the Flemish countryside. Despite significant differences, the chapters both demonstrate that the rebuilding process was very often grounded in very directive, now often largely forgotten texts. Segers and Claeys reveal that agronomists' model books promoted traditional labour divisions under the roof of newly built farms, while Welter teaches us how combat manuals were sublimated in modernist architecture.

The paper by Maarten Liefooghe takes a slightly different stand. Here, the historian is intentionally not considering the indescribable individual sufferings or personal experiences. Liefooghe – as well as Purseigle – looks at the ways war damage is dealt with from an explicitly collective point of view. Both authors explore how cities and local governments, nation-states and international administrative bodies became mediators between the material conditions and the moral wellbeing of larger collectives. In "'C'est la beauté de l'ensemble qu'il faut viser'. Notes on Changing Heritage Values of Belgian Post World War I Reconstruction Townscapes" ["It's the beauty of the ensemble one has to keep in mind"], Liefooghe explores how reconstructed cityscapes can have a commemorative ambition and perform as "memorial landscapes". He points out that post-war reconstructed towns and cities should be seen as "total monuments", similar to monuments erected to commemorate fallen soldiers. The particular care taken in making rebuilt urban environments look more beautiful than before the destruction is, in Liefooghe's opinion, to be apprehended as a commemorative aestheticisation: urban beauty was thought suitable to unlock the reconstructed total landscape as a *lieu de mémoire*. Referring to the work of Austrian art historian Aloïs Riegl – a thinker who had a profound influence on Walter Benjamin – the author acknowledges in these rebuilt but historicising urban landscapes "intentional-commemorative values". The same values also play an important role in assessing and valorising the rebuilt cities as heritage today.

Remember

The essays in the "Remember" section of this book look at a variety of practices and experiences aimed at remembering the war as well as at looking forward to the future from the vantage point of the present. Many of these practices took place at the same time as urban planners and architects were (planning) rebuilding the devastated areas, and similar issues were at stake. The commemorative practices described here are shaped by different – often gendered – war experiences and different geographical, political and social spaces. They speak of remembering and remembrance in significantly diverse but interconnected contexts or arenas of daily life, such as education, entertainment, religion, household economics.... These narratives come to the historian through different sources: from the private diary to the public stage. All four essays focus on what could be called a different "materiality" of remembrance: personal accounts, war memorials, schoolbooks and curricula and publicly performed plays. Tammy Proctor's essay "Reclaiming the Ordinary: Civilians Face the Post-war World" on how civilians reclaim and negotiate the "ordinary" or the "normal" in the face of the significant obstacles of the immediate post-war era takes individual accounts, diaries and letters as its starting point. Through these accounts she looks at how individuals were dealing with the consequences of the war against the background of political decisions, rules and regulations, (r)evolutions and societal change. In addition to foregrounding non-combatants' efforts to become visible in post-war society, Proctor pays close attention to the gendered post-war representations of the war experiences of women from all social strata, broadening our understanding of post-war recovery and commemoration.

Proctor's analysis sets the stage for the essays that follow. The commemorative practices taking place in public space, in schools or on the theatre stage – analysed in the essays by Leen Engelen and Marjan Sterckx, Kaat Wils, and Helen Brooks – are created and lived by those very same people described by Proctor as those trying to reclaim the ordinary. Her interest in the immediate post-war period – the first 18 months after the armistice – is shared by Leen Engelen and Marjan Sterckx in their essay "Expressing Grief and Gratitude in an Unsettled Time: Temporary First World War Memorials in Belgium". It is commonly known that the First World War led to a flood of war memorials in the late 1910s and early 1920s. Before permanent memorials were constructed, ephemeral monuments and temporary commemorative arrangements such as (flower) shrines and wooden or plaster structures were erected in public spaces. Engelen and Sterckx concentrate on these very first public and material acts of remembrance. In formerly occupied territories, such as Belgium and Northern France, the need to express grief as well as gratitude – which had been suppressed by the occupation regime for over four years – exploded as soon as the armistice was signed. Ideas for monuments surfaced instantly on the national and local levels. Not all of these intentions materialised, and many did so only after a long time because the financial, logistic and administrative structures required to build permanent monuments were often missing. As a consequence, this determination to commemorate resulted in temporary ephemeral memorials. Through the contextualising and analysis of several early examples, the authors demonstrate the agency of civilians in these mostly grassroots initiatives and show that the design of these memorials meandered between existing (national, religious, artistic) traditions and spontaneous ad hoc creativity. Through the ephemeral nature of the memorials, the (literal) fragility of commemoration as well as the importance of the momentum for these practices is laid bare. The moment of their creation is indeed of crucial importance.

This is also true for the British war-themed theatre described by Helen Brooks. In her essay "Remembering the War on the British Stage. From Resistance to Reconstruction" she considers the extent to which the post-war theatre either broke away from or continued wartime theatrical practices. While previous studies largely focussed on the professional London stage, Brooks casts a wider net and argues that looking beyond the British capital and at the full spread of professional and non-professional theatrical activity shows that rather than turning away from the war as a theme, theatre makers repeatedly returned to, remembered and re-staged the war throughout the 1920s. They did so not only through the production of new plays but also through continuing to stage war plays first written and performed during the war. Central to this chapter, therefore, is not simply the recovery of a post-war landscape of war-themed theatre, but rather the analysis of the distinctive ways in which the different types of productions – revivals and continuing productions of wartime plays and new war-themed plays – functioned in the context of remembrance and reconstruction. Productions of wartime plays provided a space of resistance to peace and reconciliation, whilst the production of new plays enabled the exploration of peacetime demands for rehabilitation and reconstruction.

Like Brooks, Kaat Wils shows how different remembrance practices are characterised by different temporalities and (de)mobilising processes. In her essay "A War to Learn From. Commemorative Practices in Belgian Schools after World War I" Wils takes a longer-term perspective on remembrance practices in the educational context. Her focal points are in-school commemorative practices for fallen (former) students (remembrance ceremonies, small monuments) and school excursions to the former front zone. Considering these two types of remembrance practices, Helen Brooks and Kaat Wils demonstrate that the two practices involved different concepts of memory. In the case of school ceremonies and monuments, the main aim was to link different generations. Students who had died for their fatherland and who had behaved courageously had to inspire the soldiers of the future. In field trips to the front it was not the connection between the dead and the living, but abhorrence at the sight of so much destruction, that was stimulated. Here, the past could not possibly be a model for the future. Because of this "negative" approach, this remembrance practice would survive political and cultural demobilisation and remain meaningful until well into the 1930s.

Repair

All human interactions with the past, commemorative practices and historiography included, necessarily are no more than fragmentary accounts of what exactly took place at a particular moment in time and what these events or processes meant, then and now. Trying to cope with this so-called "mutilated" account of the past is considered one of the most important challenges for contemporary historians, one which becomes very clear when taking a closer look at the third theme of this book, namely "repair". Confronted with the unimaginable scale of human suffering in relation to the First World War, one can wonder whether the acceptance of "non-understanding" is the only option for us today. Is first-hand experience the only entry point to a true understanding of history? Would it deepen our insight into large-scale human suffering – and recovery – associated with the Great War if we had experienced it at first hand, in the muddy and stinking trenches or fearfully waiting at home? Even if we had lived through all of that, the sufferings, the fears, the dreams and aspirations of all those millions of soldiers and civilians would probably still remain strange to us, intangible as it were.

What the veterans of World War One experienced is forever lost. We, of course, can try to come as close to their experiences as we can, but we will never be able to relive what they went through; we will never be capable of reviving their most intimate emotions, hopes and fears. An important reason for our inability completely to understand the atrocities of the past of course has to do with the fact that the meanings of concepts like "suffering", "pain", "happiness" and "boredom" continuously shift throughout time. Different positions are possible vis-à-vis the unavoidable strangeness of the past – as sketched out here. It can be criticised for being the unfortunate heir of postmodern thinking; it can be unmasked as an ultimate attempt to forget about or downplay previous disasters; it can be praised for the implicit epistemological humbleness or heralded for its aesthetic reconfiguration of time and space. These divergent ways of dealing with the strangeness of our past are not only legitimate, but also necessary; and perhaps also superficial. For is it not the case that whether one now believes that one can faithfully reconstruct the suffering of a veteran bleeding to death in no man's land, or that one is convinced that we can only guess what it was like, that one is capable of or interested in producing a narrative that might inspire the person who reads it; the one to whom it is being told.

The power of history has to do with the inherent capacity of reminding current and future generations of something that one has deemed important enough to safeguard for the future. The presence of those who returned from the war without a leg or two arms, without sound reason, or without the ability to hear was a constant reminder of the war and its stakes. Their presence in post-war society had consequences on an intergenerational level. How does one play with a man who says he is your father and who cannot hit a ball as both his legs were amputated after a shell exploded in the trenches? If these questions already caused a lot of anger, sadness and misunderstanding in the family context, the presence of the mutilated men and the measures taken to repair them also caused a lot of unrest in post-war societies trying to rebuild themselves as a whole. The paying of pensions, the funding of care facilities and special infrastructures, campaigns for reintegration in the workforce, etc. put a heavy financial burden on post-war societies and were often fiercely debated. These mutilated men in a sense can be considered as men that need to be "repaired". Hence the title of the third section of this book. They were repaired in the sense that they were medically fixed and professionally rehabilitated in order to make them "whole" again, the idea being that they would be able to function just as they did before the war. In many cases this complete reparation turned out to be a fiction. In contrast to the material rebuilding of cities and houses, the reparation of people was never an improvement compared to their pre-war condition.

The "repair" section brings together scholarship focussing on the ideologies, institutions, individuals and societies behind the "repairing" of war invalids after the war. While the essays of Pieter Verstaete and Marisa De Picker, and Simonetta Polenghi make their case by focusing on the rehabilitation of disabled soldiers from the First World War, Joris Vandendriessche's contribution ("Competition over Care. The Campaign for a New Medical Campus at the University of Leuven in the 1920s") rather aims to unveil the importance of ideology in the reconstruction of hospitals after the war. Despite the substantial amount of new research published in recent years on the history of disabled soldiers from the Great War, the approach taken by Verstraete and De Picker is definitely innovative.[28] In their contribution on the rehabilitation of Belgian (physically or sensorially) disabled soldiers ("High Expectations and Silenced Realities: The Re-education of Belgian Disabled Soldiers of the Great War, 1914-1921") they demythologise the contemporary rehabilitative discourse by revaluing the invalid soldier's agency and by reconsidering the importance of medical sciences for these individuals – as well as for scholars interested in the disability.

The work by Simonetta Polenghi, while also dealing with the rehabilitation of disabled soldiers, takes a more comparative approach. In her chapter entitled "Back to work. Riccardo Galeazzi's Work for the Mutilated Veterans of the Great War, Between German Model and Italian Approach" she reconstructs the international exchanges – in this case between Italy and Germany – that have led to the realisation of concrete educational practices for disabled soldiers.[29] She does so by meticulously looking into how the main Italian specialists in the rehabilitation of disabled soldiers drew their inspiration from the German tradition of taking care of so-called "crippled persons".

If the chapters by Verstraete and De Picker and by Polenghi focus on the repair of bodies and the need to distinguish between the discourse and the reality of rehabilitative practices, Joris Vandendriessche's chapter unravels the complex interplay between hospital reforms and ideologies. Medicine, whether applied to disabled soldiers or sick citizens, cannot be disconnected from ideological debates about what it means to be a human being. Making use of a Belgian case study, namely the restoration of the Leuven hospital facilities during and after the Great War, Vandendriessche demonstrates this ideological embeddedness of the different initiatives that were taken in order to revive hospital care.[30] Together, the essays in this part of the book demonstrate how the notion of "repair" is crucial to a wide and comprehensive understanding of the rebuilding of the world after the Great War.

Reform

The chapters in the fourth section testify to the truly international dimension of post-war reform. In the post-war years the global political, socio-economic and cultural imaginaries were more interconnected than ever, yet there were vast geographical differences. Local specificities led to a variety of post-war settings in which socio-economic problems, but in many cases also political instability and violence, played a major role. This was certainly the case in many East Asian or Latin American settings.[31] Maria Inés Tató's analysis ("An Argentine Witness of the Occupation and Reconstruction of Belgium: The Writings of Roberto J. Payró, 1918-1922") of writer and journalist Roberto J. Payró's post-war chronicles in the Buenos Aires newspaper *La Nación* for which he served as a correspondent in Brussels (1909-1922) focuses on the impact of post-war political and social reform and reconstruction in Belgium on discussions on political and social modernisation and reform in his home country, Argentina. Payró was particularly interested in issues such as social legislation, the recovery of an industrial economy, social housing policies and political reform, like the concept of coalition governments and the establishment of universal suffrage in post-war Belgium. Tató stresses the importance of the Belgian case in providing tools and examples for economic and political modernisation to young Latin American countries such as Argentina, and thus demonstrates the global reverberations of post-war reform.

The impact of post-war reform beyond the belligerent countries is further explored by Carolina Garcia Sanz. In her contribution entitled "The New Post-war Order from the Perspective of the Spanish Struggle for Regeneration (1918-1923)" she discusses the Spanish public representations of the conflict and the dynamics of reconstruction in Europe from 1918 to 1923. Although Spain remained neutral, the war had a profound impact on Spanish society and indirectly contributed to the implosion of the political system in the interwar years. Social activists hoped that the tumultuous international circumstances would force change in Spain as well. The war had provided statesmen, prominent thinkers, journalists and new societal groups such as the so-called "New Women" with the prospect – real or imagined – of national regeneration. In the early 1920s, public debates around Spanish modernisation in the midst of social conflict and violence leading to General Miguel Primo de Rivera's coup d'état (1923) intertwined with the post-war reconstruction elsewhere in Europe. The post-war did not just bring recovery and reform. Instability and revolution (temporarily) took hold of many countries.

The Portuguese case, described by Ana Paula Pires, fits the continuum of violence that, according to Robert Gerwarth, characterised the transition from war to peace well into the 1920s and even beyond. Once the Great War had ended, Portugal – having fought on African and Flanders' battlefields – almost vanished from the international stage (even if present at the Versailles Peace Conference) and was absorbed by political instability and (contra)revolutionary violence. In her chapter, "The Act of Giving: Political Instability and the Reform(ation) of Humanitarian Responses to Violence in Portugal in the Aftermath of the First World War", Pires focuses on the role and importance of humanitarian aid in times of post-war political instability and crisis. She demonstrates how in post-war Portugal humanitarian aid and medical assistance had to be directed not only to returning wounded soldiers but also to civilian victims of political violence and investigates the motives and implementation strategies of humanitarian aid, more particularly by the Portuguese Red Cross which acted as an intermediary between the government and revolutionary groups both during and after the war.

Finally, John Horne's contribution on reform and peace in post-war Europe can be read as a general comparative reflection on political, social and cultural transformation after the Great War. Throughout a series of case studies he covers a wide spectrum of possibilities for post-war reconstruction. Introducing the cases of the rebuilding of Salonika (now Thessaloniki) in Greece and the recovery of the universities of Leuven and Paris, Horne shows how in the years following the war architecture and urbanism got stuck between national(ist) aspirations, inter-allied cooperation and international collaboration. From the mid-1920s onwards – influenced by international initiatives such as the Locarno Treaty, the Briand Kellogg Treaty and the League of Nations – reconciliation between former enemies came to the fore. This tendency is visible in the case of Henri Sellier's plans for the garden district of Suresnes (France), which was an architectural emanation of the belief that peace and social progress were inseparable. In a final case study Horne shows that the impressive and perhaps somewhat pompous neo-classical headquarters of the League of Nations in Geneva (Switzerland) are a prime example of internationalism and cultural demobilisation.

Coda

Global conditions today – with massive displacement, climate change and growing ideological and political tensions – force us to reflect upon history, or at least ask questions with regard to the role of historical research. The international refugee crisis today incites parallels with the massive displacement taking place in the First World War, for instance in Belgium, France, Italy and Russia. The question can be raised to what extent historical scholarship related to, for instance, refugees and migrations in the 1920s and 1930s can identify continuities and divergences which might help in exposing structural historical links with current events or can at least challenge them in historical terms. Could critical understanding of this complex issue help to inspire or even define the huge task of restoring disrupted societies the world is confronted with today?

Nowadays, the societal debate frequently refers to "the new 1920s". Key topics in the post-First World War years – such as disruption by war and recovery, modernisation and traditionalism, internationalisation and globalisation, borders and refugees, radicalism and nationalism, peace and militarism, patriotism and populism, humanitarianism and oppression – are unmistakably present today too. Now, as well as in the 1920s, individual lives are heavily affected by these large, fundamental and comprehensive political, social and economic transitions and disruptions: people have to recover, rebuild, repair, remember and reform as well. A knowledge and true understanding of the 1920s' and 1930s' social history of post-war reconstruction and recovery is useful and perhaps essential to understand later and even today's political events and global developments. Histories and memories are essential also to imagining any possible future.[32]

The present book offers a wide scope of recent research that goes beyond the war itself and its military and political strategies and actually focuses explicitly on societal dimensions, particularly dealing with the everyday lives of common people in post-war times.[33] It covers a variety of societal developments in the interwar years and beyond that were prompted by the wartime destruction and disruption, also in countries outside the actual theatres of war, inside and outside Europe. The book is about the ways in which societies were rebuilt or reconstructed – in the largest sense of the word – against the background of complex post-war political, military, diplomatic, social, economic and cultural conditions. The research presented in this book tackles questions that can lead to broader, deeper and more inclusive history-based insights. Beyond mere historical understanding, they inspire us to be critical about present and future global developments, and hopefully help us to take appropriate action. More comprehensively, this raises the question about the aims of historical research and other historical practices, and about its "efficiency" to remember in any relevant way. How and why do we want to remember what about the First World War and its far-reaching consequences?

Notes

1. Robert Gerwarth, *The Vanquished: Why the First World War Failed to End, 1917-1923* (Oxford: Allen Lane, 2016).
2. "If there is a singular goal of First World War Studies, it will be to cleave the many insular, too often national particularisms, specializations, and disciplinary myopia that permeate academic fields and bring together distinctive approaches and perspectives in order to expand our horizons. This journal will approach the subject of the First World War without chronological, geographic, or topical constraints. It will embrace not merely the period associated with the years between 1914 and 1918, but will extend it to include the diplomatic, political, social, cultural, and military complexities evident before, during, and most certainly after the cessation of hostilities" (Steven Sabol, "A brief note from the editor," *First World War Studies* 1, no. 1 (2010): 1).
3. "Revolutions, the defeat of the Central Powers, and the territorial reorganization of a continent dominated by empires, created ideal conditions for new lasting conflicts – though any explanation for their escalation has to be mindful of the importance of local traditions and conditions, often deriving from much older conflicts, which shaped the violence that emerged after the war [...]. Even if Europe experienced a short lived period of stabilization between 1924 and 1929, the core issues raised but not solved between 1917 and 1923 would return, with new urgency, to the international and domestic political agenda after the onset of the Great Depression. As such, the story of Europe in the years between 1917 and 1923 is crucial for understanding the cycles of violence that characterized the continent's twentieth century" (Gerwarth, *The Vanquished*, 1-17.). See also: Robert Bevan, *The Destruction of Memory. Architecture at War*, second expanded ed. (London: Reaktion Books, 2016).
4. See for example: John Bourne, Peter Liddle, and Ian Whitehead, eds., *The Great World War, 1914-1945* (New York: Collins, 2000); George L. Mosse, *Fallen Soldiers: Reshaping the Memory of the World Wars* (Oxford: Oxford University Press, 1990); for criticism/nuance of George L. Mosse's "brutalisation thesis", see for example: Antoine Prost, "Les limites de la brutalisation. Tuer sur le front occidental, 1914-1918," *Vingtième Siècle. Revue d'histoire*. 81, no. 1 (2004); John Lawrence, "Forging a peaceable kingdom. War, violence, and fear of brutalization in post-First World War Britain," *The Journal of Modern History* 75, no. 3 (2003). The debate has also been reconstructed in historiographic works such as Antoine Prost and Jay Winter, *Penser la Grande Guerre. Un essai d'historiographie* (Paris: Éditions du Seuil, 2004).
5. In *The Lights that Failed: European International History, 1919-1933* (Oxford: Oxford University Press, 2005) Zara Steiner, for example, advocates that 1920s Europe should be assessed rather as an epilogue to the First World War than as a prologue to the 1930s.
6. See for example: Richard D. Brown and Richard Ashby Wilson, *Humanitarianism and Suffering: The Mobilization of Empathy* (New York: Cambridge University Press, 2009); Susan Pederson, *The Guardians. The League of Nations and the Crisis of Empire* (Oxford: Oxford University Press, 2015).
7. Robert Gerwarth and John Horne, eds., *War in Peace. Paramilitary Violence in Europe after the Great War* (Oxford: Oxford University Press, 2012).
8. See: John E. Tunbridge and Gregory John Ashworth, *Dissonant Heritage: the Management of the Past as a Resource in Conflict* (Chichester: Wiley, 1996); John Giblin, "Critical Approaches to Post-Colonial (Post-Conflict) Heritage," in *The Palgrave Handbook of Contemporary Heritage Research*, eds. Emma Waterton and Steve Watson (London:

9   Palgrave McMillan, 2015), 313-328; Walter G. Moss, *An Age of Progress? Clashing Twentieth-Century Global Forces* (London: Anthem Press, 2008).

9   On the differences between the commemoration in different parts of the world, see: Jay Winter, "Commemorating catastrophe: 100 years on," *War & Society* 36, no. 4 (2017).

10   Kaat Wils, "Commemorating War 100 Years after the First World War," *Low Countries Historical Review* CXXXI, no. 3 (2016): 74-75. See also: Ben Wellings and Shanti Sumartojo, eds., *Commemorating Race and Empire in the First World War Centenary* (Liverpool: Liverpool University Press, 2018); Geneviève Warland, ed., *Experience and Memory of the First World War in Belgium. Comparative and Interdisciplinary Insights*, Historische Belgienforschung (Münster: Waxmann Verlag, 2018).

11   "It was not without grim historical irony that the centenary of the great war was accompanied by civil war in Syria and Iraq, revolution in Egypt, and violent clashes between Jews and Arabs over the Palestinian question, as if to offer or that at least proof some of the issues raised but not solved by the Great War and its immediate aftermath are still with us today" (Gerwarth, *The Vanquished*, 267).

12   Sheila Jasanoff, "Reconstructing the Past, Constructing the Present: Can Science Studies and the History of Science Live Happily Ever After?" *Social Studies of Science* 30, no. 4 (August 2000): 621-631; Michael Payne and Jessica Ray Barbera, *A Dictionary of Cultural and Critical Theory* (Chichester: Wiley-Blackwell, 2013).

13   Marcel Smets, ed., *Resurgam: la reconstruction en Belgique après 1914* (Brussels: Crédit communal, 1985); Elizabeth Lebas, Susanna Magri, and Christian Topalov, "Reconstruction and Popular Housing after the First World War: A Comparative Study of France, Great Britain, Italy and the United States," *Planning Perspectives* 6, no. 3 (1991): 249-267. For the particular issue of destruction and reconstruction of historic buildings and sites, see: Nicholas Bullock and Luc Verpoest, eds., *Living with History, 1914-1964: Rebuilding Europe after the First and Second World Wars and the Role of Heritage Preservation*, (Leuven: Leuven University Press, 2011); Jeroen Cornilly et al., eds., *Bouwen aan wederopbouw 1914/2050: architectuur in de Westhoek* (Ieper: Erfgoedcel CO7, 2009); Bevan, *The destruction of memory*.

14   Modern architecture and urbanism, almost absent in post-war architectural and urban reconstruction in Belgium, found a rich field of experimentation in the Belgian Congo from about 1930 onwards, having a crucial role in the implementation of the Belgian colonialist policy (ethnic segregation included). See Johan Lagae, "'Kongo zoals het is.' Drie architectuurverhalen uit de Belgische kolonisatiegeschiedenis (1920-1960)" (PhD Diss., Ghent University, 2002); Bruno De Meulder, "Reformisme thuis en overzee. Geschiedenis van de Belgische planning in een kolonie (1880-1960)" (PhD Diss., KU Leuven, 1994). For a broader international perspective: Joe Nasr and Mercedes Volait, eds., *Urbanism: Imported or exported* (Chichester: Academy Editions, 2003); Enwezor, Okwul, ed., *The Short Century. Independence and Liberation Movements on Africa, 1945-1994* (Munich: Prestel, 2001).

15   John Horne, "The Living," in *The Cambridge History of the First World War*, ed. Jay Winter (Cambridge: Cambridge Univeristy Press, 2014), 592-601.

16   Paul Fussell, *The Great War and Modern Memory* (Oxford: Oxford University Press, 2000); Jay Winter, *Sites of Memory, Sites of Mourning. The Great War in European Cultural History* (Cambridge: Cambridge University Press, 2003).

17   For example: David Williams, *Media, Memory and the First World War* (Montreal: McGill-Queen's University Press, 2009) or, more recently Martin Löschnigg and Marzena Sokolowska-Paryz, *The Great War in Post-Memory Literature and Film* (Berlin: De Gruyter, 2014).

18 See for example: Heather Jones, "Romantic Ireland's Dead and Gone? How Centenary Publications are Reshaping Ireland's Divided Understanding of Its Decade of War and Revolution, 1912-1923," *First World War Studies* 9, no. 3 (September 2018): 344-361; Emma Hanna, "Contemporary Britain and the Memory of the First World War," *Matériaux pour l'histoire de notre temps*, no. 1 (2014): 110-117; Ben Wellings and Shanti Sumartojo, eds., *Commemorating Race and Empire in the First World War Centenary* (Liverpool: Liverpool University Press, 2018); Jay Winter, "Commemorating Catastrophe: 100 years On," *War & Society* 36, no. 4 (2017): 239-255 (this essay is part of a special issue on the centenary of the journal *War & Society*).

19 On the topic of gender and masculinity in relation to post-war recovery, see for instance: Joanna Bourke, *Dismembering the Male: Men's Bodies, Britain, and the Great War* (Chicago, IL: University of Chicago Press, 1996); Joanna Bourke, "Love and Limblessness: Male Heterosexuality, Disability, and the Great War," *Journal of War & Culture Studies* 9, no. 1 (2016): 3-19; Thierry Terret, "Prologue: Making Men, Destroying Bodies: Sport, Masculinity and the Great War Experience," *The International Journal of the History of Sport* 28, no. 3-4 (March 2011): 323-328; Wendy Gagen, "Remastering the Body, Renegotiating Gender: Physical Disability and Masculinity during the First World War, the case of JB Middlebrook," *European Review of History— Revue Européenne d'Histoire* 14, no. 4 (2007): 525-541; Sabine Kienitz, *Beschädigte Helden. Kriegsinvalidität und Körperbilder 1914-1923* (Padeborn: Schöningh, 2008).

20 David P. Forsythe, *The Humanitarians. The International Committee of the Red Cross* (Cambridge: Cambridge University Press, 2005); Brown and Wilson, *Humanitarianism and Suffering*; Gerwarth and Horne, *War in Peace*; Branden Little, "An Explosion of New Endeavours: Global Humanitarian Responses to Industrialized Warfare in the First World War Era," *First World War Studies* 5, no. 1 (2014); Bruno Cabanes, *The Great War and the Origins of Humanitarianism, 1918-1924* (Cambridge: Cambridge University Press, 2014).

21 Walter Benjamin, "Experience and Poverty," in *Walter Benjamin. Selected Writings. 2: 1927-1934*, ed. Michael W. Jennings et al. (Cambridge, MA: Harvard University Press, 1999), 731-732.

22 Studies on the afterlife of the First World War by historians such as Jay Winter or Philipp Blom and Gordon Hughes are explicitly inspired by Benjamin's take on the caesura of 1918. The title of Blom and Hughes' book, *Nothing But the Clouds Unchanged*, is directly derived from the Benjamin quote at the outset of the introduction. Also in Bloms book on the post-war, *Fracture. Life and Culture in the West, 1918-1938*, he uses the quotation from Benjamin to epitomise the post-war era. Winter links his theory of history to the famous Angelus Novus, a 1920 monoprint by the Swiss-German artist Paul Klee, which also stands central in Benjamin's philosophy of history (Winter, *Sites of Memory, Sites of Mourning*; Gordon Hughes and Philipp Blom, *Nothing But the Clouds Unchanged. Artists in World War I* (Los Angeles, CA: Getty Research Institute, 2014); Philipp Blom, *Fracture. Life and Culture in the West 1918-1938* (London: Atlantic Books, 2015).

23 Bevan, *The destruction of memory*; Gerwarth, *The Vanquished*; Luc Huyse, *Alles gaat voorbij behalve het verleden* (Leuven: Van Halewyck, 2006).

24 See, as to Europe: Robert Gerwarth, ed., *Twisted Paths. Europe 1914-1945* (Oxford: Oxford University Press, 2007).

25 For a sharp evocation of this, including a good bibliography, see: Jay Winter, "Historiography 1918-Today," in *1914-1918-online. International Encyclopedia of the First World War*, eds. Ute Daniel et al., (Berlin: Freie Universität Berlin) 2014-11-11. DOI: 10.15463/ie1418.10498.
26 Lucian Hölscher, "The First World War as a 'Rupture' in the European History of the Twentieth Century: A Contribution to the Hermeneutics of Not-Understanding," *German Historical Institute London Bulletin* 35, No. 2 (November 2013): 73-87.
27 Benjamin, "Experience and Poverty," 732.
28 For an introduction on the existing literature with regard to the history of disabled soldiers of the First World War see Pieter Verstraete, Martina Salvante, and Julie Anderson, "Commemorating the disabled soldier, 1914-1940," *First World War Studies* 6, no. 1 (Winter 2015) (Special issue): 1-7.
29 See for some comparative approaches towards the rehabilitation of disabled soldiers of the Great War: Deborah Cohen, *The War Come Home: Disabled Veterans in Britain and Germany, 1914-1939*. (Berkeley, CA: University of California Press, 2001) and David Gerber, "Disabled veterans and public welfare policy: Comparative and transnational perspectives on western states in the twentieth century," *Transnational & Contemporary Problems* 11, no. 1 (Spring 2001): 77-106.
30 See for some literature on the intersection between medicine and ideology: Henk Smaele, Kaat Wils, and Tine Van Osselaer, eds., *Sign or Symptom? Exceptional Corporeal Phenomena in Religion and Medicine, 19th and 20th Century* (Leuven: Leuven University Press, 2017); Hervé Guillemain, ed., *Diriger les consciences, guérir les âmes: une histoire comparée des pratiques thérapeutiques et religieuses (1830-1939)* (Paris: La Découverte, 2016); and Maria Pia Donato, ed., *Médecine et religion: compétitions, collaborations, conflits (XIIe-XXe siècles)*. Collection de l'École française de Rome 476. (Rome: École française de Rome, 2013).
31 See: Stefan Rinke and Karina Kriegesmann, "Latin America," in *1914-1918-online. International Encyclopedia of the First World War*, eds. Ute Daniel et al., (Berlin: Freie Universität Berlin) 2015-11-05. DOI: 10.15463/ie1418.10760; Frederick Dickinson, "Toward a Global Perspective of the Great War: Japan and the Foundations of a Twentieth-Century World," *American Historical Review* 119, no. 4 (2014): 1154-1183; Jan Schmidt, *Nach dem Krieg ist von dem Krieg. Mediatisierte Erfahrungen des Ersten Weltkriegs und Nachkriegsdiskurse in Japan (1914-1919)* (Frankfurt a.M.: Campus Verlag GmbH, 2018); Jan Schmidt and Katja Schmidtpott, eds., *The East Asian Dimension of the First World War. Global Entanglements and Japan, China and Korea, 1914-1919* (Frankfurt a.M.: Campus Verlag GmbH, 2020). Recent research has pointed to the impact of the return of thousands of Chinese workers and Indian soldiers to their native countries after the Great War on the political, cultural and economic modernisation in post-war China and India; see: Dominiek Dendooven, "Asia in Flanders. A Transnational History of Indians and Chinese on the Western Front, 1914-1920" (PhD Diss., Universiteit Antwerpen and University of Kent, 2018); Dominiek Dendooven, *De vergeten soldaten van de Eerste Wereldoorlog* (Berchem: EPO, 2019).
32 Bevan, *The Destruction of Memory*; Huyse, *Alles gaat voorbij behalve het verleden*.
33 On the occasion of the 100th anniversary of the end of the First World War, the City of Leuven organised a city-wide project featuring various events, including an exhibition and, in collaboration with the KU Leuven, an international colloquium (on which this book is based). Both initiatives focused on the post-war revival of the city and the world. See: Joke Buijs et al., eds., *Herleven. Leuven na 1918* (Leuven: City of Leuven, 2018).

PART ONE
REBUILD

The centre of the city of Leuven (Belgium),
cleared and partially rebuilt, 1921.
© City Archive Leuven

A [Paul] Klee painting named *Angelus Novus* shows an angel looking as though he is about to move away from something he is fixedly contemplating. His eyes are staring, his mouth is open, his wings are spread. This is how one pictures the angel of history. His face is turned toward the past. Where we perceive a chain of events, he sees one single catastrophe which keeps piling wreckage upon wreckage and hurls it in front of his feet. The angel would like to stay, awaken the dead, and make whole what has been smashed. But a storm is blowing from Paradise; it has got caught in his wings with such violence that the angel can no longer close them. The storm irresistibly propels him into the future to which his back is turned, while the pile of debris before him grows skyward. This storm is what we call progress.

Walter Benjamin, *Theses on the Philosophy of History* (1942)

Fig. 1. A reconstruction worker clearing away debris in Lens, France. Photographer: Lewis Wickes Hine, 1874-1940 (April 11, 1919). Library of Congress, LC-DIG-anrc-14289.

Catastrophe and Reconstruction in Western Europe
The Urban Aftermath of the First World War

Pierre Purseigle

The invasion of Belgium by the German army in August 1914 brought industrial warfare to the urban heart of Europe. Marching through its densest and most urbanised country, the German forces turned towns and cities into battlefields. Liège, Namur, Louvain, Charleroi, Mons, Antwerp, and then Ypres: for most contemporaries in Western Europe and beyond the names of these cities punctuated the unfolding story of the conflict.[1] The shocking devastation visited upon the cities of Europe by industrial warfare, the particular form of urban victimisation it brought about, is perhaps enough to consider the First World War as an urban catastrophe. One could also argue that this was a war made in cities, less in Sarajevo perhaps than in Vienna, Berlin, Paris, St Petersburg and London, where policymakers led their country into the conflagration. Provincial towns and cities were also critical sites of military, economic and social mobilisation. For all its strategic and symbolic importance however, Belgium was an outlier in a world where urbanisation still remained an uneven and incomplete process.[2] The majority of combatants were not city-dwellers but farmers and rural labourers. In market towns across the belligerent world many of the political, ethical, economic tensions created by the conflict played out on market squares and marketplaces where rural and urban populations met. By 1914, towns and cities had, like war itself, been transformed by the process of modernisation that characterised the long nineteenth century.[3] During the conflict, urban communities were, as Zygmunt Bauman noted of contemporary cities, "the battleground on which global powers and stubbornly local meanings and identities [met]".[4] Just as urban history is an important way to make sense of the war experience, it is equally central to our efforts to understand the transition from war to peace.

Recent studies of the aftermath of the First World War have demonstrated that the sharp distinction drawn between victors and vanquished, imposed by the provisions of the 1918 armistices and reinforced by Article 231 of the 1919 Treaty of Versailles asserting Germany's responsibility for the war, obscures as much as it illuminates the fraught and complex transition from war to peace after 1918. Both victory and defeat remained highly contested terms across Europe, as belligerent societies confronted the yawning gap between wartime expectations and post-war realities. For, despite its extortionate human and material costs, war was never anything but a blunt instrument of policy. Yet the cultural and ideological investment in the conflict had given credit to the notion that the war would be much more and bring about a new era of prosperity and national cohesion.[5]

Historians have long studied the frustrations and conflicts that afflicted vanquished nations and empires. Robert Gerwarth's latest book thus explores the brutal consequences of defeat. Yet his "vanquished" include nations, like Italy, whose victory soon sounded hollow, drowned out by resentful cries of betrayal.[6] Poland and Serbia also illustrate the profound tensions brought about by the victorious end to a conflict whose contested meaning continued to shape post-war politics.[7]

When the uncertain aftermath of the conflict culminated in a global crisis of liberal democracy and economics, it became apparent that no former belligerent would be spared the reckoning of peace. In this context, discourses of reconstruction did not merely reveal the need to address the material impact of the conflict but betrayed the common urge to rethink and redefine national projects and identities in the wake of war.[8] In Britain, for instance, the debate focussed on long-standing problems of social policies, including housing, and rightly underlined the centrality of the nation-state in the process of recovery.[9] As a result – and perhaps unwittingly – comparative histories of inter-war Europe, in all their diversity, have tended to paint homogeneous pictures of the national experiences of reconstruction.[10]

This chapter builds on John Horne's pioneering analysis of post-war demobilisation to challenge this persistent analytical primacy of the nation-state in the history of reconstruction and to highlight its complex geographies and temporalities.[11] To do so, it will focus on the urban transition from war to peace and shift the emphasis back to the devastated regions of Western Europe.

The Western European urban experience of demobilisation and reconstruction has thus far remained relatively neglected despite the unprecedented degree of material devastation the West faced. For those countries, too, attempted to come to terms with mass mourning, economic demobilisation and the reintegration of veterans. In Belgian and French cities laid to waste by military operations the war clearly did not end with the peace treaties and the return of war veterans. There, ruins and devastation formed the backdrop to demobilisation, whose geography was not simply defined by the boundaries of the nation-state.

In France, ten départements of the north and north-east of the country had endured such destruction that 91% of their settlements had suffered material damage. Of those, 620 communes had been entirely destroyed by military operations.[12] In Belgium, few regions had been spared the devastation and the reconstruction was a truly national undertaking: 200,000 buildings, 4,000 km of railway tracks had been destroyed.[13] While West Flanders had suffered the most extensive damage after the stabilisation of the battlefield, towns and cities in the path of the German army (Dinant, Termonde, Louvain, Malines and Namur, for instance) had suffered substantial destruction too.

Material devastation transformed both the context and the dynamics of demobilisation and forged, to use Reinhardt Koselleck's categories, specific "spaces of experience" and "horizons of expectations".[14] In the devastated regions of Europe the process of reconstruction therefore imposed its own temporalities. As local populations projected themselves into the post-war future, they were keenly aware of the particular historical trajectory of their communities. Their war experience was not just defined by mass military and social mobilisation, by collective mourning and temporary economic dislocation. It was also irremediably shaped by the destruction of their physical environment and the upheaval of their most basic, material conditions of existence. This accounts for the divergence of local and national temporalities of demobilisation, as the necessities of reconstruction imposed their own timeframes. This also explains the difficulty of offering a definite chronology of reconstruction. The planning for, if not the actual work of, reconstruction began as soon as the German army penetrated onto Belgian and French territory. Reconstruction was, in this sense, concomitant with destruction; its history therefore starts in August 1914. It is however, as we shall see, considerably more difficult to establish its endpoint. What is certain is that many communities were still completing their reconstruction when they had to face another war and its new trail of destruction.

The study of reconstruction, as an idea, as public policy, as a social experience, also demonstrates a wider point about the history of global warfare. It cannot be written from a single spatial perspective. Local, national and transnational perspectives must be combined, not because it may sound fashionable in current academic discourses, but because the belligerent societies navigated metaphorically and literally between different spaces.

It is therefore crucial to combine local and transnational approaches so as to shed new light on the process of reconstruction. In doing so, one can position the specific experiences of the devastated regions within wider debates over peace-making and reparations. Such a perspective underlines how the special status that "martyr towns" and their populations enjoyed in the wartime rhetoric gradually unravelled as Entente powers engaged in tense negotiations over German reparations. In the meantime, the pressures of national demobilisation appeared to undermine the continuing efforts required by the reconstitution of the urban battlefield. In these regions the undeniable success of relief and reconstruction belied the occasional failure of national and inter-state solidarity; it also reasserted the cultural and material importance of local and transnational civil society organisations. Moreover, it underlined the significance of translocal networks of solidarities that were born out of the war experience. This chapter will finally highlight the extent to which national cultural demobilisation and fiscal retrenchment in the 1920s impelled ruined cities to maximise their own resources and revealed the inequalities underlying the process of reconstruction.

Reconstruction and the Diverging Processes of (De)mobilisation

Although scholars have generally acknowledged that the process of reconstruction started as early as 1914, when planners and policy-makers set out the principles of urban recovery, they have considered it in isolation from the process of wartime mobilisation. Yet, as John Horne argued in relation to labour and industrial relations, it is imperative to place mobilisation and reconstruction in the same analytical framework.[15]

In a matter of weeks following the invasion of Belgium in August 1914, scores of Belgian and French towns and cities along the Western Front came to encapsulate the nature and meaning of the war. Urban devastation soon became indissociable from the "barbaric" German way of war denounced by Allied propagandists.[16] As Alan Kramer and John Horne have shown, the experience and memory of the 1914 German invasion of Belgium and France and of the subsequent "German Atrocities" were absolutely central to the shaping of the war effort among the western allies.[17] The evocation of "martyr towns" lay at the core of the rhetoric of social mobilisation in the first weeks of the conflict and was equally central to the remobilisation effort mounted in 1916-1917.[18] Intellectuals and publicists explicitly constructed the experience of urban victimhood as a symbol of national resistance; their plight confirmed in their eyes that the Kaiserreich had irremediably broken ranks with the community of civilised peoples.[19] Gabriel Hanotaux, a historian and member of the *Académie*, made this very point in a 1915 lecture, translated into 11 languages for circulation in neutral countries. His evocation of the classical and medieval history of devastated towns like Soissons allowed him to favourably compare the barbarians of the past to the modern frightfulness of German warfare. As the German army destroyed sites of national heritage like Reims, Hanotaux argued that they were attacking "the supreme expression, if not of French life, at least of French defence".[20] In the same vein, Pierre Nothomb, an important intellectual figure in Belgium, included a chapter on "the murdered cities" in his book on *The Barbarians in Belgium*.[21]

Meanwhile, Marius Vachon, a heritage specialist at the French Touring Club, reprised this trope in a series of lectures on "the martyr towns of France and Belgium" delivered in Switzerland to counter German rebuttals of stories of atrocities.[22]

The discourse of urban victimhood transparently drew on the model of Christian and catholic martyrdom so familiar to French and Belgian, as well as to many neutral, societies. In the aftermath of the conflict, the language of reconstruction would unsurprisingly continue to hark back to German barbarity and martyrdom to evoke the "great duty" of national and international solidarity.[23]

Just as urban ruins stood as local synecdoches for the global, ideological conflict, the reconstruction of devastated cities focused wider reflections on the type of social changes that the war might bring about. The language of reconstruction thus contained many of the tensions and potential conflicts that would emerge at the end of military operations. It is therefore important to distinguish between reconstruction, conceived as a re-creation, and reconstitution, the reproduction of what used to be. Although public discourses did not always explicitly endorse and elaborate on this difference, the *sinistrés* (victims) and *rapatriés* (returnees) often expressed their preference for the reconstitution of the *status quo ante bellum*. This explains the reluctance of local communities to embrace the modernising agenda of urban planners, architects and other experts who, as we shall see, aimed to seize the opportunity offered by reconstruction to transform their towns. Tensions, if not outright conflicts, inevitably erupted as modernisation was often perceived as the "best" enemy of a "good" reconstruction, that is to say, a swift and economical return to one's own home. Although French was the dominant language in Belgium, commentators and authorities there also speak of "restauration". After four years of foreign occupation, the challenge of Belgian reconstruction was, of course, not merely material but entailed the restoration of Belgian sovereignty, if not that of its flawed, pre-war political system.[24] In both cases, and indeed across the belligerent world, those debates reflected the cultural and ideological investment in the conflict. Combatants and non-combatants alike had primarily conceived the war as an existential struggle waged in defence of a nation, often experienced and framed in personal and domestic terms. Yet, as the conflict exacted unprecedented sacrifices, it also justified new calls for a post-war redefinition of the social and political compact at the national and international levels. Such reflections were part and parcel of the process of mobilisation and urban planners and architects played their role in it. In 1915-1916, Adolphe Derveaux, a noted architect and urban planner, thus contributed to a series of lectures held at the School of Higher Social Studies in Paris. These events brought together a series of prominent intellectuals to discuss the future "reorganisation" of France.[25]

To Derveaux, and indeed many of his colleagues in France, Belgium and the United States, the reconstruction of ruined cities was to be part of the wider programme of social reforms that wartime sacrifices demanded.[26]

The particular sacrifices consented to by the populations of the devastated regions during the war were also expected to frame and determine the outcome of the peace-making process. After all, as Clémentel, French Minister of Commerce, put it in a memorandum to Lord Reading in December 1918, "France has been the battlefield of the Allies" and the latter had to help her in return.[27] In diplomatic correspondence with their British counterparts, French and Belgian policy-makers regularly asserted what had become an article of faith across the devastated regions. In an enquiry carried out by the Belgian government in 1917 a host of business and political leaders made the same point: "[t]he sacrifices that the war imposed upon Belgium have created duties of gratitude" for the "great nations".[28] This rhetoric of Belgian sacrifice and Allied gratitude was of course a common trope across the Allied media and civil societies, as indicated by a letter sent to the Belgian government on 1 October 1917 by two American businessmen – arguably keen to combine profits and solidarity:

> To share in the great work of rebuilding Belgium is a privilege that appeals to the heart of every loyal American. It offers an opportunity to perform a service of inestimable value to that stricken country – a service commensurate with the debt of gratitude we owe her. [...] Who can doubt that we are obligated to Belgium for the perpetuation of our freedom, independence and democratic institutions![29]

In both public and private, British policy-makers admitted that, as Lord Cecil wrote in September 1918, "the needs of the Allied populations are a moral claim on all of us".[30] Cecil was even more explicit in a speech to the Anglo-Belgian Union on 7 November 1918: "[w]e have a debt of gratitude towards Belgium for the immense sacrifices she has made and we must apply ourselves to repay them".[31] This chapter is not intended to review or reprise the long-standing historiographical debate over post-war reparations. The issue of reconstruction does however underline in a most potent and concrete way the discrepancy between the reality of wartime and post-war international politics and the ethical discourse that underpinned the wartime cultural mobilisation. For this discourse also sustained the hope of the populations of the devastated regions.

This discrepancy – and the potential for disappointment – is well documented in the British and Belgian economic and diplomatic archives and appears as early as 1916. One good example is the debate over the potential British contribution to King Albert's Fund, an organisation created by the Belgian government to provide temporary accommodation for the population of the devastated regions. Despite the repeated efforts and pleas of Belgian diplomats, the British government refused to commit to this particular scheme or indeed to any other reconstruction scheme, even if the Foreign Office reaffirmed their "intention to assist to the utmost of their power in the reconstitution and reconstruction of Belgium".[32] Unsurprisingly, the Belgian government expressed its "profound and legitimate disappointment".[33] But the British were keen to avoid any sort of precedent that could then be invoked by other allies, like Serbia, in the peace negotiations. Typically, British diplomats soon looked across the Pond for a solution to this particular problem:

> Few things would make a greater appeal to American idealism than the rebuilding of Belgium, and extensive American contributions, whether Governmental or private, would relieve us financially at our weakest point.[34]

Therefore Belgium soon realised that inter-allied solidarity should not be taken for granted but the specificity of its experience also undermined its bargaining power. Indeed, the discussion in Paris in 1919 showed Belgium that the moral high ground that it had occupied since the invasion of 1914, or the devastation it had suffered, converted with difficulty into the hard and bloody currency of the military sacrifice that the British Empire had consented to. Material devastation counted little for Lloyd George, for instance, who discounted this in discussion with Clemenceau in March 1919. "The English public would not understand that the cost of each chimney destroyed in France be repaid in full, but not the price of lost English lives."[35]

In a matter of months, the populations of the devastated regions were forced to recognise that, in contradiction with wartime discourses, they would not be granted any special status in the post-war world. In other words, and to echo Wilsonian rhetoric, the Belgians thought they had entered into a covenant; they realised they were merely part of a strategic coalition. Sent to Belgium in April 1919 to report on local attitudes towards Britain, Herbert Samuel underlines the nature and risks of this realisation:

> The course of events at the Peace Conference at Paris had given rise to much disappointment. The internal economic condition of the country remained serious. [...] This state of affairs, four months after the signature of the armistice, was contrasted with the promises of the Allies during the war to assist the rapid restoration of Belgium, and was rapidly extending, that, the war being over the Allies in general, and the United Kingdom in particular, were indifferent to the fulfilment of those promises. [...] The enthusiasm which had existed for the Allies during the war and at the mo-

ment of the Armistice was cooling, and there was a danger that it would be replaced by a sentiment of alienation, and even of hostility.[36]

Similar sentiments were reported in the devastated regions of France: "[a]fter the efforts and sacrifice of France, the disappointment is immense".[37] By the mid-1920s, newspapers published by the *sinistrés* continued to bemoan the lack of allied – and specifically British – gratitude and solidarity.[38]

The study of reconstruction underlines the fact that demobilisation was an uneven and contested process. It underlines in particular the existence of a particular geography of demobilisation, for the populations of the devastated regions experienced the transition from war to peace in specific ways.

As the Armistice revealed the full extent of the destruction and the dire necessity of a sustained national effort, it was also welcomed in the rest of the country with relief and the desire to discontinue wartime exertions. Therefore, voluntary organisations and national and local elites took on the challenge to maintain and redirect the momentum of mobilisation towards the reconstitution of the devastated areas. And a challenge it was, particularly in France when the country was doing its best to move on, despite the continuing economic disruptions and the weight of collective and individual grief and mourning.

The real difficulty was to combine national political, economic and cultural demobilisation with a partial remobilisation directed towards the devastated regions. To achieve this, their populations used all available resources to remind their fellow countrymen and -women that they had provided a bulwark against the invaders. Like the rest of the nation-in-arms, they had mobilised their men and resources to win the war. But they also suffered the ignominy of the occupation and German oppression. And, of course, their regions, towns and cities had been laid waste by military operations. In other words, in the post-war economy of sacrifice they occupied a specific place; a place that gave them rights and placed demands upon the rest of the nation. "Who would dare betray such a duty", asked Paul Deschanel, President of the Chamber of Deputies in May 1919? "We owe [...] immortal France [...] the rebuilding of these regions."[39]

Legislators soon set out to turn the rhetoric of national solidarity into a legal and hopefully material reality: first in Belgium in October and November 1918 and then in France when on 19 April 1919 the "Charter of the *Sinistrés*" effectively created a new legal category for the populations of the devastated regions. In Belgium a law providing for the adoption of devastated towns and cities by the State was passed on 8 April 1919, followed by the creation of the Office for the Devastated Regions.

Unsurprisingly, the slow pace of reconstruction soon gave rise to endless complaints and recriminations. Regardless of the immensity and complexity of the tasks, the local populations expressed their anger at what they perceived, rightly or wrongly, to be the inadequacies, incompetence and corruption of local and national authorities.[40] Police reports in 1919 and 1920 regularly evoke the risks entailed by the growing discontent in the devastated regions. In the context marked by the rise of Bolshevism and concerns about law and order, the potential for violence loomed large on officials' minds.

As Raymond Dorgelès wrote in *Le Reveil des Morts* (1923), the fascinating and problematic novel he wrote about the reconstruction in the Aisne in 1919-1920: "For a moment, this impoverished France was allowed to believe that happy France was forgetting it".[41] Five years after the Armistice, the populations of the devastated regions were still clearly anxious not to be forgotten. "Has the time passed so fast that one has already forgotten what the *sinistrés* have suffered? Has the memory of [their] martyr disappeared?"[42] In 1925, the *Comité d'Action des Régions Dévastées*, a rather forceful and militant organisation led by left-wing and left-of-centre local politicians from the North and East launched a new publication, *Le Sinistré*, to advocate for the regions. To them, the public and official commitment to national solidarity had faded by 1920-1921. They were particularly scathing about the way in which the national press had exploited a few isolated cases of illegitimate enrichment and turned them into the so-called "scandal of the devastated regions".[43]

Reconstruction as a Translocal and Transnational Matter

This campaign for a partial remobilisation also drew on the particular resources and characteristics of imperial societies. Indeed, spared local communities and notabilities across the French Empire came to the fore to assist in the renaissance of the ruined areas of the metropole. In the aftermath of the conflict, the local elites of formerly occupied or devastated zones in northern France called on their counterparts across the French empire for their help in reconstructing the ruined regions.

The reconstruction does reveal the local, metropolitan implantation of many leaders of the colonial lobby in France. Indeed, eminent colonial administrators and eulogists of French imperialism were also heavily committed to the reconstruction of France. It is certainly worth remarking that the post-war reconstruction of France was also regularly seized upon by colonial experts and administrators to further the case for the French imperial project.

The reconstruction was also supported by a range of networks and organisations which operated across national boundaries. These initiatives can be traced back to wartime relief operations, organised in Allied as well as neutral countries. American collections document the role of international relief operations, like the Commission for Relief in Belgium. US cities often functioned as critical nodes in these transnational philanthropic and humanitarian networks. In recent years, interest in the emergence of modern humanitarianism in the era of the First World War has produced a fascinating – and growing – body of scholarship on humanitarianism.[44] It has stressed the importance of those US humanitarians who were often connected to Progressive milieus, tended to see the devastated regions as an opportunity to offer a wide range of social, educational and health services and to test out aspects of their programme for social reforms.

Another group often conceived the reconstruction as an opportunity: urban planners, architects, experts of the "urban question" also presented and almost gleefully seized the reconstruction as an opportunity finally to design and implement an ambitious programme of urban modernisation. This programme was not merely designed to meet the needs of the devastated areas. In fact, it was generally accepted that the war had exacerbated a pre-existing housing crisis across Europe and the United States, where the conflict had drastically reduced supply and prevented technicians and policy-makers from improving the quality of the housing stock.[45] In France, for instance, law-makers estimated that half a million new dwellings needed to be built to meet post-war demand.[46] Interestingly however, while experts never failed to mention the "liberated regions", they rarely acknowledged the specificities of the former battlefields. To them, the challenge they raised was primarily one of scale.[47] The provision of modern, "hygienic" housing was seen as a critical step in their pursuit of wider social reforms. Focussed as they were on architecture and urban morphology, those planners were remarkably oblivious to the specific needs of communities left reeling after years lived under fire or in exile. It is all the more surprising that urban planning, an emerging field by the war's outbreak, owed part of its dynamism to many Belgian practitioners who had fled the German invasion of 1914.

Indeed, as Pieter Uyttenhove demonstrated, it is essential to place the interwar activities of architects, planners and decision-makers into their national and international context and to trace the intellectual history of urban planning and policy-making back to the experience of war and exile.[48] Urban planning is yet another illustration of the strong transatlantic dimension of the urban reconstruction of Western Europe. In the end, the process of reconstruction reveals three types of transnationalism: caritative, municipal and urbanist.[49] The "caritative transnationalism" corresponds to the work of pre-existing organisations like the Red Cross and to philanthropic initiatives which originated in the war and continued their work after the Armistice. "Municipal transnationalism" refers to the exchanges and relationships established by local authorities across national boundaries, prefiguring twinning and other developments which prospered after World War II, and, finally, the "urbanist transnationalism" which played a key role in the reconstruction and largely shaped its intellectual and technical history.

Soon after the war, urban communities that had been spared the ravages of invasion and military operations committed to the reconstruction of the "martyr towns". Those *"villes-marraines"* thus pledged to provide financial aid and to foster the link with the devastated towns by organising charity fêtes and civic rituals. Such "adoptions" developed at a steady pace after the Armistice in the allied countries and especially in Great Britain and the USA. It is therefore essential to place the reconstruction in the context of post-war remembrance. Post-war reconstruction and cultural demobilisation, albeit geared to different phases, are strongly linked to the issue of remembrance and mourning. The adoptions by British towns and cities often revealed an attempt to inscribe the memory of dead soldiers into the place where their sacrifice was offered. Such expressions of international urban solidarity were therefore part of a larger process of mourning. Indeed, as the Lord Mayor of Liverpool put it: "You keep vigil over our dead, we will help your survivor".[50] The British system of recruiting and military mobilisation had actually reinforced the identification of British localities with a precise part of the western front since local regiments had generally fought and suffered considerable losses in one battlefield which came to symbolise their participation in the war. The same logic drove the contribution of confessional associations or of individual families. For instance, the Prince family collected money across US cities to fund the public water supply of a number of small towns in the Somme in the area where their son had fought and died.[51] Drawing on the sociology of diaspora and migration, I would like to suggest that such processes and solidarities were not so much transnational as translocal. For they were defined by the migration of soldiers across the world; soldiers whose experience connected localities to each other not simply across national borders, but irrespective of national borders.

By the mid-1920s, most towns and cities affected by military operations had made great strides towards their reconstruction, even in France. National authorities and financial institutions were keen, for different reasons, to proclaim the end of reconstruction. André Tardieu explicitly and hastily did so in November 1929 on the day he assumed the leadership of the French cabinet.[52] Yet the strategic choice made by national authorities to prioritise the reconstruction of the industrial and economic apparatus, as well as their post-war policy of fiscal retrenchment, had a direct and diverse local impact. The story of reconstruction was anything but one of linear, constant, uninterrupted progress, of the kind illustrated by the graphs in Figure 2.

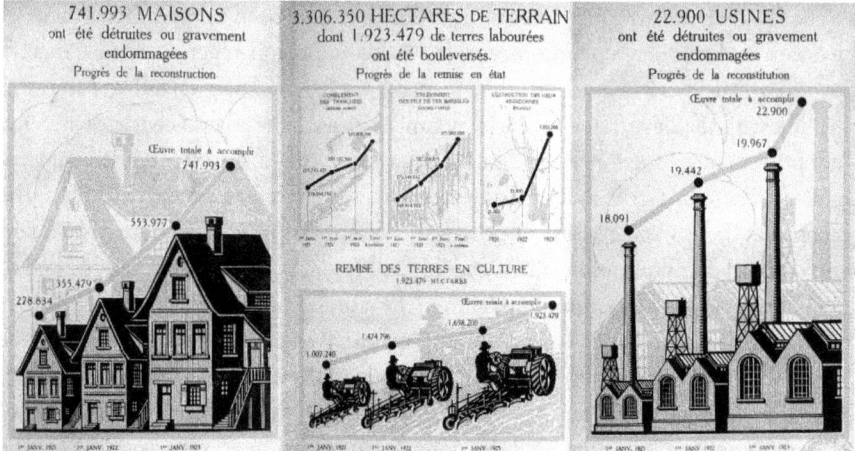

Fig. 2. A story of reconstruction. Bibliothèque nationale de France, 4-LB57-18327, *La France au travail pour réparer ses dommages de guerre*, 1923, p. 4.

Individual Trajectories: Lens and Rheims

The individual trajectories of destroyed cities often depended on the successful mobilisation of specific local resources. Urban reconstruction was therefore an uneven process and one which revealed profound inequalities. The comparison of Lens and Rheims [Reims] in France illustrates this point well. Lens lay at the centre of France's coalmining heartland. Rheims, of course, was and still is the heart of the Champagne region and was known not only for its sparkling wine, but for its Cathedral whose partial destruction during the war soon became a symbol of the "barbaric" German way of war. Both cities are included in Alex Dowdall's excellent book on urban life under fire.[53] Each suffered extensive damage as a result of military operations. At the risk of glossing over the difficulties and limitations of a straight comparison between these two towns, we can argue, I believe, that the reconstruction of Rheims proceeded at a much quicker pace. For financial and organisational reasons, the reconstruction of Lens did not take off before 1922, not least perhaps because the land registry could not be reconstituted before 1921.

Temporary shelters were dismantled in Rheims from 1923 and had disappeared by 1928. By contrast, there were still almost 1,000 temporary housing units in Lens in 1930, although Lens was only a third of Rheims's size in 1914. By 1924, builders struggled to find work in Rheims and the city could organise a parade to celebrate the return of the 100,000[th] inhabitant in 1926. In Lens, key sites of urban life, like the main Catholic church and the trade unions' headquarters, were not rebuilt before 1926.

There are at least three reasons for this which, when combined, outline the political economy of urban reconstruction. The process was indeed defined by each city's respective and unequal access to capital. Champagne producers first managed to tap into funding and support for industrial reconstruction. Money was therefore poured into the city itself, where these corporations had their headquarters and where business leaders lived. By contrast, Lens's capital-intensive mines lay on the outskirts of the city and their reconstruction certainly posed greater difficulties. Of strategic importance for the country as a whole, the reconstitution of the mines took precedence over the needs of the city. Coal extraction did not resume before 1921 and returned to full capacity only in 1923.

In Rheims, the local elite explicitly and systematically set out to exploit what Pierre Bourdieu would call the "symbolic capital" of the city, its singular status among "martyr towns". In its first meeting after the liberation on 9 November 1918, the municipal council called on the city's friends in France and abroad, and specifically in Great Britain and the USA, to fund the reconstruction, if not of the whole city, at least of a "museum, library, laboratory, high school, or hospital".[54] During and after the war, Rheims had received a number of high-profile visitors, including President Wilson on 26 January 1919, and it went on to receive the help of Chicago, New York, Los Angeles and Pasadena.

The old hospital was rebuilt as the American hospital, thanks to an initial donation of US$200,000. Each bed was sponsored by the family of a dead Sammy who had fought in France. (An interesting combination of transnational and translocal initiatives.) Ground was broken in 1922 and it was formally unveiled in 1925. By contrast, the reconstruction of the hospital at Lens was not completed before 1932. It was exclusively funded through taxation and borrowing by the municipality. Lens had, of course, been recognised by French authorities as one of the "martyr towns" and was awarded the *Croix de guerre* and the *Legion d'Honneur* in August 1919. But it never commanded the type of international resonance that Rheims or Louvain did. Neither Carnegie nor Rockefeller ever contributed to the reconstruction of Lens.

Unequal access to economic and symbolic capital also accounted for the differentiated attention that urban planning experts paid to devastated cities. Rheims soon proved to be of particular interest to French and international urban experts. The first plans were elaborated in 1915 and two projects were presented at the 1916 exhibition on the "reconstituted city". The reconstruction of Rheims was often discussed by the experts and reformers gathered in the *Musée Social* and the *Renaissance des Cités*, an organisation that played an important role in post-war planning. In 1920 the city council called upon the *Renaissance des Cités* and commissioned an American urban planner, Geo (George) B. Ford (1879-1930). A graduate of Harvard, MIT and the Beaux-Arts in Paris, Ford had been working as an architect in New York City until 1917 when he returned to France to serve as Head of Reconstruction for the

American Red Cross. He was hired by the French government as a consultant and was a popular speaker across the country. His plan for Rheims was approved in July 1920. In 1922 an amended version provided for the city we know today.

This brief, and admittedly superficial, comparison will have demonstrated that the post-war *tabula rasa* did not create an even playing field. Structural as well as contingent inequalities, unequal access to political, symbolic and economic resources, determined the urban aftermath of the First World War.

Conclusion

History thankfully does not exclusively belong to historians. In fact, historians have thus far played a limited role in the historiography of urban reconstruction, while architects, urban planners, museum curators laid the groundwork for a study like this one. Historians should also devise ways to engage with another set of practitioners, the so-called disaster-management specialists who are called upon to deal with contemporary urban catastrophes. The Great War was, after all, but one of a number of urban catastrophes in the early twentieth century: San Francisco and Valparaiso in 1906, Messina in 1908, Halifax and Salonica in 1917, the Great Kantō earthquake of 1923, Chillan in 1939. This period also witnessed the emergence of the first social-scientific studies of natural disasters. Samuel Prince, who had been a relief worker in Halifax, defended a doctoral thesis on Catastrophe and Social Change at Columbia University in 1920. At a time when cities from New Orleans to Aleppo continue to pay the price of natural and man-made catastrophes including urbicide, when discussions of urban resilience often ignore the long history of urban catastrophes, urban historians have to learn from and contribute to this most urgent interdisciplinary endeavour.

Notes

1. Sophie De Schaepdrijver. *La Belgique et La Première Guerre Mondiale* (Brussels: Archives & Musée de la Littérature, 2004).
2. Peter Clark, ed., *The Oxford Handbook of Cities in World History* (Oxford: Oxford University Press, 2013).
3. Roger Chickering and Marcus Funck, eds., *Endangered Cities: Military Power and Urban Societies in the Era of the World Wars* (Boston, MA: Brill, 2004); Stefan Goebel and Derek Keene, eds., *Cities into Battlefields: Metropolitan Scenarios, Experiences and Commemorations of Total War*. Historical Urban Studies Series (Farnham: Ashgate, 2011).
4. Zygmunt Bauman, *Liquid Times: Living in an Age of Uncertainty* (Cambridge: Polity Press, 2007), 81.
5. William Mulligan, *The Great War for Peace* (New Haven, CT: Yale University Press, 2014).
6. Robert Gerwarth, *The Vanquished: Why the First World War Failed to End, 1917-1923* (London: Allen Lane, 2016).
7. Julia Eichenberg, *Kämpfen für Frieden und Fürsorge : polnische Veteranen des Ersten Weltkriegs und ihre internationalen Kontakte, 1918-1939*. Studien zur Internationalen Geschichte 27 (Munich: Oldenbourg, 2011); John Paul Newman, *Yugoslavia in the Shadow of War: Veterans and the Limits of State Building, 1903-1945* (Cambridge: Cambridge University Press, 2015).
8. The aftermath of the US Civil War provides another locus classicus of the multifaceted nature of reconstruction. See for instance: Eric Foner, *Reconstruction: America's Unfinished Revolution, 1863-1877* (New York: Harper & Row, 1988).
9. Susan Pedersen, "From National Crisis to 'National Crisis': British Politics, 1914-1931," *Journal of British Studies* 33, no. 3 (July 1994): 322-335.
10. Charles S. Maier, *Recasting Bourgeois Europe. Stabilization in France, Germany, and Italy in the Decade after World War I* (Princeton, NJ: Princeton University Press, 1975); Arno Mayer, *The Persistence of the Old Regime: Europe to the Great War* (New York: Pantheon, 1981).
11. John Horne, ed., *Démobilisations culturelles après la Grande Guerre*. 14-18. Aujourd'hui. Today. Heute. Vol. 5. (Paris: Noesis, 2002).
12. H. Clout, "The Great Reconstruction of Towns and Cities in France 1918-1935," *Planning Perspectives: An International Journal of History, Planning and the Environment*. 20, no. 1 (2005): 11-34. La Contemporaine, F delta 874/9.
13. Laurence Van Ypersele, "Héros, Martyrs et Traîtres: Les Fractures de La Belgique Libérée," in *Sortir de la Grande Guerre. Le monde et l'après-1918*, ed. Stéphane Audoin-Rouzeau and Christophe Prochasson (Paris: Tallandier, 2008), 228.
14. Reinhart Koselleck, *Futures Past: On the Semantics of Historical Time* (Cambridge, MA: MIT Press, 1985).
15. John Horne, *Labour at War. France and Britain 1914-1918* (Oxford: Clarendon Press, 1991).
16. Stéphane Audoin-Rouzeau, Jean-Jacques Becker, Gerd Krumeich, and Jay M. Winter, eds., *Guerres et Cultures, 1914-1918* (Paris: A. Colin, 1994).
17. John Horne and Alan Kramer, *German Atrocities, 1914. A History of Denial* (New Haven, CT: Yale University Press, 2001).
18. John Horne, ed., *State, Society, and Mobilization in Europe during the First World War* (Cambridge: Cambridge University Press, 1997).

19 Paul Jarry, *Le Passé Qui Saigne : Les Villes Martyres, Hier et Aujourd'hui* (Paris: E. Champion, 1916).
20 Gabriel Hanotaux, *Les Villes Martyres. Les Falaises de l'Aisne* (Paris: Plon, 1915), 12-15.
21 Pierre Nothomb, *Les Barbares En Belgique* (Paris: Perrin et cie, 1915), 105-106.
22 Marius Vachon, *Les Villes Martyres de France et de Belgique* (Paris: Payot, 1915).
23 Paul Deschanel, "Le Grand Devoir," *Le Journal des Régions Dévastées*, 18 May 1919.
24 Henri Pirenne, *La Belgique et La Guerre Mondiale* (Paris: PUF, 1928).
25 Charles Seignobos et al., eds., *La Réorganisation de la France: Conférences Faites à l'École des Hautes Études Sociales (Novembre 1915 à Janvier 1916)* (Paris: F. Alcan, 1917). I am most grateful to Professor John Horne who brought this publication to my attention and kindly shared his notes and reflections on the topic. To place these urban reflections in context, see Cathérine Bruant, "L'École d'art public du Collège libre des sciences sociales: une formation à l'urbanisme comme « sociologie appliquée »," *Le Télémaque* 33, no. 1 (2008): 83-106.
26 La Contemporaine, O 5850; A. Daudé-Bancel, "La reconstruction des cités détruites", 1 June 1917, Excerpt from *La Grande Revue*, May-June 1917; Archives Diplomatiques du Royaume de Belgique (hereafter Arch. Dipl. Bel.) CI B 378; Harvard University, Widener Library, Fr 1870.21.5 F, *La France*, February 1921, 202-223. "Rebuilding France for Posterity. How the Renaissance des Cités is helping the people in devastated areas to plan a new life" by George B. Ford.
27 The UK National Archives (hereafter TNA), CAB 1/27/28, 12 December 1918.
28 Arch. Dipl. Belg. CI B 218, Dr Cousot, Senator of Dinant.
29 Arch. Dipl. Belg. Letter from Baron Moncheur to Minister Broqueville, 1 October 1917.
30 Anne Orde, *British Policy and European Reconstruction after the First World War* (Cambridge: Cambridge University Press, 2002), 21.
31 Arch. Dipl. Bel. CI B 267. Restauration de la Belgique. Commission for Relief in Belgium. Moncheur to Broqueville, 7 November 1918.
32 TNA, T 1/12123.
33 Arch. Dipl. Belg. CI B 267, Belgian Legation in London to Minister, 4 December 1917.
34 TNA, T 1/12123, Note to Keynes, 22 February 1917.
35 Hoover Archives, Stanford University, CA, Loucheur Papers, Box 12, Folder 34, 12 March 1919.
36 TNA, T 1/2376, Foreign Office. Public opinion on the peace treaties and reconstruction policy in Belgium: Report of the British Special Commission to Belgium, 1919.
37 *Le Journal des Régions Dévastées*, 18 May 1919.
38 *Le Sinistré*, 6 September 1925.
39 *Le Journal des Régions Dévastées*, 18 May 1919.
40 Archives Nationales de France, F7 / 1001; Marne.
41 Roland Dorgelès, *Le réveil des morts* (Paris: A. Michel, 1923), 63.
42 Lucien Hubert, *La Renaissance d'un Département Dévasté* (Paris: Boivin & Cie, 1923), 357.
43 *Le Sinistré*, 6 December 1925.
44 Annette Becker, *Oubliés de La Grande Guerre. Humanitaire et Culture de Guerre 1914-1918. Populations Occupées, Déportés Civils, Prisonniers de Guerre* (Paris: Noesis, 1998); Julia Irwin, *Making the World Safe: The American Red Cross and a Nation's Humanitarian Awakening* (Oxford: Oxford University Press, 2013); Bruno Cabanes, *The Great War and the Origins of Humanitarianism, 1918-1924*. Studies in the Social and Cultural History of Modern Warfare 41 (Cambridge: Cambridge University Press,

2014); Melanie S. Tanielian, *The Charity of War: Famine, Humanitarian Aid, and World War I in the Middle East* (Stanford, CA: Stanford University Press, 2017).

45 Elizabeth Lebas, Susanna Magri, and Christian Topalov, "Reconstruction and Popular Housing after the First World War: A Comparative Study of France, Great Britain, Italy and the United States," *Planning Perspectives* 6, no. 3 (September 1991): 249-267.

46 *Journal Officiel*, Chambre des députés, 22 July 1920, #1136.

47 Henri Sellier and A. Bruggeman, *Le problème du logement. Son influence sur les conditions de l'habitation et l'aménagement des villes*. Histoire Économique et Sociale de La Guerre Mondiale (Paris & New Haven, CT: Dotation Carnegie - PUF - Yale UP, 1927).

48 Pieter Uyttenhove, "Les efforts internationaux pour une Belgique moderne," in *Resurgam. La Reconstruction de La Belgique Après 1914*, ed. Marcel Smets (Brussels: Passage 44, 1985).

49 Patricia Clavin, "Defining Transnationalism," *Contemporary European History* 14, no. 04 (November 2005): 421-439.

50 Archives Départementales du Pas-de-Calais, B.C. 1970, *La reconstruction des régions libérées du Pas-de-Calais, suivie de la guerre sur les champs de bataille de l'Artois. Situation au premier janvier 1927*, September 1927.

51 Bibliothèque Nationale de France, 8-LK16-2390, La reconstitution de la région libérée au 1er avril 1922, exposé présenté au Conseil général par M. Alfred Morain, 1922.

52 *Le Figaro*, 8 November 1929.

53 Alex Dowdall, *Communities Under Fire: Urban Life at the Western Front, 1914-1918* (New York: Oxford University Press, 2020).

54 Archives Municipales de Reims, 6S5, Délibération du Conseil Municipal, 9 November 1918.

Fig. 1. "Belgian refugees fleeing from Louvain to Brussels" (August 1914). Reproduced from Richard Harding Davis, *With the Allies*, New York, C. Scribner's Sons, 1914.

Reflections on Leuven as Martyred City and the Realignment of Propinquity

Richard Plunz

I find it intriguing to return once again to Leuven and to the Katholieke Universiteit to reflect on the significance of the events here of a century ago that are still with us today in one form or another. We are meeting in the site of the former University Library, rebuilt after the war but no longer a library. I ask for your indulgence in reading the following account from 1914 of the fate of a professor at Leuven who would, on a regular basis, have passed through the Oude Markt and the University Library, before its destruction on 25 August 1914.

> I am the son of a Louvain Professor. I met at Furnes [Veurne], whilst I was with the army, a man who was a refugee from Louvain. […]. He came to give me information as to the happenings at my father's house, of which he had been left in charge. He told me that when the Germans arrived at Louvain they took possession of my father's house and completely looted it, taking away all portable articles of value and destroying the furniture and other contents. That they stabled horses in the drawing room. That they destroyed, tore up, and threw into the street my father's manuscripts and books (which were very numerous) and completely wrecked his library and its contents. That finally the Germans burnt the house together with all the others in the neighborhood. The Germans also destroyed the manuscript of an important work of my late father which was in the hands of a printer.[1]

Apart from the above transgressions, the professor's lifeworld in Leuven was definitively erased with the burning of the University Library and its 300,000 books and manuscripts dating back for centuries. Leuven was said to be "martyred".[2] Although the sacking of Leuven remains unspeakable today, similar atrocities have since been perpetuated elsewhere in the world. Let us reflect for a moment on our own academic worlds and imagine ourselves in the place of those Leuven faculty members in 1918 during their deliberations on rebuilding. I can imagine that we might be tempted to put everything back. There was the capacity to do so a century ago. Yet rebuilding went beyond "restoration" such that today Leuven remains an important precedent for understanding the options for urbanism that have been lost in the normative urban planning protocols of the rest of the twentieth century.

On the Western Front, the logistics of the destruction and reconstruction were immense, even by today's norms. In Belgium and France, by one estimate, 3,430,000 hectares of land were destroyed, and in Belgium alone 242 municipalities had to undergo reconstruction.[3] In Leuven, by various accounts 1,081 houses and some 2,000 buildings overall were completely destroyed, with extensive partial damage to others; 25% to 30% of the city terrain was "scorched earth".[4] In Belgium, by various estimates, up to two million people became refugees, one third of Belgium's population at that time (Fig. 1). At least half a million refugees remained in France and the UK until well after the war, and of course many from Leuven would have remained displaced for some period, given the devastation.[5] Surely the Belgian displacements of World War I were unprecedented in early twentieth-century Western Europe. Today, however, these numbers pale in comparison to the escalating wartime and climate migrations well underway.

In the Spring of 1979 Professor Marcel Smets and I were walking through the Oude Markt in Leuven. I knew almost nothing of the Belgian reconstruction, and I suggested that it should be properly studied as an important moment in the annals of twentieth-century urbanism. Our discussions continued with a "road trip" in which we visited the reconstructed World War I sites in West Flanders – including Ypres [Ieper], Diksmuide, and the Flanders Field American Cemetery at Waregem. Several years later, Marcel Smets published his pioneering study, *Resurgam*,[6] as a companion to the 1985 exhibition in Brussels. *Resurgam* further piqued my interest. It seemed that the unprecedented scale of rebuilding could be understood as consciously "modernist urbanism". On that day in 1979 I might have dismissed the Oude Markt as a picturesque but superficial scenography. Instead, I was tempted to understand the rebuilt Leuven as a unique modern urban artefact made in parallel to other, radically new urban strategies that were unfolding in the early twentieth century. I speculated that what I saw could be understood as an intentionally "modern" project, not just a historical reproduction and not just inherited nineteenth-century practice. I found it odd that the rebuilding did not occupy an important place in the context of the evolution of the cannons of modernism and regionalism. The scale of the operation alone would make it a "modern" initiative.

Marcel Smets' contribution was precisely to raise questions related to our accepted cannons of nineteenth- and early twentieth-century modernist urbanism and to ask why this moment of learning and practice in Flanders and Leuven has been so ignored and, conversely, why the emerging and radically new "modernist" tendencies in urbanism were absent in the rebuilding. As a student I had studied the radical approaches to urbanism elsewhere, concurrent with the Belgian reconstruction. There were the *villes-tours* of Auguste Perret and the Radiant City of Le Corbusier. There was the immense Russian constructivist-era urbanization. There was the beginning of the American de-urbanist movement that transformed the United States over the next half century or more. And there was the American resistance to "de-urbanism", the affirmation of nineteenth-century "urbanism as a way of life", to use Louis Wirth's phrase. But excluded was the largest single urban initiative in Europe in the 1920s.

One can suggest that the rebuilding of Leuven was a testament to complex motivations far beyond a simple reincarnation of the nineteenth-century ideals of Camillo Sitte, Joseph Stübben, Charles Buls, or the nationalistic tendencies of the German protagonists.[7] The Belgian reconstruction did engage a certain *realpolitik*, including the German attempt at post-war occupation and interference with post-war planning.[8] Yet, already in 1914 there were Belgian urban alternatives that anticipated the modernist German *Zeilenbau* planning that came into common practice only after the end of the 1920s. For example, in 1914 the completion of Émile Hellemans' housing complex in the Marollen in Brussels considerably pre-dated the *Zeilenbau* formulas. It was Bruno De Meulder's research as a graduate student at Leuven in 1983 that first made me aware of the precedent of Hellemans' *Cité* in identifying alternative modernist cannons.[9] Although such alternatives were surely well-known, Leuven represented a conscious resistance to this emerging "modernist" urbanism that has since exhibited so many signs of failure throughout the world. In some sense the rebuilding leap-frogged what was to evolve later on in the twentieth century. An important question is why this gap? And what can be some of the causes for eschewing the new modernist tendencies? One can understand that Hellemans' Marollen would have been considered too radical for the reconstruction effort in Leuven and that the realization of the emerging orthodox ideals for a Modern Movement urbanism were not yet fully operable. Instead, for Leuven one can suggest that there was a desire for historical continuity in the aftermath of war with an unprecedented scale of destruction. And this continuity can be related to revaluing the propinquity of the medieval Leuven, in opposition to the potentially alienating effects of the new urban tendencies.

By 1924, concurrent with the ongoing Belgian reconstruction, Le Corbusier was railing against the *Chemin des ânes* – the donkey's zig-zag,[10] with the implication that those who persisted in such geometries were themselves donkeys, presumably including the Belgians as well as New Yorkers. In 1924, Le Corbusier did not hesitate to rail against Lower Manhattan's zig-zag as a *paradoxe pathétique*. I suppose, however, that it was not exactly politically correct to rail against the meticulous zig-zag rebuilding next door in Belgium, although he could not resist implying the inferiority of the "Flanders House" compared to his "machine for living". In 1933 he published his Antwerp Plan for the West Bank as an affront to the Flanders reconstruction.[11] At least he did not superimpose his colossal Parisian "Plan Voisin" on the Antwerp historic center although he did have ideas for Antwerp's Cathedral Square. I am sure there can be more to say about a European *paradoxe pathétique*, and perhaps even why in the aftermath of the massive urban devastation from the war there could not yet be an operational method for implementing a "Plan Voisin" somewhere in Northern Europe. That would come to fruition after World War II. As for Le Corbusier, his "Cartesian geometry" of the "Radiant City" would supersede all other options until the 1960s, when he and even Mies van der Rohe retreated into "tradition" via their tactical advocacy of "truth" in design.[12]

Given the immense devastation in Leuven, one can hardly conceive of a rebuilding strategy that would not reaffirm historic propinquity as an antidote. Leuven could be retrieved only by deploying a spatial fabric constrained by the demands of survival of social class and culture. Seen from today's perspective, the rebuilt Leuven anticipated a new urbanism inclusive of a cohesive social vision that had its origins in its medieval core. The emerging new Modern Movement urbanism that was already obsolete by the time of its massive global implementation in the aftermath of World War II was rejected. Ironically, the urban scourges that had nurtured the "sun, space, and green" of Le Corbusier's Radiant City were already being ameliorated as modern medicine superseded hygienic design arguments against the propinquity of the historic city.[13] Given this consideration, one might postulate that the rebuilt Leuven was prescient of the next "modernist" city of the twenty-first century, rather than the other contemporary visions of the 1920s.

A legacy of the rebuilding in Flanders is the curious story of René (Renaat) Braem who prominently pioneered the new Modern Movement urbanism with a more measured variant for Antwerp in contrast to Le Corbusier's West Bank plan.[14] As a child he would have witnessed the destruction of Flanders first hand, and he would have witnessed the reconstruction of the Flemish towns first hand. Those citizens depicted in Braem's "Linear City" proposal for Antwerp were denizens of an entirely new post-industrial world. They were the modern people of leisure in an environment devoid of the regimes of nineteenth-century labor, who would have the time to frolic in the "sun, space, and green", and they rejected the propinquity of the historic Flemish towns (Fig. 2). In time this new urban world became more dystopian than the old in many cities around the world. Yet, in the post-World War I era it surely was an engaging vision and effective socio-economic instrument, as much for Flanders as for Manhattan by the 1930s. The Radiant City and the *Zeilenbau* would continue to dominate much city design practice for the next half-century, including the massive public housing that has been among my long-term preoccupations in New York City. By the 1950s in New York, however, we had arrived at a definitive impasse resulting in the "dreary deadlock of public housing" that, perhaps more than any other urban design option, cast a pall over the city.[15]

Fig. 2. Renaat Braem. Design for a *Linear City* (1934). With the permission of CIVA, Brussels, Fonds Braem.

So, apart from all else, my reflections are related to my particular interests that engage the realignment ideals of propinquity, of community, of space, and of place. Such were at the origins of medieval Leuven, and they are the ideals that lay at its recreation in the aftermath of World War I. While for sure reconstruction changed the old social fabric, seemingly what was retained was the urban crucible – the container, put back as a celebration of Flemish urban culture and as defiance of the attempt at its annihilation (Fig. 3). As crucible, Leuven has been very important to my own formation, and I include the group of faculty colleagues with whom I have shared ideas over many years. We have all been subliminally connected to the ideal of propinquity, both spatial and intellectual. I believe that this condition continues to affect this place in ways large and small, mainly unspoken, in the ether as much as in the stones. Such is the strength of this place. Yet back in 1979 and in the following years I sensed a dark side. In the Oude Markt I remember well the demonstrations: anti-nuclear and anti-racism, but also the counter-demonstrations that were pro-Flemish Nationalist and separatist. In the bookstacks of the University Library I especially remember witnessing the ongoing removal of the French language books to the new French-language Université Catholique de Louvain. For me it was a troubling encounter that still lingers in my mind today.

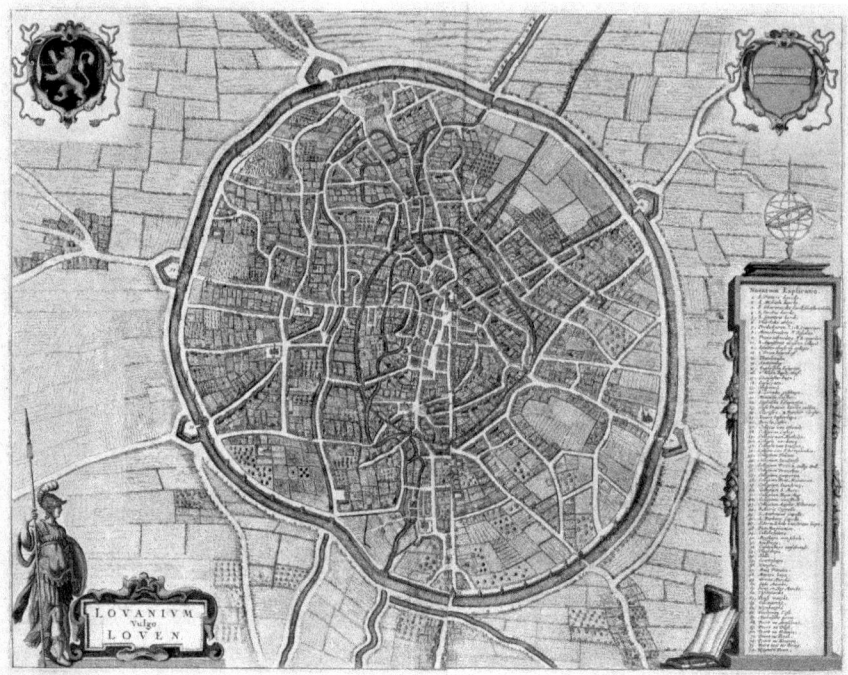

Fig. 3. J. Blaeu. Plan of Leuven from *Novum Ac Magnum Theatrum Urbium Belgicae* (Amsterdam 1649); reproduced from from *Atlas Van Loon* (1663-65). With the permission of Het Scheepvaartmuseum, Amsterdam.

Within the expanded realm of urban "martyrdom" today, the phenomenon of the "Martyred Cities" of Flanders may seem distant. For myself, perhaps the recent images that come closest to 1914 in Leuven record the burning of the National Library in Sarajevo on 25 August 1992, the exact same day as in Leuven some 78 years earlier. In Sarajevo, one and a half million volumes were lost, of which 155,000 irreplaceable manuscripts and books including the National Archive. Today when I think of Leuven my thoughts also connect to Sarajevo and the meaning of that travesty and now, with even more immediacy, to the images from Mosul, from Aleppo, from Eastern Ghouta, or from Yemen. The Syrian refugee figures currently number more than 12 million, the entire present-day population of Belgium. Today for most of the world's refugees there is little hope to achieve the extraordinary level of rebuilding that was managed in Flanders in the 1920s and 1930s. Still, one must hope that we can learn lessons from those experiences of a century ago that can be relevant for today and tomorrow, especially now that we understand that the world has not yet moved beyond such depravities – far from it. I think of the recent ISIS desecrations in Palmyra. We must ask ourselves about the meaning of the past – of the historical events that we commemorate. We might well question whether now, after the passage of a century, the commemorations of the Flemish martyred cites move ever closer to Guy Debord's *Société du Spectacle*, with the danger that the Belgian reconstruction becomes a matter of images.[16] Perhaps the most profound remembrance is the acknowledgement that urbicide is alive and well.

I have found Paul Veyne's writing on history, truth, and tribalism to be instructive in my understanding of the realignment of propinquity. Perhaps the rebuilt "new Leuven" was Veyne's "palace of imagination" in the sense of his use of the term in the context of Greek mythology as a concept, "not built in space [but] the only space available [...]".[17] One imagines that "truth" in the Leuven context was not the "truth" of Le Corbusier and Mies, but closer to the "truth" of Veyne, which is imbedded in diversity, such that "every patchwork culture, with its diversity opens the way to inventiveness". For Veyne, in describing Greek Myth, truth is the "child of the imagination" which is the "child of the constitutive imagination of our tribe", and without absolutes.[18] Truth is tribal. The tribal engages propinquity. Perhaps it is Veyne's "tribal" that best accounts for the realignment of Leuven propinquity, and from this we can gain understanding. I will take the liberty of ending with Veyne's admonition with regard to Palmyra ancient and today: "Yes, without a doubt, knowing, wanting to know, only one culture – one's own – is to be condemned to a life of suffocating sameness".[19] We can see the double edge, the dangers of the tribal then and now, but with diversity as a key to combating the dangers, and with propinquity as a key to encouraging diversity.

Notes

The author is indebted to Andrés Julian Álvarez Dávila for assistance in the editing of this manuscript.

1. Committee on Alleged German Outrages, *Report of the Committee on Alleged German Outrages Presented to Parliament by Command of His Majesty* (London: H.M. Stationery Office and Eyre and Spottiswoode, 1915), 107. Leuven Professor Léon Noël describes the events of 26 August in *Louvain, 891-1914* (Oxford: Clarendon Press, 1915), 203-241.
2. There was considerable contemporary reportage related to the sack of Leuven including the work by the Committee on Alleged German Outrages. Also useful have been Richard Harding Davis, *With the Allies* (New York: C. Scribner's Sons, 1914) and Noël, *Louvain, 891-1914*, 203-241. The characterization of Leuven among "martyred" cities in Flanders appears early on in the account of Albert Fuglister, *Louvain, Ville Martyre* (Paris: Éditions Delandre, 1916).
3. Figures referenced in Dries Claeys, "World War I and the Reconstruction of the Countryside in Belgium and France: A Historiographical Essay," *Agricultural History Review* 65, no. 1 (January 2017): 108-129. A comprehensive survey of the war damage is given in Hugh Clout, *After the Ruins: Restoring the Countryside of Northern France after the Great War* (Exeter: University of Exeter Press, 1996), 19-52.
4. Among the sources for destruction logistics in Leuven are Marcel Smets, "The Reconstruction of Leuven after the Events of 1914" (overprint, Cities in Development 19th-20th Centuries, 10th International Colloquium, Spa, Belgium, 2-5 September 1980); and John Horne and Alan Kramer, *German Atrocities, 1914: A History of Denial* (New Haven, CT: Yale University Press, 2001), 40.
5. Larry Zuckerman, *The Rape of Belgium: The Untold Story of World War I* (New York: New York University Press, 2004), 85. The scattering of the KU Leuven faculty is described in Mark Derez, "The Flames of Louvain: The War Experience of an Academic Community," in *Facing Armageddon: The First World War Experienced*, ed. Hugh Cecil and Peter H. Liddle (London: Cooper, 1996), 617-629.
6. Marcel Smets, ed., *Resurgam: la reconstruction en Belgique après 1914 (Passage 44, Bruxelles, 27 mars-30 juin 1985), Crédit communal/exposition organisée à l'initiative du Crédit communal de Belgique et réalisée par le Centre d'histoire urbaine, Leuven* (Brussels: Crédit communal, 1985).
7. A useful summary of this dynamic is provided in Wolfgang Cortjaens, "'The German Way of Making Better Cities': German Reconstruction Plans for Belgium during First World War," in *Living with History, 1914-1964: Rebuilding Europe after the First and Second World Wars and the Role of Heritage Preservation = La reconstruction en Europe après la Première et la Seconde Guerre Mondiale et le rôle de la conservation des monuments historiques*, eds. Nicholas Bullock and Luc Verpoest (Leuven: Leuven University Press, 2011), 44-59.
8. Johan Van den Mooter, "German Reconstruction in Belgium during World War I: A Regional Experiment," in *Regionalism and Modernity: Architecture in Western Europe, 1914-1940*, eds. Leen Meganck, Linda Van Santvoort, and Jan De Maeyer (Leuven: Leuven University Press, 2013), 49-73. A summary of Leuven refugee dispersal is given in Derez, "The Flames of Louvain: The War Experience of an Academic Community," 617-629.

9   Bruno De Meulder, *Galerijwoningen te Brussel. Proeve van een historisch-typologische analyse van de sociale meergezinswoningbouw in de Brusselse agglomeratie. 1870-1914* (Master's diss., KU Leuven, 1983).

10 Le Corbusier, *Urbanisme* (Paris: G. Crès & cie., 1924). The first edition published in English, translated from the 8th French edition, appeared as *The City of To-morrow and its Planning*, trans. Frederick Etchells (New York: Payson & Clarke, Ltd. 1929).

11 Le Corbusier, *La ville radieuse, éléments d'une doctrine d'urbanisme pour l'équipement de la civilisation machiniste. Paris, Genève, Rio de Janeiro, Sao Paolo, Montevideo, Buenos-Aires, Alger, Moscou, Anvers, Barcelone, Stockholm, Nemours, Piacé* (Boulogne: Éditions de l'Architecture d'aujourd'hui, 1935).

12 For example, see: Fritz Neumeyer, *The Artless Word: Mies van der Rohe on the Building Art*, trans. Mark Jarzombek (Cambridge, MA: MIT Press, 1991), 332; Le Corbusier, preface to *Architecture of Truth: The Cistercian Abbey of Le Thoronet*, ed. François Cali and ill. Lucien Hervé (New York: Phaidon Press, 2001).

13 F. B. Smith, *The Retreat of Tuberculosis, 1850-1950* (New York: Croom Helm, 1988). The obsolescence of modern "green" urbanism as a tuberculosis antidote has been variously discussed in urban ecosystem literature. See: Robert I. McDonald, Peter J. Marcotullio, and Burak Güneralp, "Urban Governance of Biodiversity and Ecosystem Services," in *Urbanization, Biodiversity and Ecosystem Services: Challenges and Opportunities*, eds. Cathy Wilkinson et al. (Dordrecht: Springer, 2013), 539-587.

14 Francis Strauven, *René Braem: Les Aventures Dialectiques d'un Moderniste Flamand* (Brussels: Archives d'Architecture Moderne, 1985), 119-124.

15 See Richard Plunz with Michael Sheridan, "Deadlock Plus 50. On Public Housing in New York," *Harvard Design Magazine* no. 8 (Summer 1999): 4-9. Republished in William S. Saunders, ed., *Urban Planning Today* (Minneapolis, MN: University of Minnesota Press, 2006), 14-23.

16 Guy DeBord, *The Society of the Spectacle*, trans. Donald Nicholson-Smith (New York: Zone Books, 1995). For the political and commercial aspects of the World War I memorials see Karen Shelby, *Belgian Museums of the Great War: Politics, Memory, and Commerce* (New York: Routledge, 2018).

17 Paul Veyne, "The Final Foucault and His Ethics," in *Foucault and his Interlocutors*, ed. Arnold I. Davidson (Chicago, IL: University of Chicago Press, 1997), 146-182.

18 Paul Veyne, *Did the Greeks Believe in Their Myths? An essay on the Constitutive Imagination* (Chicago, IL: University of Chicago Press, 1988), 113.

19 Paul Veyne, *Palmyra: An Irreplaceable Treasure* (Chicago, IL: The University of Chicago Press, 2017), 85.

Fig. 1. The completely devastated church and village center of Merkem at the end of the First World War.

Making Good Farmers by Making Better Farms:
Farmstead Architecture and Social Engineering in Belgium After the Great War

Dries Claeys & Yves Segers

During the autumn of 1914, the annual congress of the National Commission for the Embellishment of Rural Life (NCERL) was to take place in Brussels. Architects and agricultural scientists were invited to present their answers on the issue of rural housing. Since the end of the nineteenth century the Belgian countryside had been perceived as a place in peril. Not only had agriculture – a typically rural professional activity – lost its position as the "primary sector" of the national economy. Processes of urbanisation, as well as the relatively poor access to public services and amenities in rural areas, undermined the vitality of the countryside.[1] From this perspective, the national congress was one of the many activities that were organised to revitalise rural life in Belgium. However, the start of the Great War in August 1914 forced the organising committee to postpone the congress until September 1919. Although the primary objectives remained, the context in which the congress took place had definitely changed. Four years of continuous warfare and occupation had devastating effects on the Belgian territory, but also on the national economy and society.[2] Nevertheless Firmin Graftiau, a state agronomist and vice-president of the NCERL, stated that the destruction provided a unique opportunity to regenerate the Belgian countryside. In his opening address he expressed the hope that "inspired by the presented studies and previous work, the authorities that are responsible for Belgium's reconstruction will have the aim to increase the well-being of the rural population by improving their living conditions" (Fig. 1).[3]

According to Graftiau, the construction of good farms was indispensable for the creation of better farmers and, more generally, a better rural population. He believed, in other words, that it was possible to change people's beliefs and behaviour by changing their environment. This chapter explores the extent to which the reconstruction of the Belgian countryside can be considered an example of social engineering. According to the Dutch sociologists Jan Willem Duyvendak and Ido de Haan, social engineering was not so much a feature of the post-World War II welfare states but instead went hand in hand with the rise of nineteenth-century liberal societies. Starting from the hypothesis that this was indeed the case, we study the discourses that underscored the reconstruction of farmsteads – even before the end of the war – and how general ideas about farm building were put into practice after 1918.

Recent literature has shown that national governments across Europe started to govern rural communities from the nineteenth century onwards. The underlying rationale suggested that space is power-induced and could be used as a tool to control populations. In their edited volume *Governing the Rural in Interwar Europe* (2018), Liesbeth van de Grift and Amalia Ribi Forclaz showed that this idea formed the basis for practices of rural government in several European countries between the two world wars. The growing belief that spatial and social planning closely encouraged both democratic and authoritarian states to govern their countryside more actively.[4]

The tactics of governing people through space not only led to "high modernist" development plans and large-scale internal colonisation schemes, as was the case on the newly reclaimed lands of the Netherlands in the 1940s.[5] Eugen Weber's famous *Peasants into Frenchmen* (1976) described how subtler forms of governing, for example road building, were aimed at affecting the identity of the rural population in modern France and integrating them into a nation of *citoyens*.[6] In Britain, geographer David Matless revealed the role of landscape in the construction of an English national identity. Like in many other countries, the countryside and rural life were defined as the counterpart of urban, industrial society. While life in the countryside was idealised as "pure", cities were often depicted as degenerative and their populations as immoral.[7]

The garden cities movement that originated in late nineteenth-century England also incorporated spatial and social planning schemes. The advocates of the garden city believed in the creation of a new type of city that would combine the benefits from the town (presence of public transport and amenities) and the village (healthy environment). Ebenezer Howard, for example, created a model of self-sufficient and cooperatively governed towns with radial spatial planning and surrounded by agricultural land and forests.[8] During the First World War, the Belgian government remodelled the garden city idea to build the first garden suburbs shortly after 1918. Although post-war town planning in Belgium continued to be founded on private property instead of collective owenership, Louis Albrechts argued that the First World

War resulted in the application of new "philosophies of life and related reflections on the organization of space".[9]

This socio-spatial entanglement also related to the level of individual (rural) building in interwar Belgium. Recent studies on architecture in the Belgian countryside, too, have perceived rural housing as a tool for governing farmers and their families. Sofie De Caigny and Wouter Vanderstede, for example, indicated how the Belgian Women Farmers' Association explicitly related model plans of rural interiors to predefined role patterns for farmers' women. Other studies as well linked discourses on the construction of "good" housing to processes of identity building. Models of rural architecture were designed to bridge the opposition between the identity of rural dwellers and the needs of modern citizens.[10] In *Regionalism and Modernity* (2013), traditional building styles in the Belgian countryside were studied as disciplinary mechanisms as well as strategic elements that made modernity more acceptable for the rural population.[11]

Few publications have bridged the gap between theory and practice. While historians have uncovered the link between architectural guidelines and social engineering in early twentieth-century model books, little is known about the extent to which these guidelines were put into practice.[12] This is surprising, because the devastations of the First World War resulted in perhaps the most intensive construction activity in Belgian history. Contemporary statistics estimated that more than 80,000 houses were completely destroyed and 200,000 houses were at least partially damaged. Approximately 30,000 of these houses were identified as farms.[13] The geography of destruction reflected the chronology of war. While some towns in the east of the country were affected during the early months of war, the largest degree of devastation was situated in the so-called "devastated regions" in the westernmost part of the country.

By taking post-World War I farmstead architecture as an example, this article explores how the governing of society and space was entangled in architectural discourses during and after the First World War. It also studies how power-induced discourses on rural architecture found their way into practice. The reconstruction of farmsteads is an interesting case study for a couple of reasons. First, farmstead architecture played an important role in the rural idyll that conservative architects, civil society organizations and policy-makers propagated during and after the First World War. Second, there is an abundance of sources that allow us to investigate farm building in the context of post-World War I reconstruction.

Apart from the architectural model books that were mainly produced before the end of the war, the Belgian state archives have preserved a huge number of building plans and specifications from the Devastated Regions Office (DRO, 1919-1926). This was a special government institution that was established to recover the public domain – roads, communal buildings and other public property – after the First World War. Nevertheless, the government service soon became responsible for the reconstruction of private housing as well. With the integration of a Building Service as a subsection of the DRO in 1919, a large-scale turnkey building project took off that would result in the state-led reconstruction of c. 10,000 private houses. This was the first time the Belgian government had directly intervened in the housing market by building private houses with public funds.

With the reconstruction by the state, the Belgian government and its minister of the Interior, Jules Renkin, aimed to tackle some of the problems that reconstruction was facing at the time. First of all, there was the problem of bureaucracy. Every owner that had suffered war damage had the right to full compensations. In order to be compensated, they had to file a request to specially constituted courts for war damage. This could lead to an administrative bottleneck and eventually the financial draining away of reconstruction activities. Since owners who agreed to let the state reconstruct their property automatically agreed not to claim their compensation, reconstruction by the state reduced pressure on the courts for war damage. A second element in favour of reconstruction by the state was a logistic one. Letting the state take over private building sites did in fact lead to advantages of scale. Thirdly, the government hoped to improve the housing quality by committing home owners to appoint an architect to draw up the building plans.[14]

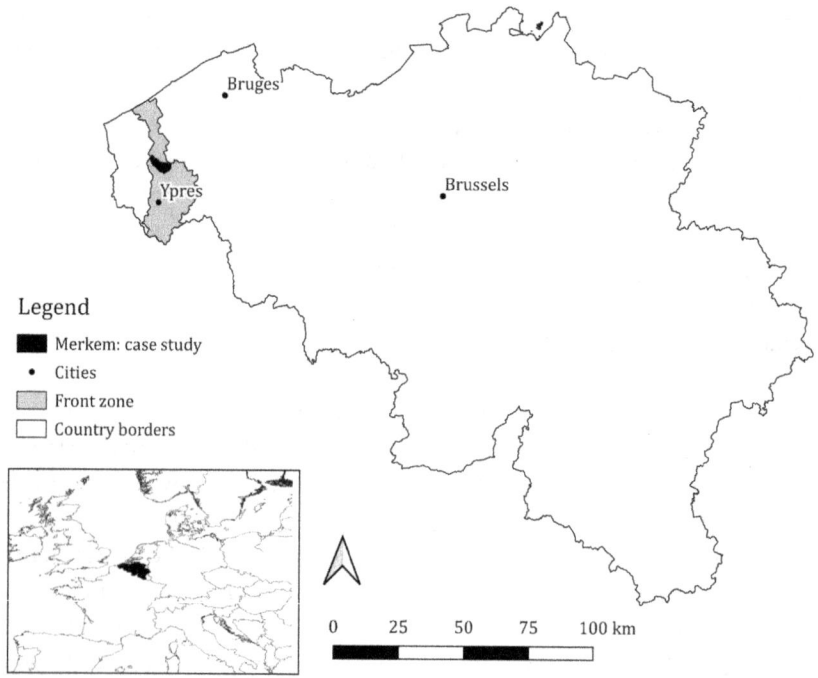

Map 1. Map of the geographical position of the case study village Merkem.

This article is based on the analysis of architectural guidebooks and 20 building documents from the archives of the DRO. The 20 documents were selected on geographical criteria. They represent the farms rebuilt by the state in a single village: Merkem. Merkem was – and still is – a rural village in West Flanders with a few thousand inhabitants. Located between Ypres and Diksmuide, the village became part of the front line in 1914 and remained under constant artillery fire for the next four years (see map). Consequently, Merkem was completely destroyed by November 1918. Since everything had to be rebuilt from scratch, Merkem is an interesting case study for investigating whether the tabula rasa of the First World War was effectively used to construct model farms and hence "increase the well-being of the rural population".

After an introductory paragraph on regionalism as an architectural style and discourse, the next paragraphs highlight three different aspects of farmstead architecture: (i) the formal language of the farm, (ii) the agricultural enterprise and its buildings, and (iii) the farmer's house. The building plans of 16 farms – four of the building documents had no plans or specifications – serve as a basis for this in-depth study, while taking into consideration that it is impossible to draw general conclusions from such a small number of cases.[15] The fact that only state-reconstructed farms were taken into account further narrow the possibilities for extrapolating the conclusions to all farms rebuilt after the First World War. Nevertheless, the conclusions will give an indication of the rationales that underscored regionalist discourses during the early twentieth century and the ways in which new ideas about farmstead building were put into practice.

Deconstructing the Regionalist Gaze

Recent literature has generally acknowledged the dominance of regionalism as "reconstruction's official ideology". From the end of the nineteenth century, it was not so much regionalism as a well-defined architectural style that developed. It was part of a modernising movement, but with respect for traditional architecture and the regional environment.[16] In Belgium, regionalist discourses perfectly fitted within conservative ideas about the countryside. They allowed the pursuit of a rural idyll with "picturesque" villages and landscapes that were at the same time adapted to modernity. This aligned with the efforts of the pre-war Catholic governments and organisations such as the NCERL to keep the rural population in the countryside and away from industrial cities. These culminated in the Modern Village that was presented at the 1913 World's Fair in Ghent.[17]

The Modern Village would later prove to inspire rural reconstruction in Belgium. From 1916 onwards, almost two years after the First World War had started, expositions on the reconstruction of rural buildings were held across occupied Belgium. The diffusion of (rural) architectural knowledge in the areas administered by the German General Government – the military government that controlled occupied Belgium and Northern France – happened via the channels of the National Relief and Food Committee (NRFC). The NRFC was established in 1914 to organise the distribution of foodstuffs and other necessities, but it also had an agricultural section aimed at the maximisation of food production in occupied Belgium. Within the agricultural section a special commission for rural reconstruction was established to investigate the issue of farmstead building.[18] Furthermore, every provincial branch of the NRFC had its own technical bureau that was responsible for farmstead building on the local level.[19]

At the exhibitions that took place in places like Brussels (Schaerbeek) and Antwerp, model plans of farms, as well as photographs of pre-war examples of "good" farmsteads, were shown to the audience. Lectures and architectural contests were also organised in the margin of these expos. Given the fact that communication was mostly in French, it can be presumed that the exhibitions in Antwerp and Brussels were aimed at both architects and civil servants. In order to connect to the farmers themselves, the technical bureau of Antwerp also organised an ambulant exposition in some ten smaller towns and villages. This time Dutch was the language of communication, which makes it even clearer that the audience to be reached was quite different. The exhibitions presented "good" examples of rural architecture next to "bad" examples, because it was "indispensable to affect the mentality of farmers by making comparisons and contrasts".[20]

Publications on rural and farmstead architecture could largely be divided into two categories. The first category contained the model books written from a merely architectural and artistic perspective. These publications were rather theoretical and first of all stressed the importance of the visual quality of the buildings in the surrounding landscape. A second type of publications was more practical in nature. Architects and agronomists developed model books and building plans that meticulously told farmers how to build their own modern farms. The Belgian Farmers' League's *Bouwen en heropbouwen van huis en stal* (Building and Rebuilding of House and Stable, 1915) is a schoolbook example of such a publication. Most of these booklets were published under the auspices of the National Relief and Food Committee.[21] The committee had branches at local and regional levels, allowing the architectural guidelines to be diffused across the (occupied part of the) country.

Certainly in the more theoretical works authors were quite clear in stating their particular aims. Regionalist protagonists such as Edward Leonard believed that if farmers were to stay away from the "immoral" cities, improve their living conditions, and continue their professional activities, it was essential to construct "good" farms. Vice-president of the NCERL Jacques Giele stressed that the emphasis on rural aesthetics went hand in hand with the improvement of rural life.[22] The regionalist definition of an "embellished" farm could in broad terms be retraced to three elements: the aestheticisation of the buildings and their integration into the environment, the improvement of living conditions, and the modernisation of the farmer's workplace. With regard to the exterior of the farm, regionalists agreed on the importance of a traditional formal language and the use of regional building materials and techniques.[23] In the specific case of Flemish farmsteads, examples of brick architecture and red-tiled roofs were omnipresent.[24]

Regionalists believed that a historicising reconstruction of the countryside would contribute to the mental wellbeing of farmers, day labourers and their families. In *De kunst op het Platteland* (Art in the Countryside, 1915), Albert Dutry – also vice-president of the NCERL – correlated the physical appearance of farms with mental virtues such as family commitment and intelligence. Furthermore, he claimed that "the physical well-being of the wage earner would encourage him to return back home after his day at work".[25] Helena Van Dorpe, one of the few female voices in the field, also linked rural aesthetics to the question of frugality. Even though the "embellishment" of rural architecture had no direct influence on the family budget, she thought that it might bring the rural population to more austerity.[26]

Secondly, architects and engineers paid a great deal of attention to the living conditions on the farm. Dutry stated that the reconstruction of the countryside was obliged to meet not only the rules of the "science of aesthetic", but those of the "science of health" as well.[27] In order to familiarise the rural population with these rules, numerous publications contained practical tips for building in a way that reduced the risk of physical disease for both the farmers and their cattle. Guidebooks particularly focused on the provision of light and air on the farm. These two natural resources were believed to kill disease-spreading microbes and vermin. Architects also proposed the construction of better – more hygienic – wells, as well as "more healthy" separated bedrooms on the top floor of the farm. Furthermore, several publications defined minimal heights and surfaces for housing accommodation and integrated separate cellars for stocks and dairy products in their plans.[28] Other modernisations, such as the provision of running water and electricity or the integration of bathrooms, were less frequently discussed.[29]

The preoccupation with hygiene on the farm aligned regionalists with the nineteenth-century sanitary movement. Decades before 1914, *hygiénistes* had already devoted themselves to the health of the population. From the perspective of the nation as a social body, they perceived that the health of all societal groups was in the public interest. This certainly was true for farmers as "feeders of the nation".[30] In another vein, regionalists were of the opinion that the physical health of the farmer affected his mental health.[31] Considering these underlying objectives, we agree with

Sofie De Caigny in recognising both the emancipatory and disciplining mechanisms that underscored regionalist building plans.³²

In the third instance, some guidebooks – especially those written by agronomists – focused on the modernisation of the farm as a place for economic activity. One of the most eye-catching changes was the modernisation of the cattle sheds: classic manure stables were transformed into group stables with fodder and manure passages bordered by individual stands. Thus, the dairying and care of the cattle could be rationalised. The installation of drainage systems for manure had to improve hygiene standards in the cattle shed and thus promote healthy livestock. The use of bricks and concrete for the construction of cattle sheds had a similar objective, as well as the presence of door and window arches. The Belgian Farmers' League explicitly condemned corners and nooks in the cattle shed as breeding grounds for pathogens.³³

The breeding of healthy livestock was mainly inspired by economic reasoning. *Handboek van Landelijke Maatschappijleer* (Manual of Rural Sociology, 1931) argued that the productivity of the dairy farm depended upon the fitness of its animals. In the handbook practical cases provided evidence for the assumption that healthy cattle delivered better milk yields.³⁴ Since stock farming had already become the largest branch of Belgian agriculture before 1914, this argument was not without significance.³⁵ It meant that the implementation of sanitary measures contributed to the profitability of the farming enterprise and, in a broader perspective, to the resilience of the agricultural sector as a whole. The fact that the "official" model book on farmstead architecture published by the Belgian government, *Enkele practische gegevens nopens het bouwen van hoeven* (Some practical measures for the construction of farms, 1920), was solely devoted to the reconstruction of sheds demonstrates the (economic) importance of stockbreeding.³⁶ The renowned Belgian zoologist Leopold Frateur rated hygiene as one of the three pillars for livestock improvement, next to the implementation of genetic theory and the prevention of diseases such as bovine tuberculosis.³⁷

The Formal Language of the Farm

The agricultural section of the NRFC made no secret of the fact that it aimed to inspire post-war reconstruction in Belgium. In its final activity report of 1919, the technical bureau of the province of Antwerp expressed its belief that "at the moment when our country [...] is thinking about letting the devastated regions rise from its ashes, it is important to look back at the activities and realizations of our organization in times of hostile occupation".³⁸ The question remains, of course, whether architects involved in post-war farmstead rebuilding were informed about the newest developments in their profession and, if they were effectively willing to implement the expertise that the NRFC had gathered during the war. This paragraph deals with the formal language of the farm.

Spokesmen for the regionalist movement regarded the urbanisation of Belgium as an imminent threat to the countryside. Regionalists regarded architecture as the culmination of three elements: work, family and the environment. The same perspective was used by the Belgian scholar – and later the first female professor in Leuven – Marguerite Lefèvre. She suggested in her thesis on rural houses in Belgium (1926) that rural architecture was the result of "actions and reactions, sometimes confusing, of physical, economic and social elements".[39] As a human geographer, Lefèvre thereby positioned herself in the school of the nineteenth-century French sociologist Frédéric Le Play. According to him there was triad between space (*lieu*), family (*famille*) and work (*travail*), which indicated that human action was always subject to environment and vice versa.[40]

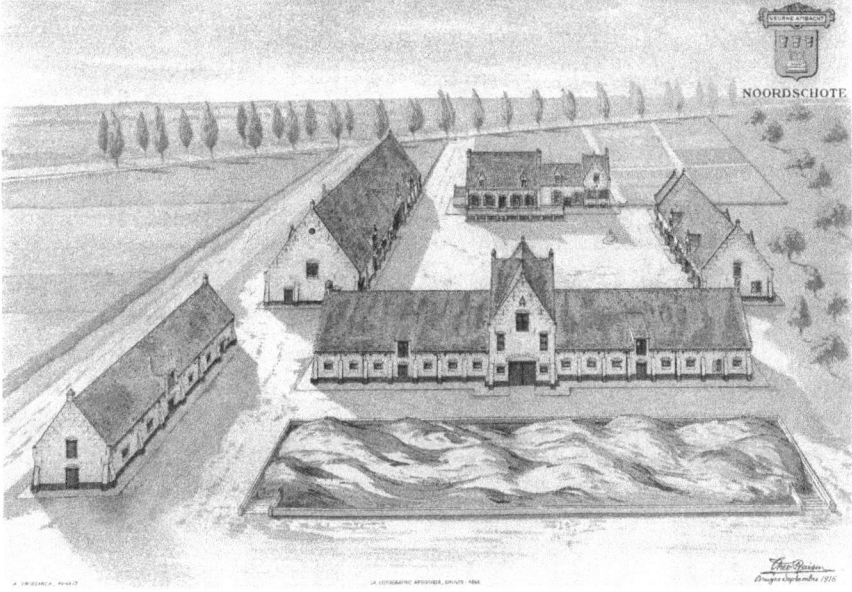

Fig. 2. Lithograph of a model farm in *Fermes-types et constructions rurales en West-Flandre* (1918) by Alfred Ronse and Theo Raison.

The idea that place and people eventually converged enabled regionalists to make a clear distinction between town and countryside, and thus between urban and rural life. While urban architecture was an expression of a specific culture and thus had to be limited to the city, the only logical place for rural architecture was in the countryside. In rural areas it was mainly the farm that served as a beacon of rural identity: "the farm is the most complete expression of rural life".[41] Regionalism, in other words, gave great importance to "harmony", a concept that stressed the connection between human culture and the natural environment. This respect for harmony and dependence on context was also clearly visible in the words of the Swiss regionalist Georges the Montenach, who was cited in 1919 by the Belgian architect Henri Vaes: "when thinking of a country [...] is a farmer or his wife that will spring to mind. And when thinking of the housing of a people, it is the rural dwelling that will be imagined" (Fig. 2).[42]

One of the main techniques for harmonising housing and architecture with their environment was the use of regional building materials. In the Flemish countryside, and in the devastated regions in particular, the use of brick was promoted by virtually every regionalist architect. Graph 1 gives an indication of the costs of building materials for a sample of five farms in Merkem. In this sample each farm represents a different price category. The graph shows that in the building specifications for small and large farms, bricks constituted more than half of total material costs. Brickwork was not only used as a construction material for walls and upright courses. Bricks were also employed as a flooring material in cattle sheds. The relative cost of roof tiles rose to 20%. Tiles generally covered all farm buildings; thatched roofs did not figure in the plans for farms in Merkem rebuilt by the DRO. The first reason brickwork and tiles were so prominent in the building plans can undoubtedly be traced back to the stylistic guidelines of regionalist architects. Furthermore, brickwork was cheaper than reinforced concrete and locally available, which made it a preferred building material in times when the national debt was increasing.[43]

	< 10000 francs	10-15000 francs	15-20000 francs	20-25000 francs	> 25000 francs
Bricks	4042,52	6026,25	7111,28	8285,84	8906,34
Mortar		212,81	617,31	630,21	1001,77
Concrete	868,12	300,43	135,76	883,72	1521,85
Floor tiles		279,39	44,34		
Paving stone			448,3		
Reinforced Concrete			75,06		
Stone	131,3	66,65	190,36	58,22	662,4
Roof tiles	1260,35	1412,09	1601,17	2816,51	2563,15
Other	81,76	346,91	415,78	1181,5	1029,56
Total	6384,05	8644,53	10639,36	13856	15685,07

Table 1. Building materials used for the construction of walls, roofs and floors in five selected farms of different price categories.[44]

A detailed analysis of the model farms' elevations reveals some recurring decorative elements. Half of the state-built farmsteads in Merkem had side walls with typical dovetail patterns. These patterns were frequently used to construct the gable ends of the roofs, but they were also a way of adding to the appeal of the farmstead architecture. In more than half of all cases there were parapets, making the side walls slightly higher than the roof itself. According to the guidebooks, this prevented wind and rain from getting under the tiles, and in this way protected the farm buildings from draught and humidity and potential roof damage. Façade plinths were constructed in order to keep the outer walls moisture-free. Subtle stylistic elements, such as flared eaves, anchors and brick cornices, further contributed to the traditional image of rebuilt farms in Merkem. Another typical decoration was door and window arches. These elements were said to add to the picturesque of the countryside but were also technically useful as they increased the bearing capacity of the lintel.[45]

Regionalist architects had to find a balance between the harmony of the rural landscape and the originality of the individual plans. According to Edward Leonard, buildings had to correspond to a "dual characteristic: the beauty of the individual house and the beauty of the area in general".[46] This translated into designs that looked very similar but were at the same time composed of a variety of building components. While the DRO produced standardised doors and windows in order to reduce production costs as well as to rationalise the workflow, different types were produced to create variety.[47] Doors were made of wood and usually had a fanlight to light the entrance. These fanlights systematically took the form of wooden cross-windows, consisting of six or eight squares. Another characteristic element of farmhouses was the presence of (painted) shutters. Shutters were not only functional but increased the esthetic qualities of rural buildings as well. The same holds true for dormers, which were integrated in almost half of the reconstructed farms. Dormers did in fact allow sunlight to warm and illuminate the top floors of the homestead, and simultaneously improved the image of the farm by breaking the monotony of the red-tiled roofs. The gable ends of the dormers were in many cases finished with spouts and shouldered gables, which were decorative elements in the first place.[48]

Becoming Modern, Remaining Rural

Rather than restoration of pre-war farmstead architecture, historians have revealed regionalism to be part of a modern movement that sought to go beyond nineteenth-century neo-styles.[49] The proposed modernisations of regionalist architects first of all related to the sanitisation of the countryside. During the course of 1919, the Belgian government issued building regulations that included minimal hygiene standards for reconstructed houses. These included the obligation to have double outer walls (without a cavity) to protect against the cold and the rain. The government also regulated the height of ceilings, which had to measure 2 (top floor) or 2.8 (ground floor) metres. The guidebooks directly correlated these compulsory measures with the improvement of in-house air quality and thus the health of the farmer's family. For the same reason the total surface of openable windows per living room had to exceed 10% of that room's area. In the same vein, bathrooms and cattle sheds were not allowed to have a direct connection with the homesteads. Neither was it permitted to construct cesspits near farmhouses.[50]

A thorough analysis of the building plans under study shows us that in all the farmhouses but one the height of the ground floor was at least 2.8 metres, with those in almost half of the studied cases being over three metres. The average window surface largely exceeded 10% of the area of the living spaces in the farms under study. As far as the construction of walls and windows was concerned, the selected sample of farmsteads built by the DRO did (unsurprisingly) meet the standards set by the government.[51] The building plans indicate that the façades of all farmhouses consisted of 1.5 brick-wide walls (or 33 cm). This was in accordance with the building regulations at that time.

Other measures to improve sanitary standards in the countryside were not taken into consideration. Since the integration of bathrooms was not mentioned in any of the model books, it comes as no surprise that not one farm in post-war Merkem was provided with a bathroom. In accordance with the building requirements issued by the government in 1919, the pit toilets installed on the farm had no direct connection to the homestead. They were usually part of the cattle sheds, which made it easier to collect the faeces in one central cesspit. Furthermore, wartime destruction was not seized upon as an opportunity to connect to public utilities such as running water and electricity. Rainwater drains and pumps were still omnipresent in the reconstructed farmsteads in Merkem.[52]

The model books testified to the beginning of a rationalisation of housekeeping and thus of the reorganisation of living spaces. Indeed, during the first half of the twentieth century housekeeping became subject to a whole new branch of science that used chronometry and management techniques to make the housewife's work more efficient.[53] In the specific case of farm building, Ronse and Raison argued that "the farmhouse had to be designed in such way that it increased its functionality for the farmer's family". A general rule in this regard was that every room was to have a single function.[54] A first indication that architects did indeed answer the call for rationalisation was the introduction of the entrance hall. While the hall was already commonplace in town houses of the nineteenth century, it was uncommon to find it in the countryside. The entrance hall not only symbolised the boundary between public and private space, but also functioned as a neutral room that gave access to the first floor and the living spaces on the ground floor.[55]

In a number of farms bedrooms were installed on the first floor of the homesteads and in two cases even on a newly constructed second floor. Nevertheless, the majority of building plans included an undefined *chambre* – presumably the parental bedroom – on the ground floor and conceived the top floor as one large dormitory. The example of the bedroom (*chambre*) suggests that the practice of linking one function to one room had not yet fully taken shape during the early 1920s. This is also clear when one looks at the "best room". This room combined a pastiche of urban furniture that was widespread in the nineteenth-century Belgian countryside. During post-World War I reconstruction, however, most architects agreed that the "best room" represented everything that was wrong with pre-war rural housing. They regarded it not only as a bad imitation of urban interior design but also as a violation of the efficiency laws, since the "best room" was rarely used in daily life. Nevertheless, the "best room" did not completely disappear after the First World War.

Regionalist discourses presented the nuclear family as the keystone of modern society. On an architectural level this led to the introduction of the living room. The living room was the centrale place of the (farm)house where all members of the nuclear family spent time together. In most cases the room was centred around a stove, the main source of heat in the (farm)house. In most rebuilt farms, the stove retained its function as a cooking instrument (certainly in the cold winter months), which gave the living room a binary function. The bourgeois ideal of disconnecting living and working spaces thus occurred only partially during the reconstruction period. Virtually every farm had a laundry room that, unlike the kitchen, was equipped with a water pump – usually the only access point for water in the house. As a consequence, this was the place where the housewife did the laundry and the dishes. Since no bathrooms were integrated into interwar farms, it also served as a place to have a wash.[56]

A Glimpse into the Farmer's Workplace

Farms built during the reconstruction period had in common that the house and the working buildings were strictly separated. In no single farm under study was there a direct connection between the stable or barn and the farmhouse. It was believed that this would increase the hygiene on the farm. According to state agronomist Honoré Vandevelde, "a farm had to be built in a manner that the smell of the stable could not penetrate into the house".[57] The physical division between the farmhouse and the stable, however, transcended the question of hygiene as it represented the detachment of the farmer's living space from the agricultural enterprise.[58]

Although dairy farming was never the sole form of agricultural activity on the farm, architects devoted far more care to the design of cattle sheds than to that of barns and other buildings. The disproportionate attention on the construction of stables corresponded to the increasing weight of dairy farming in the economic structure of Belgian agriculture. It was also in tune with the attention for the quantitative and qualitative improvement of the national livestock during the aftermath of the Great War.[59] In *Enkele practische gegevens* (Some Practical Measures, 1920), an architectural guidebook published by the DRO, author Léon Gras explicitly stated that horses had to be accommodated in special horse stables. These buildings were divided into a number of stalls or remained as a single space, which in both cases had to give animals a minimum space of 1.3 metres each. An overview of the building plans shows that only one cattle shed (out of 12) did not comply with the suggestions made by the DRO. As far as pigpens were concerned, Gras recommended avoiding direct connections with cowsheds for sanitary reasons. The farmstead architects in Merkem seemed conscientiously to follow this advice.[60]

Most attention in the DRO's booklet was given to the construction of cowsheds. In order to "correspond to the modern scientific requirements", cattle sheds had to consist of manure passages (1-1.5 metres wide) and drainage systems, individual stalls of 1-1.75 metres each, mangers, and a feed passage. This would facilitate not only feeding, but also caring for the stock and dairying.[61] The (cattle) sheds did not fully comply with the modernisations suggested by Gras. While manure passages of a sufficient size existed in practically all cowsheds, feed passages did not (only one farm was equipped with such a corridor). This finding in fact tallies with Gras' observations that feed passages were "indispensable, but rarely used in Flanders". On the other hand, deep litter barns were systematically replaced by tie-stall barns with individual stalls. In the reconstructed stables the space per head of cattle fluctuated between 0.98 and 1.59 metres.[62] These numbers demonstrate that almost every studied cowshed answered to the prescriptions of the DRO with regard to the positioning of cattle, and that the post-war reconstruction of farms at least partly complied with the modernisation of dairy farming.

After the First World War efforts were made to increase the productivity of the national livestock. This was done not only by implementing genetic theory, but also by improving the living conditions of farm animals. Léon Gras reminded his readers that the stalling of cattle involved a constant need for fresh air. Gras therefore advised the integration of air pipes in the outer walls of the cattle sheds. Another system consisted of a pipe that was placed vertically and ran through the outer wall. The latter system was implemented in at least one cowshed.[63] However, it should be remarked that not all plans were detailed enough for one to decipher which air circulation system was used. Examination of the plans nevertheless revealed that every reconstructed cowshed was provided with one or more openable windows at the tops of the walls, as was recommended by Gras' booklet. These windows would rationalise not only the ventilation inside the cattle sheds, but the distribution of natural light as well. To improve the sanitary conditions in the cattle sheds, Gras – just like other architects cited in previous sections – advocated the use of bricks and cement mortar. These building materials indeed dominated the specifications for all cattle sheds.

Concluding Remarks

> Those who witnessed the completely wild front zone shortly after the Armistice and now, in 1923, return are stunned as if confronted with a miracle. Towns and villages with churches and houses, arisen from their ashes like magic, rebuilt in stone, strong and solid. Architects have committed themselves, and have succeeded surprisingly well, to reconstructing whole villages with churches, dwellings and farms, in regional, rural style to give the region its old-Flemish character, but with respect for modern demands and techniques.[64]

In his *Land en Leven in Vlaanderen* (Land and Life in Flanders, 1923) the famous Flemish author Stijn Streuvels lyrically described the new land that had been rebuilt from the ruins of the First World War. Although Streuvels did not intend to give a scientific analysis of reconstruction, he pointed to one of the central features of regionalist architecture: the intertwining of a traditionalist formal language with modern comfort. More than any other building, the farmstead – the symbol of rural Flanders – incorporated these two characteristics (Fig. 3).

Fig. 3 A reconstructed farm in the young landscape of the former front zone. City Archive Bruges, collection Brusselle-Traen.

This article has explored the extent to which the reconstruction of farmsteads in the devastated regions after the First World War could be considered an example of social engineering. How did architectural guidelines and advice connect to ideas about governance over the rural population? This article has gone beyond discourse analysis to study if and to what degree new insights into "good" farmstead architecture were put into practice. Three elements were taken into consideration: the architecture of the farmsteads, the (re)organisation of the farmer's home, and the rationalisation of the agricultural enterprise.

Regionalists generally considered farmsteads as uncompromising beacons of rurality. Although the countryside had changed rapidly during the nineteenth and early twentieth centuries, farms – and farming – were often deemed to be the last elements that reconciled culture and nature. In architectural guidebooks the harmony of the farm with the environment was therefore stressed as a main feature of farmstead architecture. This could be achieved through the use of local building materials and techniques. Virtually every farm studied was indeed characterised by traditional Flemish brick architecture with few decorative elements. Modernisations were to be found in the details. In the farmhouse, the living room and the kitchen were sometimes disconnected, while the entrance hall was often introduced as a new space that separated private from public. The most eye-catching transformation on the farm itself occurred in the (cattle) sheds – because dairy farming became increasingly important during the twentieth century. Stables with manure passages and individual stalls had to rationalise the work of the farmer and his family – family farming was commonplace in Flanders.

The reconstruction by the state, a temporary mechanism to reconstruct private houses after the First World War, was the largest housing project managed by the Belgian government at the time. The government installed an administrative framework to manage the building programme in 1920, after it had established the DRO as an executive organisation to control the resources for the reconstruction of the devastated regions. The farms under study were all part of the reconstruction by the state and thus fitted within the framework by the state. According to Raphaël Verwilghen, the head of the Building Service of the DRO, state-led reconstruction had resulted in the reconstruction of hundreds of model farms. Although Verwilghen was not the most neutral source, the in-depth analysis of 16 building plans suggested that reconstruction by the state did indeed result in the implementation of model book advice.

Although regionalism was not an example of what James C. Scott labelled "high modernism", this article showed how spatial and social engineering intertwined. A close reading of the model books and articles published by regionalist spokesmen during and shortly after the First World War taught that their final goal was the reorganisation not of rural landscapes as such, but of rural life as a whole. This reorganisation of rural life had both disciplinary and emancipatory aspects. The preference for a traditional formal language could be traced back to the perceived need to keep the rural population in the countryside. Picturesque landscapes were believed to affect the mind of the rural dweller, thus preventing him from leaving the countryside for the city. Nevertheless, regionalist architects seemed to acknowledge that modern comfort – both at home and in the enterprise – was needed. Without denying the distinction between rural and urban housing, bourgeois elements were introduced in the farmhouse, while small adaptations (in the cattle shed) were to transform the farmer into an entrepreneur. Indeed, reconstruction in the countryside after the First World War aimed to make good farmers by giving them better farms.

Notes

1. See: Eric Vanhaute and Guy Dejongh, "Arable productivity in Belgian agriculture, c.1800-c.1950," in *Land productivity and agro-systems in the North Sea area*, eds. Bas Van Bavel and Erik Thoen (Turnhout: Brepols, 1999), 65-66; Leen Van Molle, *Katholieken en Landbouw: landbouwpolitiek in België, 1884-1914* (Leuven: Leuven University Press, 1989), 48-50; Paul Bairoch and Gary Goertz, "Factors of Urbanisation in the Nineteenth Century Developed Countries," *Urban Studies* 23, no. 4 (1986): 288.
2. For a broad overview, see: Pierre Lierneux and Natasja Peeters, eds., *Beyond the Great War: Belgium 1918-1928* (Tielt: Lannoo, 2018).
3. Firmin Graftiau, "Notice sur la Commission Nationale pour l'Embellissement de la Vie Rurale," in *Congrès national de la Restauration Agricole. Bruxelles, 28 septembre-1 octobre 1919* (Leuven: Ceuterick, 1919), 5-8.
4. Liesbeth van de Grift and Amalia Ribi Forclaz, eds., *Governing the Rural in interwar Europe* (London: Routledge, 2018).
5. Liesbeth van de Grift, "On new land a new society: internal colonization in the Netherlands, 1918-1940," *Contemporary European History* 22, no. 4 (2013): 609-626.
6. Eugen Weber, *Peasants into Frenchmen, The modernization of rural France 1870-1914* (Stanford, CA: Stanford University Press, 1976).
7. David Matless, *Landscape and Englishness* (London: Reaktion Books, 1998); Jeremy Burchardt, *Paradise Lost: Rural Idyll and Social Change since 1800* (London: Taurus, 2002).
8. For his model, see: Ebenezer Howard, *To-Morrow: A Peaceful Path to Real Reform* (London: Swan Sonnenschein & Co, 1898).
9. Louis Albrechts, "Changing aspects of Belgian public planning", in *Perspectives on planning and urban development in Belgium*, ed. Ashok Dutt and Frank J. Costa (Dordrecht: Kluwer, 1992), 27-29.
10. Sofie De Caigny and Wouter Vanderstede, "Spiegel van het hemelhuis. De wisselwerking tussen woonideaal en sociale rollen bij de Belgische Boerinnenbond (1907-1940)," *Tijdschrift voor Sociale en Economische Geschiedenis* 2, no. 1 (2005): 3-29; Fredi Floré, "Lessen in modern wonen. Een architectuurhistorisch onderzoek naar de communicatie van modellen voor 'goed wonen in België, 1945-1958" (PhD Diss., Ghent University, 2006), 162-164; Bruno Notteboom, "'Ouvrons les yeux!' Stedenbouw en beeldvorming van het landschap in België 1890-1940" (PhD Diss., Ghent University, 2009), 41-43 and 363-365.
11. Leen Meganck, Linda Van Santvoort, and Jan De Maeyer, "Introduction," in *Regionalism and Modernity. Architecture in Western Europe, 1914-1940*, eds. Leen Meganck, Linda Van Santvoort, and Jan De Maeyer (Leuven: Leuven University Press, 2013), 8-11; Pieter Uyttenhove, "Internationale inspanningen voor een modern België," in *Resurgam: De Belgische wederopbouw na 1914*, ed. Marcel Smets (Brussels: Gemeentekrediet, 1985), 38-40.
12. While Jean-Charles Cappronnier and Delorme argue that modernisations were rarely carried out in the French department of Aisne, Van Santvoort demonstrates that in Zemst, a municipality near Brussels (Belgium), attempts to build modern farms with a regionalist design were often blocked by local farmers. Jean-Charles Cappronnier and Franck Delorme, "La reconstruction des fermes dans le département de l'Aisne après 1918," *In Situ*, no. 21 (2013): 2-32; Linda Van Santvoort, "Wederopbouwarchitectuur in de fusiegemeente Zemst," *M&L. Monumenten, Landschappen en Archeologie* 33, no. 3 (2014): 20-28.

13 Dries Claeys, "Land, staat en bevolking: De wederopbouw van het Belgische platteland na de Eerste Wereldoorlog" (PhD Diss., KU Leuven, 2019), 8.
14 Georges Smets, "Les régions dévastées et la réparation des dommages de guerre," in *La Belgique restaurée: Etude sociologique*, ed. Ernest Mahaim (Brussels: Lamertin, 1926), 71-139.
15 The database with specifications for every farm is presented in: Dries Claeys, "Land, staat en bevolking," 470-490.
16 Jean-Claude Vigato, "Between Progress and Tradition: The Regionalist Debate in France", in *Regionalism and Modernity. Architecture in Western Europe, 1914-1940*, eds. Leen Meganck, Linda Van Santvoort, and Jan De Maeyer (Leuven: Leuven University Press, 2013), 15-17.
17 Bruno Notteboom, "Boeren op de wereldtentoonstelling. Het moderne dorp," in *Gent 1913. Op het breukvlak van de moderniteit*, eds. Wouter Van Acker and Christophe Verbruggen (Ghent: Snoek Uitgevers, 2013), 126-139.
18 According to reports of the National Relief and Food Committee [*Nationaal Hulp- en Voedingscomité*] at least ten contributions on the reconstruction of the Belgian countryside were published in occupied Belgium between 1914 and 1918. These books were mainly aimed at an educated audience, although a few examples – such as *The Construction and Reconstruction of House and Stable* [*Bouwen en heropbouwen van huis en stal*] of the Belgian Farmers' League – was explicitly written to be used by farmers themselves. See: *Rapport spécial sur le fonctionnement et les opérations de la section agricole du Comité National du Secours et d'Alimentation. Section agricole 1914-1919* (Brussels: Vromant, 1920), 196.
19 Claeys, "Land, staat en bevolking," 296-297.
20 Ibid., 301-302; as cited by Paul De Vuyst: Provincial Archives Antwerp, *Collection First World War*, no. 478, letter from Paul De Vuyst to Anatole de Cock de Rameyen, 17 July 1916.
21 Boerenbond, *Bouwen en heropbouwen van huis en stal* (Leuven: Belgische Boerenbond, 1915); Edward Leonard, *Land en Dorp: Aanteekeningen en wenken ter overweging bij het bouwen en heropbouwen op het land* (Antwerp: 't Kersouwken, 1916); Honoré Vandevelde, *Het heropbouwen van hoeven* (Antwerp: Land- en tuinbouwcomiteit, 1917).
22 Jacques Giele, *Nationaal Komiteit voor de Verfraaiing van het Landleven: zijn doel en zijne werking* (Leuven: Ceuterick, 1925), 4-5.
23 Leen Meganck, "Patriotism, Genius Loci, Authentic Buildings and Imitation Farmsteads: Regionalism in Interwar Belgium," in *Regionalism and Modernity. Architecture in Western Europe, 1914-1940*, eds. Leen Meganck, Linda Van Santvoort, and Jan De Maeyer (Leuven: Leuven University Press, 2013), 73-78.
24 Claudia Houben, "De wederopbouw van hoeves in de Westhoek na de Eerste Wereldoorlog. Een onderzoek naar de wederopbouwactiviteiten door de Dienst der Verwoeste Gewesten in Kemmel en Esen" (Masters' diss., KU Leuven, 2017), 100-132; Pieter Geeraert, *After the war. Het herstel van boerderijen in Oostduinkerke na de Eerste Wereldoorlog (1918-1925)* (Masters' diss., KU Leuven, 2017), 62-64.
25 Albert Dutry, *De kunst op het platteland* (Ghent: De Scheemaecker, 1915), 9.
26 Helena Van Dorpe, "Landelijke esthetica: de woning", in *Handboek van landelijke maatschappijleer* (Leuven: Belgische nationale commissie voor de verfraaiing van het landelijk leven, [1931]), vol. 1, 21.
27 Dutry, *De Kunst*, 5-7 and 42-45.

28 Jacques Giele, "Hygiène des constructions rurales," in *Cinq leçons d'embellissement de la vie rurale données pendant les travaux de jury de perfectionnement* (Brussels: Goossens, 1916), 23-29; August Poppe, *Hoe moet men op den buiten bouwen?* (Ghent: Scheerder, 1916), 21-35; *Bouwen en heropbouwen*, 5-22; Leonard, *Land en Dorp*, 18-30; Vandevelde, *Het heropbouwen van hoeven*, 10-12.

29 Although it has been argued that the introduction of bathrooms gained momentum in the interwar years, model books did not integrate these new rooms in their plans. Sofie De Caigny, *Bouwen aan een nieuwe thuis: wooncultuur in Vlaanderen tijdens het interbellum* (Leuven: Leuven University Press, 2010), 45-46; Alfred Ronse and Theo Raison, *Fermes-types et constructions rurales en West-Flandre* (Bruges: Beyaert, 1918), vol. 1.

30 Liesbet Nys, "Nationale plagen: hygiënisten over het maatschappelijke lichaam," in *De zieke natie: over de medicalisering van de samenleving 1860-1914*, eds. Liesbet Nys et al. (Groningen: Historische Uitgeverij, 2002), 220-241. On the farmers as provider of foodstuffs, see: Giovanni Federico, *Feeding the World: An Economic History of Agriculture: 1800-2000* (Princeton, NJ: Princeton University Press, 2005), 1.

31 Giele, *Nationaal* Komiteit, 16-18; Leen Van Molle, "De Belgische katholieke landbouwpolitiek voor de Eerste Wereldoorlog", *Belgisch Tijdschrift voor Nieuwste Geschiedenis* 10, no. 3 (1979), 429-430.

32 De Caigny, *Bouwen aan een nieuwe thuis*, 34-35.

33 Afred Ronse and Theo Raison, *Fermes-types et constructions rurales en West-Flandre* (Bruges: Beyaert, 1918), vol. 2, 38-51; *Bouwen en heropbouwen*, 18-28.

34 J. Van Espen, "De Gezondheid op den Buiten," *Handboek van landelijke maatschappijleer* (Leuven: Belgische nationale commissie voor de verfraaiing van het landelijk leven, 1931), 149-150.

35 Jan Blomme, *The Economic Development of Belgian Agriculture 1880-1980. A Quantitative and Qualitative Analysis*, Studies in Belgian Economic History 3 (Brussels: Royal Academy of Belgium for Science and the Arts, 1992), 197. Arable farming represented 28% of nominal production value of Belgian agriculture in 1910, stock farming 65%.

36 Léon Gras, *Enkele practische gegevens nopens het bouwen van hoeven* (Brussels: Ministry of Economic Affairs, 1920), 3-22.

37 Leopold Frateur, *De nieuwe methode tot verbetering van het vee* (Leuven: Ceuterick, 1922).

38 *Rapport spécial sur le fonctionnement et les operations*, 201-202.

39 Marguerite Lefèvre, *L'habitat rural en Belgique. Étude de géographie humaine* (Liège: Vaillan-Carmanne, 1926).

40 Claeys, "Land, staat en bevolking", 288-294.

41 "la ferme est l'expression la plus complete de la vie rurale". J. Sel, "Rapport sur la construction des fermes dans la province Anvers", in *Congrès national de la restauration agricole et de l'embellissement de la vie rurale. Bruxelles, 28 septembre-1 octobre 1919: Rapports (3e section)* (Leuven: Ceuterick, 1919), 20-21.

42 Henri Vaes, "Le sens du regionalisme," *La Cité* 1, no. 6 (1919), 103-105.

43 Clement, "De Belgische overheidsfinanciën," 123-134.

44 State Archives of Belgium, *Archives of the Office des Régions Dévastées*, nrs. 9968, 9974, 10292, 10296 and 10297.

45 State Archives of Belgium, *Archives of the Office des Régions Dévastées*, nrs. 9968, 9969, 9970, 9971, 9972, 9973, 9974, 10,290, 10,291, 10,292, 10,293, 10,294, 10,295, 10,296 and 10,297, building plans of 16 farms in Merkem.

46 Edward Leonard, *Voor 's lands wederopbouw: korte opstellen over bouwkunst* (Amsterdam: Maatschappij voor Goede en Goedkope Literatuur, 1920).
47 Such warehouses were established by the Belgian government in Merkem and neighbouring towns such as Diksmuide and Langemark. "Bestuur van den Bouwdienst – Standaarddeuren en vensters", *Beknopte bekendmaking nopens den Dienst der Verwoeste Gewesten* 2, no. 3 (1920), 162-166; "Inlichtingen nopens de gemeentemagazijnen", *Beknopte Bekendmaking* 2, no. 4 (1920), 271.
48 State Archives of Belgium, *Archives of the Office des Régions Dévastées*, building plans of 16 farms in Merkem.
49 Meganck, "Patriotism, Genius Loci", 93; Jean-Claude Vigato, *L'architecture régionaliste: France 1890-1950* (Paris: Norma, 1994).
50 "Algemeene politie verordening op de bouwwerken ten behoeve der aangenomen gemeenten", *Beknopte bekendmaking nopens den Dienst der Verwoeste Gewesten* 1, no. 3 (1919), 159-171.
51 State Archives of Belgium, *Archives of the Office des Régions Dévastées*, building plans of 16 farms in Merkem. See footnote 34 for the specific archival records.
52 Vandevelde, *Het heropbouwen van hoeven*, 10-12; Paul De Vuyst, *Le village moderne à l'Exposition Universelle et International de Gand. Notes, comptes rendus, vues et plans* (Brussels: Goemaere, 1913), 62.
53 De Caigny, *Bouwen aan een nieuwe thuis*, 75-108.
54 Alfred Ronse and Theo Raison, *Landelijke bouwingen: Algemeene raadgevingen, ontwerpen tot het opbouwen van eene kleine hofstede, mekanieke toepassingen* (Bruges: Beyaert, 1918), 8.
55 De Caigny, *Bouwen aan een nieuwe thuis*, 132-133.
56 Ibid., 93-94.
57 Vandevelde, *Het heropbouwen van hoeven*, 11.
58 Claeys, "Land, staat en bevolking", 318-319.
59 Brecht Demasure, *Boter bij de vis. Landbouw en voeding tijdens de Eerste Wereldoorlog* (Leuven: Davidsfonds, 2014), 189-202.
60 Gras, *Enkele practische gegevens*, 8-11.
61 Ibid., 2-8.
62 The size of the cowsheds under study varied wildly. The smallest cowshed had 3 stands, the largest had 20.
63 Gras, *Enkele practische gegevens*, 5; State Archives of Belgium, *Archives of the Office des Régions Dévastées*, nr. 9970, documents concerning the farm of Mr. Daniël de Haene.
64 "Alwie het front korts na den wapenstilstand in zijne woestheid gezien heeft en er nu in 1923 terugkeert, staat verpaft als voor een wonder, — men vindt er steden, dorpen, met kerken en huizen, als ware 't uit den grond getooverd, sterk en stevig in nieuw steen herbouwd. Eensdeels hebben de architecten er zich op toegelegd, en zijn er uitstekend in gelukt, heele dorpen, met kerken, woningen en hofsteden, in regionalen, landelijken stijl, volgens hedendaagsch inzicht en behoeften, weer op trekken, om zoodoende aan de streek haar archaïsch-Vlaamsch karakter te bewaren." Stijn Streuvels, *Land en leven in Vlaanderen* (Amsterdam: Veen, 1923), 326.

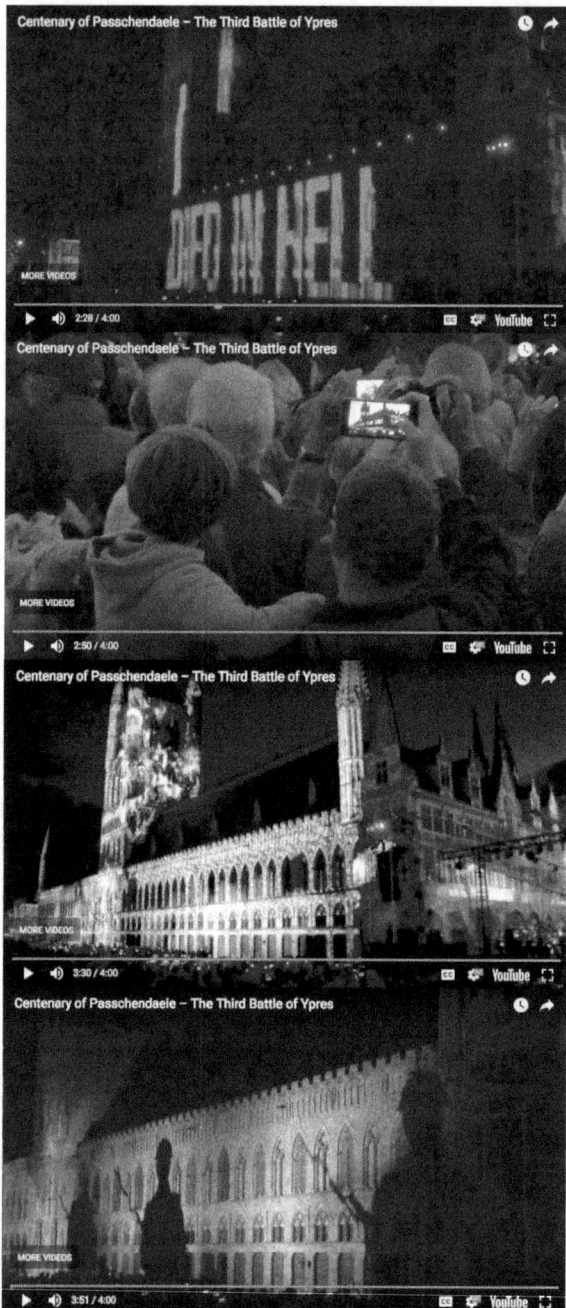

Fig. 1. Stills from the televised live spectacle to commemorate the centenary of The Battle of Passchendaele, Ypres, 30 July 2017.

"C'est la beauté de l'ensemble qu'il faut viser."
Notes on Changing Heritage Values of Belgian Post-World War I Reconstruction Townscapes

Maarten Liefooghe

Soldiers Projected on the Cloth Hall

In the evening of 30 July 2017 the United Kingdom performed a large multimedia spectacle at the Grote Markt square in Ypres as part of its centennial commemoration of the Third Battle of Ypres.[1] The infamous 100-day British offensive, which is often referred to as the Battle of Passchendaele, cost the lives of nearly 500,000 soldiers, almost evenly distributed between the British and German sides, yet yielded negligible strategic gains.[2] The formless hell of mud to which eye witnesses had testified was now remembered with musical theatre with actors in crisp uniforms, live music and breath-taking image projections on the reconstructed thirteenth-century Cloth Hall with its Belfry tower that lines Ypres's Market Square (Fig. 1). In addition to the thousands of spectators who attended the show in Ypres, many more followed the show at home via British and Belgian television. While more commemorative events were programmed in nearby Passchendaele itself – with notably distinct commemorations for the Canadian, Australian and New Zealand nations, but without major German involvement – the event in Ypres confirmed this West-Flemish reconstructed town as key *lieu de mémoire* for British Great War commemoration and war tourism. The commemoration also confirmed the reconstructed Cloth Hall in its status as a war memorial of sorts, but the projections on its façade perhaps also underlined the limited expressiveness, and the under-defined meaning of the building as a war memorial.[3]

For the reconstructed stone façade with its endless repetition of gothic bays bears none of the inscriptions that cover the Portland stone surfaces of the nearby Menin Gate Memorial to the Missing, the city's second memorial epicentre which bears the names of 54,395 Commonwealth soldiers who died in the Ypres Salient but whose bodies were never found or identified. It is because of this, perhaps, that the Cloth Hall was deemed acceptable to serve as the backdrop for the theatrical narration and as a screen onto which word messages and static and moving images could be projected. The projections of fire, or of the silhouette of the Hall in ruins, onto the reconstructed building however also activated its memorial significance as a testimony of those suffering from war destruction and to the resilience of "Poor Little Belgium".

Ms. Karen Bradley, then the UK's Secretary of State for Digital, Culture, Media and Sport, also hinted at this significance of the Cloth Hall as a marker of destruction and reconstruction in an online video announcing the commemoration spectacle:

> The thing for me about being here today, in Ypres, a hundred years from the start of the Passchendaele offensive, is that you're standing in a town that was utterly destroyed. It is almost impossible to imagine just what happened in this town and how it's been completely reconstructed. And what we will see tonight is part of that reconstruction, and part of what it meant at the time.[4]

The near impossibility "[of] imagin[ing] just what happened in this town and how it's been completely reconstructed" is a characteristic yet most ambiguous quality, not just of contemporary Ypres, but of the townscapes and landscapes across the entire former Belgian war front zone, and of other repaired towns further inland, such as Louvain, Dinant and Visé. The opening words of the catalogue of the 1985 Resurgam exhibition about the post-1914 reconstruction in Belgium also raise the issue of forgetfulness of post-war generations:

> Few people are aware of the enormous devastation caused in Belgium by the First World War. One remembers the Yser Front, the trenches and the many victims who have lost their lives in this unscrupulous battle. However, people rarely realize that, in the front region alone, the war has destroyed an area of approximately 60 kilometres long and 20 kilometres wide.[5]

That the front area has been reconstructed so as to form a somehow convincing image of its pre-destruction past, even if this proves to be a highly idealised historical image that masks various infrastructural modernisations, could be evaluated as a successful recovery from the destruction of war. What I want to evaluate here, though, is how the reconstructed cityscapes perform as a memorial landscape or a "total monument" perhaps, commemorating the sufferings from the war and demonstrating the national resilience in recovering from it.[6] I want to argue that this double memorial programme in the historicist rebuilding of war damaged or devastated towns and villages turns out to have *rather failed* in the long run. Its readability as a resilient reconstruction was fragile from the start, and it has only diminished with each passing decade. Yet, acknowledging the ambiguous and diminishing significance of the reconstruction fabric as a commemorative monument should not keep us from acknowledging other heritage values that should equally inform our contemporary appreciation and critical appropriation of towns like Ypres or Diksmuide and villages like Slijpe or Westouter. Nor should we be ignorant or uncritical of the commemorative monument that slumbers under the surface of everyday built environments in the former war front area, and in rebuilt urban areas further inland, like Dinant, Louvain and Mechelen.

Rebuilding Monumental Ensembles

Official initiatives to stimulate and coordinate repair started as soon as 1914, soon after the German invasion. A Service for Devastated Areas was established in 1919 to coordinate the rebuilding and existed until 1926. It would however take several more decades to finish the reconstruction of major historical monuments like the Cloth Hall, completed only in 1967. The institutional complexities and the ideological aspects of the Belgian reconstruction have been discussed amply in the existing literature.[7] Let me refer only, schematically, to the opposition between a traditionalist camp which advocated a historicist reconstruction of devastated towns and villages, based on their pre-war historically grown layout, and a more progressive camp which called for rebuilding the devastated regions according to the new town planning ideas. Two institutions confronting each other along these lines were the Royal Commission of Monuments and Sites and the Union of Belgian Cities and Municipalities. In the main the same fault line also divided the visions of the desirability of reconstructing historical monuments or, alternatively, of preserving selected ruins of major monuments as commemorative relics of war events. The traditionalist views eventually determined the Belgian reconstruction approach, confining modern town planning in practice to a limited number of *cités-jardins* outside the reconstructed historical centres.

The rebuilding of the devastated towns and villages, each to a convincing image of its idealised pre-destruction past, was generally realised "in a two-tier pattern" which also marked the rebuilding of some of the historic towns in the French Front area, like Bailleul and Arras, while for other "martyr towns" like Rheims another approach was adopted.⁸ Only a selection of key historical monuments like the cathedral in Ypres, the Cloth Hall and the Biebuyck House were reconstructed "*à l'identique*", based on documentation from earlier restoration campaigns or from the wartime documentation campaigns like the one headed by architect Eugène Dhuicque.⁹ "*À l'identique*" however rarely means an absolute correspondence to the pre-war state, as "corrections" would still often mark those reconstructions just as they marked contemporary restorations. These reconstructed monuments were set in an "ameliorated" local historical townscape that was not so much a receding background for these reconstructed historical monuments, as it produced an internally varied fabric and a historic image in itself into which the monuments would merge almost seamlessly. In this two-stage yet integrated approach, ultimately both major monuments and urban houses contribute to the desired effect of the whole: to upholding the image of a historical, region-specific town.

The pre-existing historical urban layouts and plot divisions were generally taken as the point of departure for rebuilding towns, save for local aesthetic optimisations and adjustments to the building lines in view of the modernisation of the road network. This approach matched with the organisation of war damage indemnification on the basis of individual ownership, but it also continued pre-war ideals and practices of urban beautification. In addition to an older practice of corrective historicist restorations of historic monuments, by the end of the nineteenth century also organically grown urban ensembles had become the object of conservation and corrective restoration. Inspired by the work of Camillo Sitte, mayor of Brussels Charles Buls expounded his influential vision of the *esthétique des villes* in an 1893 brochure.¹⁰ This urban aesthetics approach was originally mobilised to counter the threats of a levelling urban modernisation. At the outbreak of the war the Royal Commission of Monuments recommended it to counter the levelling effects of modern warfare. Repairing damaged or completely demolished urban centres according to this same aestheticising historicist agenda now amounted to a programmatic gesture of cultural resilience, of imbuing the reconstructed fabric with the charge of a phoenix rising from the ashes. As early as in 1914 engineer Charles Lagasse de Locht and architect Paul Saintenoy, president and member of the Royal Commission of Monuments and Sites respectively, had published an article sketching a programme of how the war-devastated towns and villages were to be reconstructed: "*Il convient que notre Patrie se relève, plus belle et plus magnifique, de ses ruines passagères!*"; "*nous appliquerons, dans des cas particuliers, les règles générales de l'esthétique des villes et villages*"; "*C'est la beauté de l'ensemble qu'il faut viser*".¹¹ A 1910 lecture on the subject by Charles Buls was added as an annexe, to be studied by all parties called to the task.

The article by Lagasse de Locht and Saintenoy however also opened another line of thought that would be pursued in the following years: that of preserving and restoring a regionalist diversity to buildings and building patterns. The 1914 article might seem to limit this regionalist concern to rural architecture, as it calls for surveying "*les types caractéristiques des Campines anversoise et limbourgeoise, du Brabant, du Pays de Herve, de l'Ardenne, etc., etc., plutôt que d'innover, tout à fait, à la hâte et sans inspiration régionale*".[12] Yet, a few months later, Paul Saintenoy published a short follow-up article in the architecture magazine, *Le Home*, in which he further emphasised the regionalist concern and also applied it to the rebuilding of historic towns:

> Rebuilding our fatherland in beauty! Resurrecting cities by drawing largely, as you say, on the deep resources of tradition and using as much as possible the materials offered by the area itself.
>
> This is my dream that will be realized tomorrow.
>
> I would like to see Dinant, Andenne, Louvain, Aarschot rebuilt as cities of Walloon and Flemish art. […] cities that will remind us of our glorious past of freedom and independence and our old and dear cities of yesteryear, whose urban evocations at the exhibitions in Antwerp (1894) and Ghent (1913) gave the public imperishable images.[13]

Saintenoy is referring to the Oud-Antwerpen (Old Antwerp) and Oud Vlaendren (Old Flanders) precincts at the International Exhibitions in Antwerp and Ghent: collages of reconstructed façades and local, region-specific building types modelled on extant or lost historical buildings from Antwerp's Golden Century and from historic Flanders respectively.[14] Not only was the popular Oud-Vlaendren a highly significant feat that would influence the post-1914 reconstruction approach. Equally relevant was the redesign of Ghent's urban centre aimed at enhancing the picturesque appearance of its restored medieval monuments on the occasion of the international exhibition. This demonstrated how the *esthétique des villes* approach was already being put into practice to similar integrated effect to that obtained in the temporary Oud-Vlaendren décor.

Despite the daunting scale of the war-devastated areas to be rebuilt and the administrative and logistic challenges this involved, the rebuilding campaign did manage to achieve the "beauté de l'ensemble" aspired to in each of the rebuilt villages and towns. The campaign was centrally coordinated by the Service for Devastated Areas. High Royal Commissioners, associated with that Service, each supervised the rebuilding on the ground in a number of municipalities which had temporarily ceded many of their powers to the central body in return for financial and administrative support. Representatives of the Royal Monuments Commission not only supervised the reconstruction of lost major monuments, but also advised the High Royal

Commissioners on development plans – which were rarely more than building line plans. Temporarily appointed municipal architects often not only designed the main public buildings, but also supervised the façade designs of submissions for building permits. In the resulting reconstruction fabric, generic white neo-classical façades largely disappeared from the reconstructed townscapes of Ypres, Diksmuide and Nieuwpoort. Instead, a vague "Ypres style" or "Nieuwpoort style" came to dominate the streetscapes, with a proliferation of local variants of stepped gable silhouettes or motifs like the yellow-brick aedicula windows presumed to be typical of Veurne. This infill fabric set the stage for scientifically reconstructed monuments and for newly designed public buildings in prominent locations in the city whose structure they co-articulated.

The regionalist-historicist reconstruction of the territory, extending from farmsteads to entire historic towns, then added up to a comprehensive national memorial.[15] We could compare its modern, encyclopaedic yet fictitious assemblage of historical images with that achieved in the 1913 Oud-Vlaendren exhibition experiment or with an intriguing yet unexecuted project for a war monument in Liège, published in the architecture magazine, *L'Emulation* in 1921[16] (Fig. 2). It was designed by Liège architect Paul Jaspar together with the sculptor Georges Petit, developing an idea formulated by local senator Remouchamps. *La Grosse Tour,* the big tower, featured a complex sculptural programme of emblems and symbols that were to honour *la défense nationale*: the destroyed cities, the heroism of soldiers and civilians, the return of refugees, the acquired fame and the saved values of freedom, justice, law and, crowning the whole monument, democracy. Yet, the monument's architecture carrying all these sculptures was already most programmatic in itself, and it was so in a twofold way. First, because of the choice to adopt the belfry typology for this commemorative monument, because it was an architectural symbol of the freedoms that medieval cities enjoyed and cherished vis-à-vis feudal princes and celebrated in an established Belgian nation-building narrative as the precursor of a popular democracy. In his eulogistic review of the project, Eugène Dhuicque applauded the concise eloquence of Jaspar's belfry-like tower and its simple expression that was intelligible to the masses:

> a big tower, a kind of monumental and definitive landmark of the invasion, a belfry proudly rising in the sky, symbol of an unbeaten pride, of a faith that does not let itself be defeated, emblem of freedom, dressed, in the popular feeling, in all the majesty of the centuries![17]

The belfry motif can be found in many reconstruction projects too, for example it is integrated in the new City Hall (Joseph Viérin and Valentin Vaerwyck) in the rebuilt town of Diksmuide, and as one of the references echoed in the new university library

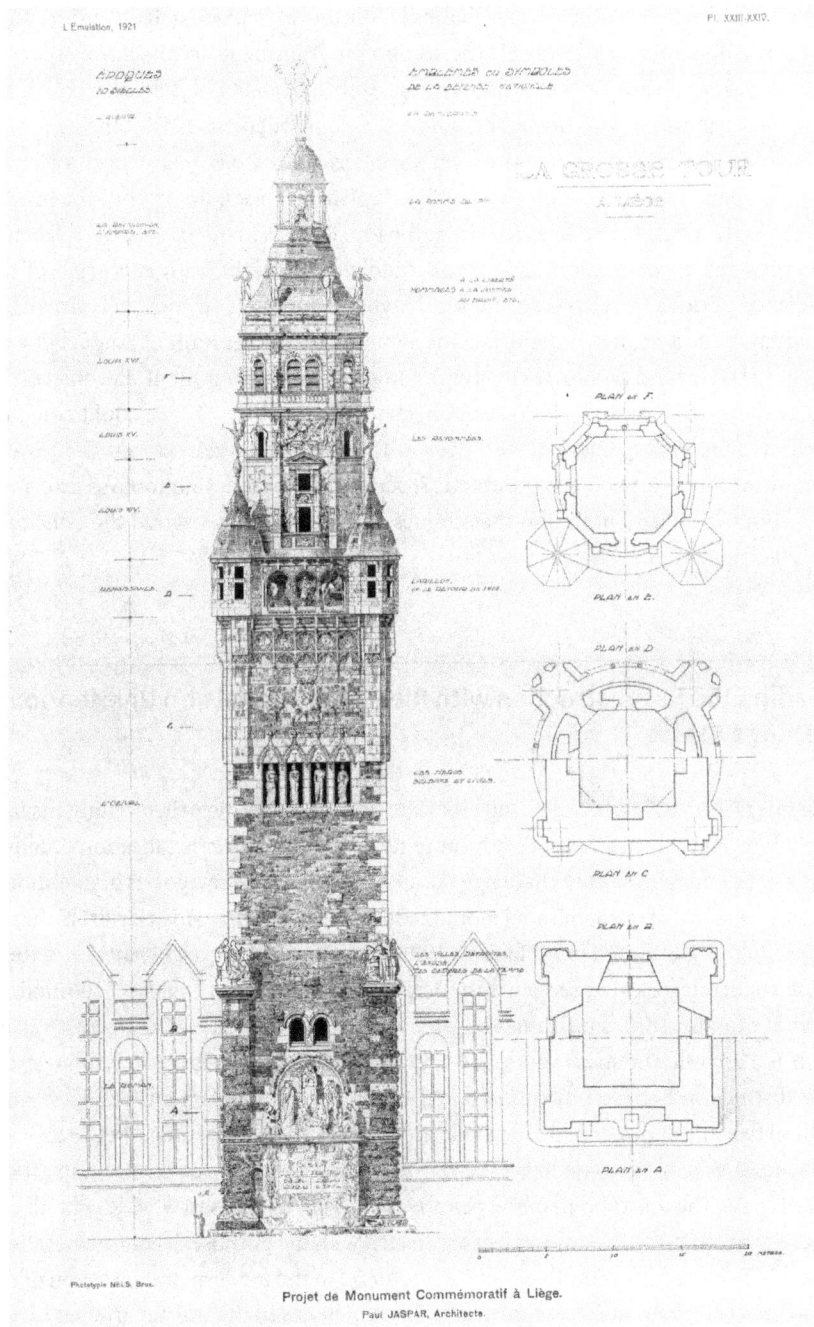

Fig. 2. Unexecuted project of Paul Jaspar for a monument commemorating Belgium's national defence, to be erected in Liège. Plate from *L'Emulation* 41, no. 12 (1921).

in Louvain (Withney Warren and Charles D. Witmore), replacing, if on another site, the burnt-down historic library.[18] The second programmatic architectural aspect of *La Grosse Tour* is the one that mirrors the assemblage quality of Belgian reconstruction. Jaspar projects onto the belfry silhouette – but independently of the historical phenomenon of belfry architecture itself – a historical sequence of architectural styles from Romanesque at the base and Gothic – *ogivale* – taking up most of the tower's height, all through to the *Style Empire* at the top. Jaspar's juxtaposition of styles thus exceeded the chronological limit – the middle of the eighteenth century – of the reference periods that marked the local stylistic bouquets of most reconstructed towns and quarters, but it manifests the same supple integration of (vaguely local) historical styles and typologies to craft a comprehensive monument. Reconstructed Nieuwpoort, Diksmuide, Lo, Ypres, Aarschot, Dinant, Visé, …: we could compare each of them with Jaspar's tower. Even if these towns largely lacked the tower's sculptural allegories and programmatic inscriptions, their design too was informed by a commemorative ambition that chimes with but extends beyond the *esthétique des villes* approach.

Reading the Reconstruction with Riegl: Intentional and Unintentional Heritage Values

The integration of selected facsimile reconstructions of key historic monuments into the towns and villages rebuilt with more liberty and historic idealisation entails a number of ambiguities that challenge the applicability of the categories of intentional monuments and of unintentional monuments as formulated by Austrian art historian Alois Riegl (1858-1905). In his famous 1903 essay *Der moderne Denkmalkultus*, Riegl related both categories to a series of historically variable monument values.[19] The modern "cult of monuments" is informed by a set of present-day values (*Gegenwartswerte*), such as a use value or an art value, and a set of recollection values (*Erinnerungswerte*). The distinction between intentional and unintentional monuments results from a split between the three distinct recollection values that differentiate between ways in which a structure is valued for the way it allows a beholder to recollect (an aspect of) the past. The *intentional commemorative value* corresponds to what Riegl calls the intentional monument – any work of art erected with the purpose of commemoration. The other two commemorative values correspond to the modern phenomenon of the unintentional monument: a *historical value*, which lies in the way an artefact serves as an irreplaceable historical document attesting to, but also evoking, an episode in the history of some aspect of human culture; and an *age value*, which is essentially an aesthetic-existential appreciation of the way in which the traces of an artefact's ageing – patina, fading colours, crumbling walls, etc. – reminds us of time passing, and of the cycle of natural degeneration of human constructions. It is on the basis of one or both of the latter two values that modern societies, Riegl argues, denominate and try to preserve an artefact as a (historic) monument, even if it was never realised with the purpose of serving as a monument.

According to Riegl, *Alterswert* or age value was the most recent value being taken into consideration in the care and protection of monuments, and he felt its importance was still questionable. Riegl however predicted an important future for it, that would not only further expand the category of the unintentional monument, but also change its (ageing) face. The promise and societal importance of the age value lay for Riegl in the way it made a time-worn artefact speak directly, in a sensorial fashion, to a viewing subject, and could therefore also appeal to the "uneducated masses". Riegl also predicted that the ascent of *Alterswert* would further diminish the importance of the commemorative monument. Yet, the post-1914 destructions and reconstructions of entire historic towns proved how soon the course of history contradicted Riegl's speculations. Miles Glendinning has pointed out how "one immediate effect [of the war destruction] was to revitalise and radicalise the intentional-commemorative values that Riegl had pronounced obsolete", since "an intensely politicised 'memory landscape' of mass conflict, focused on the Western Front" was now cultivated with conventional-style war memorials, but also with ruined and rebuilt monuments and towns.[20]

Riegl's conceptualisation, however, remains a powerful lens through which to map and read the heritage values mobilised or sacrificed in the Belgian approach taken to the reconstruction and memorialisation of the Front area and of damaged monuments and towns further inland. Here it is important to point out that there are no indications that Riegl's essay was familiar to Belgian architects and preservationists at the time of the war and the rebuilding debates. Dinstinguishing between heritage values was however a common practice in Belgian heritage discourse, also in the context of war devastations.[21] A first illustration is Henri Kervyn de Lettenhove's wartime pamphlet, *La guerre et les oeuvre d'art en Belgique: 1914-1916* (1917), in which the German army is accused of the conscious destruction of important monuments and towns with particular heritage values – historical, archaeological and artistic values defined differently, however, from Riegl's definitions.[22] Another illustration can be found in a 1918 letter inquiry that architect Huib Hoste, who spent the war in the Netherlands, organised into the opinion of 68 Dutch architects, artists, art historians and societies, asking: "Should the Ypres Cloth Hall be rebuilt or not after the war, if considered from an aesthetic, art historical, national and international perspective?".[23]

If we first assess the Rieglian present-day values, the *use-value* perspective highlights how functional modernisation measures were injected into the reconstruction endeavour, from adjusting street sections or crossings to facilitate modern traffic through the (reconstructed) historic centres to the introduction of modern building typologies in historicist dress. The *art value* is subdivided by Riegl into a *relative art value* which concerns the extent to which a monument meets a present-day *Kunstwollen* and a *newness value* which Riegl calls an "elementary art value" and which results from a work being intact. Newness value must have abounded in the freshly reconstructed monuments, towns and villages. Yet, as the *passe-partout* pejorative appellation of *vieux-neuf* for post-1914 reconstruction fabric suggests, this new, flawless execution of a historical-looking design was also exactly what made the reconstruction landscapes indigestibly inauthentic to some commentators. Turning to an assessment of the recollection values, we should first notice that Riegl's cherished *age value* informed objections to reconstructing damaged or entirely lost historic monuments and towns, but was clearly not decisive.[24] Indeed in the reconstructions a *newness value* would become intimately interwoven with the *historical value* in much the same way as happened in nineteenth-century interventionist restorations epitomised by the projects of French restoration architect Viollet-le-Duc, aimed at completing a stylistically unified and idealised version of a monument, in a state that may have never existed before and at the expense of preserving a building's authentic material substance.[25] Historical value, however, played out very differently in a range of preservation and rebuilding initiatives: its evidentiary dimension was respected in preserved war sites – like trenches, craters or shelters – and in the occasional preserved war-damaged monument, whereas this concern for preserving "material evidence" was readily passed over in the reconstruction of historic monuments or in rebuilding an entire historic town starting from a historical blueprint of its layout. Riegl's relatively wide concept of historical value can, however, not be reduced to evidentiary values – and this width invites us to make a more benign evaluation of how historical value informed the reconstruction. For Riegl still accords documentary value to an "identical" copy of a monument, and even to historicist restorations and reconstructions to which he still ascribes the historic monument's power to evoke particular historical episodes.[26]

Intentional commemorative values, of course, pertain to the numerous war cemeteries and war memorials within and beyond the Front region, but they also shimmer in general contours and specific details of the reconstructed cityscapes. Lagasse de Locht and Saintenoy had already suggested the possible application of a phoenix iconography with such commemorative intent in their 1914 programme: "*Que du sommet de ses pignons s'élance l'oiseau renaissant de la cendre!*"[27] One rather rare example crowns the façade of *In het Woud* on the Grote Markt square in Louvain (Fig. 3). It echoes the Phoenix atop one of the ornate guild houses on the

Fig. 3. Louvain, Grote Markt. A phoenix on top of *In het Woud* (Léon Govaerts, design 1922) and date indications on the adjacent façade. (Photo: Author)

Brussels Grand Place, itself entirely reconstructed after the French bombing at the end of the seventeenth century. Another and much more frequently applied type of commemorative accent is building years inscribed in stone or in figure-shaped wall clamps. To limit the intentional commemorative aspirations to these explicit and small-scale elements, however, would be to fail to acknowledge various more extensive logics that infuse a programmatic commemorative ambition into entire buildings, villages, towns and landscapes: bringing back only a *selection* of historic monuments that are supposedly representative for the local architecture history; developing and applying to other buildings an eclectic "reconstruction style" loosely inspired by building materials, styles and motifs from regional architectural history, such as city architect Jules Coomans' so-called "Ypres style"; and, finally the overall *curation of townscapes and streetscapes* in the organically grown image of the destroyed historical cities and in accordance with the already discussed *esthétique des villes* views. All of these dimensions cross each other and interact in an economy of recollection that turns entire towns into intentional monuments, "total" monuments in which the commemorative drive runs from some of the smallest ornaments to aspects of the entire urban structure. And these towns-as-total-monuments in turn co-sustain, together with rebuilt farmsteads, the dispersed war cemeteries and war relics, the reproduction of the former Front area, if not the Belgian territory, into a diffuse memorial landscape.

And Moving Beyond Riegl

This extensive logic of commemoration without clear focal points risks inflation. Yet, the instability of Diksmuide, Ypres, Nieuwpoort etc., as commemorative monument-towns is not only the result of this inflationary stretching. The very gesture of rebuilding an (idealised) pre-war state, of reconstructing "more beautiful than was before", also contained a return to normality, to taking up daily life, and suppressing the traumatic memory of the historical events. The historicist-commemorative stage set would in time be able to recede into the background, to form a backdrop to the daily life that was to be continued once war refugees had returned and the rebuilding of the area was finished. In short, the adopted mode of reconstruction yielded a remarkable "total monument" that could, however, easily shift into an "absent monument", which it did more and more over subsequent decades, as the emphatic newness of the historical simulation started fading. If it were not for narratives in other media – history books, documentaries, museums – that recall the destruction and subsequent reconstruction, today's inhabitants and visitors of Nieuwpoort, Lo and other picturesque reconstructed towns and villages in rural West Flanders could easily *not* read the loss, the reconstruction and the intended commemoration in the built environment they are traversing.

Riegl's relatively sophisticated monument conceptualisation clearly has its limits when it comes to charting this flickering of the reconstruction fabric as monument. It is a flickering between scales, between omnipresence and absence, but also between intentional and unintentional monuments. With regard to the latter, Riegl was obviously right that any intentional monument – each phoenix or soldier statue – is also an unintentional one – a document of historical interest. But more critical with regard to the historical reconstructions after the war is the way each unintentional monument (document) "hides" an intentional monument we might fail to notice, to paraphrase Jacques Le Goff's argument about the *document-monument*.[28] This also forces us to acknowledge the nationalist (and regionalist) values and rationales that are conspicuously absent from Riegl's cosmopolitan heritage framework, developed in the context of the pre-war multinational Austro-Hungarian monarchy, and to acknowledge the symbolic gestures of resilience performed in the rebuilding of entire historic towns (just like symbolic gestures were also at stake in the preservation of wartime ruins, an option which happened almost nowhere).[29]

Epilogue: Valuing the Post-1914-18 Rebuilding Project as Twenty-first-Century Heritage

As the post-1914-18 construction fabric is now itself a century old, it is clear that its heritage values should also be reassessed from a contemporary vantage point. In 2007 I took part as a junior researcher in a consultancy procedure with Ghent University advising the Province of West Flanders and the municipalities of Ypres and Heuvelland on how to assess and valorise the various aspects of reconstruction heritage on their territories.[30] We were also asked to advise on how contemporary spatial developments could find a place in the still largely extant reconstruction landscape.

As is often the case with rediscoveries of heritage, a perception of threat catalysed the initiative. Local authorities were alarmed by the upscaling in agricultural industry that would overwrite a landscape dotted with sometimes historicising reconstruction farmsteads, or by a wave of renovations to improve comfort standards in housing. These and other spatial processes were increasingly putting pressure on what was vaguely understood as post-war reconstruction heritage by these authorities, but for which few comprehensive policies had ever been developed. The dynamics of change posing a threat all concerned a questioned *use value* of particular sections of the historical built environment – of farmsteads left without active farming or ill-suited to contemporary farming, of town halls of municipalities that had long been merged, of parsonages in villages left without parish priests, but also of plain working men's houses facing major renovation.

Not formulated in our consultancy brief were considerations of the use value of the heritage of the reconstructed towns and buildings as economic resources for (war commemorative) tourism. In 2007, there was no anticipation of a valorisation of reconstruction heritage in view of the four-year-long war commemorations we have seen of late. Arguably, the use value of this heritage for war tourism is limited in comparison to that of war cemeteries or battle relics for instance, but this might also be a matter of heritage management. Now that we have also reached the centennial birthday of (physical) reconstruction activities, reconstruction architecture and urbanism have started being thematised in local commemorative events over the past few years, with exhibitions, catalogues and books about the rebuilding of Louvain, Nieuwpoort or the Ypres area among others.[31]

Recognition of the *(architecture) historical value*, including the architecture historical value, of the reconstruction building stock seems long to have been hindered by two reproaches. A first objection was that even the archaeologically reconstructed pre-war historical monuments were only reconstructions, lacking the original material substance that could authenticate them as historical document. Yet, a number of precisely such reconstructed major historic monuments constitute a group of buildings that were the first to be given legal protection. A second obstacle to recognition of especially the architecture historical value was the rather negative appreciation of the rebuilding architecture as retrograde. Here preservation's predilection for what once was innovative and avant-gardist architecture – at least when it comes to more recent heritage – ran parallel to an architecture historiography with a modernist bias that used to stigmatise the rebuilding after the First World War as the Modern Movement's missed appointment with history.[32] Hence, the second group of listed buildings: a number of modernist exceptions to the overriding historicist and regionalist agenda. Luckily a more nuanced and inclusive point of view has been growing at least since 2007. Notable research and publication initiatives in West Flanders and other Belgian provinces have since followed, which helped the development of an appreciation of what was now increasingly called *wederopbouwarchitectuur* (reconstruction architecture).[33] This denominator transcends the progressive versus reactionary opposition, and brings the association with post-war repair more to the foreground. This hesitant thematic re-appreciation of *wederopbouwarchitectuur* is today largely associated with the local history this architecture issued from.[34] Yet, from a wider angle, this post-1914 rebuilding architecture could also be historicised within a wider history of heritage reconstructions after calamities and war. In the past two decades the subject has been given major attention in architecture and preservation circles in the German-speaking world, mainly due to contentious monument reconstructions in Berlin and other major cities since German reunification.[35]

Already in 1985 urban planning historian Marcel Smets stressed how the rebuilt urban fabric demonstrates exceptional care on the level of the urban design of public space: "[t]he whole of observations that the rebuilt urban areas release onto viewers, bespeaks an undeniable concern for coherence and décor. Every building is both a component and a building block of the total environment".[36] This key quality of the reconstructed towns and villages as integrated cityscapes was a quality that we gave a central place to in our 2007 study. We believed that the close interaction between the positions and designs of public buildings, façades of private buildings, and the way they co-construct public space was not only critical to the value and meaning of individual buildings. We also argued that the carefully crafted cityscapes in themselves should be attributed heritage value, and that this was a valuable basis upon which future urban developments could be grafted. The study therefore presented maps that analysed the interaction of buildings and urban structures for Ypres and for selected villages in the area. We also proposed to add to the Rieglian heritage values a *locus value* which concerned the degree to which a construction contributes to the cityscape or is a decisive part in a larger urban whole. Constructions with high locus values should then be maintained in their configuration to preserve the larger cityscape coherence, but they could also be replaced by new structures that take up a similar role. And the larger urban structures can develop towards new qualitative cityscapes. Through this locus value we acknowledged the planned coherence of the *wederopbouw* as total monument, while singling out the *esthétique des villes* level as a key to unlock this total landscape for future development.

Looking back, I feel our 2007 study did not sufficiently overthink the importance of the *intentional commemorative value* of the rebuilt towns, villages and buildings today. As argued above, the rebuilt War Front area is a total monument that is however only perceived as such when one realises the gesture of rebuilding entire towns, of reconstructing an entire cultural landscape. In the decades after the war, no one needed to be reminded of the size of the devastation and the scope of rebuilding efforts. For later generations however the *vieux-neuf* newness has started weathering while contrasting recent constructions bestow an aura of undefined pastness onto the reconstruction fabric. Date inscriptions and occasional phoenixes might not be enough to clarify the historical status of the rebuilt towns and the commemorative aspiration that infused it. This memorial dimension, and its ideological messages of a threatened but in the end reinforced local identity and of a victor's national resilience do not disappear for that matter. The total monument never completely shifts into an absent monument, but more into "a total monument in stand-by mode" with a rhetorical power only to be reactivated. The use of the Cloth Hall and the Grote Markt square for the Passchendaele commemorative spectacle illustrates this possibility.

Riegl was clear: while the logic of the historical value demands the unconditional conservation of the historical document, the logic of the intentional commemorative value demands only continuity on the condition that contemporary society still endorses the monument's message and cause. Yet, even if today we would probably no longer subscribe to the nationalist ethos of the reconstruction as intentional commemorative project, because so many other heritage values are also involved, we cannot simply give up the rebuilt towns and landscape as obsolete memorials. Rather, just as contemporary urban planning and architectural projects can further develop the cityscapes of Visé, Louvain, Diksmuide and Ypres, contemporary memorial practices could and should engage critically with this monument in stand-by mode. Site-specific artistic interventions and curatorial projects are a first option to do so. With more than a dozen exhibitions in Ypres and other towns in the Belgian Front area, with thematic routes, theatre projects and publications, the current project *Feniks2020. De groote wederopbouw van de Westhoek / Reconstruction of Flanders Fields* (March 2020 – October 2021) sets out to claim and to historicise the former Front area not just as a former war but also as a reconstruction landscape. It remains to be seen whether some of the artistic and curatorial projects within this large-scale cultural touristic programme will also question the reconstruction as lingering monument in the way Krzystof Wodiczko's *Leninplatz-projection* (1990) did during the *Die Endlichkeit der Freiheit* exhibition in Berlin. Like the 2017 British projections on the Cloth Hall in terms of media but critical instead of celebratory, Wodiczko's projection addressed the obsolescence of one of the many Lenin monuments in former East Berlin. It is but one in a series of 1990s *Kontextkunst* projects that are currently revisited as projects of "experimental preservation".[37]

Even architecture and urban planning, the very media used during the *wederopbouw*, could be a means to articulate a corrective or a questioning contemporary stance. The redesign of Skanderberg Square (completed in 2018) in Tirana by Brussels-based firm 51N4E shows how an urban ensemble of public space and communist representative architecture can be formally demonumentalised and at the same time infused with a new symbolism. In the Belgian former Front area, recent examples of a critical appropriation of the reconstruction fabric are much smaller and less outspoken. A first example can be found in the architectural design for the conversion of a wing of the Ypres Cloth Hall from municipal offices into a new city museum. This particular wing of the Cloth Hall complex was the last part of the monument to be reconstructed between 1957 and 1967. Architect Pierre Pauwels opted for a concealed reinforced concrete structure which FVWW and Callebaut Architecten chose to lay bare in their 2014 adaptive re-use project of this *vieux-neuf* monument. Exposing the ceiling's grid of concrete beams in the spaces where visitors now marvel at the gigantic model of medieval Ypres was a way of highlighting the defiant historicity of the Cloth Hall complex, a quality that extends to the entire city. Yet, in the gloomily lit gallery spaces this exposed modern construction may remain hardly noticed. A different and more challenging response to the local reconstruction fabric can be found in the Schaerdeke social housing estate (2019), just outside the small historic town of Lo, 20 kilometres north of Ypres. There Architectenbureau Bart Dehaene addressed the West Flemish town's invisible quality as (part) post-war reconstruction, as he adorned the eight new semi-detached yellow-brick houses with four entrance portals, each marked by round arches and a Brancusi-like concrete column, a combination of elements that refers to the portal of Lo's reconstructed historical town hall. The Schaerdeke housing estate, however, also recalls the garden city ideal championed by the modernists in opposition to the *reconstruction à la identique*. In its combination of building typological and ornamental motifs, then, the Schaerdeke housing transcends the traditionalist-modernist division that marked the Belgian official rebuilding campaign, and becomes a modest, local, critical supplement to the reconstruction fabric of Lo and the many other reconstructed towns and villages, just as ambiguous as the reconstruction fabric itself.

Notes

1. For Ypres (Ieper) and Louvain (Leuven), I will use the French toponyms despite their location in present-day Flanders, as these are most common in English usage. Other towns will be referred to by their Dutch or French names, respecting present-day official languages in Belgium.
2. The Battle of Passchendaele of 12 October 1917 is however only part of this larger offensive. See Spencer Jones, "Ypres, Battles of," in *1914-1918-online. International Encyclopedia of the First World War*, eds. Ute Daniel et al. (Berlin: Freie Universität Berlin, 2015-02-13).
3. We can contrast this limited vocality with Baron Joseph Kervyn de Lettenhove's appraisal of the (prewar) monument as symbol of the medieval communal guilds in his *Histoire de Flandre* (1847-1850): "Sur le Beffroi et les Halles d'Ypres […] se trouvent écrites en caractères ineffaçables la grandeur et la puissance des corps de métiers de cette ville autrefois si florissante", as quoted by his son: Henri Kervyn de Lettenhove, *La guerre et les oeuvres d'art en Belgique: 1914-1916* (Paris & Brussels: Van Oest, 1917), 132. Some statues on the façade of the reconstructed monument make the monument speak of its dual historical identity as medieval and twentieth-century structure: a Lady Mary in a niche above the gate to the belfry, corresponding to the fourteenth-century original, and statues of Boudewijn IX and Margareta of Champagne under whose reign the Hall was build, are complemented by statues of the war royals King Albert and Queen Astrid. An unrealised war-time proposal by mayor Colaert was to mark the façade of the reconstructed Hall with shaming effigies of the leaders of the enemy responsible for the destructions, as had also been the case in the seventeenth century. Johan Meire, *De stilte van de Salient: de herinnering aan de Eerste Wereldoorlog rond Ieper* (Tielt: Lannoo, 2003), 116.
4. Quoted from the youtube video UK Culture Media and Sport Department for Digital, "Centenary of Passchendaele. Ypres Menin Gate and Market Square 30 July 2017" (28 March 2018). https://www.youtube.com/watch?v=PyoEutlmZ60.
5. François Norman, "Woord Vooraf," in *Resurgam: de Belgische wederopbouw na 1914*, ed. Marcel Smets (Brussels: Gemeentekrediet van België, 1985), 7.
6. Indeed, the reconstruction of devastated towns and villages shows a commemorative ambition and should therefore also be considered in the historiography of the postwar commemoration, next to the numerous monuments erected by municipalities to commemorate fallen soldiers as war heroes and civilians as martyrs, as discussed in Laurence Van Ypersele, "Commemoration, Cult of the Fallen (Belgium)," in *1914-1918-online. International Encyclopedia of the First World War*, ed. Ute Daniel et al. (Berlin: Freie Universität Berlin, 2014-10-08).
7. For an overview, see: Herman Stynen, "De rol van de instellingen," in *Resurgam: de Belgische wederopbouw na 1914*, ed. Marcel Smets (Brussels: Gemeentekrediet van België, 1985).
8. Miles Glendinning, *The Conservation Movement: A History of Architectural Preservation: Antiquity to Modernity* (Abingdon & New York: Routledge, 2013), 194-198.
9. Herman Stynen, Georges Charlier, and An Beullens, *15-18, het verwoeste gewest: Mission Dhuicque, the devastated region* (Bruges: M. Van de Wiele, 1985).
10. Charles Buls, *Esthétique des villes* (Brussels: E. Bruylant, 1893).
11. Charles Lagasse de Locht and Paul Saintenoy, "La reconstruction des villes et villages détruits par la guerre de 1914. Rapport sur les devoirs administratifs incombant aux

Pouvoirs publics," *Bulletin des Commissions Royales d'Art et d'Archéologie* 54 (1914): 254, 259, 262.

12   Lagasse de Locht and Saintenoy, "La reconstruction des villes et villages détruits," 254.

13   "Rebâtir notre patrie en beauté! Y ressusciter des villes en puisant largement, comme vous le dites, dans les profondes ressources de la tradition et en utilisant autant que possible les matériaux offerts par la contrée elle-même. C'est là mon rêve qui sera réalisé demain. Je voudrais voir rebâtir Dinant, Andenne, Louvain, Aerschot, comme des cités d'art wallon et flamand. [...] des cités qui rappelleront notre glorieux passé de liberté et d'indépendance et nos vieilles et chères villes d'antan dont les évocations citadines des expositions d'Anvers (1894) et de Gand (1913) ont donné au public d'impérissables images." The article had an almost unworldly title: Paul Saintenoy, "Rebâtissons en Beauté !" *Le Home*, no. 1 (1915), 9.

14   We could also refer to Bruxelles-Kermesse (1897) and Vieux-Liège (1905). See Herman Stynen, *De onvoltooid verleden tijd: een geschiedenis van de monumenten- en landschapszorg in België 1835-1940* (Bruxelles: Stichting Vlaams erfgoed, 1998), 228-231.

15   "The entire rebuilt environment, and in any case the city or village centre as the most representative part, thus becomes one large memorial. Its architectural perfection symbolises the artistic and intellectual level of the nation." Marcel Smets, "De Belgische wederopbouw op de overgang tussen stadsbouwkunst en stedebouw," in *Resurgam: de Belgische wederopbouw na 1914*, ed. Marcel Smets (Brussels: Gemeentekrediet van België, 1985), 93.

16   Eugène Dhuicque, "Un monument commémoratif de la défense nationale à eriger à Liège," *L'Émulation* 41, no. 12 (1921).

17   "une grosse tour, sorte de borne monumentale et définitive de l'invasion, d'un beffroi orgueilleusement dressé dans le ciel, symbole d'une fierté invaincue, d'une foi qui ne se laisse point abattre, emblème de liberté, revêtu, dans le sentiment populaire, de toute la majesté des siècles !" Dhuicque, "Un monument commémoratif de la défense nationale à eriger à Liège," 178.

18   Jeroen Cornilly explains how the main building volume of the Diksmuide City Hall mirrors on each side of the entrance a stepped gable that was modelled on a lost sixteenth- or seventeenth-century house from Diksmuide; and how a tower evoking the belfry tradition was asymmetrically integrated into the building complex. Jeroen Cornilly, "Gevraagd: architecten. Kiezen tussen alternatieven," in *Bouwen aan wederopbouw 1914/2050: architectuur in de Westhoek*, eds. Jeroen Cornilly et al. (Ypres: Erfgoedcel CO7, 2009), 137.

19   Alois Riegl, "Der moderne Denkmalkultus. Sein Wesen, seine Entstehung [1903]," in *Alois Riegl. Gesammelte Aufsätze* [re-edition of the 1929 edition of essays published with Filser Verlag] (Vienna: WUV-Universitätsverlag, 1996): 139-184.

20   Glendinning, *The Conservation Movement*, 191-192.

21   Stynen, *De onvoltooid verleden tijd*, 172-173.

22   Kervyn de Lettenhove, *La guerre et les oeuvres d'art en Belgique: 1914-1916*.

23   Huib Hoste cited in Herman Stynen, "Opvattingen over het herstel van de hal te Ieper," *Wonen/TABK*, no. 4-5 (1983): 37.

24   When it comes to age-value, we should be careful, though, not to overlook the difference between a time-worn building or "natural" ruin on the one hand and a ruin resulting from man's deliberate intervention, as with war-time deliberate destruction. Riegl suggests that in the latter case the cycle of becoming and perishing, in which man faces nature, is not evoked and *Alterswert* would not apply. Riegl, "Der moderne Denkmalkultus," 156-157.

25 Note that Viollet's far-reaching idealist restorations can also be thought of as reconstructions, as in Alexander Stumm, *Architektonische Konzepte der Rekonstruktion*, Bauwelt Fundamente (Basel: Birkhäuser, 2017), 19-46.
26 Riegl, "Der moderne Denkmalkultus," 164-165.
27 Lagasse de Locht and Saintenoy, "La reconstruction des villes et villages détruits," 264.
28 Jacques Le Goff, "Documento/monumento," in *Enciclopedia Einaudi*, eds. Ruggiero Romano and Alfredo Salsano (Torino: Einaudi, 1977).
29 Johan Meire structures the historical debate about the rebuilding of Ypres around the functional, the culture historical, and the symbolic values of Ypres. Johan Meire, *De stilte van de Salient*, 114-117.
30 David Schmitz et al., *Omgaan met wederopbouwarchitectuur in de Frontstreek van 1914-1918: Ieper en Heuvelland*, Labo S - Department of Architecture and Urban Planning (UGent) (Ghent, 2008).
31 Joke Buijs et al., *Herleven: Leuven Na 1918* (Louvain: Stad Leuven, 2018); Erwin Mahieu, *Een stad vol stellingen. De wederopbouw van Nieuwpoort-Stad na WOI* (Ghent: Academia Press, 2018); *herSTELLINGEN* (Ypres: Yper Museum), 2020 and Piet Chielens, Dominiek Dendooven, and Jan Dewilde, *Antony d'Ypres, fotografen van de wederopbouw* (Ghent: Tijdsbeeld, 2020).
32 This was the case at least until the early 1980s, when the Resurgam research and exhibition project directed by Marcel Smets signalled shifting views.
33 Jeroen Cornilly et al., eds., *Bouwen aan wederopbouw 1914/2050: architectuur in de Westhoek* (Ypres: Erfgoedcel CO7, 2009); Nicholas Bullock and Luc Verpoest, eds., *Living with history 1914-1964: Rebuilding Europe after the First and Second World War and the Role of Heritage Preservation* (Louvain: Leuven University Press, 2011).
34 For an overview of this gradual reappreciation in heritage management, see: Jo Braeken, "The Remains of War and the Heritage of Post-war Reconstruction in Flanders Today," in *Living with History 1914-1964: Rebuilding Europe after the First and Second World War and the Role of Heritage Preservation*, eds. Nicholas Bullock and Luc Verpoest (Louvain: Leuven University Press, 2011).
35 *Arch+ 204: Krise der Repräsentation* (Berlin, 2011); Adrian von Buttlar et al., eds., *Denkmalpflege statt Attrappenkult gegen die Rekonstruktion von Baudenkmälern - eine Anthologie* (Gütersloh: Bauverlag, 2013); Winfried Nerdinger, *Geschichte der Rekonstruktion - Konstruktion der Geschichte* (Munich: Prestel, 2010); Stumm, *Architektonische Konzepte der Rekonstruktion*.
36 Smets, *Resurgam: de Belgische wederopbouw na 1914*, 11.
37 Jorge Otero-Pailos, Erik Langdalen, and Thordis Arrhenius, eds., *Experimental Preservation* (Zürich: Lars Müller Publishers, 2016).

Fig. 1. Lucien Coppé and Stephen Rowland Pierce, *Zeebrugge: Projet de la Ville pour la Reconstruction du Port*, October 12, 1917, ink and water color on paper, mounted on backing paper. With kind permission of RIBA Collections.

Rebuilding, Recovery, Reconceptualization:
Modern architecture and the First World War

Volker M. Welter

The effects fighting on the battlefields of the First World War had on soldier-artists and their works have often been analyzed.[1] Missing from many such accounts, however, are architects and architecture; a lacuna that becomes somewhat understandable if one considers that battlefields as sites of destruction are the ultimate opposite to architecture and building, two of humanity's most constructive endeavors. As soldiers who actively participated in the war, architects and members of cognate disciplines like town planning experienced the same battlefields as writers, poets, painters, musicians, and indeed any other soldier. Accordingly, the question remains after architects's experiences of fighting in the war and the possible consequences of their experiences on their architectural work, on the ways they saw their discipline and profession.

This paper presents three case studies of how architecture and the First World War intersected, each offering an aspect of a possible comprehensive answer to the above question which this essay, however, does not attempt. The first case study discusses a summer school entitled *The War: Its Social Tasks & Problems*, which the Scotsman, Patrick Geddes, a biologist who had meandered via sociology into city design, co-organized in London. Held in July 1915, the event debated the larger cultural meaning of the war and was attended by various architects and soldier-architects from Britain and Belgium.

The following two examples illuminate how the experience of actively fighting in the war influenced individual architects. The second case study looks at an example from the western front where the English architect Adrian Berrington was shell-shocked in Flanders in July 1917. Subsequently treated at Craiglockhart War Hospital near Edinburgh, Berrington was a patient of Captain Dr. Arthur Brock, a Scottish medical doctor who had developed a shell-shock therapy that relied on Geddesian ideas about the interaction of human beings with their environment.

The final case study turns to the Austrian architect Richard Neutra for whom fighting in and experiencing the First World War contributed to an understanding of modern architecture as a means to position man in a hostile environment; a perception that many years later resulted in a radical new way of organizing architectural space.

Reconstruction

The summer meeting 'The War: Its Social Tasks & Problems' was held at King's College in London from July 12-31, 1915.[2] The event offered a "sociological interpretation of the war" to which end the lectures of the first week focused on geographical and educational fundamentals of the warring nations, those of the second on historical aspects of the war, and of the third on civic, or socio-cultural, and constructive rebuilding of the destroyed nations and their cities. During the second week, a half-day conference on the "Reconstruction in Belgium and Northern France" was hosted by Émile Vandervelde, the Belgian Secretary of State, and the Belgian architect Victor Horta. Another speaker was Herbert C. Hoover, the Chairman of the American Committee for Relief in Belgium and future President of the United States of America.

In attendance at the summer school were many representatives of architecture, urban planning, and housing, among them the architects Henry Vaughan Lanchester, Frank Mears, Geddes's son-in-law, Alfred Portielje (*Société Royal des Architectes d'Anvers*), and Raymond Unwin. Also attending were Lawrence Weaver, the editor of *Country Life*, and representatives of the Garden City and Town Planning Association, the National Housing and Town Planning Council, the Rural Housing Organization Society, and the Outlook Tower Edinburgh. In the audience was the architect Charles Rennie Mackintosh.[3]

Geddes and his co-organizer, the economist Gilbert Slater, principal of Ruskin College in Oxford, argued that among the pressing problems was "real reconstruction [which] is ... essentially ... a renewal of social life".[4] The rebuilding of Belgium (and northern France) required that architects should aim "at no mere restoration, nor merely more efficient re-planning, roads, railways and all; but nobler and grander designs also".[5]

The German invasion of Belgium had attacked a nation and her citizens, and a century-old, spatial-geographic, and socio-economic order. On a large scale, this order had historically found visible expression in a network of villages, towns, and cities that existed harmoniously with and within their natural surroundings. On the scale of individual towns, Geddes often resorted to images of town squares when he wanted to symbolically represent the social order underpinning the physical fabric of individual cities. The churches and cathedrals that rose on these squares were for Geddes complementary symbols of the spiritual order these communities enjoyed.

To reconstruct a historically grown socio-spatial order required, according to Geddes, two distinct though closely intertwined stages. First, a survey from high above would offer a synthesizing view of a larger territory. Second, on the ground, local, detailed surveys had to be conducted in order to familiarize oneself with the specific urban environments, individual communities, and their cities. Geddes had propagated this two-pronged approach ever since he installed the Outlook Tower in Edinburgh which offered far-reaching, surveying outlooks from the top floor complemented by ever more inward-directed looks at the history of Edinburgh and Scotland on the lower levels, ending with a meditation cell on the ground floor for final reflection before exiting.

In addition to the fighting on the ground, the modern battlefield necessitated reconnaissance from above, as the military service of Geddes's oldest son, Alasdair, a geographer, illustrates. The size of the battlefields of the First World War had expanded almost indefinitely in comparison to those of earlier European history. For example, the terrain of the battle of the Somme that was fought from July to November 1916 "was ten times more spread out than Waterloo",[6] the site of Napoleon's defeat. Before Major Alasdair Geddes was killed in France in May 1917 he had surveyed the frontline from a balloon that floated high above the battlefield while being anchored to the ground. Geddes's wartime duty transformed into a military task his father's idea of surveying from above vast territories as a basis for a regional or urban masterplan. Coincidentally, the architect Frank Mears, Patrick Geddes's son-in-law, also surveyed enemy territory from above with the same unit as Alasdair Geddes.

Other architects immediately saw the potential of the aerial view for reconstruction proposals. In October 1917, for example, the Belgian architect Lucien Coppé (1892-1975) drew up a scheme to rebuild both the city and port of Zeebrugge. His English colleague, Stephen Rowland Pierce (1896-1966), visualized the scheme with an aerial view depicting the new city and port as they would be seen through the fuselage of a biplane (Fig. 1).

The smaller, local scale of Geddes's two-pronged approach was addressed by war memorials which the circle of architects around Geddes conceived following the summer meeting. Sometime in 1915 or 1916 Mackintosh designed a war memorial for soldiers fallen in France and a design for a memorial fountain.[7] If built, both would have inserted into the urban fabric and the civic realm spaces for personal commemoration, reflection, and memory. After the war, Frank Mears conceived a comparable commemorative space for an entire community when he drew up plans for a *Via Sacra* for his home town of Edinburgh. To be located just below Edinburgh

Castle, the unrealized design envisioned a ceremonial street leading up the lower slopes of Castle Rock and ending in a neo-Gothic memorial chapel.

Recovery

The two protagonists of the second case study, the English architect Adrian Berrington (1886-1923) and Captain Dr. Arthur John Brock (1879-1947), were both acquainted with Geddes. Berrington had been in contact with Geddes from approximately the mid-1900s onward. Brock had studied medicine at the University of Edinburgh and also practiced in the city where he moved in Geddesian circles.[8]

Adrian Berrington was born in Birkenhead, near Liverpool, in 1886. From 1903 to 1905, he studied at the Liverpool School of Architecture. In 1907, Berrington moved to London where he worked for architect R. Frank Atkinson, who that year collaborated with Daniel H. Burnham on the Selfridge's department store in London's Oxford Street,[9] enrolled in evening classes at the Royal Academy of Arts, and rendered designs conceived by Geddes, for example a temple of the Greek gods and a garden for the nine muses.[10] While transforming lofty ideas into perspectival drawings, Berrington met in London the Scottish poetess, Rachel Annand Taylor (1876-1960), an acquaintance of Geddes from Aberdeen and knowledgeable on both mythology and classical antiquity. Berrington deeply admired Annand Taylor, and the two began a lasting correspondence by letter.

Berrington enlisted in January 1915. As a member of signaling units of the Royal Engineering Corps, one of his duties was to establish and maintain communication lines on the battlefields. Three letters to Taylor illustrate how Berrington tried to make sense of the spatial and environmental settings of his military service. On September 8, 1916, Berrington described how he had reached St. Ouen, France, by train on a journey that had taken him through a "slowly – very slowly – unfolding panorama of harvest fields & streams which run [through] this meadow … The machine sustains one however & the train keeps to its rails". He adds that "standing about in a camp or a station whilst one might be seeing a cathedral or the church of St. Ouen almost makes a conscientious objector".[11]

Clearly, Berrington did not want to be where he found himself to be, yet when recapitulating his travels, they transformed into an image of Geddes's valley section, following the course of a river through a landscape until it reached a *city*, that is a human community huddled around a cathedral or church, a Geddesian symbol as explained earlier.

On October 22, 1916, Berrington was in an unidentified and undistinguished location: "A hard bitten little place of stone & cobbled streets. No '*place*' with cafes

& so on. A big village really". He continues: "I know smaller places which are towns – by virtue of that *place* & perhaps a boulevard".[12] Relying again on Geddesian concepts to describe and analyze his surroundings, Berrington conveyed once more his alienation from the landscape of war. This example, however, focused on the social interactions between human beings as symbolized by a square or *place*, French for square, of a town rather than a spiritual community as represented by a cathedral.

Finally, on October 25, 1916, Berrington was occupied with the "gratuitous labour to make cosmos in chaos",[13] a phrase that summed up his efforts to arrange a livable space in a dugout. Already three days earlier, Berrington had reported that he was working on "quite a decent dugout" located below the cellar of a house:

> By the time I have finished it, it will be a jolly good dugout. White & warm with wires in neat rows & so on.[14]

He continued explaining his motivation for spending much time and energy on this abode:

> [I] Hate disorder like the Devil – a good big chunk of the devil is just pure disorder. [...] Even if we move out next week it is a good work to make a white[,] clean[,], well[-]lit[,] orderly dugout in place of a [illegible word] confusion.[15]

Life in the trenches was bearable only by creating a space that through its orderly arrangements could perhaps resemble a home.

Berrington's attempts to root himself in an environment rendered hostile through the war came to naught near Nieuwpoort (Nieuport), Flanders, on July 14, 1917. Nearby to the south-west is the town of Veurne (Furnes), even further to the south Ypres is located. Early in July 1917, just before the Third Battle of Ypres or the Battle of Passchendaele began, this part of Flanders was the site of the German army's first deployment of Blue Cross and Yellow Cross (or mustard gas), two new chemical weapons.[16]

The German attacks began on July 10, the same day on which Berrington's unit was exposed near Nieuwpoort to heavy fire with High Explosives and gas shells as minutes from a medical board meeting in December 1917 retrospectively report. A few days later, on July 14, Berrington "was startled by what appeared to be the quick sound of a high velocity shell, and he tripped and fell. Subsequently his mind became blank as regards practically the whole of his war experiences".[17]

The notes were most likely written by Dr. Brock, Berrington's medical doctor, who elsewhere described his understanding of shell-shock (or neurasthenia) as "a privation or relative absence of life". A shell-shocked human being's life is "broken up and dispersed into its constituent elements" because "its unity in space and time both gone". With the usually harmonious integration of a human being (or any other living organism) into the environment violently interrupted, a soldier is rendered incapable of "utilizing and profiting by his environment, his circumstances" because he can no longer adapt to or even shape his surroundings.[18]

This environmentally oriented definition of shell-shock called, accordingly, for a treatment that focused on the re-synthesis of the disparate experiences of and reactions to the environment, though not on the large scale of the surveying gaze from high above but on the small scale of being eye-to-eye with one's everyday surroundings. In short, Brock wanted to nudge his patients to re-engage through work and other physical activities with their daily, man-made and natural environment and thereby regain the capacity to synthesize again what the violence of the battlefield had torn apart.

Berrington came to Craiglockhart War Hospital in August 1917; shortly before him the poet Wilfred Owen, another of Brock's patients, had been admitted.[19] At the time of Berrington's arrival, Owen had taken on as part of his therapy the editorship of *The Hydra: The Magazine of Craiglockhart War Hospital*. Responding to an editorial call "for an attractive cover design – a promising futuristic thing",[20] Berrington depicted the (possibly autobiographic) moment when a blast suspends a soldier in mid-air above a barren battlefield in the foreground. (Fig. 2) The soldier's, and also the viewer's, gaze goes into the distance where the silhouette of the Pentland Hills to the south-west of Edinburgh again recalls a Geddesian Valley Section. Between the hills and the human body a multi-headed hydra entangles the soldier and obscures the edifice of the war hospital. Even if not a futuristic design, the drawing was selected as the title cover for the new series of *The Hydra* from November 1917 to August 1918, when the magazine folded.[21]

Berrington's other contribution to the new series of *The Hydra* was small line drawings illustrating regular columns on activities of various clubs and societies the patients could join. The clubs were more than social opportunities, for participation was part of the treatment regime, especially but not only of Brock's patients. Viewing Berrington's small vignettes, the drawings illustrate parts of the treatment that Brock hoped would stimulate the recovery of the lost unity between patient and environment. Patients arrive in a reception area of what could almost be a country club, they participate in indoor activities such as the debating society or writing for and producing the magazine. Outdoor activities comprise sports, nature walks and study, photography, but also surveying of the surrounding territory and exploring the nearby city of Edinburgh.

Brock himself published in *The Hydra* on the history of Edinburgh and prescribed participation in activities of Geddes's Outlook Tower.[22] He coined for his shell-shock therapy the term ergotherapy – *ergo* being the Greek word for work. In the context of his and Berrington's involvement with Geddes and his circle, the term "occupational" also refers to Geddes's notion of natural occupation which underpinned the valley section and indicated environmentally well-integrated ways for humans to exist in different areas of a valley region.²³

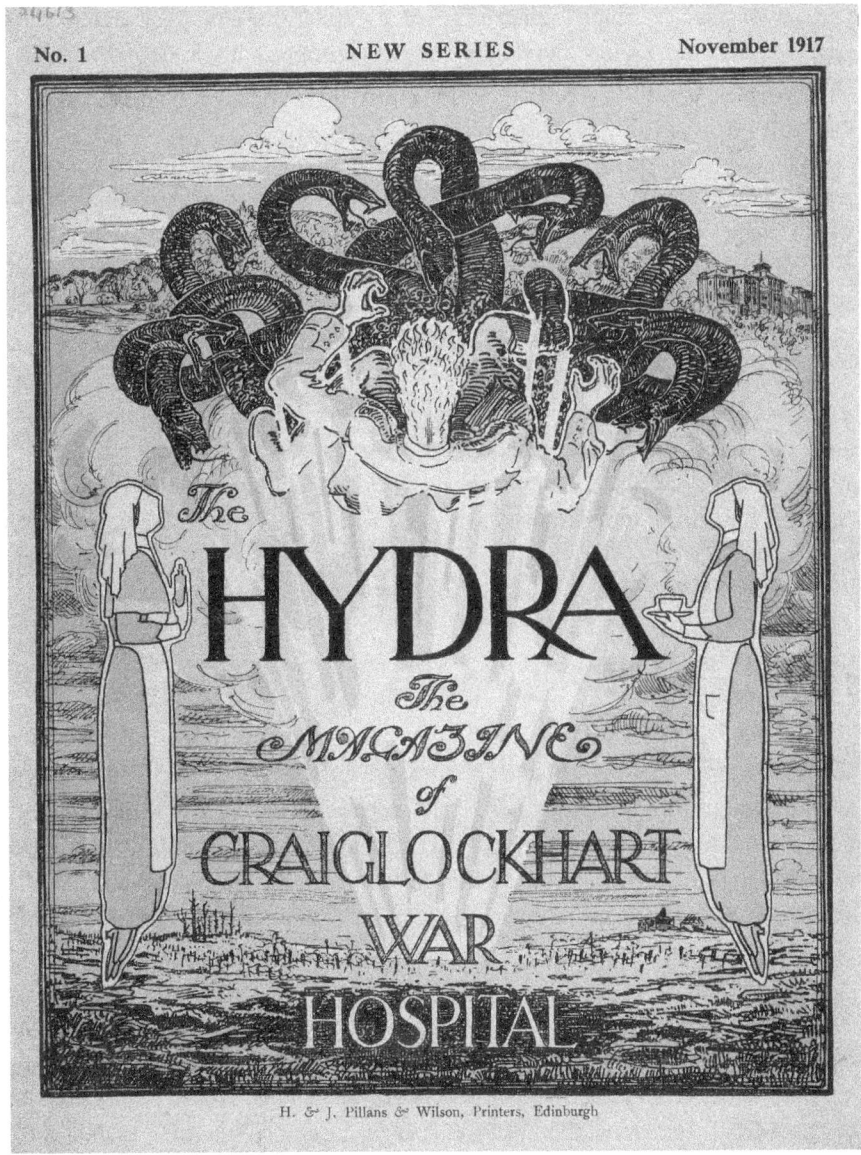

Fig. 2. Adrian Berrington, Cover Design for *The Hydra*, November 1, 1917. The first issue of the magazine with Berrington's cover. With kind permission of The Wilfred Owen Trust and The Bodleian Libraries, The University of Oxford, MS. 12282/35, No. 1 November 1917, Front Cover.

Berrington embarked on ergotherapeutical activities such as hiking on the hill behind the hospital. Surveying from high up the surrounding countryside and city elated his mind while also bringing up painful memories of Alasdair Geddes. Berrington traveled to Edinburgh, visited local artists such as Charles Mackie, another acquaintance of Geddes, and explored the countryside. During the latter, he painted watercolors of regional architecture emphasizing the geometric solids underneath all architectural and ornamental dressings. Berrington also drafted imaginary buildings such as a Duke's house for a hill in the Scottish countryside; the whereabouts of the design is presently not known.[24]

A final vignette for *The Hydra* shows departing patients passing the ticket booth of a train station upon leaving Craiglockhart War Hospital. Brock's goal was that patients would regain their ability of "synoptic[ally] seeing" the environment which, if attained, indicated the recovery of an "Organism's constant active Interplay with Environment", as Brock paraphrased Geddes's triad of Place-Work-Folk.[25] The ultimate tragedy for Brock (and his fellow doctors) was the death on the battlefield of patients who had been discharged after successful treatment. Wilfred Owen was killed a week before Armistice Day. Berrington also went back to military service, though not to active fighting. After the war he was appointed professor for Urban Design and Planning at the University of Toronto on October 1, 1920. He took medical leave a year later and died suddenly in London in 1923.

Reconceptualization

The third and final case study deals with the Balkans, far away from Belgium and the United Kingdom. However, Richard Neutra, the Austrian, later American, architect and protagonist of this section, shared with Berrington an experience of the battlefield and fighting in the war that was determined by the relationship between the soldier-architect and his environment. In Neutra's case, this gaze was initiated by the architect's early interest in the physio-psychology of, for example, Wilhelm Wundt; Neutra read selected works of the Leipzig psychologists while studying architecture in Vienna from 1910.

Four phases of active military service can be reconstructed for Neutra. From the beginning of the First World War to the end of 1915 Neutra was stationed mainly in forts and defense installations, often in isolated locations, along the southern and on the Adriatic borders of the Austro-Hungarian Empire. In January 1916, Neutra participated in the offensive against Montenegro, and until the end of April 1916 he was a member of the forces occupying the mountainous country. From then on, a malaria infection repeatedly enforced prolonged hospital stays and Neutra essentially ceased to serve actively in the military.

The Balkans posed a unique set of military challenges and dangers. Contemporary sources point out that the war in the mountainous regions of the Alps and the Western Mountain Barrier of the Balkans was second only to the Western Front.[26] War in a mountainous terrain spatially expanded the battlefield even more than on flat land, as the topography often separated positions by distance *and* height, and required foremost trenches that were sometimes just short, unconnected segments. According to the German general lieutenant, William Balck, mountain war was harder because it was a struggle with the enemy *and* a "fight against nature". The latter was a consequence of the addition of height to distance and the unpredictable swings of the weather. In addition, "troops had to learn a different way of … breathing" as the circumstances forced them to interact more intensely on a physio-psychological level with the environment.[27]

Neutra's war diary and autobiographical writings record the specific dangers and fear the war theater triggered. For example, the imbalance between modern weaponry and more traditional techniques of warfare and weaponry was a worrisome potential threat. The commanding, but exposed, mountain-top position of Fort Kravica, for example, faced "a savage guerilla-trained enemy", who, in the night, burned down farm buildings and "frontier hamlets".[28] When wired dynamite charges supplemented barbed wire entanglements around his company's position, Neutra wondered about their effectiveness against enemies who were "mountaineers of Montenegro, who had knives with which to cut our throats, pistols, guns, and matches";[29] in short, much simpler weapons that allowed the enemy to get as close as possible to Neutra and his fellow soldiers.[30] Accordingly, Neutra's gaze remained fixed on the landscape that crept right up to this outpost as it was the immediate danger zone from which partisans might attack.

The ways soldiers perceived the surroundings also determined their experience of the landscape of war. Comparing the war diary with diaries Neutra had written before the war, an important difference concerning the architect's view of the landscape becomes apparent. As I have analyzed elsewhere, Neutra's pre-war landscape observations differ little from those of a painter who studies a landscape by looking at a scene with a canvas or sketch pad between him and the scenery.[31] Neutra's war diary complements such directed gaze with one that perceives the landscape as surrounding space, a totality into which the soldier-architect is immersed and of which he takes measure primarily with regard to any physical characteristics that may hinder or help in traversing the terrain in pursuit of a military mission or survival.[32]

Other soldiers recorded comparable experience; for example, the gestalt psychologist Kurt Lewin. Recuperating from wounds received on the western front, Lewin wrote *The Landscape of War*. The essay reflects on the space of a battlefield, most notably the fundamental changes in the perception of both general landscape characteristics and details as seen through the eyes of an individual soldier. To the latter, the modern, extended battlefield appears as a relative, surrounding space that changes constantly depending on where the solider is located or moving to, and never fully comprehensible.[33]

Militarily speaking, the phenomenon Lewin analyzed and which echoed through Neutra's war diary was the open order of the modern battlefield that had emerged in the late nineteenth century.[34] Advances in technology, reach, and accuracy of modern weapons spatially expanded the battlefield and revolutionized the position of individual soldiers within it. Modern weapons increasingly rendered obsolete traditional shoulder-to-shoulder formation because tight groups of soldiers were obvious and easy targets for machine guns, for example. Instead, soldiers on the battlefield were now "farther apart from one another than had been custom for most of recorded history".[35] Consequently, soldiers learned to fight differently, maneuvering more and individually, scanning the terrain for the slightest cover offered by topography and nature, crawling and hugging the ground while moving forward or backward; in short they engaged in activities that imposed close and persistent physical contact with nature.[36]

The German architectural and cultural critic, Karl Scheffler, pointed out already in 1915 that any likely effect of the First World War on art and architecture would be felt only "in a certain temporal and spatial distance, when the disgust of the moment, the efforts, in short the All-too-Human have been overcome".[37]

While this conclusion is arguable for some art forms, it holds for literature. Soldier-authors such as, for example, Edmund Blunden and Erich-Maria Remarque published their ground-breaking works about the war only towards the end of the 1920s.[38] Neutra's architectural response to his experience of the landscape of the First World War happened even later, in the 1940s, when the immersive perception of battlefield space developed into one source of Neutra's novel approach to architecture.

Survival Through Design, Neutra's lengthy, quasi-philosophical statement of his approach to design and architecture, was published in 1954 but compiled after the United States had entered the Second World War at the end of 1941. It contains a remarkable passage that discusses four stages of a process of perpetual exchange between sensory stimulations and corresponding reactions or design decisions. The stages are "Orientation Response", "Defense Response", "Control Response", and, finally, "Precision Response".[39] The passage can be read as an architect envisioning a well laid-out, functionally arranged modern house, for example, when Neutra refers to conveniences and other practical items being within reach. But it also describes how Neutra tried to control nearby dangers and, when that effort failed, to deal with their possible consequences, for example when checking whether he could still control his limbs, gather his tools, and flee, and was not confined because not entrapped.

The second perspective sheds an interesting light on Neutra's architectural projects from the 1940s; a time when, as the late Esther McCoy once remarked,[40] Neutra's California œuvre entered a distinct new period as exemplified in the Nesbitt house (Los Angeles, 1941-42) – which Neutra called the "war house" – and the Kaufmann Desert House (Palm Springs, CA, 1946-47). Both houses are characterized by a dissolution of the building and its constituent elements. Enclosed rooms, fixed walls, and defined interior spaces spill over into and merge with the surroundings. Individual rooms form almost stand-alone pavilions, linked by views through generous and often moveable floor-to-ceiling glass walls and doors, outdoor terraces, and walkways, partially covered with projecting roofs and pergolas.

Almost everywhere within the environment of the Kaufmann House an occupant is placed into the open plan of modernist space without, however, being exposed to the dangers of the open order of the modern battlefield as Neutra had experienced them first-hand. Instead, Neutra allowed the inhabitant to constantly survey, for example, the immediate space around the house with the help of direct, indirect, and mirrored views. (Fig. 3) Situating his clients in an exposed, but now safe spatial position suggests that Neutra was re-enacting his precarious positions in the dangerous landscapes of the First World War, and the consequent need for prospect and refuge. The design of the house is less an ingenious response to an intriguing local landscape. Instead, it is inextricably linked to the malevolent nature that Neutra had experienced during the First World War; an experience the Second World War reawakened and for which California's desert landscape offered the perfect laboratory to come to terms with architecturally, if not psychologically.

Fig. 3. Richard Neutra, *Kaufmann House*, Palm Springs, California, 1946-47. The photograph by Julius Shulman shows in the foreground to the right the wall-mounted mirror in the bathroom of the master bedroom. In the middle ground the sliding glass walls of the adjacent living room can be seen through the bathroom window. © J. Paul Getty Trust. Getty Research Institute, Los Angeles (2004.R.10).

Conclusion

Reflecting on the possible consequences of the Great War on contemporary art, Scheffler distinguished three responses which are helpful to classify the three case studies presented. Scheffler claims that artists who did not or could not actively participate in the war responded symbolically.[41] Thoughts about the war by Geddes and memorials designs like Mackintosh's fall into this group, tough comparable designs by Mears indicate that symbolic responses were not restricted to non-participants in the war.

Scheffler's second group refers to young artists who actively fought in the war, were impressed and formed by the events, and subsequently often rejected established art forms. Berrington and, by extension of his dealing with shell-shocked soldiers, Brock come to mind. Trying to make sense of the experiences of the battlefield and treating the traumatic consequences of those experiences, both men resorted to Geddesian thought. This move, however, placed their responses into a long tradition of cultural critique of modern society. The effects the experience of the war may have had on a soldier-architect's post-war work are difficult to decide in the case of Berrington because of his sudden death. That after the war Brock gradually broadened his environmentally based shell-shock therapy into a general critique of the ills of modern life[42] suggests that, perhaps, the traumatic experiences of the First World War did not inevitably result in a *revolutionary* rejection of established understandings of one's art or environment.

Finally, Scheffler hints at artists who initially appeared rather untouched by their experiences of the war. Scheffler expected new forms of art to emerge over time, yet he also suspected that they would draw less on obvious war motives but more on new moral sentiment (*sittliche Gesinnung*) and a contemplative world view (*grosse Anschauung*). As Neutra's case illustrates, even two or three decades later soldier-architects's experiences of the First World War could be resolved in new concepts of modernist architecture. At first sight, Neutra's new architecture proclaims to revolutionize man's relationship with benevolent nature, but as it turns out it was deeply rooted in the architect's experience of nature as a malevolent, man-made environment.

Notes

1. My thanks for the support of my research on Berrington go to the late Dr. Louise Annand, Glasgow; Catherine Walker, MBE, curator of the War Poets Collection, Napier University, Edinburgh; and David Whiting of the Berrington family.
   Referring only to the most recent literature, see for example: Gerhard Finckh, ed., *Das Menschenschlachthaus: Der Erste Weltkrieg in der französischen und deutschen Kunst* (Wuppertal: Von der Heydt-Museum, 2014); Gordon Hughes and Philipp Blom, eds., *Nothing but the Clouds Unchanged: Artists in World War I* (Los Angeles, CA: Getty Research Institute, 2014); Robert Cozzolino, Anne Classen Knutson, and David M. Lubin, eds., *World War I and American Art* (Philadelphia, PA: Pennsylvania Academy of the Fine Arts, 2016); Emma Chambers, ed., *Aftermath: Art in the Wake of World War One* (London: Tate Publishing, 2018).
2. Unless noted otherwise, all factual information about the summer meeting comes from *Syllabus and Time-Table of Summer Meeting at King's College, Strand, July 12-31, 1915, on The War: Its Social Tasks & Problems* (London: Co-operative Printing Society, 1915).
3. Volker M. Welter, "Arcades for Lucknow: Patrick Geddes, Charles Rennie Mackintosh and the Reconstruction of the City," *Architectural History* 42 (1999): 316-332, see especially endnote 9.
4. Patrick Geddes and Gilbert Slater, *Ideas at War* (London: Williams and Norgate, 1917), 59-60.
5. Ibid., 51.
6. Stéphane Audoin-Rouzeau and Annette Becker, *14-18: Understanding the Great War*, trans. Catherine Temerson (New York: Hill and Wang, 2002), 26.
7. Welter, "Arcades for Lucknow," especially at 327-328 and endnote 43.
8. For Brock see David Cantor, "Between Galen, Geddes, and the Gal: Arthur Brock, Modernity and Medical Humanism in Early-Twentieth-Century Scotland," *Journal of the History of Medicine and Allied Sciences* 60, no. 1 (January 2005): 1-41 (including a comprehensive bibliography). Geddes wrote the introduction to Arthur J. Brock, *Health and Conduct* (London: Williams and Norgate, 1923), vii-xiii.
9. James Steven Curl, *Oxford Dictionary of Architecture* (Oxford: Oxford University Press, 2000), 41.
10. Volker M. Welter, *Biopolis: Patrick Geddes and the City of Life* (Cambridge, MA: MIT Press, 2002), 199.
11. Letter from A. Berrington to R. A. Taylor, 8 September 1916. The late Dr. Louise Annand, Glasgow, kindly let me read and excerpt Berrington's letters to her aunt, R. A. Taylor. Taylor's letters to Berrington remain missing.
12. Letter from A. Berrington to R. A. Taylor, 22 October 1916, italics added.
13. Letter from A. Berrington to R. A. Taylor, 25 October 1916.
14. Letter from A. Berrington to R. A. Taylor, 22 October 1916.
15. Letter from A. Berrington to R. A. Taylor, 25 October 1916.
16. Simon Jones, "Yellow Cross: The Advent of Mustard Gas in 1917," 4 February 2014, *Simon Jones Historian*, (simonjoneshistorian.com/2014/02/04/yellow-cross-the-advent-of-mustard-gas-in-1917/; accessed 21 July 2018).
17. "Proceedings of a Medical Board, Edinburgh, December 19, 1917," signed A. Brock, Captain; George Stewart, Lieutenant; and a third, illegible signature (National Archives United Kingdom, WO 374/6051).

18 Arthur J. Brock, "The Re-Education of the Adult. I/The Neurasthenic in War and Peace," *The Sociological Review* 10, no. 1 (Summer 1918): 25-40, reprinted in *The Re-Education of the Adult/Papers for the Present* issued by the Cities Committee of the Sociological Society, Second Series, No. 4 (London: Headly Bros. Publishers, [1918]), 1-19 (2).

19 For Berrington's arrival, see: *The Hydra*, no. 10, 1 September 1917, 18, and for Owen's, see: *The Hydra*, no. 6, 7 July 1917, 16. For Dr. Brock's treatment of Owen, see: Dominic Hibberd, "A Sociological Cure for Shellshock: Dr. Brock and Wilfred Owen," *The Sociological Review*, 25, no. 2 (May 1977): 377-386.

20 *The Hydra*, no. 11, 29 September 1917, 1.

21 The May 1918 issue omitted Berrington's cover for economic reasons as noted on page 18.

22 Arthur J. Brock, "Evolving Edinburgh," *The Hydra*, n.s., no. 7, May 1918, 4-7; no. 8, June 1918, 10-12; and no. 9, July 1918, 4-7.

23 Welter, *Biopolis*, 60-65.

24 Letter from A. Berrington, Bowhill Auxiliary Hospital, Selkirk, to R. A. Taylor, 9 September 1917.

25 Brock, "The Neurasthenic in War and Peace," 8, 15.

26 See for example: William Balck, *Entwickelung der Taktik im Weltkriege* (Berlin: R. Eisenschmidt, 1922), 164-172; Douglas Wilson Johnson, *Topography and Strategy in the War* (New York: Henry Holt, 1917), 144-176; Douglas Wilson Johnson, *Battlefields of the World War. Western and Southern Fronts. A Study in Military Geography* (New York: Oxford University Press, 1921), 605-632.

27 Balck, *Taktik*, 165.

28 Neutra, *Life*, 106.

29 Ibid., 107.

30 Ibid., 107.

31 For example, Richard Neutra Diary, vol. 2, 1912-1917, 124-125 (Richard and Dion Neutra Papers, Department of Special Collections, Charles E. Young Research Library, University of California at Los Angeles). See also: Volker M. Welter, "From the *Landscape of War* to the Open Order of the Kaufmann House: Richard Neutra and the Experience of the Great War," in *The Good Gardener? Nature, Humanity, and the Garden*, eds. Annette Giesecke and Naomi Jacobs (London: Artifice Books on Architecture, 2014), 216-233.

32 Most notably the entry 1/30/1916 (p. 37), but also 1/26/1916 (pp. 31-32), 1/31/1916 (pp. 39-40), 2/1/1916 (pp. 40-41), Richard Neutra Diary, vol. 4, 1915-1916 (Richard and Dion Neutra Papers, Special Collections, UCLA).

33 Kurt Lewin, "The Landscape of War" [1917], trans. by Jonathan Blower, introd. by Volker M. Welter, in *Art in Translation* 1, no. 2 (2009): 199-209.

34 See for example: John A. English and Bruce I. Gudmundsson, *On Infantry. Revised Edition* (Westport, CT: Praeger, 1994), chapters 1 and 2; Balck, *Taktik*, 120; and John A. English, *A Perspective on Infantry* (New York: Praeger, 1981).

35 English and Gudmundsson, *On Infantry*, 1.

36 Balck, *Taktik*, 9, 52-53.

37 Karl Scheffler, quoted in Bernd Küster, *Der erste Weltkrieg und die Kunst: Von der Propaganda zum Widerstand* (Oldenburg: Merlin Verlag, 2008), 101.

38 Brian Bond, *Survivors of a Kind: Memoirs of the Western Front* (London: Continuum, 2008), xiv.

39 Richard Neutra, *Survival Through Design* (Oxford: Oxford University Press, 1954), 332, italics in original.

40 Esther McCoy, *Richard Neutra* (New York: George Braziller, 1960), 12, 16.
41 For this and the following references to Scheffler, see: Küster, *Der erste Weltkrieg*, 100-101.
42 See Cantor, "Between Galen, Geddes, and the Gael," 16-38.

PART TWO
REMEMBER

Family photograph of a patriotic *tableau vivant* re-enactment, Leuven (Belgium), 1919.
© Family Archive Kristien Stals

Now all roads lead to France
And heavy is the tread
Of the living; but the dead
Returning lightly dance:

Whatever the road bring
To me or take from me,
They keep me company
With their pattering,

Crowding the solitude
Of the loops over the downs,
Hushing the roar of towns
and their brief multitude.

Edward Thomas, excerpt from *Roads* (1915-1917)

Fig. 1. Governments honored widows by presenting to them their husbands' posthumous medals. Yet widows continued to struggle with material deprivation and emotional trauma in the post-war world. Source: Imperial War Museum, Q56741.

Reclaiming the Ordinary
Civilians Face the Post-war World

Tammy M. Proctor

In her diary an elderly female author in Ghent, Belgium, carefully records the destruction of her grandparents' house and with it a lifetime of memories; she describes her birthplace as having been mauled or battered.[1] An Englishwoman married to a German aristocrat laments: "The few people I have already spoken to were depressed and horrified at the terms of the armistice, especially that the blockade is not to be raised, which means for so many people a gradual death from exhaustion".[2] Finally, in a letter to the British War Office intelligence bureau, a Belgian official pleads for a certificate of service for wartime agents, noting that "we are flooded with demands" from men and women for concrete evidence proving that they were soldiers in the British service.[3] Each of these accounts was penned in the days after the official armistice on the Western Front on November 11, 1918, and each touches on fundamental themes that faced civilians in the aftermath of the First World War.

With the end of war, combatants and civilians alike confronted a need to reclaim the ordinary or, in other words, to return to normalcy. Yet there was a clear problem: what constituted normal in a world transformed by violence and disruption? This essay looks at the tension between remembering and forgetting in civilian lives in the post-war world, paying close attention to the gendered representation of their war experiences in personal accounts and examining how ordinary people defined normalcy after 1918 in the face of significant obstacles. In particular, this essay explores two main pressures that emerged within a gendered framework. First, despite many ways in which normal life resumed in the streets and households of Belgium, for some people continuing deprivation and widespread devastation delayed the resumption of "normal" life. This was especially true for civilians who had been traumatized or whose breadwinners had died or who now cared for severely disabled returned soldiers. Second, returning to a pre-war ideal of an ordinary or normal life suggested forgetting or minimizing the impact of the war. However, most civilians felt compelled to remember their dead and wounded while also seeking recognition of their own patriotic service and sacrifices. As Drew Gilpin Faust argued in her influential study of the US Civil War, modern war led to a crisis of language, knowledge, and understanding, and survivors often felt "sentenced to life".[4] This rupture between pre-war understandings of life and death also marked the First World War and its aftermath.

Many historians have examined the strains of the immediate post-war period, often with an eye to the long-term impact of the war, especially in terms of the precedents set for later conflicts. Some scholars have dissected the question of violence, particularly as it pertains to civil society as well as on the battlefield, in order to understand the watershed that was the First World War.[5] Others look to questions of trauma in individual lives by examining widowhood, grief, injury, and disfigurement, often through the lens of gender.[6] A related field of study places this trauma into the framework of claims for compensation in the form of pensions, long-term medical care, and reparations.[7] With the surge in scholarship surrounding the centenary of the war, there has been a trend towards investigating the violence unleashed by the war that continued into the 1920s. In particular, historians have examined the phenomena of civil war (Ireland, Soviet Union), population exchange and violence (Turkey, Greece, Poland), and paramilitary action (Germany, Italy, Hungary).[8] Finally, a robust area of historical work explores the culture of memory that emerged after 1918.[9]

In spite of all the historical work published on the post-war period, the question of how individuals and families negotiated the challenges of post-conflict life remains an elusive and thorny problem. In their article on mourning in France that was published in the *14-18 encyclopedia online*, Rémi Dalisson and Elise Julien provide compelling statistics and analysis of the scope of the trauma. For French communities, roughly two-thirds of the population experienced the loss of either a family member, a colleague, or a friend; officially there were 600,000 widows and a million war orphans. As they note, expressions of grief and mourning were omnipresent, from the clothing of mourners to the special services and monuments devoted to the dead[10] (Fig. 1). Again, this ever-present memory of the war daily challenged the idea of normalcy. In Belgium, war losses (60,000) included both soldiers and civilians, many of whom had been killed during the 1914 invasion. Public political wrangling over the question of the repatriation of bodies and community mourning marked the immediate post-war period, while families privately grieved.[11] As John Horne has argued: "The dead thus defined the living…", and he makes it clear that negotiating the future was a challenge for those who survived, caught between anxious remembrance of the war and cautious hope for the years to come.[12]

While drawing on many of these important historical works, this essay takes a slightly different angle. Rather than examining the long-term impact of the war, instead I focus on the first 18 months following the armistice on the Western front in November 1918. In particular, this chapter examines the challenges of reconstructing life within the framework of a gendered narrative strongly articulated in the aftermath of violence. My argument relies on evidence from only three locales: an occupied zone (Belgium), a nation living with defeat (Germany), and a victorious nation (Britain), although these themes certainly resonated in other post-war settings. While each of these states experienced war and its aftermath in profoundly different ways, all sought to reconstruct the family in order to reconstruct society.

According to many memoirs and diaries, the armistice of November 1918 was both surprisingly abrupt and long awaited. Promises of peace had abounded for more than a year in the media, so when rumours became reality many civilians had trouble processing this change. In Brussels, diarist Mary Thorp described the cautious anticipation of early November: "[w]e are living on our nerves at high pressure, expecting every moment to hear the armistice is signed…".[13] In Germany as well, civilians waited to hear news. As one young woman wrote in her diary on November 2, "The war is as good as over, but fighting goes on".[14] Newspapers also awaited the armistice. *The Times* of London published a short piece on November 8, entitled simply "Suspense", that described the eager anticipation and breathless attention to rumor as Britain expected to hear of a peace.[15] In much post-war memory of the war, the November 11, 1918 armistice has a totemic quality: the eleventh hour of the eleventh day of the eleventh month, but for those living through the war it was simultaneously anticipated and anti-climactic.

Although many expressed joy and looked forward to the future, the end of war also brought anxiety and fear for soldiers and civilians alike, but often for different reasons. Male combatants feared that normal home life might be beyond their grasp or that their families would no longer recognize or want them. They also faced enormous economic insecurity. Women, on the other hand, worried about how their male loved ones might have been transformed by war, both physically and emotionally, and thousands waited for prisoners of war to come home or hoped that their loved ones who were presumed missing might still be alive. On top of these concerns, many women faced loss of employment and severe hardship. The instability that citizens perceived was often real.

Violence and its threat accompanied soldiers home; in Epsom, England, for example, soldiers waiting to leave the army attacked a police station and killed a man in June 1919.[16] Women still working in wartime jobs experienced verbal or physical abuse from veterans. Even those seen as keeping the peace and controlling other women and children, such as policewomen, faced threats and ridicule in the streets.[17] In formerly occupied Brussels in the days following the armistice officials worried about socialist revolution during the period before the resumption of civil government.[18] In Germany, the disorder was much more severe in 1918 and 1919, as many soldiers left for home without formal demobilization. Labor instability, revolutionary activity, and civil unrest, as well as the return of six million men during a period of political collapse, was difficult to control (Fig. 2). Media accounts of the moral rot brought about by the war made many people fear for their futures – venereal disease, young people running wild, petty crime, drunkenness, marauding soldiers – all these featured prominently in the discourse about soldiers returning in 1918.[19] For Germans in particular, the shocking loss from the war and the humiliating terms of peace exacerbated tensions as families were reunited in the midst of unemployment and shortages. Men wanted to return to ordinary family life, but many had very little to which they could return, or they simply did not know how to regain normalcy.

Fig. 2. Instability in 1918 and 1919 led in some cases to outright revolution. The violence and uncertainty of post-war life, especially in defeated nations, made it difficult to know what "normal" looked like. Here, revolutionary activity on 9 November 1918 marks the end of the German Empire. Source: Imperial War Museum, Q88164

Historian Jason Crouthamel documented some of the challenges soldiers now faced as they struggled both to remember and to forget their experiences. One particularly poignant set of letters between a soldier and his wife expresses both the longing for a return to pre-war family life and a dread that it could not be recaptured. This soldier worried that upon returning to Germany he would feel "like a tourist" in his own country.[20] Veterans described fears that the world had changed and the normal could not be recaptured. Men, unlike women, often articulated this idea of dislocation through an angry focus on the betrayal of the home front; they feared that men who had not served or women who had taken on male jobs had gotten ahead. For German and Irish soldiers, for instance, the civil disorder and revolution they encountered at home in 1919 only reignited their sense of alienation. Again, Crouthamel aptly described this disruptive return, noting that soldiers had idealized home while serving at the front, but in 1918 that fantasy "collided with the reality of a desperate, fractured home front".[21]

It was not just German soldiers who felt that they were returning to a foreign country. Phyllis Bentley, an educated British woman who had got a well-paying clerical job during the war, explained bluntly that her reality had changed with the armistice:

> Suddenly it became the duty of all women to clear out – I use the vulgar expression advisedly because it represented the opinion of the man in the street at the time – and leave the jobs open for the returning men [...] So we all cleared out and returned home.[22]

Women who lost their livelihoods with the armistice often had difficulty receiving governmental help because of the emphasis most states placed on a male breadwinner. In Britain, for instance, married women could receive benefits through their husbands as dependents, but unmarried women lost their right to government assistance if they rejected jobs such as laundry work or domestic service.[23] This put women in a difficult situation in multiple ways. Unmarried women who had previously earned an income now faced returning to their parents' home (as Bentley did) or finding work that might be unsuitable or poorly paid. Bentley, an unmarried, middle-class, educated woman, had little to fear because her family could support her.

While middle-class women felt a sense of grievance, poor women faced particular anxieties, and many lived a different reality in the weeks and month after the war than their wealthier counterparts. Many women faced loss of employment and severe hardship. Married women, especially if they had minor children, often could receive public assistance only as wives and mothers. Their dependence on male breadwinners meant that many women were unwilling or unable to leave bad domestic situations, this at a time when some men returned with psychological trauma. Sometimes, too, relief payments for widows and pensions did not cover basic needs. Government officials worried, too, about rising divorce rates, which they perceived as an attack on the nuclear family and "normal" households. In Britain and in Germany divorce rates spiked in the years following the war, and they never returned to their pre-war levels.[24] For many, such an increase in family dissolution required a redrawing of gender lines to build an ideal family model, often remembering something that had never really existed.

In Germany, where the economic blockade continued into the immediate post-war period and where the return of prisoners of war was often slow, the hardships of the war lasted beyond the armistice. One remarkable set of accounts helps expose such difficulties and anxieties in the period between the armistice and 1920. A Quaker team visited German homes of POWs who had worked for the Friends in French war relief schemes in devastated areas. This German mission brought financial payment for the prisoners' work and a message from the POWs to families whom they could locate. Prior to this journey, the three representatives (two Quakers and a Mennonite volunteer) took more than 200 photos of POWs and also recorded personal messages for their families. While this was designed to create reconciliation and spread the message of peace, this mission also provided testimonials and photos to use in fundraising literature in the United States for post-war relief efforts in Germany.[25] The three relief workers recounted moving stories of their visits with families, some of which were in remote and hard-to-reach areas. One example of such a visit comes from Solomon Yoder who visited the Grassler family in Losnitz, a coal mining district. The father was bed-ridden and the family of four was surviving on the wages of two teenaged children in the household. When Yoder showed her the photo of her son the mother seemed transfixed. Then Yoder gave her Otto's pay and she just sobbed. Despite Yoder's assurances that Otto wanted her to spend the money on the family, she assured him that she would put it in Otto's savings account for his return home.[26]

The Friends' representatives also encountered stories of the unbearable waiting for news of the missing. Yoder, a Mennonite relief worker, wrote home to his mother about the heart-rending situation of a Russian Mennonite woman living in the Berlin suburbs. Her husband, a German, had served in the food department of the army and had disappeared more than a year earlier in southern Russia. As Yoder noted, "Frau Sperling hopes and worries each day. She says if she only knew whether he was dead or alive, it would be better than this uncertainty".[27] Frau Sperling was also supporting twins aged 13, and Yoder commented on the meager food they had in the household more than a year after the war ended.

States recognized that such hardships contributed to political and social problems, and officials developed plans to address shortages, unemployment, and infant and maternal mortality rates. In Germany, the Law for Maternity Benefits and Maternity Welfare (1919-1920) provided basic stipends as well as food and healthcare for mothers, but this only began to deal with the scope of the problem.[28] Foreign aid organizations such as the American Relief Administration also set up feeding centers for children and delivered more than a million meals weekly, but again, this was a short-term, limited solution.[29] Government officials also worried considerably about the fall in birthrates at the end of the war and about the poor health of children. In Britain, the birth rate dropped from 24.1 births per 1,000 in 1913 to 17.7 in 1918.[30] While British women did have more children in 1920, the new average birth rate of the 1920s never returned to the levels prior to World War I. In Germany, the birth rate dropped even more precipitously during the war. The 1911 rate was 29.5 per 1,000, but it had dropped to 14.7 in 1918. By 1924, the rate had risen to only 21.1.[31]

Another lingering worry in the immediate post-war period was what a "normal" household now looked like after the cataclysm of war. For Belgians, especially those living in war zones or those who returned from a time as refugees, home was no longer a physical reality. The physical devastation from the war meant a long rebuilding period for homes and livelihoods. As in Germany, many Belgian soldiers merely left for home when news of the collapse of the front came; they wanted their ordinary lives to resume as quickly as possible.[32] However, militarization had deeply affected Belgian towns, cities, and landscapes, thereby slowing down the process of normalization. Many transport lines were destroyed or inoperable, and factories had been looted by departing troops. It was also a time of revenge for angry civilians who had lived through enemy occupation. Mary Thorp described the scene in Brussels in mid-December 1918:

> The shop-keepers who traded kindly with the Germans, have had their shop & windows smashed & goods plundered – the La Faire comestible shop, Rue de Namur, the 2 grand & "expensive" pork-butchers & the pastry-cook at Porte de Namur, & others of course in other neighbourhoods.[33]

Those who may have profited by the war or who had actively or passively collaborated felt the sting of post-war retribution. This was particularly true of women accused of "sexual treason" or friendly relations with enemy men, and as societies drafted a script of war remembrance women often found themselves as either good victims or bad perpetrators.[34]

As individuals and families sought to manage the effects of four years of war on their physical and psychological wellbeing, communities and states set to work remembering and making meaning of the war, often through memorials and public commemoration. With the armistice, states emphasized combatant dead, placing them at the center of post-war commemoration and defining non-combatants as "objects" of war. Most memorials and celebrations of service focused on male fighters, leaving others who had served and who had experienced losses without closure and sometimes without a sense of whether their war service mattered. Almost from the beginning, the language of these memorials articulated a heroic male combatant and a sacrificial female civilian, each playing a role in the ongoing gendered narrative of war. Individual monuments showed uniformed men, male graves, and female caretakers, while state-sponsored cemeteries and monuments to the dead inscribed the names of the men who had died. Implicit and explicit in the iconography was a gendered vision of sacrifice. This left many male civilians without a way to tell their stories that did not paint them as cowardly or complicit in the deaths of so many. Male conscientious objectors, workers in industries of national importance, and men with medical conditions faced post-war guilt and shame. Women, on the other hand, had difficulty demonstrating their own heroism as providers, defenders, and workers. Female medical personnel, for instance, who had endured air raids and dangerous conditions near the front, were often redefined in the public narrative as nurturing angels. The post-war stories of remembrance served multiple purposes: as a focal point for societal grief, as a guide to rebuilding families through a gendered understanding of war service, and as a necessary interpretation of the losses suffered.[35]

In Belgium, which had suffered under enemy occupation, the post-war commemoration included civilians as heroes and heroines, but most of the time their heroic acts focused around resisting victimization rather than on patriotic service. In the context of German occupation, Belgian civilians had trouble contesting the idea of "poor little Belgium" that had dominated wartime accounts of the nation (Fig. 3). The publication of wartime atrocity accounts, the massive wave of refugees who fled the country, and the deportation of male workers and officials during the war all pointed to a tale of victims triumphing over repression. Resistance activities, patriotic manifestations, intelligence gathering, and other active war service became relegated to a few individual stories of outstanding individuals. Often, too, the search for collaborators and war profiteers tainted the post-war narrative of civilian heroism. In their book investigating post-war disciplining of those considered to be unpatriotic, Xavier Rousseaux and Laurence van Ypersele listed multiple ways in which Belgians policed each other's war actions. In some communities popular vigilantism in the immediate aftermath of war punished "bad" Belgians with physical attacks and property destruction. Also, several official judicial proceedings also raised the issue of economic and moral collaboration in the months following the war.[36] In such an atmosphere, proving one's active war service was important in order to show loyalty.

Both Belgian men and women sought recognition for their patriotic activities. For instance, civilians submitted detailed depositions along with supporting documents from eyewitnesses in order to prove their work in resistance and intelligence networks run by allied governments. Some submitted their testimony as part of official inquiries into wartime service, while others proactively offered evidence in the hope of post-war recognition and possibly payment. One good example is the dossier of Marie Pierson, a 40-year-old Belgian housewife who filed a claim for recognition for her service in the Sedan region of the front where she was "actively occupied in espionage".[37] She went on to explain that she secretly gathered information on the movements of German troops for British intelligence. To support her claim, she included a statement from a local curate who had encountered her during her 1918 spying activities. Pierson's dossier demonstrates the painstaking documentation of war service by civilians hoping to show their patriotic commitment and the danger that they had undertaken during their nation's crisis.

Reclaiming the Ordinary 135

Fig. 3. Forgetting did not come easily in areas where major physical destruction had displaced populations, yet the question of "how" to remember the past became politicized in questions of rebuilding. Printed postcard from 1914-1918. Source: Library of Congress Prints and Photographs

In Britain, too, women demanded recompense and recognition for their war work. Six thousand female munitions employees marched on November 19, 1918 to Parliament "to convey to the prime minister and the Ministry of Munitions their demand for 'immediate guarantee for the future'".[38] Other smaller groups staged later demonstrations, marches, and petitions in the immediate aftermath of the armistice, trying to preserve their jobs and to demand recognition in the form of pension or out-of-work insurance. These demonstrations did little to stop the mass unemployment of former female war workers. Angela Woollacott estimated that in Birmingham and Newcastle tens of thousands of women faced unemployment by mid-December.[39]

Conclusion

In her well-known memoir, *Testament of Youth*, Vera Brittain spends a full chapter on the difficulties of reclaiming a normal life after the war. Yet even as she decried the celebratory mood and dwelled on all she had lost, Brittain also recognized that the year 1919 represented a rebirth with which all had to reckon:

> [1919] appeared to an exhausted world as divine normality, the spring of life after the winter of death, the stepping-stone to a new era, the gateway to an infinite future – a future not without its dreads and discomforts, but one in whose promise we had to believe, since it was all that some of us had left to believe in.[40]

For Brittain's generation, the First World War functioned as a break between the ordinary existence they remembered before the war and the unfulfilled promise of the post-war, in which violence, trauma, and anxiety continued to plague them. Brittain's experience was not entirely representative, however, and other people just got on with life. They went to the cinema, they worked, they attended church, they raised families even if they continued to mourn losses from the war.

In reflecting on 1918 and its consequences, it is hard not to conclude that the war did not really end for many families and societies. Belgium's post-war reckoning and rebuilding helped shape its response to a second occupation in 1940 in profound ways. In Germany the rise of National Socialism, whose core early supporters were war veterans, placed the scars of war on full display. British veterans, too, sought an outlet for their feelings of displacement, as is evident in the fledgling Boy Scout movement, which experienced major growth especially among adult members in the 1920s.[41] For women across Europe, the gendered work of rebuilding society that became their responsibility remains elusive in the historical records, and the striving for normalcy became an ongoing struggle, also largely hidden from view. Likewise, the building of monuments and the commemorative impulses of the 1920s could never quite provide the meaning or the closure that combatants and civilians sought. Even the gendered reclaiming of war service for the heroic male soldier ultimately failed to restore a sense of order to the home, the workplace, or the community.

Notes

1. Ludo Stynen and Sylvia van Peteghem, eds., *In Oorlogsnood: Virginie Lovelings Dagboek 1914-1918* (Ghent: Koninklijke Academie voor Nederlandse Taal-en-Letterkunde, 1999), 749 (13 November 1918).
2. Evelyn Blücher, *An English Wife in Berlin* (New York: E. P. Dutton & Co., 1920), 292 (12 November 1918).
3. Archives Générale du Royaume (AGR) P-207, Correspondence, Folder #1; Services Observation Anglais to the War Office, 25 November 1918.
4. Drew Gilpin Faust, *This Republic of Suffering: Death and the American Civil War* (New York: Random House, 2008), 267.
5. See: Alan Kramer, *Dynamic of Destruction: Culture and Mass Killing in the First World War* (Oxford: Oxford University Press, 2007) and Stéphane Audoin-Rouzeau and Annette Becker, *14-18, retrouver la Guerre* (Paris: Éditions Gallimard, 2000).
6. Works include Joy Damousi, *The Labour of Loss: Mourning, Memory, and Wartime Bereavement in Australia* (Cambridge: Cambridge University Press, 1999); Erika Kuhlman, *Of Little Comfort: War Widows, Fallen Soldiers, and the Remembering of the Nation after the Great War* (New York: New York University Press, 2012); and Robert Whelan, *Bitter Wounds: German Victims of the Great War, 1914-1939* (Ithaca, NY: Cornell University Press, 1984).
7. See for example: Susan Pedersen, *Family, Dependence, and the Origins of the Welfare State: Britain and France, 1914-1945* (Cambridge: Cambridge University Press, 1993).
8. For an overview of much of this literature, see: Robert Gerwarth and John Horne, eds., *War in Peace: Paramilitary Violence in Europe after the Great War* (Oxford: Oxford University Press, 2012).
9. The book that launched much of this scholarship is Jay Winter, *Sites of Memory, Sites of Mourning: The Great War in European Cultural History* (Cambridge: Cambridge University Press, 1995).
10. Rémi Dalisson and Elise Julien, "Bereavement and Mourning, Commemoration and Cult of the Fallen (France)," in *1914-1918-online. International Encyclopedia of the First World War*, ed. Ute Daniel et al.,(Berlin: Freie Universität Berlin, 8 October 2014. DOI: 10.15463/ie1418.10378. Translated by: Jocelyne Serveau. On mourning rituals and war in Britain, see: Pat Jalland, *Death in War and Peace: Loss and Grief in England, 1914-1970* (Oxford: Oxford University Press, 2010).
11. Laurence Van Ypersele, "Bereavement and Mourning (Belgium)," in *1914-1918-online*, 8 October 2014. DOI: 10.15463/ie1418.10176.
12. John Horne, "The living," in *The Cambridge History of the First World War, volume III: Civil Society*, ed. Jay Winter (Cambridge: Cambridge University Press, 2014), 592.
13. Sophie de Schaepdrijver and Tammy M. Proctor, *An English Governess in the Great War: The Secret Diary of Mary Thorp* (New York: Oxford University Press, 2017), 146 (8 November 1918).
14. Piete Kuhr, *There We'll Meet Again: A Young German Girl's Diary of the First World War*, trans. Walter Wright (Gloucester: Walter Wright, 1998), 309.
15. "Suspense," *The Times*, 8 November 1918, 7.
16. Susan Kingsley Kent, *Making Peace: The Reconstruction of Gender in Interwar Britain* (Princeton, NJ: Princeton University Press, 1993), 98.
17. Philippa Levine, "'Walking the Streets in a Way No Decent Woman Should': Women Police in World War I," *The Journal of Modern History* 66:1 (March 1994), 63-64.

18	De Schaepdrijver and Proctor, *An English Governess*, 246 (11 November 1918).
19	Richard Bessel, *Germany after the First World War* (Oxford: Clarendon, 2003), 235-245.
20	As quoted in Jason Crouthamel, *An Intimate History of the Front: Masculinity, Sexuality, and German Soldiers in the First World War* (New York: Palgrave MacMillan, 2014), 158.
21	Crouthamel, *An Intimate History*, 155. For similar feelings regarding alienation and dislocation, see: Jessica Meyer's study of Britain, *Men of war: masculinity and the First World War in Britain* (Basingstoke: Palgrave Macmillan, 2011).
22	Phyllis Bentley, *O Dreams, O Destinations: An Autobiography* (New York: Macmillan Company, 1962), 106.
23	Pedersen, *Family, Dependence*, 126.
24	Britain allowed for divorce on equal terms with the Matrimonial Causes Act of 1923, at which time divorce rates grew. In Germany, divorce rates tripled after the war. Bessel, *Germany after the First World War*, 231.
25	AFSC Press Release (for German-American papers), "Love Finds a Way," 1920; Folder: Germany Prisoner of War Family Visits, BOX General Administration 1920 Foreign Service Country – Germany, American Friends Service Committee Archives (AFSC), Philadelphia, PA.
26	Tammy M. Proctor, "Repairing the Spirit: The Society of Friends, Total War, and the Limits of Reconciliation," *Peace & Change: A Journal of Peace Research* 45, no. 2 (2020): 209.
27	S. Duane Kauffman, ed., *Your Son and Brother Sol* (Morgantown, PA: Masthof Press, 2011), 121-122. Letter from December 1919.
28	Michelle Mouton, *From Nurturing the Nation to Purifying the Volk: Weimar and Nazi Family Policy, 1918-1945* (Cambridge: Cambridge University Press, 2007), 155-156. The infant mortality rate in Germany in 1918 was 38.9 per 1,000 births, Mouton, 154 n.3.
29	Tammy M. Proctor, "An American Enterprise: British participation in U.S. food relief programmes (1914-1923)," *First World War Studies* 5, no. 1 (2014): 31.
30	*Statistical Abstract for the United Kingdom: No. 72 (1913-1927)* (London: HMSO, 1929), 18-19, 26.
31	Bessel, *Germany after the First World War*, 229.
32	Sophie De Schaepdrijver, *La Belgique et la Première Guerre mondiale* (Brussels: Peter Lang, 2004), 288.
33	De Schaepdrijver and Proctor, *An English Governess*, 252. (15 December 1918). See also: Xavier Rousseaux and Laurence Van Ypersele, "Leaving the war: popular violence and judicial repression of 'unpatriotic' behaviour in Belgium (1918-1921)," *European Review of History* 12, no. 1 (March 2005): 3-22.
34	For an excellent book on this topic, see: Lisa M. Todd, *Sexual Treason in Germany during the First World War* (Cham: Palgrave Macmillan, 2017).
35	In her recent book, Alison Fell examines the narratives that a few women in France, Belgium, and Britain constructed in the post-war period in order to make their case as veterans of the conflict. Alison Fell, *Women as Veterans in Britain and France after the First World War* (Cambridge: Cambridge University Press, 2018).
36	Xavier Rousseaux and Laurence Van Ypersele, *La Patrie crie vengeance! La Répression des 'inciviques' belges au sortir de la guerre 1914-1918* (Brussels: Le Cri, 2008). See also: Emmanuel Debruyne, *'Femmes à Boches': Occupation du corps féminin, dans la France et la Belgique de la Grande Guerre* (Paris: Les belles lettres, 2018).

37 Archives Générale du Royaume (AGR) P-2224, Services Patriotique; Deposition of Marie Augustine Pierson to the Commission des Annales des Services Patriotiques, May 1919.
38 Angela Woollacott, *On Her Their Lives Depend: Munitions Workers in the Great War* (Berkeley, CA: University of California Press, 1994), 106-107.
39 Ibid., 107.
40 Vera Brittain, *Testament of Youth* (New York: Penguin, 1989), 467-468.
41 Tammy M. Proctor, *On my Honour: Guides and Scouts in Interwar Britain* (Philadelphia, PA: American Philosophical Society, 2002), 35. Scout membership in the UK rose from 194,331 in 1917 to 270,110 in 1923 to 480,379 by 1933.

Fig. 1. Karl Gläser, *Monument to German Field Marshal Paul von Hindenburg*, executed in snow, 1915, Stuttgart, Ice skating rink. Picture postcard, F. Hinderer Verlag. (private collection)

Expressing Grief and Gratitude in an Unsettled Time
Temporary First World War Memorials in Belgium

Leen Engelen & Marjan Sterckx

Introduction: Temporary Monuments and the Great War

> There will be, there would be, if one is not careful, something atrocious: memorials! Let's denounce this peril. Certainly, let's write the names of the martyrs in bronze and marble on the threshold of our village halls; let's plant commemorative trees [...]; let's erect in some larger cities the column or temple that eternalises the painful image of this grand era. But, let's be wary of cheap memorials of poor quality, a threat that is surrounding us on all sides. [...] Can you see that? [...] on all the squares, a Lady Belgium in bronze by a local artist [...] To make things worse, no doubt every Lady Belgium will be accompanied by a lion, that formidable Belgian lion.[1]

This warning against a deluge of average-quality war memorials was published in the Belgian satirical magazine *Pourquoi Pas?* as early as December 1918. In his bantering critique, the author was referring to the thousands of memorials that had been erected in French villages after the Franco-Prussian war. Alas, his warning fell on deaf ears. As of November 1918, and continuing well into the 1920s and 1930s, a large number of monuments commemorating the Great War were erected throughout France and Belgium. Although the act of commemorating conflict through monuments indeed long predated the Great War, no previous war had instigated the creation of such a large number of memorials.² In formerly occupied territories such as the majority of Belgium and Northern France, the need to express grief as well as gratitude had been actively suppressed by the occupational regime for over four years. The occupation army's departure triggered a rapid and intense surfacing of the need to create monuments. Instantaneously and enthusiastically, ideas began to surface on both the national and local levels and many of these initiatives involved active and intense public participation. Plans were forged by formal as well as informal local associations such as parishes, professional guilds, schools, (sports) clubs and neighbourhood associations. Occasionally, independent initiatives were taken by bereaved families or individual artists. Only a minority of these intentions actually materialised and many took a long time to develop.³

This essay looks into a phenomenon which slightly predates the large-scale postwar "statue mania" that flooded municipal squares and parish grounds starting in the early 1920s. We will explore the emergence of temporary public memorials in Belgium during and immediately after the First World War, assessing how they developed and established a commemoration trajectory which lasted for decades. Although ephemeral monuments were an international phenomenon characterised by a great diversity, they took on a specific form in (previously) occupied territories such as Belgium, both during and after the war. These monuments – made of temporary materials such as greenery, wood, earth and plaster – were created with the intention of alleviating the urgent (and sometimes long repressed) need for a place of remembrance, a *lieu de mémoire*. They emerged from a deeply felt and shared desire to mourn, remember and commemorate singled-out (groups of) people, specific war-related events or causes. They emerged from below in the absence of official permanent monuments – which usually came about via top-down procedures – and were often conceived to structure collective commemorations and commemorative practices according to familiar, ritualised patterns. In his essay on "The Living", John Horne describes people's coming to terms with death in wartime as a process which takes place in three concentric circles: the innermost circle is the private loss of a loved-one, the second circle is the formation of temporary mourning communities (small-scale to nationwide) and, finally, the third circle – public commemoration – gives mourning an enduring public form. In general, the early temporary monuments are firmly rooted in the innermost circle. They develop within small mourning communities and sometimes – if their replacement by a permanent structure is envisaged – they are the harbinger of enduring commemoration.⁴ As such, they play their part in private, collective as well as public processes of mourning and healing. Through involvement people gained the opportunity to do more than just visit the monuments and leave flowers and wreaths: in what were often grassroots initiatives, they could also participate in their conceptualisation and collaborate in their creation. At the same time, hierarchical committees (such as parish groups or *comités de patronage*) often played some part in their realisation. These memorials often were conceived and constructed in a short time. Therefore, they mostly by-passed the generally cumbersome official procedures for erecting public monuments and were able to disregard conflicting agendas of official bodies as well as aesthetic discussions. It was often hoped that before these ephemeral monuments deteriorated, regular top-down procedures would lead to their replacement with permanent structures in stone or bronze. In a way, the ephemeral character of the monuments created a kind of a space "in between": their presence eased an immediate need and thereby gave communities and authorities time to think about durable monuments and future commemorative practices. When in the early 1920s an increasing number of permanent memorials were built, their temporary predecessors quickly began to disappear.

In order to contextualise the emergence and meaning of ephemeral First World War memorials in Belgium, we will shed light on the different historic and international manifestations of this phenomenon before, during and after the First World War. First, we will show that in the context of the Great War temporary memorials were an international phenomenon that manifested itself in many different forms depending on the place where they emerged and those involved in their conception. Next, we will show that these temporary monuments took a specific shape in occupied areas such as Belgium, both during and after the war. In our discussion we will pay attention to the variable temporalities of different types of temporary monuments and to the changing roles played by the various stakeholders (the public, the authorities, the artists).

Wartime Temporary Memorials: An International Phenomenon

The specific nature of the Great War partly accounts for the popularity of temporary monuments in the countries directly involved in the conflict. For the first time, a total war was being fought and the consequences of war were forced home on civilians. The massive involvement of citizens revealed that the general population had a pressing urge to commemorate or celebrate specific and often local events or to come together to publicly express and share grief. These needs had already begun to arise during the conflict. Although the circumstances differed depending on the country or region, the erection of ad hoc, co-created, do-it-yourself memorials, such as flower shrines or modest wooden columns or crosses, was an international phenomenon that manifested itself in many different forms. Some early British instances are well documented. As early as October 1914, for example, the London fire brigade proposed to honour its fellow firemen who fell in the first weeks of the war (five by then) by erecting a temporary memorial at the brigade's headquarters.

The memorial was erected as an immediate, emotional response to the loss this local community of firemen was confronted with and became a tangible symbol for their grief.[5] In 1916, likewise in London, inhabitants of a working-class neighbourhood in the East End marked the voluntary enlistment of 65 of their boys and men with a street shrine. Their example was followed by several other neighbourhoods in the area and led to what came to be called the "war shrine movement".[6] As the movement caught on, institutional (funding) bodies such as parishes and local governments quickly became involved and a standard design was proposed. By the end of October 1916, more than 250 shrines had been erected or were planned and many more would follow.[7] Evidently, public wartime shrines such as these British examples were rare to non-existent in occupied or frontline areas. In Britain, these early initiatives often already carried within them the intention for a later permanent memorial. In August 1916, the British parish of Dorking for example erected "a handsome oak cross with a figure of bronze representing Christ crucified" along with the roll of honour of the parish. Immediately, it was made clear that this was "only intended to be a temporary memorial, to suffice until the end of the war, when, doubtless the town will desire something of a more enduring character shall take its place", as indeed many communities envisaged.[8] As Mark Connelly argues, the war shrines indeed laid the foundations for later remembrance, but this was by no means a paved way and many hurdles lay ahead.[9] A case in point is the Hyde Park memorial shrine: a 24-foot spire with Allied flags around the top placed on a Maltese-cross-shaped base. It was inaugurated on 4 August 1918 and attracted vast audiences.[10] Due to its popularity, the shrine remained in situ for over a year and prompted debates on official war memorials. Architect Edwin Lutyens (1869-1944) was asked to design a monument to replace the temporary shrine, but this project never materialised.[11]

Some temporary memorials inscribed themselves in more vernacular practices. An out of the ordinary example are the snow memorials. These are at once rooted in the popular pastime of snow sculpting and in the artistic tradition of open-air snow and ice sculpture exhibitions, commonly organised during frost fairs. The latter were quite popular in the Low Countries during the Little Ice Age that struck Europe from the fourteenth to the nineteenth century. In some cases, the extremely ephemeral nature of snow sculptures occasioned more daring or even provocative designs or themes.[12] This was not the case when, in January 1915, a snow sculpture of the German Field Marshal Paul von Hindenburg (1847-1934) – at that time already known in Germany as "the victor of Tannenberg" – was unveiled in Stuttgart. The large bust of Hindenburg in uniform (complete with iron cross) was placed on a massive rectangular plinth and flanked by pine trees (Fig. 1). The structure was approximately three metres high. The almost alabaster or marble white of the snow as well as its transient qualities stood in stark contrast to the serious posture of the bust and the stately elaboration of the plinth in an imitation granite texture. As it was placed in an outdoor ice rink, people skated around the statue, which was guarded by two guards on ice skates. Before it melted, this first memorial to Hindenburg in Germany was documented in articles in the local press, press photos, a Messter Woche newsreel item and picture postcards.[13]

Fig. 2. Georg Marschall, *Der Eiserne Hindenburg zu Berlin*, erected in 1915 in Berlin. Picture postcard, Oscar Peters Verlag, Darmstadt. (private collection)

This type of documentation – more long-lasting than the objects themselves – also exists in relation to a so-called *Nagelman* (nail man) sculpture of the same Hindenburg which was erected in Berlin in the autumn of 1915. In the years that followed, the 13-metre-high wooden structure by German painter and sculptor Georg Marschall (1871-1956) was covered with 14.000 kg of nails (Fig. 2). The *Eiserne Hindenburg von Berlin*, as the monument came to be known (later "the wooden Titan"),[14] was removed and put into storage after the war and reportedly largely used as firewood (except for the head which was placed in the Deutsche Luftfahrtsammlung in Berlin in 1938).[15] The nail men are a typical phenomenon that gained popularity during the First World War. The first *Nagelmänner* emerged in the spring of 1915; by 1918 hundreds of nail figures had been made, mostly in Germany and Austria Hungary. They represented not only military figures, but also symbols such as coats of arms and iron crosses.[16]

Often these resulted from grassroots initiatives by local communities (for instance schools or charity organisations) raising money for war-related aid organisations. The communities participated either directly in the nailing itself, or indirectly by purchasing or supplying iron silver- or gold-plated nails.[17] The ephemerality of these sculptures is complex. On the one hand, the wooden sculpture is made more durable through the application of nails; on the other hand, the massive application of nails eventually destroyed the wooden structure.

Temporary Memorials in Occupied Belgium

As the examples above demonstrate, temporary memorials were conceived in a remarkable variety of shapes, materials and sizes. In occupied territories like Belgium, monumental or eye-catching memorials, even when temporary, were largely forbidden. One thus had to resort to inconspicuous improvised shrines or memorials.[18] We can assume that a lot of ephemeral memorials in this fashion were created in the private or domestic space, to be seen only by the members of a specific family or association: a photograph or postcard on the wall adorned with a candle, a cockade or a flower arrangement… These mostly stayed under the radar. The (censored) press was not likely to report on this phenomenon either, making it even more difficult to grasp. On the (semi)public level, it is noticeable that under the occupation religious celebrations and gatherings often took on patriotic undertones and cemeteries became important loci of remembrance. This was reluctantly tolerated by the occupier.[19]

From early on, local inhabitants, parishes, patriotic associations and occasional groups began to erect improvised funerary steles and temporary monuments in cemeteries. These were likewise covered by the mourners with chrysanthemums and wreaths. A few months after the invasion, for instance, in the cemetery of Kessel-Lo near Louvain a fugitive gravestone-like memorial made from earth, flowers and wood was created to mark the mass grave of the 65 Belgian soldiers[20] who died in nearby Kessel-Lo(o) in August and September 1914[21] (Fig. 3). As of December 1914, the grave was managed by the local veteran society (*De Bond van Oud-Soldaten van Blauwput-Kessel-Loo*) and it is likely that the memorial was created under their auspices. In 1915, they placed an additional temporary wooden cross on the grave, with the inscription "to the memory of our Belgian heroes who died for their country in Kessel-Loo" ("*à la mémoire de nos héros belges tombés pour la patrie à Kessel-Loo*"). In mid-1915, the group pleaded for a permanent memorial with the city council, but the latter decided it preferred to wait until the end of the war.[22]

Fig. 3. Temporary memorial at the cemetery of Kessel-Lo (Leuven), 1914. (Leuven City Archive)

The Catholic tradition of laying flowers on the tombs in the local cemetery on All Souls' and All Saints' Day (1-2 November) developed into massive commemorations of the fallen during the war. On those days, monuments related to the allies, such as the French monument for the fallen of 1870 (inaugurated in 1880) and the Wellington Memorial (inaugurated 1890), both at the cemetery of the Brussels commune of Evere, became sites of mourning and patriotic manifestations. In a solemn procession, people walked quietly before the monuments, leaving flowers or lighting candles. At the same cemetery, for All Saints' Day in 1915 a chrysanthemum flower carpet representing the Belgian lion and the initials of the Belgian royals was laid around the graves of the Belgian officers and soldiers who died in Brussels' hospitals following the invasion. At another Brussels cemetery (Saint-Josse-ten-Noode), a temporary monument (probably in plaster) by an unnamed sculptor (the press mentions only that he was a pupil of the famous Thomas Vinçotte (1850-1925)), representing a Belgian lion holding the Belgian flag in its claws mounted on a stone plinth was erected.[23] A year later, in November 1916, a pyramid-shaped wooden memorial was erected at the cemetery of the Brussels district of Ixelles, and a temporary sculptural group embellished the soldiers' cemetery in the nearby municipality of Etterbeek.[24] Participating in these events was not only a religious token, but also an act of patriotic resistance.

Meanwhile, the occupying regime occasionally celebrated its own heroes with temporary monuments on Belgian soil. In December 1915, a bas-relief of the German general Otto von Emmich (1848-1915) – celebrated as responsible for the fall of Liège – was inaugurated in the city's courthouse. It was executed in the traditional *Nagelmänner* style and came to be called the "Eiserne Emmich".[25] Von Emmich, who was already gravely ill at the time, died barely a week later. On this occasion, a cast iron bust on a nailed wooden pedestal was erected in Liège as well.[26] The Belgian exiled press was not impressed by the (particularly German) nail men tradition. A few days before the inauguration of the "Eiserne Emmich", a journalist had commented on the "Eiserne Hindenburg" in terms that can hardly be misunderstood: "this crouched Hindenburg, made out of wood, in which the faithful push nails in iron or gold. A ridiculous spectacle for which the *boche* illustrated magazines made ample and ludicrous publicity".[27]

What most of these wartime ephemeral sculptures, both in Belgium and abroad, have in common is their co-creation by the local community. While the model of financing public sculptures by subscription was already well-established in the nineteenth century, the tangible and hands-on involvement of the public at large is a feature that came to prominence during the war. The people were involved in both the decision-making process and the actual construction of the memorials and monuments. The *nail men* – which were literally nailed by the public – are probably the most radical emanation of this trend. But their involvement is also palpable in the snow sculptures, cemetery memorials and street shrines. A second, closely connected feature is their ad hoc nature. These monuments emerge almost unexpectedly and are the result of improvisation. They are built for the most part with non-durable materials that are readily available, such as snow, greenery and derelict wood or metal, and that have been effectively repurposed. As such, they might be considered early examples of "upcycling" and of what design theorists such as Charles Jencks and Nathan Silver, and Joseph Grima call "adhocism" or "adhocracy", which they describe as the art of doing things ad hoc – tackling problems at once, using materials at hand, rather than waiting for the perfect moment or "proper" approach.[28] Such an ad hoc approach questions authorship, standardisation and bureaucracy; and favours collaboration, sharing and bottom-up initiatives.[29] This is exactly what also happened in the wartime emanations of ephemeral monuments.

November 1918: An Abrupt Series of Temporary Sculptures in Brussels

As the Armistice and the end of the war approached, the nature of temporary memorials changed. Design was increasingly prioritised, the prospect of eternalising became more prominent, and official bodies became more and more involved.[30] The end of the occupation of Belgium in November 1918 was above all a cathartic moment. People were finally able to speak out, give in to ecstatic patriotism, and publicly ventilate anti-German sentiments. At the same time, space was created for mourning and commemoration which was no longer limited to the private inner circle or local community. A feeling was shared by many that places of commemoration were important and necessary. Almost instantly, questions arose about whose efforts should first be eternalised in monuments: soldiers, high ranking military, the royals, civilian victims or resisters…? This, of course, brought up the matter of who was to build and finance these memorials, where they should be placed, and what they should look like. It was clear that local or national authorities would play a role in this, but in a state where they were overwhelmed with financial and logistic problems, they initially did not consider monuments a priority and were reluctant to make decisions. As a consequence – and despite the urgency felt by the population – the building of official monuments did not start immediately after the Armistice.[31] At this point, temporary monuments provided an answer. They were less cumbersome to realise and allowed at least temporarily for actual *lieux de mémoire* to emerge.[32] Realising that it would take a considerable time to finance and conceive official and expensive permanent monuments, local authorities were interested in involvement in the realisation of these temporary counterparts. These not only offered a possibility quickly to acknowledge military effort and sacrifice but they were also instrumental in the legitimation of the victory of the nation state, and in some cases in consolidating the emerging post-war world order.

In this respect, they were reminiscent of the longstanding tradition of political use of temporary sculpture. Already in the sixteenth century the contribution of artists to patriotic celebrations – such as Joyous Entries or anniversaries of nations and rulers[33] – through the design of ephemeral sculptures was customary in countries such as Belgium:

> In every epoch of our history, Belgian art has largely contributed to rejoicing the fatherland, and the grandest artists have not looked down upon attaching their name to ephemeral creations whose glory helped to perpetuate the memory.[34]

This type of work involved artists from many different trades: architects, stage set designers, decorators, craftsmen, painters, sculptors… In Antwerp, for example, painter Pieter Paul Rubens (1577-1640) created and oversaw the ephemeral decorations for the festive entry of Archduke Ferdinand of Austria in 1634 and turned it into "what was beyond doubt the most splendid of all princely pageants".[35] Temporary sculptures and architectural contributions remained part of the pomp and circumstance of official celebrations over the centuries.[36] The close involvement of artists in patriotic celebrations further intensified with the foundation of the nation state in 1830. Every year on this national holiday the streets of Brussels underwent a true metamorphosis. The capital was reshaped into a grand open-air fair with flags and pennants, large flower arrangements, paintings and temporary sculptures and architectural structures. These ephemeral artworks had a legitimising, educational and commemorative function: they represented the grandeur and the history of the nation while at the same time contributing to it. The mostly short-lived constructions and adjoining sculptures depicted the glorious past and future of the country and focussed on the monarchy and the constitution to legitimate the nation state.[37]

The use of ephemeral sculptures was also customary in traditional religious, folkloric and historical pageants (which had been common since the late Middle Ages),[38] and in International and World Exhibitions which Belgium enthusiastically organised in the late nineteenth and early twentieth centuries (Antwerp 1894, Brussels 1897, Liège 1905, Brussels 1910, Ghent 1913).[39] Joyous Entries, patriotic celebrations, historic and religious pageants and International Expositions were all temporary spectacles, built to be wondered at and then dismantled. To a greater or lesser extent, official bodies were involved in their creation as commissioners and financiers. Through their spectacular qualities, artistic merit and the use of well-known iconographies they consolidated political ideologies.

The first temporary memorials which were erected in Belgium after the war were direct exponents of these traditions. On the occasion of the festive re-entry of the Royal Family into the Belgian capital on 22 November 1918 an exceptional series of ten temporary monuments was made.[40] Although this event took place 11 days after the actual signing of the armistice (on 11 November 1918), this day was considered the real end of the occupation and marked the beginning of the post-war era in Belgium.[41] The monuments were commissioned by the city of Brussels and placed in the historic centre as part of the festal decorations. Compared to most wartime temporary memorials, their emergence was obviously less spontaneous and less bottom-up. The enterprise was supervised by city architect François Malfait (1872-1955), assisted by *peintres décorateurs* Jean Delescluze (1871-1947) and Albert Dubosq (1864-1940).[42] Next to these lavish decorations, the military parade and the festive atmosphere, the public monuments were an important attraction – they were also photographed and as such disseminated via postcards. The monuments were made in plaster, following the traditional "staff" technique that was also used for the temporary buildings and monuments for the Belgian International Exhibitions and World Fairs. As the project was conceived in the short transitional period between the armistice and the Royal Entry, the usual commissioning procedures for public monuments were not followed, which resulted in fewer restrictions than usual and more freedom for the participating artists.

As late as mid-November 1918, local newspapers reported that the city council had voted a budget of 500,000 francs for the city's decoration on the occasion of the Royal Entry, including the monuments.[43] According to the newspaper *Le Soir*, the sculptors completed their plaster projects in only a fortnight – an almost impossible exploit, as just the casting in plaster of such large models takes a considerable time.[44] *Le Soir* spoke of "improvised" monuments,[45] but it seems – and this is only logical – that most artists involved creatively reused or adapted existing models or designs from their studios. Art critic Sander Pierron (1872-1945) formulated it as such: "[a] not so quite spontaneous flowering, for if some of these works were realised as quickly as the victory of our armies asserted, others had been long conceived and executed in the silence of the workshops".[46] For instance, Charles Samuel (1862-1938) corresponded already in 1916 with the Brussels' *Compagnie des Bronzes* concerning his statuette *La Brabançonne*, which he reworked into a larger, more detailed statue in 1918[47] (Fig. 4). Pierron spoke of "sketches" that would have to be reworked or fine-tuned when later realised in marble or bronze.

Fig. 4. Charles Samuel, *La Brabançonne*, plaster and wood, November 1918, Brussels, Grand-Place, photograph Sylvain. (Ghent University Library)

Apparently, no clear programme, formal guidelines or templates were provided, which left room for improvisation in the design and iconography on the part of the sculptors. As a consequence the monuments varied remarkably in style, genre, height and format, and featured reliefs and busts as well as full-length statues. The all-figurative statues represented personalities as well as small realist groups (the troops, the wounded or grieving women) and semi-nude historical and abstract allegories (e.g. Lady Belgium – sometimes called La Brabançonne – with different qualities, triumphant, fierce or grieving). Moreover, the statues were adorned with patriotic attributes such as flags, lions, Adrian helmets and laurel wreaths in various combinations. The monuments paid homage to a variety of causes in the military sphere: to the heroism and sacrifice of the Belgian soldiers, the wounded soldiers, the British nurse Edith Cavell executed in Brussels[48] (Fig. 5), King Albert I, the Allies (monuments dedicated to France, Italy, England and the United States) and more abstract subjects such as "liberty", "law" and "peace". By honouring the Allies, international diplomatic concerns were covered. This was much less the case for internal sensibilities regarding the suffering of different groups in the civilian population, who had lived different war experiences (at the front, as resisters in occupied Belgium, in German labour camps, as refugees abroad…). After the war tensions rose between them as to who had suffered most and which experiences should be commemorated (first), influencing post-war decisions about monuments.[49] Thus, the only semi-improvised nature of the monuments as well as the fact that they were official commissions makes them very much an "in between" series, bridging the transition from war to peace, from ad hoc remembrance to orchestrated commemoration.

Compared to the international avant-garde *en vogue* at the time, most of the temporary monuments described above were designed in a fairly academic or realist-allegorical style indebted to the nineteenth-century sculptural tradition. After all, these were artworks aimed to appeal to the public at large, to local communities, with particular demands concerning form and content and with a specific function. This led to straightforward, uplifting and recognisable figurative designs. Moreover, several of the authors of the 1918 monuments belonged to the "older" generation (born in the 1850s and 1860s) and had well-established careers. Many were trainees from the Brussels Academy (most of them being pupils of Charles Van der Stappen (1843-1910)) and stemmed from higher social classes. The 1918 project provided them with not only an opportunity to show generosity and patriotism, but also the chance to obtain visibility and remuneration after a grim financial period. The *Fédération Professionnelle des Beaux-Arts*, set up in September 1914, provided sculptors in occupied Brussels with plaster and a monthly sum in order to help them survive, but they could hardly work and sell during the war. Marble was scarce, and bronze was requisitioned by the occupier from late 1915.[50] Whereas exhibitions and salons were still organised during wartime in some Brussels museums and galleries, for the benefit of the artists in need, they mainly exhibited portraits and *salonfähige*, charming paintings. Sculptures – even in plaster or terracotta – were largely absent, as were avant-garde works that were considered too much of a risk and thus less attractive for buyers and collectors of art seeking secure investments in times of devaluation.[51]

Fig. 5. Jacques Marin, *Monument to Edith Cavell*, plaster and wood, November 1918, Brussels, Grand-Place, picture postcard. (Brussels City Archive, Guerre 1914-1918 [Monuments provisoires érigés dans la Ville de Bruxelles (en 1918 ou 1919) en reconnaissance aux soldats et victimes de la guerre], C-1879)

Progressing Towards Permanent Memorials… But Not Just Yet

The statues erected in Brussels in 1918 were made without any immediate prospect of making them permanent, even if *Le Belge Indépendant* called them "plaster models of future commemorative monuments".[52] According to the same newspaper, the statues were intended to remain in place until Christmas. Some stayed a few weeks longer, but by February 1919 all sculptures were removed from the public space and most likely returned to their authors or demolished.[53] However, the monuments had struck a chord, and several plans to perpetuate them were initiated.[54] Three out of the ten temporary monuments would ultimately be given a permanent character, albeit only after a considerable time and with some minor changes. Not surprisingly, only "unproblematic" monuments representing Belgium in the most general sense were retained: Jules Lagae's (1862-1931) monument to King Albert, Guillaume Charlier's (1854-1925) *La Belgique reconquise,* and Charles Samuel's *La Brabançonne* (the latter two represent Lady Belgium holding the national flag). Monuments referring to specific groups (*À nos blessés* by Jos Van Hamme, or *À nos soldats morts pour la patrie* by Jules Mascré) or to the allies, and monuments airing anti-German sentiments (*La Belgique repoussant l'invasion des barbares* by the French-born Marquis Jean de Pouilly) disappeared after the festivities.

Samuel's *La Brabançonne* seems to have been the most popular of the series. It was the last stucco monument to be removed and already before that a possible permanent location was discussed by the Brussels city council. In January 1919, François Malfait suggested the Place de la Chapelle in the popular Marolles neighbourhood, but this idea did not materialise.[55] In April 1920, on the occasion of the first post-war Brussels Commercial Fair, the plaster monument reappeared briefly in the Royal Park, only to be quickly removed afterwards.[56] Finally in 1930, Samuel's *Brabançonne* model was cast in bronze to mark the Belgian centenary. Prior to the festivities, money had been raised by public subscription. It was then relocated to the slightly peripheral Surlet De Chokier Square where it still stands today.[57] The statue was put on a new pedestal and reframed by a new inscription: the first couplet of the national anthem, *La Brabançonne.*[58]

That only a few of the November 1918 temporary monuments were re-used later is remarkable. Nevertheless, several of the sculptors, most notably Georges Vandevoorde (1878-1964), Léandre Grandmoulin (1873-1957) and Jacques Marin (1877-1950), as well as architect François Malfait, moved on to make war memorials in Brussels and elsewhere in the 1920s and 1930s. Commonplace dedications like "*à nos soldats morts pour la patrie*" or "*à nos héros*", which were featured on the early temporary monuments, as well as representations of King Albert, personifications of the Belgian *poilu* or *La Brabançonne*, allegories such as the Belgian lion devouring the German eagle, as well as symbols such as the Belgian flag or laurel wreaths were commonly reused in the permanent war memorials. Yet, most of these elements can hardly be considered original. They had been common throughout the war and stemmed from laic iconographical imagery predating the First World War. In that respect, the impact of the 1918 temporary monuments on post-war sculpture was limited.

The temporary monuments erected in Brussels in November 1918 were the first, but certainly not the last, post-war emanation of the urge to commemorate. They were quickly followed by other initiatives, material as well as immaterial. Several patriotic associations established after the war, such as the *Ligue des patriotes* (Patriotic League) and the *Ligue du Souvenir* (Remembrance League), aimed for the commemoration of war heroes through immaterial commemorations such as public funerals and remembrance ceremonies. Some associations, such as the *Bond der Politieke Gevangenen van den Oorlog* (League of Political Prisoners of War), specifically focussed on the commemoration of civilian heroes. The latter also became the focal point of remembrance in towns that had suffered exceptionally during the war, such as the *villes martyres*. In the Walloon village of Tamines for instance, which lost over 380 inhabitants overnight in August 1914, a large wooden cross with a commemorative plaque was erected on the Place Saint Martin immediately after the armistice[59] (Fig. 6). Although discussions about a permanent official monument of a more suitable design to remember the civilian victims had been ongoing since January 1919, the deteriorating wooden cross was replaced with an almost identical concrete one in 1923. It took another three years, until August 1926, before an official monument in honour of the civilian victims was inaugurated: a sculptural group by Louis Mascré (1871-1927) (also one of the sculptors involved in the 1918 Brussels temporary monuments). In Louvain (Leuven), another *ville martyre*, a wooden column was erected in the municipal cemetery on 12 January 1919 on the occasion of a patriotic manifestation in honour of the city's civilian martyrs.[60] Already in December 1915, the city had been planning a permanent memorial for its civilian victims after the war. What followed was a ten-year agony. Finally, the permanent and large-scale "monument to the martyrs" was inaugurated in April 1925.[61]

Fig. 6. Temporary monument (cross) erected in memory of the victims of the 22nd August 1914, wood, 1918, Tamines. Picture postcard, Nels, Brussels. (private collection)

On a different scale, a robust temporary cenotaph (an empty tomb) was placed in the park in front of the Royal Palace in Brussels on the occasion of the national jubilee and the subsequent *Marche de la Victoire* (21 and 22 July) in 1919. The cenotaph gave death a literally massive presence amid the victory celebrations. This temporary structure was erected in anticipation of a great national war memorial to be built in Brussels later on – a project that would be abandoned altogether in 1924.[62] The Brussels cenotaph was designed by city architect François Malfait, and put on the same spot where in November 1918 one of the temporary monuments had stood: Philippe Wolfers's (1858-1929) group of two female nudes, *À nos héros*.[63] Some ceremonies took place at the cenotaph and it was removed immediately thereafter. Following the capital's example, in 1919 and 1920 provisional cenotaphs appeared in numerous Belgian cities, such as Arlon, Bouillon, Engin, Halen, Halle, Koekelberg, Marcinelle and Mechelen.[64]

As a common typology for a funerary monument, the laic and solemn design of the cenotaph had wide international appeal. In the summer of 1919 temporary cenotaphs were erected in many different countries on the occasion of memorial festivities. For the French national holiday, on 14 July, cenotaphs were raised in several French cities, such as Nancy, Lisieux and Paris, where a short-lived cenotaph was placed under the Arc de Triomphe.[65] In London, the Peace Parade on 19 July, celebrating the Versailles Peace Treaty, was the occasion for placing a cenotaph by architect Sir Edwin Lutyens in the middle of Whitehall. It remained in situ until it was replaced with a permanent stone cenotaph of roughly the same design in 1920.[66]

Conclusion: Temporary, Untimely and yet Timeless

This essay has explored the phenomenon of temporary memorials erected during and immediately after the Great War in Belgium. These temporary memorials initiated a trajectory of material commemoration of the Great War that strongly marked the 1920s and 1930s and is still ongoing today. They were conceived to share grief and structure collective commemorations at an "untimely time". During and immediately after the war the grief was overwhelming, and the need for these memorials was deeply felt by the people. At the same time official bodies were paralysed by not only occupation, cumbersome procedures and the lack of financial means and debate, but also a lack of consensus as to who or what was to be commemorated and in what way. Temporary monuments immediately provided for people's commemorative needs and intentions with a locus – a place to grieve and gather. As such, they had a lot in common with their permanent counterparts, from which they differed mostly in terms of their immediacy and their often bottom-up genesis.

Despite their variety, the temporary memorials discussed here shared some important characteristics. First, their creation interactively involved three different actors: the people (usually united in informal or ad hoc groups), (commissioning) local authorities or official committees, and the artists and artisans involved in their conception and design. The degree to which each actor was involved depended on both the place and the time the monument was conceived and created. Small and simple memorials emerging during the war – such as street shrines or graves decorated with flowers – were much more bottom-up and the result of ad hoc co-creation by local inhabitants than larger more official memorials such as the November 1918 series of temporary monuments in Brussels and the post-war temporary cenotaphs, created by professional sculptors and architects. The momentum they created allowed for a creative investment of the people and the artists in public space that was hitherto seldom seen.

Yet – and this is a second feature – despite their spontaneous and temporary nature, these temporary memorials were generally not original: their concepts and designs were mostly traditional and timeless. Abstract shapes such as steles, crosses or cenotaphs that could appeal to all were open to a variety of commemorative needs and interpretations and therefore did not require – or instigate – extensive debate. Nor did these designs require the input of the most skilled, famous artists, who were not always readily available. This might also explain why the fleeting character of the temporary memorials did not inspire more daring experiments. Only the larger and more official, top-down initiatives – such as the November 1918 series of temporary monuments in Brussels – displayed considerable artistic and political ambition and as such echoed a long tradition of the use of temporary sculptures and architectural structures in patriotic festivities.

A third shared characteristic of the temporary monuments is their ad hoc character and improvised nature. They went against the grain of bureaucratic procedures and long consensus-oriented debates and were characterised by quick decision-making processes, creative workarounds and the use of readily available materials. Even if their design was traditional, their execution (process) could still be original. This makes the November 1918 series in Brussels all the more exceptional. Thanks to the short time-span and lack of a clear programme, there was room for improvisation and recuperation on the artists' part. No fewer than ten figurative plaster monuments were quickly made, some hastily created from scratch, others based on existing elements or fragments that were recuperated, adapted or reoriented for this purpose. Each monument was dedicated to a specific cause. The series and its "pop-up" wartime precedents preceded or avoided debates about worthy causes, finances and aesthetics that would erupt in full force barely a few months later. They were improvised ad hoc solutions for an "untimely time".

Notes

1. "[...] et puis il y aura, il y aurait, si on ne prenait garde quelque chose d'atroce : les monuments commémoratifs !... Dénonçons ce péril. Certes, inscrivons dans le bronze et le marbre, au seuil des maisons communes, les noms des martyrs ; plantons des arbres du Souvenir [...] ; édifions dans quelques grandes villes la colonne ou le temple qui perdurera l'image véhémente et douloureuse de cette époque grandiose. Mais, méfions-nous du monument commémoratif, de prix et de talents réduits, dont nous sommes menacés de tous les coins de l'horizon. [...] Voyez-vous ça ? [...] sur toutes les places, une Belgique en bronze, due à l'enfant du pays, [...] N'en doutez pas, d'ailleurs, que chaque Belgique serait aggravée par un lion, le redoutable lion Belgique." (B. L. Souguenet, "En attendant...", *Pourquoi Pas?*, 12 December 1918.) According to the introduction to the article, the piece was first published by the Parisian weekly *La Chronique* a few weeks earlier.
2. See for example: David G. Troyansky, "Monumental Politics: National History and Local Memory in French 'Monuments aux Morts' in the Department of the Aisne since 1870," *French Historical Studies* 15, no. 1 (1987); Annette Becker, "Monuments aux morts après la Guerre de Sécession et la Guerre de 1870-1871: Un legs de la guerre nationale?," *Guerres mondiales et conflits contemporains*, no. 167 (1992), https://doi.org/10.2307/25730854; James E. Young, "Écrire le monument: site, mémoire, critique," *Annales: Économies, Sociétés, Civilisations* 48, no. 3 (1993); Alan Borg, *War Memorials from Antiquity to the Present* (London, 1991). For an overview of war memorials in the North of France and Belgium see the online database constructed by a research team of the Université de Lille 3: http://monumentsmorts.univ-lille3.fr/. The database is work in progress but aims to be exhaustive by the end of the project.
3. Stéphanie Claisse, "Pouvoir(s) et mémoire(s). L'État belge et les monuments aux morts de la Grande Guerre," in *Une guerre totale? La Belgique dans la Première Guerre Mondiale. Nouvelles tendances de la recherche historique*, ed. Serge Jaumain et al., Études sur la Première Guerre Mondiale (Brussels: Algemeen Rijksarchief, 2005); Antoine Prost, "Les monuments aux morts: Culte républicain? Culte civique? Culte patriotique?" in *Les lieux de mémoire*, ed. Pierre Nora (Paris: Gallimard, 1984).
4. John Horne, "The Living," in *The Cambridge History of the First World War*, ed. Jay Winter (Cambridge: Cambridge University Press, 2014), 594.
5. "Firemen's role of honour," *Daily Gazette for Middlesbrough*, 20 October 1914, 3.
6. Jay Winter, *Sites of Memory, Sites of Mourning. The Great War in European Cultural History* (Cambridge: Cambridge University Press, 2003), 80; Mark Connelly, *The Great War, Memory and Ritual: Commemoration in the City and East London, 1916-1939* (London: Boydell & Brewer Ltd, 2015), 25-35. *East London Observer*, 4 November 1916, 4; 23 December 1916, 5; 10 March 1917, 5.
7. Connelly, *The Great War, Memory and Ritual*, 25.
8. "Memorial Cross," *Dorking and Leatherhead Advertiser*, 12 August 1916, 5.
9. Connelly, *The Great War, Memory and Ritual*, 35.
10. A photograph of the inauguration is in the *Daily Mirror*, 5 August 1918.
11. Jeroen Geurst, *Cemeteries of the Great War by Sir Edwin Lutyens* (Rotterdam: 010 Publishers, 2010), 51-53; Alex King, *Memorials of the Great War in Britain: The Symbolism and Politics of Remembrance* (London: Berg Publishers, 1998), 55-56.
12. In the extremely harsh winters of, among others, 1660, 1671 and 1672, artists and students from the Antwerp Academy organised an open-air snow sculpture exhibition in the city of Antwerp. The winters of 1511, 1892 and 1901 saw the emergence of the

snow sculpture exhibitions in Brussels. On this phenomenon, see: Frits Scholten, "Malleable Marble: The Antwerp Snow Sculptures of 1772," *Netherlands Yearbook for History of Art / Nederlands Kunsthistorisch Jaarboek Online* 62, no. 1 (2012), https://doi.org/10.1163/22145966-06201011; "Les hivers rigoureux," *L'Événement Illustré*, 3 February 1917; Herman Pleij, *De sneeuwpoppen van 1511. Literatuur en stadscultuur tussen middeleeuwen en moderne tijd* (Amsterdam: Meulenhoff, 1988); Martin Warnke, "Schneedenkmäler," in *Mo(nu)mente. Formen und Funktionen ephemerer Denkmäler*, ed. Michael Diers (Berlin: Akademie Verlag, 1993).

13 The *Messter Woche* 1915, no. 8 is part of the film collection of the Österreichisches Filmmuseum. It can be consulted online through the European Film Gateway (http://www.europeanfilmgateway.eu).

14 John W. Wheeler-Bennett, *Wooden Titan. Hindenburg in Twenty Years of German History (1914-1934)* (New York: William Morrow & Co., 1936).

15 Karl-Robert Schütze, *Der eiserne Hindenburg. Bildergeschichte in Postkarten. Chronologie der Ereignisse und Berichte* (Berlin: Schütze, 2007); Hugo Ball, "Der benagelte Hindenburg", *Freie Zeitung*, 4 May 1918.

16 For a list of *Nagelmänner* (by Dietlinde Munzel-Everling), see: http://www.munzel-everling.de/pr_nag.htm (last consulted on 7 July 2020); Dietlinde Munzel-Everling, *Kriegsnagelungen, Wehrmann in Eisen, Nagel-Roland, Eisernes Kreuz* (Wiesbaden: Munzel-Everling, 2008), 12-34; Gerhard Schneider, *In eiserner Zeit. Kriegswahrzeichen im Ersten Weltkrieg* (Schwabach am Taunus: BD Edition, 2013).

17 Michael Diers, "Nagelmänner. Propaganda mit ephemeren Denkmälern im Ersten Weltkrieg," in *Mon(u)mente. Formen und Funktionen ephemerer Denkmäler*, ed. Diers Michael (Berlin: Akademie Verlag, 1993); Munzel-Everling, *Kriegsnagelungen*.

18 Stéphanie Claisse, *Du soldat inconnu aux monuments commémoratifs belges de la guerre 14-18* (Brussels: Académie Royale de Belgique, 2013), 31.

19 Louis Gille, Alphonse Ooms, and Paul Delandsheere, *Cinquante mois d'occupation allemande* (Brussels: Librairie Albert Dewit, 1919), Tôme 1, 128-129.

20 Later on, this number would be adjusted to 71.

21 Leuven City Archive, Modern Archive, Coll. Uytterhoeven. The authors wish to thank Liesbeth Coimans for locating the memorial and providing valuable information.

22 A permanent stone memorial was finally erected on the same spot in May 1922. Marc Veldeman, "Voorbijganger gedenk… Monumenten en gedenkstenen rond de Eerste Wereldoorlog te Leuven," in *Aan onze helden en martelaren… Beelden van de brand van Leuven (augustus 1914)*, eds. Marika Ceunen and Marc Veldeman (Leuven: Peeters Publishing, 2004), 267.

23 "À Bruxelles," *L'ami de l'ordre*, 20 October 1915; "À Bruxelles. Le jour des morts," *Le XXe siècle: journal d'union et d'action catholique*, 11 November 1915.

24 "Le jour des morts à Bruxelles," *Le XXe Siècle: journal d'union et d'action catholique*, 14 November 1916.

25 "Une statue de von Emmich à Liège," *La métropole d'Anvers: paraissant provisoirement à Londres* (London), 15 December 1915.

26 "À Liège. Le service funèbre de von Emmich," *La Belgique nouvelle: journal quotidien indépendant* (London), 3 January 1916.

27 "*Ainsi cet Hindenburg accroupi, en bois, où des fidèles enfoncent des clous de fer ou d'or. Spectacle risible auquel les illustrés boches ont fait la plus large et plus sotte publicité*". Charles Bernard, "L'idole," *L'écho belge: journal quotidien du matin paraissant à Amsterdam*, 11 December 1915.

28 Charles Jencks and Nathan Silver, *Adhocism: The Case for Improvisation* (New York: Doubleday/Anchor Books, 1973).
29 Joseph Grima, "Adhocracy," *M+ Matters* 1, no. 1 (2012), https://www.mplusmatters.hk/ (last accessed 7 July 2020).
30 In October 1918 a plaster model of François Sicard's (1862-1934) *Au poilu* was erected on the Champs Élysées in Paris. The model was put in this central place to attract funding. A sign reading "subscribe to the loan" was mounted on its pedestal. The monument was however never realised. In the 1920s Sicard did design several different memorials in France (in Saint-Symphorien, Fécamp and Blois). For pictures of the temporary model on the Champs Élyseés, see the cover of *L'Illustration*, 26 October 1918. For an eye-witness account, see: H. Pearl Adam, *Paris Sees it Through. A Diary, 1914-1919* (London: Hodder and Stoughton 1919), 251.
31 The quarrels about the monuments between the authorities on different levels are discussed in detail in Claisse, *Du soldat inconnu*, 133-175.
32 For a discussion on how (temporary) monuments created *lieux de mémoire*, see: Leen Engelen and Marjan Sterckx, "Herinneringen in steen en op papier. Monumenten en prentbriefkaarten voor twee heldinnen van de Eerste Wereldoorlog: Gabrielle Petit en Edith Cavell," *Volkskunde* 111, no. 4 (2010): 379-403.
33 John Rupert Martin, *The Decorations for the Pompa Introitus Ferdinandi*, vol. XVI, Corpus Rubenianum Ludwig Burchard (London: Phaidon, 1972), 27.
34 Louis Hymans, *XXVe anniversaire de l'inauguration du roi. Les fêtes de juillet, compte rendu des solennités et cérémonies publiques célébrées à Bruxelles les 21, 22 et 23 juillet* (Brussels: Alexandre Jamar, 1856), cited in Jeroen Janssens, *De Belgische natie viert: de Belgische nationale feesten, 1830-1914* (Leuven: Leuven University Press, 2001), 23.
35 Martin, *The Decorations for the Pompa Introitus Ferdinandi*, XVI, 17, 178-186.
36 On the occasion of the entry of Charles-Alexandre de Lorraine into Brussels in 1749, for example, several triumphal arches with tableaux representing the prince were erected in Brussels. Christel Stalpaert, "The Entry of Charles-Alexandre de Lorraine into Brussels: Monarchical Discourse in Public Ceremonies and Theatrical Performances," *Eighteenth-Century Life* 26, no. 2 (2002): 75-76. This article focusses on the role of theatre and ballet during the entry of the prince, highlighting the wide variety of artistic disciplines involved in these ceremonies.
37 Stefan Huygebaert, "The Quest for the Decisive Constitutional Moment (DCM)," in *Sensing the Nation's Law. Historical Inquiries into the Aesthetics of Democratic Legitimacy*, eds. Stefan Huygebaert, Angela Condello, and Sarah Marusek (Cham: Springer, 2018); Janssens, *De Belgische natie viert* 23-39.
38 Parades such as the *Holy Blood Procession* in Bruges, the *Ommegang* in Brussels, the *Virga Jesse Parade* in Hasselt and the *Cortège historique des comtes de Flandre* in Ghent featured pageant wagons adorned with monumental decorations and sculptures in stucco in between which figurants in historical costume performed historic or religious scenes. Mario Damen, "The Town, the Duke, his Courtiers and their Tournament: A Spectacle in Brussels, 4-7 May 1439," *Studies in Medieval and Early Renaissance art history* 69 (2013); Gerard Verbeek, *Virga Jesse, schat van de Hasselaar* (Hasselt: Comité Zevenjaarlijkse Virga-Jessefeesten, 1988); Davy Depelchin, "De ontwerper als redacteur van een nationale geschiedenis. Het concept van de Gentse Cortège historique des Comtes de Flandre (1849)," *Tijdschrift voor Interieurgeschiedenis en Design*, no. 40 (2018): 47-67; Chrétien Dehaisnes, *Fêtes et marches historiques en Belgique et dans le nord de la France* (Lille, 1893).

39 Jana Wijnsouw and Marjan Sterckx, "'Een machtige veropenbaring der jeugdige Gentsche kunst'. Publieke kunst in het kader van de Gentse Wereldtentoonstelling van 1913," *Handelingen der Maatschappij voor Geschiedenis en Oudheidkunde te Gent*, no. 66 (2012).

40 For a longer analysis of this case study, see: Leen Engelen and Marjan Sterckx, "An Ephemeral Open-Air Sculpture Museum: Ten Temporary Monuments for the Festive Return of the Belgian Royal Family to Brussels, November 1918," *Sculpture Journal* 26, no. 3 (2017): 321-348.

41 Chantal Kesteloot, "Une nouvelle joyeuse entrée dans Bruxelles libérée," in *Albert & Elisabeth. Le film de la vie d'un couple royal*, ed. C. Kesteloot (Brussels: Mardaga, 2014), 86-97.

42 Bruno Forment, "In kleur en op ware grootte. De operadecors van Albert Dubosq," in *Opera. Achter de schermen van de emotie*, ed. Francis Maes and Piet De Volder (Tielt: Lannoo, 2011), 228-247.

43 *Le Matin*, 20 November 1918.

44 "Pour le retour de nos souverains. Les décorations de Bruxelles: un demi-million de crédit voté," *Le Soir*, 18 November 1918.

45 *Le Soir*, 23 November 1918.

46 *Le Peuple*, 4 December 1918: "*Floraison pas tout à fait spontanée, car si d'aucunes de ces oeuvres furent réalisées aussi rapidement que s'affirma la victoire de nos armées, d'autres avaient été longuement conçues et exécutées dans le silence des ateliers*."

47 Cor Engelen and Mieke Marx, *Compagnie des Bronzes de Bruxelles. Archief in beeld* (Brussels: Algemeen Rijksarchief, 2002), 348.

48 Engelen and Sterckx, "Herinneringen in steen en op papier," 379-403.

49 Claisse, *Du soldat inconnu*, 54; Laurence Van Ypersele, Emmanuel Debruyne, and Chantal Kesteloot, *Brussel. De oorlog herdacht (1914-2014)* (Waterloo: Renaissance du Livre, 2014), 94.

50 "Among the sculptors, there was great commotion after the requisition of bronze materials. I know folks who keep their best pieces under water in the water tank. Others covered their bronzes with plaster to make them look like plaster casts and put them in between the wet clay sketches on the highest shelves in their studios." ("*Chez les sculpteurs, il y eu grand branle-bas par suite de la réquisition des bronzes. J'en connais chez qui des pièces admirables sont au fond de l'eau dans la citerne. D'autres ont recouvert des bronzes d'une couche de plâtre les assimilant à des moulages et les ont mêlés à des ébauches en terre glaise sur les plus hautes planches de leurs ateliers*"). Gille, Ooms, and Delandsheere, *Cinquante mois*, Tôme 4, 288.

51 Werner Adriaenssens, "Belgian Art During the First World War: Exhibitions and Salons in Brussels," in *14-18 Rupture or Continuity. Belgian Art Around World War I*, ed. Inga Rossi-Schrimpf and Laura Kollwelter (Leuven: Leuven University Press, 2018), 143-159.

52 *Le Belge Indépendant*, 13 December 1918. ("*des maquettes en plâtre de futurs monuments commémoratifs*").

53 *Le Belge Indépendant*, 1 February 1919.

54 In early December 1918, an enthusiastic reader of *Le Soir* advocated in a published letter to the editor the casting of the temporary monuments in bronze and financing them by public subscription. As an answer, *Le Soir* recommended the selection of the most meritorious monument: "but one could select one of the best and erect it by public subscription". "Une suggestion", *Le Soir*, 8 December 1918. ("*mais on pourrait en distinguer un entre les meilleurs, et l'élever par souscription publique*").

55 Letter from the city architect of Brussels to an alderman, 8 January 1919, Brussels City Archives, A, D8, nr. 71; as mentioned by Cathérine Leclercq, "Standbeelden en monumenten van Brussel na 1914," in *De beelden van Brussel*, ed. Patrick Derom and C. Marquenie (Brussels & Antwerp: Patrick Derom Gallery - Pandora, 2000).

56 As appears from a rare picture postcard of this Fair, the statue was then installed in the Royal Park facing the Royal Palace, almost where Lagae's King Albert memorial was positioned in November 1918. The monument was now placed on a new plinth, with the same inscription but without the explicitly war-related bas-relief decoration.

57 The statue was inaugurated on 16 November 1930. See: Leclercq, "Standbeelden en monumenten," 207-209.

58 "ô Belgique, ô mère chérie, À toi nos cœurs, à toi nos bras, À toi notre sang, ô Patrie ! Nous le jurons tous, tu vivras!". Initially there existed only a French version of the anthem. In 1938 an official Flemish translation was accepted. This text was added to the plinth of *La Brabançonne* later on.

59 During the German siege of Tamines on 21-22 August 1914, 383 civilians lost their lives and another 98 were wounded. Tamines was first mentioned as a martyred city in 1915: Marius Vachons, *Les villes martyres de France et de Belgique: statistique des villes et villages détruits par les Allemands dans les deux pays* (Paris: Payot et Cie 1915), 166-167.

60 Veldeman, "Voorbijganger gedenk," 261.

61 Marika Ceunen, "Wat een monument lijden kan... Oprichting, lotgevallen en restauratie van het oorlogsmonument op het Martelarenplein," in *Aan onze helden en martelaren... Beelden van de brand van Leuven (augustus 1914)*, ed. Marika Ceunen and Marc Veldeman (Leuven: Peeters Publishing, 2004), 305-320.

62 On 14 July 1919, a resolution was adopted confirming the intention to build a great national war memorial in Brussels. In the following years, several locations and artists were proposed but no consensus was reached. Eventually, the state settled for the burial of an Unknown Soldier in 1922 at the foot of the Congress Column in Brussels. The latter was built in the 1850s to commemorate the founding of Belgium and the Belgian Constitution in 1830. In 1924, this grave was completed with an eternal flame and the project to build a national war memorial was abandoned altogether. Claisse, "Pouvoir(s) et mémoire(s)".

63 Stéphanie Claisse, "Les monuments aux morts," in *De la guerre de l'ombre aux ombres de la guerre*, eds. Laurence Van Ypersele and Emmanuel Debruyne (Brussels: Éditions Labor, 2004), 65.

64 Cited in Claisse, *Du soldat inconnu*, 63-64.

65 This location was used for temporary monuments on several occasions. In 1885, for example, a catafalque for Victor Hugo (by Alexandre Falguière and Marguerite Syamour) was erected on the same spot. In July 1919 an additional, peculiar temporary memorial was installed at the roundabout of the Champs Elysées: *The Coq Gaulois of 1914 Surveying the Pyramid of German Guns*, consisting of a plaster sculpture of the Gallic rooster triumphing over a pile of captured German canons.

66 Jay Winter, *Sites of Memory, Sites of Mourning*, 102-105; Geurst, *Cemeteries of the Great War*, 52-55.

Duke of York's Theatre

Licensed by the Lord Chamberlain to Mr. PHILIP MICHAEL FARADAY

Sole Proprietors - - - Mr. & Mrs. FRANK WYATT
(Miss VIOLET MELNOTTE)

General Manager - - - - Capt. WM. GIFFARD-BARRY
Assistant Manager - - - - Mr. WALTER HENDERSON

NIGHTLY at 8.30
MATINEES: WEDNESDAY and SATURDAY at 2.30

In conjunction with
PHILIP MICHAEL FARADAY
OWEN NARES and B. A MEYER
present

The Enchanted Cottage
A FABLE IN THREE ACTS
BY
ARTHUR PINERO

Oliver Bashforth (late Lieut. 8th Bn. Royal ———— Regt.)	OWEN NARES
Mrs. Smallwood (his Mother)	WINIFRED EMERY
Rupert Smallwood Smallwood (his stepfather)	NORMAN FORBES
Major Murray Hillgrove, D.S.O., M.C.	NICHOLAS HANNEN
Revd. Charles Corsellis (Rector of Fittlehurst)	O. B. CLARENCE
Mrs. Corsellis	MAY WHITTY
Laura Pennington	LAURA COWIE
Mrs. Minnett	JEAN CADELL
Rigg	RONALD SIMPSON
First Married Couple	GRIZELDA HERVEY / GEOFFREY BEVAN
Second Married Couple	MARGOT BARFF / WILLIAM CULFF
Third Married Couple ... *Shadows*	MARJORIE HOPKINS / CEDRIC OSMOND
The Second Witch	VIOLA MARCH
The Third Witch	DOROTHY MILLAR
The Three Bridesmaids	SYBIL HAWKES / K. STANLEY-ALDER / LILA MARIVAN
The Fourth Bridesmaid	DOROTHY STEPHEN

CHERUBS, IMPS, CHILDREN

Fig. 1. Programme for production of *The Enchanted Cottage* at the Duke of York's Theatre (St Martin's Lane, London), Friday 3 March 1922 (collection of the author)

Remembering the War on the British Stage
From Resistance to Reconstruction

Helen E. M. Brooks

One week after the armistice, in an article entitled "Peace and the Theatre: The Outlook for the Future", a columnist for *The Times* confidently predicted that "one immediate result of the armistice will undoubtedly be the disappearance of the 'war play'", adding dismissively that "few productions of this kind will be remembered".[1] Over the next ten years, the declining interest in war-themed plays was a repeated theme in critical commentaries on theatre. "As the war recedes into the past, the less interest do people take in war plays", reported the *Daily Herald* in 1920, whilst in 1923 the *Gloucester Citizen* reflected on the "prejudice attached to plays which bring in the war".[2] In October 1928 *The Scotsman* went so far as to declare that J. M. Barrie's, *The Old Lady Shows Her Medals*, then being performed at the Lyceum, Edinburgh, "must be one of the very few literary or dramatic works of art to survive the war period [...] Most war plays have been left high and dry by the receding tide".[3]

Alongside contemporary accounts of the disappearance of wartime plays, histories of British theatre also suggest that the decade following the armistice saw the war, and its consequences, being rejected as a theme for new plays. "The war seems to have passed across the stage making little impact outside a handful of plays", concluded Michael Woolfe in 1993, whilst more recently Maggie Gale has argued that 1920s playwrights and audiences seemed "to shy away from the 'war' itself as a setting", with dramatic analyses of the effects and consequences of the conflict becoming common only in the 1930s.[4]

The result of these twin historical threads is a dominant narrative which positions the war as largely absent from – or forgotten by – the British stage in the years following the armistice. It is a narrative, however, which is brought into question when we look beyond London and at the full spread of theatrical activity taking place across the nation. As I argue in this chapter, by examining a range of plays staged in both regional and metropolitan theatres and by both professionals and amateurs, we can see that rather than turning away from the war as a theme, theatre-makers repeatedly returned to, remembered and re-staged the war. Equally importantly, not only did they do this through the production of new plays about the conflict and its aftermath, as Rebecca D'Monte has indicated, but they also did so through continuing to stage war-plays first written and performed during the war.[5] Central to this chapter, therefore, is not simply the recovery of a post-war landscape of war-themed theatre, but an analysis of the distinctive ways in which the two different types of productions – revivals/continuing productions of wartime plays; and new plays – functioned in the context of remembrance and reconstruction. Productions of wartime plays, I argue, provided a space of resistance to peace and reconciliation, whilst the production of new plays enabled the exploration of peace-time demands for rehabilitation and reconstruction through, in particular, the figure of the wounded veteran. Whether looking backwards or forwards, what is clear is that the theatre, like the literature and cinema of the period, played an important cultural role in how and why the war was remembered.

The re-evaluation of early 1920s theatre in the context of what Mark Connelly has described as the "Great War's cultural imprint" is long overdue.[6] Whilst scholars of cinema and literary history have begun to question the idea, as Samuel Hynes put it in his seminal *A War Imagined*, that for "nearly a decade, there was a curious imaginative silence" about the war, the theatre has been notably absent from such work.[7] Yet the argument made by Janet Watson, that whilst 1928 saw the floodgates opening on war books, war-themed works had in fact been appearing steadily, although garnering little attention, since the end of the conflict, could be made almost word-for-word about the theatre of the period.[8] As I argue here, theatre-makers, both amateur and professional, repeatedly returned to the war after the armistice, literally and imaginatively "re-membering" the conflict on the nation's stages and, by doing so, positioning the theatre as a space in which the experience of war, its consequences and the challenges of peacetime could be exposed and examined, even if they could not always be resolved.

War Plays on the Post-War Stage: Resisting Peace

Even a very brief trawl through engagement notices and reviews of 1920s theatre productions reveals that the end of hostilities did not immediately result in war-themed works being cancelled. Moreover, a number of popular wartime spy melodramas went on to be staged in regional theatres for much of the following decade. These included the earliest wartime success, Lechmere Worrall and J. E. Harold Terry's *The Man*

Who Stayed at Home, a play which had been performed over 1,500 times, not only at the Royalty and Apollo theatres in London but also at theatres across Britain, by late June 1916.[9] After the armistice it continued to prove popular, and not only with professional companies but also with amateurs. With its one-scene drawing-room setting and strong range of parts for both male and female performers, the play lent itself easily to production by amateur groups. Throughout the 1920s it was repeatedly staged in aid of various war-related charities including district nursing associations, hospitals, orphans' homes, regiments and the British Legion.[10]

Less easily adaptable by amateur groups – not least due to its spectacular third act featuring a U-Boat surrounded by British destroyers with guns blazing – but equally popular in the period following the armistice was Walter Howard's 1917 spy melodrama, *Seven Days Leave*. Featuring a captain returning home on leave to his coastal village where two supposed Belgian refugees – in fact undercover German spies – are planning to kidnap the hero, the play premiered at the Lyceum, London, on 14 February 1917. Acclaimed as being "one of the best new melodramas which the Lyceum has had for years", in a review which also predicted the post-war revival of the play, *Seven Days Leave* was performed at the Lyceum over 700 times under the guidance of the melodramatic leaders of the day, Fred and Walter Melville. It also toured nationally and internationally for the rest of the decade and throughout the 1920s.[11] In total it was performed at more than 226 theatres and over 1,400 times, continuing to meet, as the *Burnley Express* commented in April 1923, with as much "enthusiasm as it ever did in the early days of its production" despite the fact that the days of the spy menace might seem "rather remote now".[12]

Seven Days Leave was not alone in continuing to appeal to regional audiences after the armistice. Emilie Clifford's play *The Luck of the Navy*, written under the pseudonym Clifford Mills and first performed in London at the Queen's Theatre on 5 August 1918 – after a preview week at the Theatre Royal, Bournemouth – was another melodrama which continued to attract audiences despite the end of hostilities. This "thrilling little spy drama" which bore, as the *Tatler* put it, "a certain resemblance to *Seven Days Leave*", with its kidnap plot and German spies – in this case a German woman and her son posing as a sub-lieutenant in the navy – featured the popular actor Percy Hutchinson in the leading role. It was an immediate hit in London, where it was performed until spring 1919, before being toured by two concurrent companies until early 1921.[13] In total, between 1919 and 1930 *The Luck of the Navy* was staged in at least 148 theatres over 900 times, not including the international tours or the 1927 film adaptation.[14]

The examples discussed above are just a small selection of the melodramas which, having been performed in London during the war, continued to tour and attract audiences throughout the rest of the country, and internationally, after the armistice. For many critics, however, the ongoing popularity of these productions and the apparent desire of new audiences to repeatedly return to and remember the war through theatre, jarred with the perception of a nation – or indeed a world – moving beyond the war. As one Coventry critic commented on going to see a production of *The Man Who Stayed at Home* in August 1924, "when the Armistice was signed there was a widespread determination to forget the war", yet as there was "no sign of declining popularity" for this play or for other recent war-themed hits, it must be concluded that "plays centred around the war are not de trop".[15] Whilst public discourse might be focussed on forgetting and moving forward, regional and sometimes international audiences, it would appear, felt differently and found in the theatre a communal space through which to return to and remember the war.

The version of the war which audiences remembered, or reimagined, through these productions was, however, to draw on Michael Booth's description of melodrama, an "idealisation and simplification of reality".[16] Presenting a thrilling world where heroic British men (accompanied by plucky British heroines) faced up to the barbaric, villainous Hun, these melodramas existed apart from the complexities of post-war reconstruction and reconciliation in which the former enemy was now to be seen, as S. N. Sedgwick put it in his 1929 peace-play, *At the Menin Gate*, as part of "a League of bruders who haf all suffered and learnt der lesson".[17] For those suffering in the wake of the war, whether through bereavement, disability, unemployment, strikes or the reinforcement of traditional gender roles, the melodramatic "world of absolutes where virtue and vice coexist in pure whiteness and pure blackness" provided a temporary, contained and safe outlet for resistance to reconciliation and reconstruction.[18] Here audiences could, and indeed did, cheer the patriotic sentiments of the heroes, and boo and hiss at the villainous Hun. As one critic commented after watching a performance of *Seven Days Leave* in Burnley in April 1923, "there is still a considerable public for plays of the sensationally patriotic order".[19] Nor was the appeal of patriotism confined to the regions. At the Queen's Theatre, London, in November 1920, the popularity of a revival of *The Luck of the Navy*, was evident, as one critic put it, through "the enthusiasm with which the incidents in the play and the patriotic sentiments are received nightly", adding that "the German sentiments appeal so strongly to the playgoers that one realises that hostility to the Hun is still profound among the British people".[20]

With their expression of patriotic ideals and anti-German attitudes, post-war productions of wartime melodramas provided a space in which audiences could express their ongoing antipathy towards the former enemy. Yet melodramas were not alone in resisting the demands of post-war reconciliation, as we see with Maurice Maeterlinck's 1918 drama, *The Burgomaster of Stilemonde*.[21] Particularly popular between 1919 and 1923, *Burgomaster* is set during the invasion of Belgium, and depicts the last hours of the titular burgomaster who is executed at the end of the play as a reprisal for the shooting of a German officer. Written during 1917, *Burgomaster* was translated into English by Alexander Teixeira de Mattos and first performed in English at the Lyceum, Edinburgh, on 1 October 1918. It was an immediate success and the Burgomaster soon became an iconic role for the celebrated actor John Martin Harvey. For the following five years he performed it repeatedly in regional theatres across Britain and during a one-year tour in Canada, as well as reprising the role in a 1929 film of the play.[22]

For some, the appeal of *Burgomaster* was its examination of the impotence of men caught up in the military machine. It was a play in which, as the Examiner of Plays Ernest A. Bendall noted, "murderers as well as murdered are shown to be victims of a hideous system of militarism".[23] Throughout, the Burgomaster refuses to blame the Germans for their actions, describing them as men "caught in the cogs of the machine" (131) who "can't act differently" (121) and who are "to be pitied" (141). Yet whilst through its titular character, Burgomaster calls for an understanding of the mechanisms of warfare and their impact on men, as well as for reconciliation and forgetting, it was not this which appears to have resonated with the majority of spectators. Rather it was the figure of the Burgomaster's daughter who, traumatised by her father's death, is fuelled with an inexpressible rage and hatred of those who have destroyed her life. As one ex-soldier put it in 1920, "Maeterlinck's play simply reeks with hate, acrid, flaming hate of the German, of all Germans".[24] As another commented, in a review which speaks to a conscious resistance to the wider rhetoric of forgetting, the play was "performing a national service in helping to perpetuate in the minds of us all what the politicians would like us to forget – the horrors of military aggression".[25] Audiences certainly seem to have responded to this reminder. As a critic at a performance at the Lyceum, London, commented in 1921, audiences watching the play were "roused to demonstrations reminiscent of unhappier times" and the play was serving to "fan the old antagonisms now slowly waning into well-deserved oblivion".[26] Whilst the text of the play called for reconciliation and reconstruction, in live performance *Burgomaster* created a space of resistance to these demands. It is hardly surprising that the German press expressed serious concern when the play was being adapted for the screen, ten years after the armistice.[27]

New Plays: Reconciliation and Reconstruction

Where post-war productions of wartime plays returned to the war, and in doing so gave audiences a space in which they could temporarily resist the demands of post-war reconciliation, new plays about the war and its aftermath spoke to the need to move forward and adapt to post-war society. Most often they did so through the central character of a wounded serviceman whose impaired or damaged body, ultimately rehabilitated, became a proxy for the nation and its reconstruction. Indeed, so ubiquitous was the stage character of the wounded or maimed serviceman that in May 1927 the *Era* could go so far as to state that "everyone has, of course, the deepest sympathy for the maimed or blinded soldier, but regarded strictly as a stage character, he has become stale".[28]

One of the earliest post-war plays to use the figure of the wounded soldier to explore the demands of reconstruction was Major C. T. Davis's one-act play, *The Silver Lining*, performed at the Ambassadors Theatre, London, in a charity matinee for British refugees from Russia, on 24 February 1921. Set in a hospital where blinded soldier-artist Harry has been undergoing surgery to repair his sight for the last two years, the play gives voice to the pain and despair felt by many wounded veterans. Physically and mentally stuck in the war, Harry may have survived but there is, as he puts it, "nothing before me but years of blankness", with life being "one long endless tunnel" (5). He only wishes, he tells his nurse, that as a blind man it were easier to commit suicide: a bold statement considering the criminal nature of this wish.[29]

The response of the nurse – as well as of Harry's sweetheart – makes clear how Harry should deal with these feelings. He must, as the nurse points out, not give in but go on "bearing it with a smile" (4). You must "think more of others and less of yourself" (6) she advises, whilst Harry's sweetheart goes further and describes the thrice-decorated wounded veteran as a coward for wallowing in the past and refusing to face life beyond the war. With British soldiers being expected to experience pain stoically, as Wendy Gagen has demonstrated, and those who did not being "thought of as cowardly or childlike", the attitudes expressed by the women in the play directly reflect those of wider society.[30]

By encouraging Harry not to remember but to forget and look to the future, the women in the play voice an important message about national reconstruction and the individual's role within it. "The past is past and you and I can't alter it", the nurse admonishes Harry:

> But we can look to the future and we can help in the reconstruction [...]
> You must start by reconstructing your own life. [...] Banish all these morbid ideas. Reconstruct your own life and then you will be able to help in the reconstruction of others. (6)

Accepting the love of his sweetheart is the first step in this self-reconstruction. Being reassured that "blindness today is not a great infirmity" and that his sweetheart's "womanly tenderness" will be dedicated to caring for him and will "make up to him for his loss" (11), Harry is able to turn away from his wartime experience and look to the ways in which he can contribute to post-war society. In a clear signal of his rediscovered masculinity and virility, his first contribution, as he tells the nurse euphemistically, will be to embark on a large reconstruction scheme to "rebuild the empire" (11). Ending on this hopeful note, with Harry transformed through the care and love of the women around him and turning away from his past to work towards the production of a new post-war generation, the play offers a clear message. And whilst the theme of love as cure would have been familiar to audiences from a number of wartime plays, unlike in those plays, where blinded soldiers would often miraculously recover their sight, here it is not physical recovery that love enables, but rather a mental recovery from a temporary failure of courage: a temporary failure to cope with the consequences of war.[31]

Whilst *The Silver Lining* appears to have been performed only once and there is little evidence of its reception, a year later the theme of "love as cure" and the exploration of post-war rehabilitation through the figure of the wounded serviceman was developed further in Arthur Pinero's "fantastic fable", *The Enchanted Cottage*.[32] Premiering at the Duke of York's Theatre, London, on 29 February 1922 and running there until 22 April, including a "flying visit" to the King's Theatre, Portsmouth, on 13 April 1922, *The Enchanted Cottage* did not have an extended run.[33] It was, however, subsequently staged by both professional and amateur companies, as well as premiering in New York in 1923 and being adapted for film in 1924.[34] At the heart of the play are two "relics of the war": Major Hillgrove, who was blinded at Vimy in August 1917, and Lieutenant Oliver Bashforth, who was wounded at La Boiselle in August 1918.[35] Serving as an exemplar of the "correct" way of dealing with the wounds of war, Hillgrove is cheerily reconciled to his new state, despite being a former champion tennis player who is now unable to play (an echo of the blinded artist who can no longer paint in *The Silver Lining*). Oliver, on the other hand, represents the dangers of remembering and failing to move beyond the war. Described as a "wreck of a handsome young man, broken by the war", who loathes his "shrivelled face and shrunken carcass" (19) and cannot even bear to catch sight of himself, Oliver hides himself away in a remote cottage, with his "chief object for the future" (12) being to "avoid those who have known me as I was!" (19). In a parallel to accounts of wounded soldiers like Second Lieutenant C. E. Healey who found it "a terrible strain to try and be normal and not show I was in pain",[36] Oliver physically hides himself away in order to avoid having to perform the acceptable face of the wounded soldier to the world. As such he offers, as one reviewer commented, "a poignant exhibition of that loss of hope and interest in life which is begotten in so many war victims by physical affliction".[37]

As in *The Silver Lining*, *The Enchanted Cottage* allows sympathy for the wounded soldier but ultimately demands that he move beyond his war-wounds and reintegrate into society. Once more it is women who facilitate this. Under the "magic" influence of the cottage and its housekeeper, Oliver falls in love with Laura, an unattractive young woman from the village. It is through this love that his perception of his disfigurement, as well as his actual physical experience of it, is transformed.[38] To each other, although as they discover to their surprise, not to others, the couple are beautiful. The moral, as one reviewer commented, was that "beauty lives in the seeing eye, and that love's illusion is a reality".[39] What no review commented on, however, was the way that the play spoke to the figure of the wounded soldier. Through love Oliver's experience of his injury is transformed and he is emboldened to re-enter society rather than hiding himself away. And in the ultimate sign of his rediscovered masculinity and contribution to social reconstruction, the final scene of the play sees the figure of a tiny baby being placed in the arms of the sleeping Laura by an angel.

These romantic, reassuring narratives present love as the medium by which the physically wounded could move forward, leave the war behind and be reincorporated within the gender and social norms of post-war Britain. A notable absence within post-war drama, however, is the facially wounded soldier. As Suzannah Biernoff has argued, the disfigured face is almost entirely absent from British art.[40] The same is largely true of the theatre of the period. Playwrights on the whole were reluctant to tackle facial injuries and their consequences, and in the few cases where they did there was a marked difference from the way in which other physical injuries were treated. Charles McEvoy's play, *The Likes of Her*, is an apt example. First performed by the Lena Ashwell Players during their Bath season in 1923, and receiving rave reviews in London where it was performed at the St Martin's Theatre in August and September of the same year, the comedy is set in the East End during demobilisation. Attitudes towards the wounded run throughout, yet a distinction is drawn between bodily and facial wounds, as is clear when Alfred, himself a wounded veteran, describes a man he has found in a shell-hole. He has "got one leg left", he tells his friend, Sally:

> this arm was blowed away at the shoulder, he's got just a little sight in one eye, and that must go in time. And – and – something worse than that [...] It ain't nice to tork abart, but his fice is all gorn like. (873)

Alfred can list the physical wounds this soldier has received; yet he can barely find the words to describe the facial disfigurement. Listening to the account makes Sally feel "faint and sick". "Why do they sive them like it?" (874), she asks: a provocative question which taps into the concern over how those men suffering what was described as the "worst of all injuries" could be rehabilitated and reintegrated within society.[41] The answer is given at the end of the play when this wounded man returns home with a glass eye, and a new face and voice. He is "tall, bronzed, and seemingly intact [...], a pleasing figure" (887): literally having moved beyond his war wounds. Ultimately, and in a marked contrast to *Silver Lining* and *Magic Cottage* where veterans can move forward *with* their bodily wounds, in *The Likes of Her* the facially mutilated soldier can only be rehabilitated when his wounds are "patched up" (874).

A very different treatment of the facially wounded veteran is offered in *The Person Unknown*. First performed in 1920 for the Grand Guignol season at the Little Theatre, London, H. F. Maltby's one-act horror play features as its main character a "hopeless – incurable" (15), facially disfigured veteran. Set in the early hours of the morning, after actress Daisy has returned from a masquerade ball, *The Person Unknown* depicts the fatal attack on this "bright young thing" by the wounded veteran she had inspired to sign up when she kissed him and sang "Your King and Country Need You" à la Vesta Tilly. Now, having returned from the war, wounded so badly that he can not even be helped by "bits of wax" (15) and with the lower half of his face covered in bandages, he seeks out the woman who promised, in the words of the song, to "love you, hug you, kiss you, when you come back home again". Removing his bandages to her horrified screams (although the audience are left to use their imagination) he cries out "I ain't so pretty as I was – but that is what you 'ave got to love and hug and kiss – 'cause I've got back home again" (15-16). In the final moments of the play he then attempts to hold her to her promise: struggling to kiss and hug her and, through his forced intimacy, killing her.

In a deliberately horrific twisting of the trope of love rehabilitating the wounded and enabling them to move past the war, here the wounded veteran's attempt to reintegrate into society through "love" does not create life, as in previous plays, but rather destroys it. For a man suffering "the worst of all injuries" there is, the play suggests, no escape from the war and no reintegration within post-war society through love.

In undercutting romanticised accounts of the rehabilitation and reintegration of the war-wounded, *The Person Unknown* tapped into post-war anxieties around the competing demands of remembering and forgetting. Questioning the limits of reconstruction with its ominous ending in which the unrepentant murderer disappears into the darkness, the play leaves unresolved the threat posed by unrehabilitated figures within society. At the same point, the audience were prompted to consider the dangers of forgetting. The wounded veteran, physically and emotionally stuck in the war, hiding in the shadows and obsessed with the promise made in the recruiting song, is placed in sharp contrast to Daisy and her friends who begin the play returning from a party, drinking champagne and laughingly dismissing the song as "that old thing" which it was about time "everyone had forgotten" (9). It is a contrast that offers a stark warning as to what might happen if society moves on from the war and leaves behind, or fails to remember, those who cannot. As one critic reflected on seeing *The Person Unknown* a second time and once they had got past the horror of it, it was a play which highlighted the extent to which "the world easily promises, easily forgets", adding thoughtfully that "the hero of yesterday has lost his halo. The feeling of intense pity, the feeling of enthusiasm, the feeling of interest in the fate of the men who fought and bled for us has faded fast".[42]

Through the genre of horror, which as Joseph Grixti argues provides a "safely distanced and stylised means of making sense of and coming to terms with phenomena and potentialities of experience which under normal [...] conditions would be found too threatening and disturbing", *The Person Unknown* forced audiences to face the limits of social reconstruction and the dangers of forgetting.[43] In the titular character, "turned [...] adrift" and having to keep in the shadows (15), audiences were presented with a figure of both pity and terror. "Men want to spew when they see me", the Person Unknown tells Daisy, "but I'm a man just the same, and 'as feelings same as other men" (15). He is, at one and the same time, both a victim of the war as well as a monster created by it. As such he is the ideal figure through which to explore the contradictory and complex challenges of peacetime.

It seems appropriate to end with this analysis of *The Person Unknown*, a play that exposes the tensions between remembrance, rehabilitation and reconstruction. Over the course of this chapter I have argued for a distinction between the ways in which revivals of wartime plays and new post-war plays engaged with these competing demands: suggesting that whilst wartime plays clung on to the past and provided a regressive space in which to resist the demands of peace, new plays examined the possibilities for reconciliation and rehabilitation through the figure of the wounded soldier. The number of plays examined here is, however, necessarily limited. Far more work remains to be done in examining the ways in which post-war theatre engaged with the experience and aftershock of the Great War, both in national and transnational contexts. By looking at regional and amateur productions, international tours and film adaptations, new and revived plays, and middlebrow and popular theatre, it is clear that there are plenty of plays and productions which might be the subject of such analysis. Rather than being absent from the theatre of the period the war was a recurrent theme. It is time, therefore, that we reinstate the theatre within our cultural histories of remembrance.

Notes

1. "Peace and the Theatre: Outlook for the Future". *The Times*, 18 November 1918.
2. *Gloucester Citizen*, 8 November 1923; *Daily Herald*, 2 September 1920.
3. *Scotsman*, 9 October 1928.
4. Michael Woolfe, "Theatre: Roots of the New," in *Literature and Culture in Modern Britain: Volume 1, 1900-1929*, ed. Clive Bloom (London: Longman, 1993); Maggie Gale, "The London Stage, 1918-1945," in *The Cambridge History of British Theatre, Volume 3 Since 1895*, ed. Baz Kershaw (Cambridge: Cambridge University Press, 2015), 144.
5. Rebecca D'Monte, *British Theatre and Performance 1900-1950* (London & New York: Bloomsbury, 2015), 118.
6. Mark Connelly, *Celluloid War Memorials: The British Instructional Films Company and the Memory of the Great War* (Exeter: University of Exeter Press, 2016), 1.
7. Samuel Hynes, *A War Imagined. The First World War and English Culture* (London: Pimlico, 1992), 423.
8. Janet S. K. Watson, *Fighting Different Wars: Experience, Memory, and the First World War in Britain* (Cambridge: Cambridge University Press, 2004), 188.
9. *Era*, 21 June 1916; for more information and a full list of performances, see: https://www.greatwartheatre.org.uk/db/script/122/, accessed 30 May 2020. My thanks go to Michael Waters for his work in tracing these performances for the Great War Theatre project.
10. To give a few examples, in April 1920 it was performed by a mixed cast of soldiers and women at the Royal Marine Barracks in Devon; in 1921 by the Burnley Amateur Comedy Company in aid of the 5th East Lancs Regiment and the House of Help; and in 1927 by the Sidmouth Amateur Dramatic Society in aid of the Waifs and Strays Home and the local Benevolent Fund of the British Legion. For further examples, see: www.greatwartheatre.org.uk/db/script/122/, accessed 12 August 2019.
11. *Tatler*, 28 February 1917. During the autumn of 1917 *Seven Days Leave* played in both Melbourne and Sydney, Australia. In January 1918 it opened at Broadway's Park Theatre where it played until June 1918 for a total of 156 performances. It then toured several major American cities.
12. *Burnley Express*, 28 April 1923. For a full list of performances, see: www.greatwartheatre.org.uk/db/script/1776/, accessed 12 August 2019.
13. *Tatler*, 28 August 1918.
14. For a full list of performances, see: www.greatwartheatre.org.uk/db/script/2700/, accessed 12 August 2019.
15. *Coventry Evening Telegraph*, 26 August 1924.
16. Michael R. Booth, *English Melodrama* (London: H. Jenkins, 1965), 14.
17. Sidney Newman Sedgwick, *At the Menin Gate: a melodrama* (London: Sheldon Press, 1929).
18. Booth, *English Melodrama*, 14.
19. *Burnley Express*, 28 April 1923.
20. *Western Morning News*, 1 November 1920.
21. Maurice Maeterlinck, *The Burgomaster of Stilemonde* (New York: Dodd, Mead and Company, 1919), 121.
22. *The Burgomaster of Stilemonde*, dir. by George J. Banfield. Walthamstow Studios: British Filmcraft Productions, 1929.

23 Ernest A. Bendall, Lord Chamberlain's Plays, British Library, Add MS 66198 HH, in *Great War Theatre*, www.greatwartheatre.org,uk, accessed 1 October 2018.
24 *Aberdeen Press and Journal*, 17 March 1920.
25 *Western Morning News,* 3 June 1922.
26 *Daily Herald,* 27 October 1921.
27 The *Daily Herald,* 27 June 1928, reported that "several German newspapers have protested that the film should not be exhibited" and quoted one paper calling it a "new war and hate film".
28 *Era*, 25 May 1927.
29 Suicide was illegal in Britain until the Suicide Act of 1961.
30 Wendy Jane Gagen, "Remastering the Body, Renegotiating Gender: Physical Disability and Masculinity During the First World War, the Case of J. B. Middlebrook," *European Review of History: Revue européenne d'Histoire* 14, no. 4 (2007), 530, https://doi.org/10.1080/13507480701752169.
31 See for example: Anon. *The Rapid Cure,* 1916, Lord Chamberlain's Plays, British Library, Add MS 66128 G, in *Great War Theatre*, www.greatwartheatre.org,uk, accessed 1 October 2018.
32 Arthur Wing Pinero, *The Enchanted Cottage* (London: William Heinemann, 1922).
33 *Era*, 1 March 1922.
34 On 19 April 1923 the *Stage* reported a performance on 31 March 1923 at the Ritz Theatre, New York, presented by William A. Brady.
35 *Aberdeen Press and Journal*, 2 March 1922.
36 Healey, C. E. Second Lieutenant, *My Terrible War,* 1960, IWMD 94/50/1 quoted in Gagen, "Remastering the Body," 530.
37 *Aberdeen Press and Journal,* 2 March 1922.
38 Laura is described as "a thin, exceedingly plain young woman with a sallow, unhealthy complexion, colourless lips, and poor flat chest […] dull, scanty hair is drawn tightly from her temples and she is so pronouncedly round-shouldered as almost to give the impression that she is deformed". Pinero, *Enchanted Cottage*, 5.
39 *Illustrated Sporting and Dramatic News,* 11 March 1922.
40 Suzannah Biernoff, "The Rhetoric of Disfigurement in First World War Britain," *Social History of Medicine* 24, no. 3 (2011), 667.
41 "Worst Loss of All", *Manchester Evening Chronicle*, press clipping dated May-June 1918, London Metropolitan Archives, cited in Biernoff, "Rhetoric of Disfigurement", 670.
42 *Illustrated London News,* 3 February 1921.
43 Joseph Grixti, *Terrors of Uncertainty: The Cultural Contexts of Horror Fiction* (London & New York: Routledge, 1989), 164.

Fig. 1. Patriotic school notebook with King Albert I in uniform. (Ghent, Fonds Municipal Schools, Primary School Hippoliet Lammenstraat, Notebook Suzanne Braeckman).

A War to Learn From
Commemorative Practices in Belgian Schools After World War I

Kaat Wils

In March 1919, barely four months after the armistice, Alphonse Harmignie, the Catholic Belgian Minister for Arts and Science, provided all state schools with a publication describing the course of the war. The document, published by the War Ministry, was intended to help teachers to "explain to young people the huge task that had been carried out by our armed forces".[1] The publication emphasised the difference between the German forces, well-oiled and superior in numbers and technical knowledge, and the small Belgian army. It was made to sound as though the latter, running on pure determination, had succeeded in slowing down, hindering, challenging and ultimately ambushing the German war machine. In that same year, Harmignie's socialist successor, Jules Destrée, sent out a circular to all public, state-funded secondary schools (athenaee). In it he encouraged school boards and teaching associations to think about the way in which lessons learned from the war could be applied for the "*œuvre de l'éducation patriottique*", or patriotic education.[2]

In the days immediately following the conflict the Belgian government set great store by the distribution of a patriotic discourse of the war. Both in primary schools, where compulsory education had been in force since 1914, and in secondary schools, where the nation's future elite were being educated, the memory of the war was to be kept alive. Four years of trench warfare had to be given some meaning. History education seemed like an obvious place to address the subject and nurture patriotism. From an international perspective, Belgian history teaching had never had a pronounced nationalistic profile. Unlike the educational systems in France and Germany, education in a small, and moreover neutral, country like Belgium had surrendered far less to an open nationalism aimed at an external enemy. National history was mainly taught at primary school. No more than a third of the history lessons in state and free secondary education were dedicated to the nation's past, the major part being devoted to so-called "universal" history, which was mainly European in scope.[3]

World War I was introduced into traditional history lessons quite soon after it ended and was subsequently included in the curriculum for secondary education in 1926. In the years immediately following the war's end a number of textbooks dedicated exclusively to the war appeared. They were recommended by the government for use both in the classroom and in the school library.[4] The use of visual teaching aids, such as wall panels, illustrations and slides, was encouraged, with the idea that it would stimulate the pupils' empathy. For example, every school in the public network had at its disposal, from 1920, the film *La Belgique martyre*, a patriotic drama made in 1919 by Charles Tutelier. The film painted a dramatic picture of the tortured country, a topos that had been popular during the war and in which the German atrocities were a central theme.[5] Germany was the perpetrator and Belgium the victim. The dichotomy, as postulated by the government, was now established in the new curricula. In this way, a public, political memory took shape.[6]

The war had to be studied in school but should certainly not be reduced to a subject of scholarly study. It had also to be kept in the heart, constantly remembered. Only by surrounding the youth daily with this message could one be certain that they would take their task of remembrance to heart, now and later. In 1920, for example, the government made it compulsory for portraits of King Albert in his uniform and helmet and Queen Elisabeth as a nurse to be hung in every classroom.[7] The following year, two more portraits were added: that of Léon Trésignies, the soldier who had sacrificed his life in 1914 in a military operation at the "Verbrande Brug" (Pont Brulé) in Grimbergen, and that of Gabrielle Petit, resistance heroine, who was executed by firing squad in 1916 at the National Shooting Galery. In the years after that, every time a hero or heroine died, schools were expected to dedicate half a day to them. Future generations must be prevented from losing the memory of national unity during the war: anyone who had no personal memories of it because they had been too young at the time the events took place would learn to commemorate at school. Teachers also took initiatives and sometimes turned classrooms into shrines.[8]

The whole school experience was coloured by commemorating the war in the post-war years. Books and textbooks, walls and playgrounds and even extra-curricular activities revolved around the preceding conflict. This was certainly not only the case within the network of public schools, which fell under the authority of the government. It was equally true for the private, Catholic schools, which were in the majority in early twentieth-century Belgium, and which were in theory not bound by the prescriptions of the government. In the following pages we will look at two types of ritualised remembrance practices in both public and Catholic secondary education: the commemoration of the fallen and the organisation of excursions to the region of the front. These two very different practices – one bringing the war into the school and the other taking the school to the battlefield – embodied two different expressions of remembrance (Figs. 1 and 2).

Fig. 2. Patriotic school notebook. The text reads: "the war of national defence. How the barbarians exposed themselves. The armory of the Palace of Justice in Brussels during the occupation (1914-1918)". (Ghent, Fonds Municipal Schools, individual notebook)

The cases discussed in this article are national in scope, but the practices they represent were certainly not confined to Belgium, as international historiography suggests. Much research has been done on the ideological and physical mobilisation of children and the transformation of education during the war, demonstrating the profound impact of the war on classroom practices all over Europe. The decisive role of the war in post-war educational reform towards more comprehensive forms of schooling has also been analysed.[9] In the growing body of scholarship on post-war commemoration and historical culture, however, education has not played a prominent role, except for a few studies, mostly on primary education, such as Mona Siegel's *The Moral Disarmament of France*.[10] Within this broader field of commemoration studies, both the importance of local communities and the role of field excursions and tourism have been stressed. A further exploration of these themes from the perspective of the history of education thus promises to be of interest. Such studies will probably also nuance the recent claim by Andrew Donson that the wartime patriotic mobilisation of schoolchildren did not have any permanent effects on schools in the immediate post-war period.[11] At least with regard to war memorials and the ritualised practices that developed around them in schools, there seemed to be much continuity with the "war education" that had been installed during the war, a tendency confirmed by research on France and Britain.[12]

Names for Eternity

In July 1919, after the years of gloom and doom in which each school year ended on a low note without the usual final awards ceremony, Belgian Minister Harmignie hoped for large-scale patriotic festivities in every school.[13] At Antwerp's Our Lady secondary school, for instance, on 31 July pupils gathered in the school courtyard for the first post-war graduation ceremony. As the head of a Jesuit school, Father Rutten was not obliged to take into consideration the festivities guidelines drawn up by the ministry. But non-state schools also glowed with patriotic pride in the days following liberation. The attitude of the Roman Catholics during the war had shown that they too were prepared to fight for the homeland, despite the anti-militaristic stance taken by the Catholic Party since the middle of the nineteenth century. In fact, thanks to his relentless resistance to the German occupier, Cardinal Mercier had emerged as an example to all devout and patriotic Belgian citizens.[14]

Father Rutten marked the occasion by printing an apology entitled *For Liberty and Justice* in which he praised all his fallen boys.[15] In his apology, Rutten took the reader on a pilgrimage along the places where pupils and former pupils had been killed, along the graves of martyrs. In this way, this specific Catholic school war commemoration became firmly rooted in the West Flanders war landscape. Just as patriotic children's songs since the nineteenth century had honoured the battlefield and the heroes that perished there, calling upon the listener to be prepared to die, now the sense of duty of those who had perished was held up as an example.[16] Rutten's text ended by calling for the names of all those who had been killed to be immortalised in a stone memorial (Fig. 3).

Fig. 3. Commemorative plate for the deceased students and former students of the Antwerp Our Lady secondary school. From P. Taelman, *En souvenir de nos morts* (Antwerp, 1920).

Setting up memorials and memorial plaques in memory of World War I was a postwar custom that was not restricted to the world of education. All across Europe and beyond memorials were inaugurated as an acknowledgement of the debt owed by society to those who had perished and its duty to keep the memory alive.[17] On 11 November 1922, the Tomb of the Unknown Soldier was inaugurated in Brussels. Together with the massive war cemeteries, characterised by their uniformity, the tomb became a symbol for the democratic nature of war memorials, in which military rank and position were relatively unimportant. During the inauguration ceremony pupils of Brussels schools formed a guard of honour and joined wholeheartedly in the singing of the national anthem, the Brabançonne. The Tomb and the Place of Honour for the Executed ("*Ereperk der Gefusilleerden*") at the National Shooting Range that was inaugurated on 10 April 1921 were the two national war memorials of the Great War. A class visit to one or both sites was strongly recommended.

Brussels schools were invited to march past the monument according to a strict schedule. A reading was given in the classroom with the intention of getting the boys and girls into the right frame of mind. They had to understand that the unknown man buried there represented all the defenders of the country. He represented the victor in the mammoth battle for justice and liberty against foreign tyranny and oppression.[18] In December 1922, in order to complete the pupils' connection to the unknown soldier, Emile Jacqmain, the liberal education alderman in Brussels, sent a photo of the monument to every school in his area of office.

At a local level, cities and municipalities were committed to setting up memorials designed to appeal specifically to their own communities. The larger cities did this by announcing architecture and design contests. Given the financial problems often accompanying such projects, it sometimes took until the mid-1920s before a prestigious commemorative monument, such as the one on "Martyrs' Square" in Leuven, actually appeared.[19] By that time, more modest memorials had been fulfilling their function as mourning places and commemorative monuments for the village community for years. Factories, churches, sports clubs, patriotic societies and schools took the initiative in commemorating the victims of the conflict within and beyond their own small communities. Even in larger cities commemoration was often a bottom-up phenomenon, which in the course of the process came to be supported by local authorities.[20]

The iconography of the monuments displayed much continuity with the pre-war period: traditional images were used to represent the sacrifice, the hero and the homeland. Moreover, an explicitly religious dimension was added to the memory of the war.[21] While the modernistic sensitivity of a great many intellectuals and artists may have been born in the trenches of the war, practices of mourning and commemoration displayed much more continuity with pre-war traditions, as Jay Winter pointed out in his landmark 1995 study, *Sites of Memory, Sites of Mourning*.[22] One new and democratic aspect of the commemorative practices around World War I was the hyper-nominalism in the exhaustive lists of names on the monuments.[23] Each of those names referred to a person, an individual who perished by the war machine. The strength of such memorials was in the sum of all the names together, which symbolised at a higher, more abstract level, the qualities of the "patriotic soldier", faithful to his homeland to the end. The surviving population was able to relate to the figure of "the soldier" to whom they owed their liberty. The future generation was expected to take inspiration from his patriotic heroism.

There was no place more suitable for getting that last message across than the school buildings in which the fallen soldiers had sat at their desks. Calling out the names of former pupils who had been killed in the war was not uncommon: the practice had started during the war itself. Years later, in 1921, during the inauguration of a commemorative plaque, a senior student at the athenaeum in Liège described his memory of those school moments as "an endless list of names, to which our hearts responded as sombre death bells: 'Morts pour nous' (They died for us)".[24] The athenaeum in Antwerp also had a plan to honour former pupils who had been killed. To ensure that no-one was forgotten, the head of the study group placed an appeal in the *Le Matin* newspaper, in which he asked the parents of those former pupils who had been killed to send their names and portraits to the school. Various parents responded to the appeal with emotional expressions of gratitude for this recognition of their sons' sacrifices. The school collected money from teachers and former teachers to pay for the sculpture, which was made by the Antwerp stonemason Clément Jonckheer.[25] The monument was inaugurated on 26 July 1920.

The scripts for the inauguration ceremonies of such commemorative plaques and monuments were similar in both state and non-state schools, with the exception of the mass that accompanied the ceremony in Catholic colleges. Catholic schools congratulated themselves on the fact that they had now made it impossible to doubt the scope of their patriotism. State schools, in turn, enthusiastically took their inspiration from the religious repertoire of sacrifices and martyrs, elevating the national war story to a new kind of salvation history. Various players addressed those present during the ceremony: the school headmaster or director, the dignitary (preferably a former pupil of the school itself), the veteran, the father of a pupil or former pupil killed in the war and a representative of the senior year pupils. They all had their own clearly marked positions in the relay race of remembrance.

The school headmaster or director was the guardian of the school memory. In his speech he often interwove personal memories of the boys who had died with traditional elements from the patriotic discourse, such as civic duty and heroism. His eulogy to the qualities of the fallen boys was generally repeated and confirmed during the ensuing speeches by the dignitaries present. These might have been a prominent politician, such as the Christian-democrat Henri Carton de Wiart at the Sint-Jan

Berchmans school. High-ranking military personnel also fulfilled the role, as in the case of Lieutenant General Cabra, at the Our Lady school in Antwerp. The ceremony at the athenaeum school in Liège, on 17 July 1921, was attended by Prince Leopold.

Je recueille en mon cœur votre gloire meurtrie,
Je renverse sur vous les feux de mes flambeaux,
Et je monte la garde autour de vos tombeaux,
Moi qui suis l'avenir parce que la Patrie…

Emile VERHAEREN.

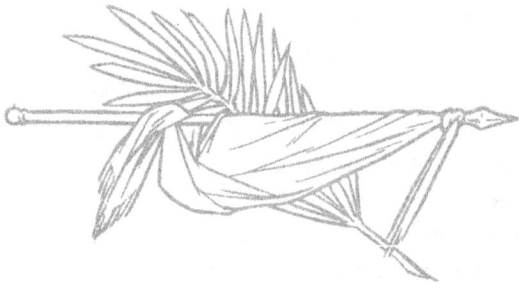

Fig. 4. Commemorative plate for the deceased students and former students of the atheneum school of Liège. From Athénée Royal de Liège, *Liber memorialis rappelant la participation des élèves et des anciens élèves à la Grande Guerre 1914-1918* (Liège, 1921).

The school board invariably declared that the enormity of the soldier's actions reflected on the performance of the secondary school, college or athenaeum school that he had formerly attended. The number of former pupils who had been killed in action was elevated to a seal of quality for the school itself. "If we doubt the future, we only have to follow the example shown by the dead", according to headmaster Gerard of the athenaeum school in Liège. Thus, the names of the dead became signposts for future generations.[26] By way of illustrating that important future, a pupil from the senior year also addressed the audience. "Our predecessors' task remains uncompleted, and we must bring that work of liberty, progress, magnificence and vitality to a successful conclusion – for God and country" is how a pupil at the Sint-Jan Berchmans school in Brussels put it.[27] The younger generation at other colleges also acknowledged its duty (Fig. 4).

The government discourse on the war, repeated during the speeches in schools, was one of unity and vigilance. Remembrance was an especially appropriate task aimed at the future: the willingness to repeat the sacrifice of the dead if need be. General Glotz made no bones about this at the athenaeum school in Liège: if the pupils genuinely wanted to pay their debt to their fallen friends they would register *en masse* as reservists in the military. The remembrance shaped here was aimed at linking various generations. The dead were to set an example for the living. It was a remembrance aimed at prompting deeds, or at the very least inspiring the willingness to perform patriotic, heroic deeds.

The school excursions to the front were given a very different interpretation. They were concerned not with solidarity between the dead and the living, but with disgust at the material ravage the war had caused. There was no way that the past here could set an example for the future.

A School Excursion to the Front

In post-war educational circles experts were increasingly of the opinion that pupils remembered a living lesson best. Despite modern media such as photos, slide shows and films, there was no technology that could match the actual experience of World War I. School excursions to the front were the ultimate experience for schoolchildren and would undoubtedly have the desired patriotic effect, so it was thought. Incidentally, school excursions to "national" battlefields were nothing new. As far back as 1870, the period in which concepts of visual education began to gain a foothold, school excursions to locations such as Waterloo had been promoted in educational circles.[28]

Raising a glass to toast the publication of the first Michelin tourist guide to the Battle of the Marne in 1917, French historian Ernest Lavisse called the organised trips to the battlefield "living history lessons".[29] In Belgium, the national division of the Touring Club promoted front tourism from the summer of 1919, with moralising and patriotic reflections.[30] In the same year the Belgian Touring Club also published a two-part guide for the individual traveller entitled *Things you must see on the battlefields and in the destroyed towns of Belgium*. This historic and documentary guide was put together by Henriette Dirkx (née Coenraets), a teacher of history and geography at a public girls' secondary school in Brussels, and Jean Massart, professor of biology at Brussels University.[31]

Henriette Dirkx was a teacher who spent as much time as possible visiting museums and monuments with her pupils. Massart had given a series of extra-curricular biology lessons every year at Dirckx's school since its establishment in 1908. Dirkx continued to teach history and geography to the girls who still attended school during the war. Together with Massart she was committed to publishing the ultimate guide to the front for Belgium. Dirkx wrote the first part, entitled *Up to the fall of Antwerp*; Massart wrote the second part, entitled *The front of Flanders* (Fig. 5).

In the first part Dirkx meticulously lists the unjustly killed citizens, the frightening reprisals and the unnecessary destruction. The attention to detail gives the impression of objectivity but was actually intended to act as a wall of horror against the destructive power of time, since anyone wishing to see the devastation with their own eyes would have to hurry. "In some regions, certainly in Brabant, the traces of the German rage are disappearing", according to Dirkx. The guide was, above all, a memorial to the tragedy of the war.[32] Massart summed up his part of the guide the same way: "[i]t is not a guide for the rushed tourist, not a guide designed for speed; it is a book for those who wish to investigate the range and specificity of the war in Flanders. Nothing is more educational and saddening than a walk along the front". Massart had first come into contact with the Westhoek landscape before the war, for his own geo-botanical research, charting the Belgian landscape.[33] His knowledge of the region made him a unique observer of the battlefield after the war. As he looked at the plain around Hill 60, he did not describe manoeuvres or battles, but sank into sadness at the picture of abandonment and wasteland: "[n]ot a sign of a tree, a house or a field in a radius of eight kilometres. Only broken-down tanks, with the corpses of their drivers still in them. Concrete bunkers with silenced machine-guns and vegetation in full bloom, adding cruel flashes of colour to this landscape of tears".[34]

Although there was some criticism of the potentially morbid and voyeuristic side of the new front tourism, it did not seem to apply to school excursions: there seemed to be no doubt of the educational value of a classroom visit to bunkers, barbed wire and scorched earth. When in 1927, for instance, two boys and a priest teacher at a secondary school in the border town of Tourcoing in northern France were killed as a result of the detonation of war ammunition, they were not so much accused of reckless behaviour as praised for their patriotic attitude. Had they not proved that the war was still remembered?[35]

Fig. 113. — Tanks anglais démolis par l'artillerie allemande, à Poelcappelle. Arbres bordant la route, réduits à l'état de moignons. Mai 1919.

Fig. 114. — Route à Poelcappelle, réparée à l'aide de planches. Arbres réduits à l'état de moignons. Mai 1919.

Fig. 5. Images from the travel guide of Henriette Dirkx en Jean Massart. Touring Club de Belgique, *Ce qu'il faut voir sur les champs de bataille et dans les villes détruites Belgique* (Brussels, 1919-1920).

Soon after the armistice, in the primary and secondary schools in Brussels there was already enthusiasm for the "real-life" experience of a visit to the front. In January 1919, Victor Devogel, general director of the Brussels schools, addressed the subject with the alderman for education, Emile Jacqmain.[36] In his letter asking permission from the Minister of Arts and Sciences, Jules Destrée, Jacqmain wrote, "I do not have to remind you what admirable lessons in history, morality and patriotism the children receive when viewing the places at which the fate of our country and the world was decided".[37] The Minister approved the plan and in the Easter holidays of 1919 Devogel travelled to the area together with the Brussels history professor Leon Leclère, who had also written a textbook about the war. The tour of inspection made it clear that the organisation of the excursions would be more difficult than anticipated. It was almost impossible to organise transport on site, there was no drinking water within a radius of seven kilometres of Diksmuide and the sea threw a fresh load of unexploded ammunition up onto the beaches every day.[38] In response, the municipality cautiously suggested that it might be better to keep the girls far from the horror and danger of the front and, instead, give them a guided tour of the civilian suffering in Brussels. Devogel remained convinced about the usefulness for the pupils of the excursion to the front. The organisation of the trip was merely an exercise in balance between minimum risk and maximum effect. Leclère also regarded the trip as an opportunity: it was both an excursion to the living locations of history and a reward for an unfortunate generation that had experienced the saddest of school lives. After the tour of inspection, Devogel made Ypres the destination, rather than Diksmuide. "If the trip is well-prepared and guided, it will leave an indelible imprint in the minds of the pupils", he believed.[39] In the course of June 1919, the project was realised: Brussels' primary and secondary school children travelled for two or three days to the front region.

The main aim of these and so many other school excursions to the front region or nearer war ruins was indeed "to leave an indelible imprint". Being physically and emotionally impressed by the desolation of the ruins and the devastated landscape was seen as the most effective lesson in remembering the war. What this lesson further entailed was not always made explicit. Was it about feeding hatred of the Germans who were at the root of the violence or rather instilling abhorrence of war violence as such? While the former might have been prominent in 1919, the latter aim would become dominant in the longer run.[40]

Epilogue

Throughout the interwar years students indeed continued to go on school trips to regions which had been badly hit by the war. Soon, however, remembrance of the Great War was no longer the only aim of these trips. Henriette Dirkx had not exaggerated when she warned readers of her war tourist guide to make haste to visit the war destruction in the country. Not only in the occupied territories but also on the actual battlefields in the Westhoek there was a return to ordinary life. Reconstruction covered the wounds. The former site of conflict was evolving into a tourist attraction, alongside cathedrals, museums and the wonders of nature. In June 1925, a student of the public teacher training school in Ghent summed up a visit to Dinant as a visit to the "wonderfully-situated and cruelly-ravaged town". Five years later, a pupil from the same school noted that during their excursion to the coast they had also learned "a few facts about the war".[41]

The war seemed to lose the omnipresence and urgent religious expressiveness it had been granted from the early post-war days. What is more, the carefully constructed, government-supported patriotic remembrance possibly never had a complete monopoly. Indeed, within the Flemish Movement, a cultural and political national movement that since the 1840s had defended the use of Flemish in education, justice and government, anti-Belgian sentiments had grown as a result of the war, during which some Flemish nationalists had collaborated with the German occupier and its *Flamenpolitik*. In some schools with a long-standing tradition of sympathy for the Flemish Movement, teachers with more radical Flemish-nationalist sympathies were certainly not enthusiastic supporters of a Belgian patriotic discourse on the war. Flemish schoolchildren who stopped at the explicitly Flemish memorial site of the Yzer tower (*IJzertoren*) in Diksmuide (built in 1929) did not necessarily commemorate the heroes who had fallen for Belgium. It could also be an exclusively Flemish memory: "[i]ron monument, wonderful statue that tells us of the heroic deeds by Flemish bravery … where Flemish blood has flowed for so many years for our Flanders' liberty", as a pupil of a school in Bruges noted in 1935 in an excursion report.[42] When, during the 1930s, the government continued to initiate projects with which to keep the national war remembrance alive among students, this was partly in response to signals of deviating local educational practices.

It was not just the advancing time and the tensions between different (sub)national allegiances that worked against the patriotic commemoration of war. There was also criticism of the militaristic logic inherent in the culture of remembering and the formal education about the war, a tendency that has also been noticed by Mona Siegel in France.[43] Immediately after the war, the Belgian government had tried to channel the memory of the war by putting the emphasis on patriotic education, rather than on a message of hate. That channelling was only partially successful. Criticism grew in international networks of intellectuals – pacifists, pedagogues and, increasingly, historians. History education had contributed to nationalistic sentiment, and that was what had made the war possible, according to the reasoning. Was it not high time to replace education about war with education about peace?

The League of Nations was one of the organisations that emerged during the interwar years as a proponent of peace education.[44] Partly in that same context, an international movement for the revision of textbooks emerged. By way of a system of international recommendations, it was hoped that textbooks could be "cleansed" of any hostile depictions of other nations.[45] This led, in Belgium, to a cautious adjustment of the virulent anti-German nature of textbooks from the period immediately after the war.[46] Patriotism and commemoration of victims of war were allowed to keep their place in education, but they were to be enhanced by education about international cooperation and mutual dependence, as described by the recommendations. In many cases, however, these recommendations remained a dead letter.

UNESCO followed the same path with more success, from 1950 on. In contrast to its predecessors, the organisation immediately received an official mandate to concentrate its efforts on the revision of history education. Bilateral committees between previously warring countries started in the early 1950s to look for mutually acceptable interpretations of, among other things, World War I. The central issue was not so much the question of guilt, but rather the long-term causes, the political and socio-economic contexts that had made the war possible. Although patriotism and the promotion of national unity remained high on the education agenda, and the Belgian government expressed the wish to keep the memory of King Albert and those who died in the war alive in history education, a cross-schools culture of remembrance, aimed at cultivating military sacrifice, seemed increasingly inappropriate.[47]

In the meantime, the commemorative school monuments to the fallen were gradually being neglected. What had been their strength was now their weakness: they were linked to the concrete experiences and memories of a single well-defined generation of pupils and teachers. The central message, that these pupils had died for their country and that their courage offered an example worth following, was difficult to fit into the new peace paradigm. This was not the case for the school excursions, a practice of remembrance in which the horror of the war was central. As long as that horror remained "empty" and was no longer accompanied by anti-German sentiments, these excursions offered an ideal starting point for peace education. This transformation was to break through from the 1960s onwards. Excursions to the front region with its aesthetically designed and well-maintained cemeteries now became a reflection on the pointlessness of war. From now on, education about the war was resolutely about peace.[48]

Notes

This text is based on a more extensive Dutch article published as: Tine Hens, Saartje Vandenborre and Kaat Wils, "De oorlog maakt school. Herinneringspraktijken in het Belgische onderwijs na de Eerste Wereldoorlog," *Volkskunde* 115, no.1 (2014): 5-25.

1 *Bulletin du Ministère des Sciences et des Arts: circulaires et dépêches* 13 (1919): 20; Ministère de la guerre, *Aperçu général des opérations de l'armée belge d'août 1914 au 11 novembre 1918* (Brussels: Imprimerie H. Mommens, 1919).

2 Archive Royal Atheneum Bruges, Report of a teachers' meeting, Bruges, 21 January 1920; Circular of the Ministry of Arts and Sciences, Brussels, 27 December 1919.

3 See Kaat Wils, "The Evaporated Canon and the Overvalued Source. History Education in Belgium, An historical perspective," in *National history standards: the problem of the canon and the future of teaching history*, eds. Linda Symcox and Arie Wilschut (Charlotte NC; Information Age Publishing, 2009), 15-31.

4 Godefroid Kurth. *La patrie belge, y a-t-il une nationalité belge? La Belgique dans la Grande Guerre* (Brussels & Namur: Albert Dewit Lambert-Deroisin, 1922); Léon Leclère. *La grande guerre, 1914-1919* (Brussels: Vanderlinden, 1919); Mlle. C. Perlès. *Histoire de la Grande Guerre racontée aux enfants belges. Causeries* (Brussels: Lebègue & Cie, 1919); F. Sosset. *La Guerre de 14-18 en Belgique et l'occupation allemande* (Brussels: A. De Boeck, 1921).

5 On the film, see: Leen Engelen, Erik Martens, and Bénédicte Rochet. *14'18. De grote oorlog in de Belgische film* (Brussels: Cinematek, 2014). On the topos of "La Belgique martyre", see: Sophie De Schaepdrijver, "Gemartelde steden en verwoeste gewesten. Twee legaten van 1914-1918," in *België. Een parcours van herinnering*, vol. 2: *Plaatsen van tweedracht, crisis en nostalgie*, eds. Jo Tollebeek et al. (Amsterdam: Bert Bakker, 2008), 195-207.

6 For the concepts of "political memory" and "cultural memory", see for example: Aleida Assmann, "Re-framing memory. Between individual and collective forms of constructing the past," in *Performing the Past. Memory, History, and Identity in Modern Europe*, eds. Karen Tilmans, Frank van Vree, and Jay Winter (Amsterdam: Amsterdam University Press, 2010), 35-50.

7 *Catalogue des ouvrages classiques dont le Gouvernement a autorisé ou recommandé l'emploi dans les établissements d'enseignement moyen soumis au régime des lois organiques sur la proposition du conseil de perfectionnement de l'instruction moyenne et des moyens matériels d'enseignement et d'ornementation des classes* (Brussels: Ministère des Sciences et des Arts, 1920), 15.

8 See for example: Gustaaf Segers, "De Belgische Volksschool en de Heropbeuring van ons Vaderland," *Verslagen en Mededelingen der Koninklijke Vlaamsche Academie voor Taal- en Letterkunde* (1921): 550.

9 See for example: David Parker, "Talent at its Command: The First World War and the Vocational Aspect of Education, 1914-1939," *History of Education Quarterly* 35 (1995): 237-259; Andrew Donson. *Youth in the Fatherless Land. War Pedagogy, Nationalism, and Authority in Germany, 1914-1918* (Cambridge, MA: Harvard University Press, 2010); Barry Blades. *Roll of Honour: Schooling & The Great War, 1914-1919* (Barnsley: Pen & Sword Military, 2015).

10 Mona Siegel, *The Moral Disarmament of France: Education, Pacifism, and Patriotism, 1914-1940* (New York: Cambridge University Press, 2004).

11 Andrew Donson, "Schools and Universities," in *1914-1918-online. International Encyclopedia of the First World War*, eds. Ute Daniel et al. (Berlin: Freie Universität Berlin, 2014). DOI: 10.15463/ie1418.10346.
12 Stéphane Audoin-Rouzeau, "Children and the Primary Schools of France," in *State, Society and Mobilization in Europe during the First World War*, ed. John Horne (Cambridge: Cambridge University Press, 1997), 39-52; Mark Connelly, *The Great War, Memory and Ritual. Commemoration in the City and East London, 1916-1939* (London: Royal Historical Society, 2001), 75-97; Siegel, *The Moral Disarmament*, 51-91.
13 *Bulletin du Ministère des Sciences et des Arts*, 13 (1919): 46-48.
14 See most recently: Jan De Volder. *Cardinal Mercier in the First World War. Belgium, Germany and the Catholic Church* (Leuven: Leuven University Press, 2018).
15 J. Rutten. *Voor Vrijheid en Recht. Verslag gegeven op de plechtige prijsuitreiking van het Onze-Lieve-Vrouwcollege den 31sten juli 1919* (Antwerp: De Winter, 1919).
16 For these songs, see: Josephine Hoegaerts, "'Op 't bloedig oorlogsveld, is ied're man een held.' Hoe kinderen het slagveld verbeeldden en beleefden aan het eind van de negentiende eeuw," *Volkskunde* 113, no. 3 (2012): 306-324.
17 The literature on war memorials is vast. See for example: Bruce Scates and Rebecca Wheatley, "War memorials," in *The Cambridge History of the First World War*, vol. 3: *Civil Society*, ed. Jay Winter (Cambridge: Cambridge University Press, 2013); Stéphane Tison, "Commemoration, Cult of the Fallen," in *1914-1918-online. International Encyclopedia of the First World War*, eds. Ute Daniel et al. (Berlin: Freie Universität Berlin, 2019). DOI: 10.15463/ie1418.11340. Specifically on Belgium, see: Laurence Van Ypersele, "Commemoration, Cult of the Fallen (Belgium)," *1914-1918 online*, 2014. DOI: 10.15463/ie1418.10313.
18 City Archives Brussels (SAB), *Instruction publique*, II 1869. Minutes of meeting, Brussels, 24 October 1921.
19 See Marika Ceunen, "Wat een monument lijden kan… Oprichting, lotgevallen en restauratie van het oorlogsmonument op het Martelarenplein," in *Aan onze helden en martelaren… Beelden van de brand van Leuven (August 1914)*, eds. Marika Ceunen and Piet Veldeman (Leuven: Peeters, 2004), 305-338.
20 See for instance: Karla Vanraepenbusch and Matthias Meirlaen, "Van trauma sites naar herinneringsplekken. De integratie van de executies en de gefusilleerden in de stedelijke ruimte van Antwerpen, Luik en Rijsel (1914-1940)," *Stadsgeschiedenis* 11, no. 2 (2017): 146-164.
21 Axel Tixhon and Laurence Van Ypersele, "Du sang et des pierres. Les monuments de la guerre 1914-1918 en Wallonie," *Cahiers d'Histoire du Temps Présent*, no. 7 (2000): 83-126; Stéphanie Claisse, "Visages de la Patrie belge à travers les monuments aux morts de 14-18," in *Comment (se) sortir de la Grande Guerre? Regards sur quelques pays 'vainqueurs': la Belgique, la France et la Grande Bretagne*, eds. Stéphanie Claisse and Thierry Lemoine (Paris: L'Harmattan, 2005), 37-58.
22 Jay Winter. *Sites of Memory, Sites of Mourning. The Great War in European Cultural History* (Cambridge: Cambridge University Press, 1995).
23 Daniel J. Sherman, "Bodies and Names. The Emergence of Commemoration in Interwar France," *American Historical Review* 103, no. 2 (1998): 443-466.
24 Athénée Royal de Liège, *Liber memorialis rappelant la participation des élèves et des anciens élèves à la Grande Guerre 1914-1918* (Liège: Bénard, 1921), 20.
25 State Archives Antwerp, *Archive Royal Atheneum Antwerp*. 2428-2429. Correspondence on the war memorial, 1919.
26 Athénée Royal de Liège. *Liber memorialis*, 20.

27 Jesuit Archives Heverlee, Sint-Jan Berchmans School Brussels, C 33/6 A.2. A la mémoire de nos héros.
28 Hoegaerts, "Op 't bloedig oorlogsveld", 310-311.
29 Susanne Brandt, "Le voyage aux champs de bataille," *Vingtième Siècle. Revue d'Histoire* 41(1994): 18-22.
30 See also Johan Meire, *De stilte van de Salient. De herinnering aan de Eerste Wereldoorlog rond Ieper* (Tielt: Lannoo, 2003).
31 Jean Massaart and Henriette Dirkx, *Ce qu'il faut voir sur les champs de bataille et dans les villes détruites de Belgique*. 2 vols. (Brussels: Touring Club de Belgique, 1919-1920).
32 Henriette Dirkx. *Jusqu'à la chute d'Anvers* (Brussels: Touring club de Belgique, 1920), 4.
33 See Bruno Notteboom, "De verborgen ideologie van Jean Massart. Vertogen over landschap en (anti-) stedelijkheid in België in het begin van de twintigste eeuw," *Stadsgeschiedenis* 1, no.1 (2006): 51-68.
34 Jean Massart. *Le Front de Flandre* (Brussels: Touring Club de Belgique, 1919), 137.
35 Sherman, "Bodies", 448.
36 SAB, *Instruction publique*, II 658. Letter from V. Devogel to E. Jacqmain, 22 January 1919.
37 SAB, *Instruction publique*, II 658. Letter from E. Jacqmain to J. Destrée, 25 March 1919.
38 SAB, *Instruction publique*, II 658. Letter from V. Devogel to E. Jacqmain, 28 May 1919.
39 SAB, *Instruction publique*, II 658. Permission for school trip to Nieuwpoort and Ostend (s.l., 1919).
40 On these school excursions, see more extensively: Tine Hens in collaboration with Saartje Vanden Borre and Kaat Wils. *Oorlog in tijden van vrede. De Eerste Wereldoorlog in de klas (1919-1940)* (Kalmthout: Pelckmans, 2015), 24-41.
41 State Archive Ghent, Funds Rijksmiddelbare Normaalschool Ghent, 458, reports of school trips.
42 Quoted in Marc Constandt, "We reizen om te leren: schoolreizen in het interbellum," *Brood & Rozen. Tijdschrift voor de Geschiedenis van Sociale Bewegingen* 14, no. 2 (2009): 56. For the Ijzertoren, see: Frank Seberechts, "Slechts de graven maken een land tot vaderland. Van Heldenhulde tot IJzertoren: een stenen hulde aan de Vlaamse IJzersoldaten," in *Duurzamer dan graniet. Over Monumenten en Vlaamse Beweging*, ed. Frank Seberechts (Tielt: Lannoo, 2003), 123-154; Karen Shelby, *Flemish Nationalism and the Great War: The Politics of Memory, Visual Culture and Commemoration* (London: Palgrave, 2014), 83-111.
43 Siegel, *The Moral Disarmament*, 79-92.
44 See, for the initiatives of the League of Nations and their impact on Belgian education: Hens et al., *Oorlog in tijden van vrede*, 147-204.
45 See for example: Mona Siegel and Kirsten Harjes, "Disarming Hatred: History Education, National Memories, and Franco-German Reconciliation from World War I to the Cold War," *History of Education Quarterly* 52, no. 3 (2012): 370-402.
46 Christophe Béchet, "La révision pacifiste des manuels scolaires. Les enjeux de la mémoire de la guerre 14-18 dans l'enseignement belge de l'Entre-deux-guerres," *Cahiers d'Histoire du Temps Présent* 20 (2008): 49-101; Hens et al., *Oorlog in tijden van vrede*, 77-146.
47 See: Tessa Lobbes, "Het Belgische geschiedenisonderwijs en de uitdaging van de eigentijdse geschiedenis (1945-1961)," *Tijdschrift voor Geschiedenis* 126, no.1 (2013): 76-91; Tessa Lobbes. *Verleden zonder stof. Strijd om het geschiedenisonderwijs in België (1945-1989)* (Ghent: Academia Press, 2017).

48 See Silke Saey. *De 'Groote Oorlog' in het onderwijs. Herinneringseducatie over de Eerste Wereldoorlog in het Vlaams secundair onderwijs (1970-heden)* (unpublished MA thesis, University of Leuven, 2012), 34-59.

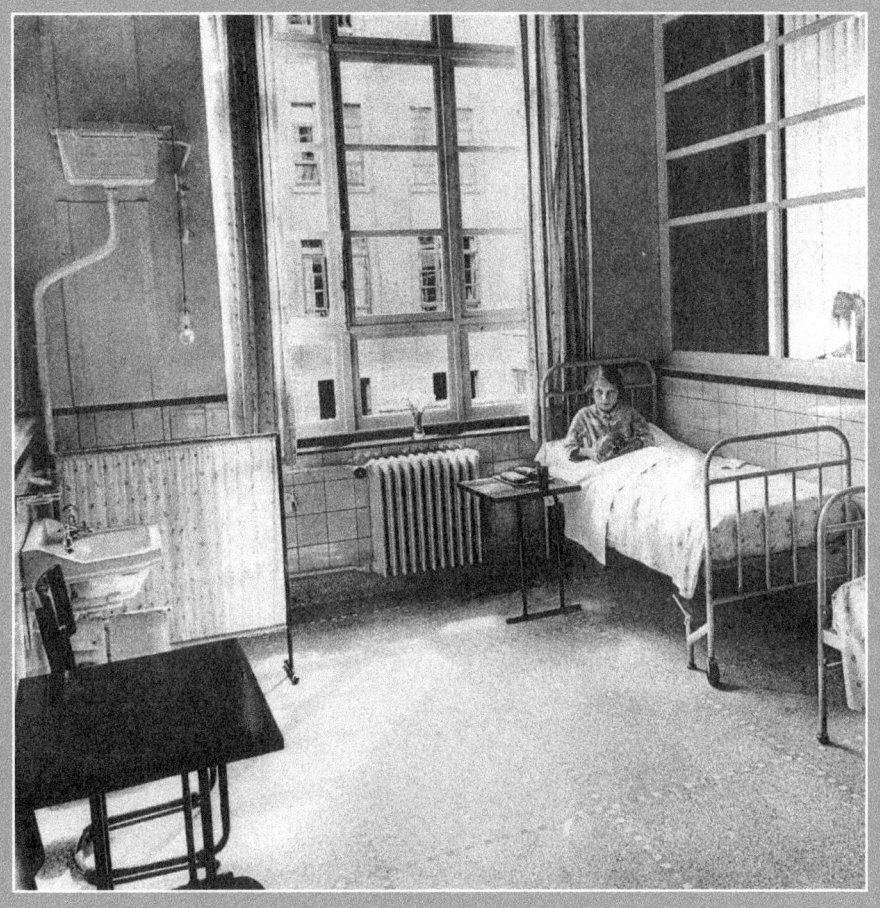

PART THREE
REPAIR

Paediatric ward of the St. Rafael Hospital in Leuven (Belgium), opened in 1936.
© City Archive Leuven

Behind the blind walked the one-armed, and behind them those without arms, and behind the armless the ones who were hit in the head …

There they stood, the invalids, whose whole face was a single gaping big hole, wrapped in white bandage, with reddish wounded folds instead of ears.

There they stood, the clogs of flesh and blood, soldiers without limbs, torsos in uniform, the empty sleeves tied together on the back in an expression of coquettish horror …

Behind the car the insane were walking. They still had everything, eyes, nose and ears, legs and arms, only the mind had flowed out of them, they did not know why or for what they had been brought here, they looked like brothers, they all experienced the same great destructive emptiness.

> Joseph Roth on a mass demonstration of war invalids in Lviv (Galicia) shortly after the war, quoted in Geert Mak, *In Europe. Travels Through the Twentieth Century* (2004)

Fig. 1. Raymon Haesebrouck and his wife
© Private archive of the Van Eenooghe Family.

High Expectations and Silenced Realities
The Re-education of Belgian Disabled Soldiers of the Great War, 1914–1921

Pieter Verstraete and Marisa De Picker

11 November 1922. It was on this day that, in imitation of other Allied Powers such as Britain and France, the Belgian Unknown Soldier was finally laid to rest.[1] The place of his interment was the Congress column in Brussels, where the eternal flame would afterwards also be lit, and the fact that the chosen pall-bearers were eight war-disabled Belgian veterans lent the event an even greater degree of symbolism.[2] The four pall-bearers on the left-hand side had lost their right arms, whilst those on the right-hand side had lost their left arms. In addition, Raymon Haesebrouck, the man who had originally chosen the coffin which would become that of the Unknown Soldier, was himself a disabled veteran of the Great War.[3] Haesebrouck was a war-blinded Belgian soldier who, during a visit to the trenches by the Belgian King Albert I, had thrown himself over the king to protect him when sudden gunfire was heard. 10 November found Haesebrouck at Bruges station, indicating with his white stick which one of the five coffins on display would be sent by train to Brussels to become that of the Unknown Soldier (Fig. 1).

That the role played by Belgian war-disabled soldiers in the ceremonial funeral of the Unknown Soldier is almost unknown, both in the academic world and in society at large, is indicative of the specific position afforded to impaired persons in Belgian historical research. It is often the case that disability history is regarded as being a topic of little interest or importance – although there are, of course, exceptions to this.[4] The contribution we would like to make to this is to show how the oft-cited quotation by the American historian, Douglas Baynton, is also applicable to the situation in Belgian historical research: "[d]isability is everywhere in history, once you begin looking for it, but conspicuously absent in the histories we write". One of those places was the First World War. The Great War disabled 8.5 million soldiers. Of the approximately 6 million mobilised English soldiers, 750,000 (12.3%) became disabled. Germany had to face 1.5 million (11.6%) disabled soldiers after the Armistice was signed. According to one official document dated December 1918 it was said that of the 170,000 mobilised Belgian soldiers 5,200 (3.06%) were invalided due to the military conflict. It needs, however, to be emphasised that this official number is an underestimation of the real impact of the Great War as in the 1930s almost 37,000 men were members of the Belgian National Association for Disabled Soldiers. Since the 1990s – and partly in response to the previously described growing interest in disability history – an increasing number of historians have dedicated themselves to uncovering the history of disabled war veterans.[5]

Although the impact of the Great War on the Belgian army in terms of deadly casualties and mutilated bodies/minds, in comparison to that on the other Allied and Central Forces, was relatively limited, the Belgian case nevertheless deserves to be studied, and this for at least the following two reasons. Belgium, first of all, was the only belligerent country which needed to care for its mutilated soldiers abroad. Besides this particular challenge, Belgium is also portrayed in the primary literature with regard to the rehabilitation of disabled soldiers as a "pioneering country" when it came to tackling what was called the "problem of the invalid soldiers".[6]

In order to find out what was to become of men who, before the outbreak of war, had been bakers, tram drivers or builders but who, because of an exploded shell, an illness or a bullet wound, had now lost both legs, we will examine the pedagogical component of the medical, juridical and political measures taken both during and after the Great War to address the "problem" of Belgian war-disabled soldiers. This pedagogical element was described as either re-education or retraining.[7] The first part of this paper will look at the initiatives that were developed to assist physically impaired soldiers to repair both their broken bodies and shattered working lives. The second part will do the same with regard to those who were blinded as a result of their war service. In order to get a better view of the history of Belgian disabled soldiers we made use of the following sources and archives: local (digitised) newspapers, city and district archives, the memories of the children and grandchildren of disabled soldiers, the archives of the Royal Museum of War and the Armed Forces, the Archives of the Royal Palace and the Documentation Centre of the In Flanders Field Museum.

Re-education, Professional Reorientation and Prosthetics

By the first months of the war the "invalid question" had already made it onto the Belgian political agenda. In November 1914, Speaker of the Chamber of Deputies Frans Schollaert supported the creation of a home and re-educational institute for disabled soldiers in Sainte-Adresse – that being the temporary capital of Belgium during the Great War. In June 1915, Minister of War Charles de Broqueville decided to set up another re-educational institute nearby, in Port-Villez (île de France). The Belgian government hoped that this initiative would show soldiers who had been seriously injured in the German advance and the Belgian field war that their lives were not over. Physically impaired soldiers could follow a course of professional re-education in these institutes, a course which was supplemented by general training lessons and medical gymnastics or physiotherapy sessions.

While these two schools were being built, another re-education institute was being set up in occupied Belgium. It was in Woluwe, a suburb of Brussels, and it was the brainchild of a sub-department of the Belgian Red Cross: the *Oeuvre d'Aide et Apprentissage aux Invalides de Guerre* (Organisation for the Assistance and Training of War Invalids).[8] From 1919 on the buildings became the responsibility of the state, which left the day-to-day operation of the school to the *Nationaal Werk voor Oologsinvaliden* (National Employment Organisation for War Invalids).[9]

The aims of these retraining initiatives were twofold. Firstly, to ensure that as many war-disabled soldiers as possible would eventually be able to return to work, despite their physical limitations. Their work-related difficulties were described as a national problem to which an effective solution needed to be found. Both within Belgian politics and within the press, the idea that the country owed these disabled war veterans a debt of gratitude for their service and proven sacrifices at the Front gained considerable currency; secondly, to create as many workers as possible to assist in the reconstruction of the devastated fatherland.[10]

The following pages will use photographs and concrete examples to give in insight into what retraining was actually like for the soldiers of Port-Villez, Sainte-Adresse and Woluwe. It is based upon publications from Belgian newspapers, publications by the soldiers themselves, information contained in their personal archives, as well as publications dealing directly with war and invalidity. Examples of the last include *De Belgische Gebrekkelijke (*The Belgian Invalid; later renamed as *De Belgische Verminkte/L'invalide belge)*, which was the periodical of the study group of disabled soldiers of the Belgian institute for re-education in Port-Villez during the war and taken over from 1919 by the advocacy association *Fédération Nationale des Invalides et Mutilés de Guerre* (National Federation of War Disabled Soldiers). The association originated from the study group and different unions set up in occupied Belgium during the war. The organisation quickly became the only veterans' association uniting most disabled ex-servicemen. These periodicals give a unique insight into the lives of war-disabled Belgian soldiers during and after the First World War and are a fantastic source for anyone wanting to begin researching the topic.[11] By far the most comprehensive study of the retraining institute at Port-Villez is Léon de Paeuw's 1917 work entitled *La Rééducation Professionnelle des Soldats Mutilés et Estropiés*.[12] Thanks to de Paeuw, this article can give a much fuller picture of life at Port-Villez than would otherwise be possible. De Paeuw's study is also an excellent source for anyone who wants to learn more about the world of soldiers disabled in the Great War, more specifically about those who attended the Port-Villez retraining institute. It is illustrated and paints an extremely detailed picture of the day-to-day running of the institute. The archive of the school at Port-Villez is also worth investigating, even though many of its documents have been lost over time. The archive as it is now comprises a trio of boxes concerning the setting-up and running of the institute. It also contains a limited number of documents concerning the schools of Sainte-Adresse and Woluwe.[13]

The first candidates for re-education arrived at Vernon station near Port-Villez on 21 August 1915. These wounded men had, until very recently, been at the Front. As far as de Paeuw was concerned, this could only be an advantage. Men who had spent a long time before being looked after were less motivated to learn, "for nothing is more injurious to men's mentality and character than a prolonged period of 'dolce far niente' (sweet idleness)".[14] Nevertheless, the school was built in an oasis of calm, at a respectable distance from the Front. De Paeuw wrote that the nerves of many invalids could easily be put on edge as a result of the terrible conditions they had endured in the trenches. It was necessary for their recovery to ensure that these men did not become over-stimulated.[15]

After their arrival at Port-Villez, all the "pupils" underwent a comprehensive medical, pedagogical and work-related examination, the purpose of which was to map out their previous history. To this end, every one of the wounded men had to appear before the Vocational Guidance Committee, which would determine which job workshop he should be assigned to. Wherever possible, the Committee took the invalid's own wishes into account, provided that his choice was physically and economically feasible.

In addition, the Committee was driven by three guiding principles, which were also kept in mind in the Sainte-Adresse and Woluwe institutes. The first and most important question to be considered was whether or not a physically impaired soldier would be able to resume his former occupation, albeit with some degree of adaptation. When this was found to be possible, the soldier was allowed to follow his choice. At Port-Villez were developed various applications designed to mechanise work processes. Indeed, the school received international praise for its sewing table, which enabled a tailor with an injured pelvis and a paralysed left leg to work at a sewing machine without straining his body. An air cushion made it possible to work while sitting and while leaning on crutches (Fig. 2).[16]

In situations where adjustments were insufficient, the Committee instead tried to find an alternative trade or profession for a disabled soldier. It tended to recommend work which contained or actively used skills which the soldier had used in his pre-war work. An example of this given by de Paeuw involved the construction sector. During their time at Port-Villez, various disabled soldiers chose to retrain as architects or structural engineers.[17] The last of the three key principles was that a disabled soldier should be in a position to earn a sufficient living from his chosen profession or trade.

Fig. 2. Sewing-table made at Port-Villez for disabled tailors © University Library KU Leuven.

To this end, the Committee took account of the type of place in which the soldier proposed to practise the work for which he had trained. They were conscious that, in some respects, a different type of workforce was required in towns as opposed to in the country. Disabled soldiers could count on assistance from the institutes in finding suitable jobs with trustworthy employers once they had completed their retraining. They were strongly encouraged to keep in contact with the institute, "for they are not discharged from the army, they are simply on leave without pay and can be recalled for any misbehaviour".[18]

The men at Port-Villez had the option of choosing from 73 professions as well as from various administrative specialisms.[19] Those who wanted a university education were sent to Paris, where they stayed at the Belgian *Home Universitaire de*

Paris, which had been set up with support from Charles de Broqueville, the Minister for War. Twenty and 14 vocational training courses were available in Woluwe and Sainte-Adresse respectively. The majority of soldiers with physical impairments of the lower limbs chose to retrain as cobblers, tailors or basket-makers, as these were all trades which could be carried out sitting down and were needed just as much in the country as in towns. Standing for long periods whilst wearing a prosthetic leg was not possible for everyone, de Paeuw wrote:

> among the men (in Port-Villez) with perfected artificial legs 48 per cent manage very well; 18 per cent manage fairly well, and 34 per cent dislike it and do not use it. Of the others who have had a leg amputated, 34 per cent manage very well with a peg leg; 26 per cent manage fairly well; 6 per cent dislike it, and 34 per cent do not possess one.[20]

Fig. 3. Disabled soldiers with a work prosthesis in an adjustment workshop at Port-Villez, 1917. © Private Collection Pieter Verstraete.

The orthopaedic workshop at Port-Villez also developed a number of artificial arms for upper-limb amputees, for example designed for use in woodwork, metalwork and agricultural work.[21] Instead of an artificial arm or hand, a complex and rather difficult-to-manage work-tool was attached to the amputee's stump (Fig. 3). De Paeuw reasoned that these arms were particularly useful for trades that required many uniform movements, and sometimes they could be of great service to skilful workmen who keenly wished to continue their former trade. On the other hand, de Paeuw warned that artificial limbs were far from an ideal solution:

because one man may have succeeded in using an artificial arm, it does not follow that every man who has lost an arm, if given this apparatus, will be able to employ it for any trade he may wish to practice. The truth is quite different. These perfected arms are not only very costly, but too delicate and intricate to use working in a shop. Moreover very few men are dexterous enough to manipulate these arms properly. [...] In most cases it would be much better to re-educate the man as he is, with the limbs that he still possesses, and to choose a profession adapted to his physical limitations.[22]

Soldiers who had a disabled arm often chose a profession requiring little in the way of physical strength or hard manual work, and some of them chose to retrain for a profession in the arts sector. At both Woluwe and Port-Villez, for example, men could train to be decorators or artistic painters. Others chose a non-technical job in the public or service industries, such as postman or telegraph operator, and sat recruitment tests set by the authorities (Fig. 4).

Fig. 4. 27-year-old disabled soldier Martin. © University Library KU Leuven.

As well as their practical retraining, disabled soldiers received daily medical gymnastics or physiotherapy and general physical training in order to maximise their physical capabilities.[23] There was a general conviction that a healthy and thoroughly-taught disabled soldier would stand a much better chance both in the job market and in getting used to his new profession.[24] The theoretical training offered by the institutes comprised, for example, language, arithmetic, chemistry, design and technology lessons. Men who had an impairment in their right hand or arm took special lessons in order to learn to write left-handed. This was certainly no picnic (Fig. 5).

The closure of the retraining institutes in Northern France began in 1919, a few months after the Armistice. Those disabled soldiers who remained there were transferred to retraining institutes in Belgium. Besides that in Woluwe, there were two more re-education institutes in Belgium, both of which had been set up before the outbreak of war and were intended specifically for young and adult men with physical impairments, both congenital and those sustained in work-related accidents.[25] Next to be set up – on 11 October 1919 – was the *Nationaal Werk voor Oorlogsinvaliden* (National Work for War Invalids), which the authorities tasked with supporting the war disabled in finding retraining opportunities and work. It was also responsible for organising re-education at the Woluwe institute.[26] This school remained open until the end of 1924. No-one knows the total number of men who studied at the institutes. The *Nationaal Werk voor Oorlogsinvaliden* documented the re-education and reintegration of war victims, but unfortunately there are no surviving archives for the early interwar years. It is, however, possible to find some stray figures in the publications and archive material of the institutes, and to use these to build up a picture of just how many men were assembled in these schools. For example, we know that in 1916 there were around 700 and 1,500 disabled soldiers in Sainte-Adresse and Port-Villez respectively.[27] Woluwe retrained an average of 148 disabled soldiers per year during the war.[28]

Next to re-education, the *Nationaal Werk voor Oorlogsinvaliden* would offer several other work-related services to stimulate disabled soldiers' reintegration into society

Fig. 5. M. Charlier, a disabled inmate of Woluwe, in 1919. © University Library KU Leuven.

as re-training was only a partial solution to the "problem of the invalids". Examples of these services include assistance in finding a job in the industrial, commercial or public sector, loans to buy a property or work equipment, reimbursement of medical costs and permission for orthopaedics and wheelchairs. In addition, the *Fédération Nationale des Invalides et Mutilés de Guerre* (National Federation of War Disabled Soldiers) advocacy association strove for sufficient disability pensions to allow every veteran to live well together with his family. After all, not every disabled soldier could be helped by the emancipatory initiative of orthopaedic and vocational rehabilitation. Some required constant nursing help or assistance with day-to-day activities for various reasons such as continence problems, great difficulty moving around on their own and the loss of more than two limbs.[29]

Blindness and the Ideal of Independence

Just as was the case with physically disabled soldiers, so the rehabilitation discourse around blind soldiers also emphasised that the ultimate goal was to return these men to full economic productivity. Reconstructing the way in which retraining was discussed is not easy. What is still more difficult is to find out what the disabled soldiers themselves thought about their re-education. The sources that can be used for this are scattered and very incomplete. A keen researcher can look in the archives of the institute for war-blinded soldiers which are housed in the Royal Archives (Secretary Queen Elisabeth) in Brussels. Further sources of information include the periodicals for a blind readership which were published during the interwar period – *Vers La Lumière*, *l'Alexandre Rodenbach* and the *Roomsche Licht*, for example.[30] Finally, where possible a researcher can try to track down the children and grandchildren of disabled soldiers and use their memories as the basis upon which to build up a picture of the lives of disabled soldiers.

In 1932 Léopold Mélis, who had been Inspector-General for Healthcare in the Belgian army during the war, claimed that there were 47 war-blinded Belgians. We can, however, be fairly confident that, at the end of hostilities, there had been 88 war-blinded military servicemen.[31] This group received a great deal of publicity, just as they did in other countries, and both during and after the war they were the public face of charitable campaigns to "improve their circumstances". One good example of this is the art portfolio brought out by Samuel De Vriendt in 1919 to benefit war-blinded men (Fig. 6). In the introduction to these reproductions of drawings by blinded ex-servicemen, De Vriendt referred to both the severity of the men's impairments and the chances which re-education offered them, stressing:

We offer this art album to the world, and in so doing, it is our earnest hope that the world will continue to think of these brave men, who so willingly sacrificed their sight in defence of their beloved Fatherland. It proclaims the severity of their handicap, but is also a testament to how appropriate re-education, under the motherly gaze of Her Majesty the Queen, can prepare them to enjoy life once again as useful and productive members of society.[32]

The above quotation shows that, during the First World War, blind people were still seen as individuals who, unlike sighted people, struggled to be happy. This was a widespread misconception, and one which those who set up the first institutes for blind people had made full use of in order to justify taking this step.[33] During the nineteenth century, blindness was certainly regarded as being one of the severest impairments that it was possible to have. The very visual nature of society meant that blind people had little chance of being able to compete on anything like equal terms. So the enormous sacrifice that the war-blinded had made to repel the German invader made them amongst the most conspicuous of all the country's heroes (Fig. 6).

Fig. 6. Samuel de Vriendt's sketch – La toute petite amie/Het vriendinnetje/Making friends. © Private Collection Pieter Verstraete.

War-blinded soldiers were seen as heroes, albeit as vulnerable heroes who, without professional care and re-education, were doomed to lead lives full of difficulty and suffering. Specific measures were taken with regard to them from the beginning of the Great War. Initially, war-blinded soldiers were sent to the Saint-Victor hospice in Amiens. It was only later that they were sent to Port-Villez, where the majority of physically disabled soldiers were taken for retraining. From official documents pertaining to the transfer of war-blinded soldiers it appears that this happened because the advance of German troops meant that the situation in Amiens was becoming too dangerous.[34] However, it can be inferred from a document in the Royal War Museum (Brussels) that the war-blinded soldiers had no real desire to engage in retraining, and that they had instead succumbed to depression.[35]

There is not a great deal of information that can be found regarding the rehabilitation of war-blinded soldiers during the First World War. Unlike that of those with physical impairments, war-blinded soldiers' care was centralised, at the institute for the war-blinded at Bosvoorde. This was run under the auspices of Queen Elisabeth and was headed by Captain Delvaux. The institute was set up in opposition to the prevailing idea that rehabilitating blind people was of no benefit to society as a whole. There are documents in the Royal Archives which show that, as far as the Minister for Economic Affairs was concerned, it would be quite sufficient merely to ensure that war-blinded soldiers had some degree of diversion.[36] If it was up to him, the war-blinded soldiers would be looked after by women who would read aloud and play music to them. Fortunately, Queen Elisabeth – probably influenced by the experiences of her father who was himself an ophthalmologist – took a far more sensible view of the situation. She fought hard for a centralised rehabilitation institute where war-blinded soldiers could learn a new profession, could learn to walk independently, and could learn to read Braille.

The sources give us little concrete information about the running of the institute. We do know that it existed from 1919 to 1921, and that it functioned with the help of generous gifts from abroad. One of the photographs of the institute shows the Kesslerzaal, or Kessler Room. This functioned as the main classroom for the war-blinded men and was called after the American industrialist George Kessler (1863-1920), whose Permanent Blind Relief War Fund had donated a substantial subsidy to the institute (Fig. 7).

As shown in a collection of postcards given out to drum up financial support for the institute, war-blinded soldiers were re-educated for traditional trades such basket-weaving, brush-making, cigarette-rolling, machine knitting, breeding chickens and piano-tuning. Although the 88 soldiers at Bosvoorde were expected to be willing participants in their own re-education, some documents kept at the Royal Archives in Brussels demonstrate that this was not always the case. Isidore Van Vlasselaere, for example, was one soldier who was unwilling to leave the comfort of his home and family to spend an extended period retraining in Brussels:

> Van Vlasselaere is a brave man whose morale is good, he seems happy and is much engaged with the education of his son. He would be very happy to be re-educated, but is unwilling to leave his wife and child. If circumstances permitted, he would voluntarily come to the institute at Bosvoorde.[37]

For other war-blinded soldiers, and particularly for those with additional psychological and physical problems, retraining for another profession was simply not possible. Julien Dhont was a case in point, as his dossier clearly shows:

> His life is very difficult – like that of an involuntary hermit: both from a physical and a moral point of view; he has all his intelligence, he hears everything but he no longer has any way of communicating with the outside world: neither by speaking nor by writing, he cannot express a wish or make his needs known. Dhont always has a huge appetite and needs extra rations, an ordinary amount of food is not enough for him.[38]

Clearly, the dream of re-education could not always become a reality. But even for the war-blinded soldiers who stayed in the institute, it was not certain whether, after their release, they would be able to put the ideal of an individual able to live and work independently into practice. Interviews with the children and grandchildren of disabled veterans of the Great War are one way to shed light on this topic.[39] From the interview carried out with the grandchildren of Désiré Stas, who was blinded during his war service, it became clear that Stas did everything he possibly could to avoid being recognised as blind.[40] Although he did have a white stick, two of his grandsons both said that they never saw him use it in public. And the niece of Maurice Haesebrouck – the war-blinded serviceman who had chosen the Unknown Soldier – clearly remembered that her uncle would never leave the house without a companion, even though he had learned to find his own way to the adjacent café.[41] The way in which the retraining of war-blinded soldiers was perceived needs to be placed in perspective – just as is also required for the image of war-blinded soldiers more generally. Photographs such as those contained in the collection entitled *Une promenade dans l'institut* (*A Stroll in the Institute*), in which war-blinded men are shown strolling independently, expressed the dream of rehabilitation, rather than the reality for blind people in the inter-war period (Fig. 8).

High Expectations and Silenced Realities 213

Fig. 7. Salle Kessler in the institute for war-blinded soldiers at Bosvoorde. © Private Collection Pieter Verstraete.

Fig. 8. Aveugles sortant des salles des cours (The blind leaving the classrooms). © Private Collection Pieter Verstraete.

Conclusion

Almost from the very outbreak of the Great War, the large number of soldiers whose active service had left them with lasting physical, mental or sensory wounds was described as an extremely pressing problem. The solution to making these men independent and economically productive once again lay, at least in part, in retraining them. In the main, this retraining took the form of either introducing the soldiers to work that would make use of their remaining physical capacities or of training them to use prostheses to enable them to return to their pre-war jobs.

In spite of the paucity of source material, we can say with certainty that these aspirations could not always be fulfilled. For soldiers with a physical or sensory impairment finding suitable work was a process of give and take – a question of finding a balance between their own wishes and physical capabilities on the one hand, and the expectations of society, the authorities, their doctors and families on the other. Many of the available sources – the periodical *De Belgische Verminkte*, the information held at the Royal Archives and the interviews carried out with the children and grandchildren of war-disabled soldiers – bear witness to the huge gulf which often existed between the ideals of rehabilitation and how it worked in practice. Following Sarah Rose, who studied the mixed results of the rehabilitation programmes for disabled veterans in the United States in the 1910s and 1920s, we could say that "disability and its relation to the labor market proved a far more fluid and complex concept than either the framers of rehabilitation programs or rehabilitation officials had expected".[42] Neither, however, is it possible to say that all disabled soldiers lived tormented, troubled lives – further research is needed to give us a nuanced view of the experiences, both of re-education and of life more generally, that the Belgian war-disabled had during the post-war period. The following sources are a good place to start for anyone who wants to research the topic further: local (digitised) newspapers, city and district archives, the memories of the children and grandchildren of disabled soldiers, the archives of the Royal War Museum in Brussels, the archives of the Royal Palace, and the Documentation Centre of the In Flanders Field Museum in Ypres.

Notes

1. Stéphanie Claisse, *Du soldat inconnu aux monuments commémoratifs belges de la guerre 14-18* (Brussels: Académie Royale de Belgique, 2013).
2. The congress column was built between 1850 and 1859 in order to commemorate the creation of the Belgian constitution by the national congress in 1830.
3. See the Bruges City Archive [Raymon Haesebrouck Bequest] and the private archive of the Van Eenooghe family.
4. Some of these exceptions are: Patrick Devlieger et al., "Visualising disability in the past," *Paedogogica Historica*, 44 (2008): 747-760 and Liesje Raemdonck and Ingeborg Scheiris, *Ongehoord Verleden. Dove frontvorming in België aan het begin van de 20ste eeuw* (Ghent: Fevlado-Diversus, 2007). There have been similar developments within the history of medicine. See for example: Joris Vandendriessche, "Ophthalmia Crossing Borders: Belgian Army Doctors between the Military and Civilian Society, 1830-1860," *Belgisch Tijdschrift voor Nieuwste Geschiedenis. Journal of Belgian History* 46, no.2 (2016): 48-71. What is still very much needed, however, is approaches which incorporate the perspective of the disabled person him- or herself into the analysis.
5. It would be impossible to provide an exhaustive list within the confines of this paper, but the following works will serve as a good introduction: Joanna Bourke, *Dismembering the Male: Men's Bodies, Britain, and the Great War* (London: Reaktion Books, 1996); Suzannah Biernoff, "The Rhetoric of Disfigurement in First World War Britain," *Social History of Medicine* 24, no.3 (2011): 666-685; Heather Perry, *Recycling the Disabled: Army, Medicine and Modernity in WW1 Germany* (London: Oxford University Press, 2014); Julie Anderson and Neil Pemberton, "Walking alone: Aiding the war- and civilian blind in the inter-war period," *European Review of History – Revue européene d'Histoire* 14, no.4 (2007): 459-479.
6. Garrard Harris, *The redemption of the disabled. A study of programmes of rehabilitation for the disabled of war and of industry* (New York: D. Appleton & Company, 1919).
7. These two terms will be used interchangeably in this article. They both indicate the way in which attempts were made to fit disabled soldiers for a new trade or profession. Given that these were purely professional initiatives, an incredible amount of emphasis was placed on morality – hence the resurgence of specific norms and values explained in terms of "education" and "training".
8. *Une visite à L'oeuvre Aide et apprentissage aux invalides de la guerre durant l'occupation* (Brussels: Laurent, 1918).
9. Brussels and the Surrounding Area, BIM [Brussels Institute for Conservation], "The Parmentier Park," *Infofiches over de Groene Ruimten in het Brussels Hoofdstedelijk Gewest*. 4 January 2011. http://document.environnement.brussels/opac_ccs/elecfile/IF%20EV%Parcs%20Parmentierparc%20NL (14 August 2017).
10. Pieter Verstraete and Christine Van Everbroeck, *Verminkte Stilte [Mutilated Silence]* (Namur: Presses Universitaires de Namur, 2014), 46-47.
11. The periodicals can be consulted at the Koninklijk Museum van het Leger en de Krijgsgeschiedenis in Brussels.
12. Léon de Paeuw (1873-1941) was inspector general of Belgian primary education when the war broke out. He then became Cabinet Manager of the Ministry of War (Minister de Broqueville) and would, in the interwar years, play an important role in the reception of Montessori education in Belgium. In 1915 de Paeuw was entrusted by de Broqueville with overall responsibility for the Port-Villez project.

13 The archives of the retraining institutes form part of the Moscow Archive, so called because it had been transported to Moscow by the Russian troops who liberated Berlin in 1945. It was only recently returned to Belgium as a gift from the Russian authorities. It can now be found in the Koninklijk Museum van het Leger en de Krijgsgeschiedenis, Brussels.
14 Léon de Paeuw, *La Rééducation Professionnelle des Grands Blessés de Guerre et l'Institut Militaire Belge de Rééducation Professionnelle de Port-Villez-les-Vernon (Eure)* (Port-Villez: Imp. I.M.B.R.P., 1916), 23.
15 De Paeuw, *La Rééducation Professionnelle des Soldats Mutilés*, 48-50; Verstraete and Van Everbroeck, *Verminkte Stilte*, 55.
16 De Paeuw, *La Rééducation Professionnelle des Soldats Mutilés*, 105; Emile Galtier-Boissière, *Larousse médical illustré de guerre* (Paris: Larousse, 1917), 317-318.
17 De Paeuw, *La Rééducation Professionnelle des Soldats Mutilés*, 114-116.
18 Ibid., 228.
19 Until February 1916, those training for administrative careers were taught in the *Institut militaire belge d'instruction des grands blessés de guerre* at Blanche Abbey in Mortain. From October 1916, this section was combined with the technical École des métiers at Port-Villez.
20 De Paeuw, *La Rééducation Professionnelle des Soldats Mutilés*, 147.
21 Stassen and Delvaux, "La rééducation agricole à l'Institut militaire belge des invalides et orphelins de la guerre à Port-Villez (Armée Belge)," *Revue interalliée pour l'étude des questions intéressant les mutilés de la guerre* 4 (1918): 375-386.
22 De Paeuw, *La Rééducation Professionnelle des Soldats Mutilés*, 139-140.
23 F. Thiébaut, *La Rééducation Professionnelle des Invalides de la Guerre à l'Institut Militaire Belge de Port-Villez* (Port-Villez: Imp. I.M.B.R.P., 1918), 84-85.
24 Van Avermaet, "Jongens! leert goed uw vak," *De Belgische Gebrekkelijke*, 1 October 1917, 3; Alleman, "Port-Villez. Technisch Onderwijs II," *De Belgische Verminkte*, 15 April 1918, 1.
25 These two schools were called *L'École Provinciale d'Apprentissage et Ateliers pour Estropiés et Accidentés du Travail de Charleroi* (opened in 1908) and *L'Institut Provincial Pour Estropiés du Brabant* in Brussels (opened in 1916).
26 "L'Oeuvre Nationale des Invalides de la Guerre," *L'invalide belge*, 1 June 1920, 1; Œuvre Nationale des Invalides de la Guerre, *25 ans d'activité 1919-1945* (Liège: Œuvre Nationale des Invalides de la Guerre, 1945).
27 De Paeuw, *La Rééducation Professionnelle des Soldats Mutilés*, 197; De Paeuw, *La Rééducation Professionnelle des Grands Blessés de Guerre*, 16.
28 Royal Museum of the Army and Military History, Moscow Archive Box 1814 185-14-1441.
29 Stassen, "Ontwerp voor inrichting in België van een Nationalen Dienst voor Verminkten en Gebrekkelijken van den Oorlog," *De Belgische Verminkte*, 10 May 1919, 2.
30 See for more information about these journals: Pieter Verstraete, "Remastering independence: The re-education of Belgian blinded soldiers of the Great War, 1914-1940," *Educació i Història: revista d'història de l'educació*, no.32 (2018), 257-277.
31 The archives of the Royal Palace contain a list, dated 1 April 1938, in which every war-blinded man who was then known is listed by name: Liste des Aveugles de Guerre (Liste au 1er avril 1928)//AE806//Archives Palais Royales). This list contains only the names of war-blinded military servicemen, although undoubtedly there were also civilians who became blind as a result of their war-service. We have not been able to find any further information about this.

32 Samuel De Vriendt, *Croquis, schetsen, sketches* (Boitsfort: Institut des Aveugles de Guerre, 1919).
33 The history of blind people in Belgium badly needs to be written. Senator Alexander Rodenbach was blind himself and fought hard against existing misconceptions about blind people. For an introduction to the history of blindness in France see Zina Weygand, *Vivre sans voir: les aveugles dans la societé française, du Moyen Age au siècle de Louis Braille* (Paris: Creaphis Editions, 2003).
34 "Bij onze blinden soldaten," *De Belgische Verminkte*, 15 May 1918, 3.
35 Pieter Verstraete, "Disability, Rehabilitation and the Great War: Making Space for Silence in the History of Education," in *Educational Research: The Importance and Effects of Institutional Spaces*, ed. Paul Smeyers and Marc Depaepe (Amsterdam: Springer, 2013), 107.
36 Letter from the Queen's private secretary to Velge, Cabinet Chief of the Ministry of Economic Affairs (Minister Jaspar),Queen Elisabeth, Archives, no.134 (Royal Archives, Brussels).
37 Confidential file on Isidore Van Vlasselaere, Queen Elisabeth Archives, no. AE 806 (Royal Archives, Brussels).
38 Confidential file on Julien Dhont, Queen Elisabeth Archives no. AE 806 (Royal Archives, Brussels).
39 Between February 2012 and 8 April 2015, a total of 15 interviews were conducted with the children or grandchildren of war-disabled soldiers of the Great War.
40 Interview with the Stas family, 27 February 2012.
41 Interview with Maria de Blaere and Martine Van Daele, 23 May 2015.
42 Sarah Rose, *No right to be idle: The invention of disability, 1840s-1930s* (Chapel Hill, NC: UNC Press Books, 2017), 221-222.

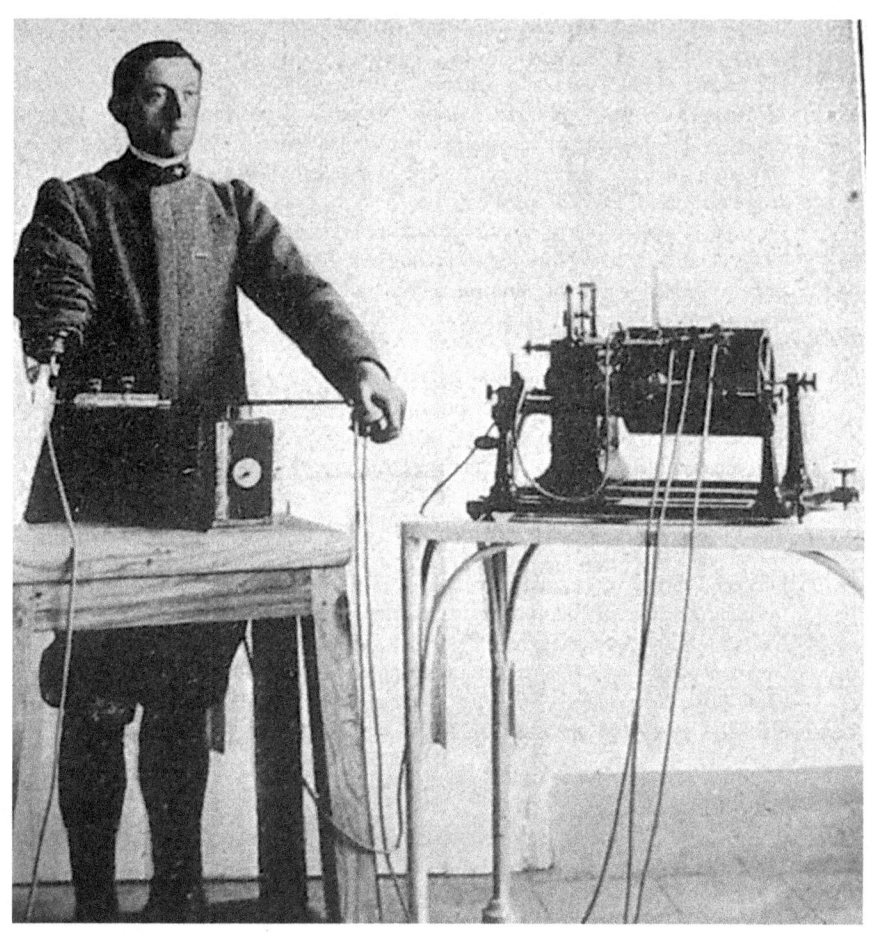

Fig. 1. Workshop for professional re-orientation in the Finzi Ottolenghi Refuge. Training to use the left-hand. Riccardo Galeazzi, *L'Italia provvede ai suoi figli mutilati in guerra*, Milano: Tipografia del Corriere della sera, 1916, p.5.

Back to work

Riccardo Galeazzi's Work for the Mutilated Veterans of the Great War, Between German Model and Italian Approach

Simonetta Polenghi

The question of disabled veterans of the Great War has many aspects: the surgical advancements stimulated by the war; the post-war social reintegration of invalid ex-service men; their political role; the social acceptance of disfigured bodies. All European countries shared a huge number of dead and disabled, to the extent that the interwar period has been described as a process of collective mourning.[1] The integration of maimed veterans was not only a medical, political and economic question, but also a cultural and educational one. Belonging to a country that had won or lost the war was a key point. In France and in England the community supported invalid veterans, who were recognised as symbols of national strength.[2] In the Weimar Republic, on the other hand, they became a symbol of defeat. So whereas the welfare policy in favour of war invalids was very poor in France and England but the social recognition was high, in Germany the war's victims were totally protected and integrated in the work system, but were also socially marginalised by the community, not being recognised with visible rituals of thanksgiving. Being considered victims of the war instead of heroes, they incarnated the humiliation of the defeat in their shattered limbs, rather than the pride of courage.[3]

This paper focuses on the Italian case in general, and on the work of the Italian orthopaedist Riccardo Galeazzi (1866-1952) in particular. Galeazzi's pioneering work for the rehabilitation of maimed soldiers and his ideas on repairing bodies as well as minds will be compared to the approach of the German orthopaedist Konrad Biesalski (1868-1930). The latter was one of those doctors and orthopaedists who did not confine their work to medical cure, but extended it to educational care and social provision, an approach deemed progressive at the time. To illustrate the relationship and the difference between these two giants in the field we will first go back to their attitude towards born cripples[4]. We will underline Galeazzi's debt to Biesalski, but also his originality, particularly in the role played by work in education and rehabilitation and in repairing not just bodies, but also minds.

German Educational Views On Cripples' Education: Biesalski and Würtz

When Germany declared war, Biesalski was already the reference point for cripples' education. Paediatrician, orthopaedist, surgeon, he cared about the destiny of the lame and the cripple. He was the author of an analytical census about young cripples published in 1906. The study showed that nearly 100,000 young Germans (under 15 years old) were deformed, a number that meant that the total number of cripples in Germany, young and adult, rose to circa 500,000.[5] In spite of the fact that Germany could boast the first school for crippled boys (*Technische Industrieanstalt für krüppelhafte Kinder*), opened in 1832 in Munich by Johann Nepomuk Edler von Kurz with private means and taken over by the Bavarian State in 1844 (now named *Königliche Zentralanstalt für Erziehung und Bildung krüppelhafte Kinder*),[6] the number of homes for lame, paralysed and deformed people in Germany was limited to 39. Only 3,371 places were therefore available, a hugely inadequate number. In 1906 in Berlin Biesalski opened his Home for the cure and education of cripples (*Krüppel-, Heil- und Erziehungsanstalt für Berlin-Brandenburg*, then named *Oskar-Helene-Heim*)[7] that became famous, thanks also to the work of the teacher Hans Würtz (1875-1958), who joined Biesalski in 1911.

Biesalski advocated social provision and legal recognition for crippled people and spread his ideas in the German Union for the Cure of the Cripples (*Deutschen Vereinigung für Krüppelfürsorge*), founded in 1909, in which he soon became a leading figure. He strongly defended the right of deformed people to be considered "infirm", but also to receive special education and job training. He rejected mere assistance and believed in the importance of linking medical and surgical therapies with educational action in special and vocational schools in order to make cripples able to earn their living. He eventually managed to see his ideas materialise in the German Law of 6 May 1920. This law accepted his definition of cripples as infirm, thus eventually recognising their right to receive help from the state.[8]

Biesalski distinguished between the feeble minded, who could not reason properly and therefore could not work, and cripples, who could not work because of physical deformation. It was thus possible to train the latter in order to enable them to earn their living instead of begging. They would be recognised as citizens, since they would be taxed like other healthy people. Darwinist conceptions crept in in the idea of "useful" and "non-useful" people, who were a burden for society. Being able to support themselves and to pay taxes was for Biesaslki the way for cripples to obtain equality. Striving towards this aim, he believed that not only had the deformed body to be cured, but the soul too. In this respect he was influenced by Würtz, who was the theorist of the *Krüppelpädagogik*. Würtz thought healthy people were utterly different from deformed ones, whose souls were crippled as well as their bodies.[9] The disfigurement of their bodies was so bad that it altered their way of thinking and of perceiving the world. According to him, every departure from normal wellbeing clouded the person's self-esteem so that crippled people ended up with typical character traits: egocentrism, feelings of discrimination and impairment, morbid sensitivity, irritability, envy, mistrust, intransigence, harsh self-assertion.[10]

These "weaknesses of the soul" made the cripple envious of healthy people and incapable of living in society, whereas work could redeem the deformed man, giving sense to his life and putting him in a condition to bear life's struggles with healthy men. According to Würtz's *Krüppelpädagogik* only years of segregation in special school-homes could mould crippled children's souls: inside the school progressive education was applied, but children had to live segregated for years to be able to enter into society when adults.[11]

Biesalski and Würtz and the *Kriegskrüppel* Re-education

As soon as the war started, Biesalski began to act for the mutilated soldiers. Already in September 1914 welfare services for invalid soldiers were opened up everywhere in Germany. In November 1914, four months after the start of hostilities, Germany had more than 2,500 places for the cure of maimed soldiers. The Oscar-Helene-Heim offered 100 beds for the treatment of the seriously injured. A workshop for prosthesis-making was opened in the Oscar-Helene-Heim, as well as a school for soldier amputees, where two teachers were mutilated soldiers.

In 1917 the number of German disabled soldiers had already reached one million.[12] The burden for the state, in terms of pensions and welfare, was enormous (not taking civilian invalids into account). Before World War I, invalid soldiers who received a pension lived in centres far from cities, segregated from society. If they worked they would lose their pensions. Biesalski was firmly opposed to this concept. He travelled all over Germany and held countless conferences proving the necessity of making the mutilated able to go back to work and regain their place in society. According to Biesalski what threatened rehabilitation was not the severity of the injury, but rather the manner in which the maimed was perceived and treated by the general public.[13]

Returning to work was important for the economic independence of the amputee as well as for the prosperity of the nation. In 1915 Biesalski wrote a pamphlet on the subject, stressing the importance of both orthopaedic care and vocational training, which had enormous success. In 1916 140,000 copies had already been sold, and it was translated into Hungarian, Slovenian, Polish, Bulgarian and Turkish.[14] The Oscar-Helene-Heim was recognised as a model institute in Germany and abroad.[15] In 1916 Würtz published an article on the example of a train driver who lost an arm and with great determination managed to build himself an artificial arm that worked so well that after an official medical examination he was allowed to go back to work. Moreover, he could see to his kitchen garden and carry on a normal life as a husband and father.[16] Würtz underlined the importance of man's will – the article's title was "The will wins!".

But the examples of the war-mutilated gradually outnumbered those of civilian invalids, so that after the war the former came to overshadow those born crippled, as Würtz lamented in 1925.[17] But Würtz himself had to some extent contributed to this change, for when describing historical and literary examples of crippled people Würtz had exhibited a rather ambivalent attitude, both describing as heroes war amputees, like Götz von Berlichingen, who carried on fighting, and depicting as morally deformed and antisocial other cripples, such as Richard III and Lord Byron, thus distinguishing between those whose healthy bodies were deformed in adult years and those born cripples.[18]

The massive presence of war cripples required a shift in mental attitude and linguistic choice, for the war invalids could not be seen as morally guilty and deceptive by birth; quite the opposite, they had to be honoured for their sacrifice for the nation. In Germany, the use of the word cripple (*Krüppel*) for war invalids (*Kriegskrüppel*) had its difficulties, since the word *Krüppel* was perceived as a negative, "with a hideous sound" (it was a swearword in South Germany), so much that Biesalski asked to turn to other European languages and use more neutral words, like *Kriegsgeschädigt* (war-damaged) or *Kriegsinvalide*. The change was not easy, so that Biesalsky and Würtz decided to reverse the discourse, altering the perception of the word *Krüppel* and making it a positive one. Whereas the concept of the deformed man was associated with being unable to work and being a beggar, possibly with a nasty soul, it had now to remind people of heroic attitude, iron will and the ability to go back to work: it had to become a name of honour.[19] This did not actually happen.

The Weimar Republic, with the national Pension Law of 1920, was actually the European state that spent the most on invalid veterans (between 1922 and 1932 war pensions accounted for nearly 20% of total governmental spending).[20] Nonetheless, it failed to win their gratitude, for economic support was not the only answer to the needs of mutilated soldiers, who asked for social recognition as well, recognition also linked to a cultural attitude.[21] National Socialism publicly recognised and distinguished mutilated soldiers and presented them as heroes for their sacrifice (*Opferhelden*). Nevertheless images of severely wounded war cripples were censored, and only mild images of superficially wounded heroes were allowed.[22]

Galeazzi, Director of the Pious Institute for Rickets Sufferers of Milan

In Italy, the Pious Institute for Rickets Sufferers (*Pio Istituto dei rachitici*), now the Orthopaedic Hospital (*Istituto Ortopedico Gaetano Pini*), was founded in 1874 in Milan by Dr. Gaetano Pini (1846-1887), a leading figure of the Italian democratic wing of Free-masonry and a patriot (he had fought with Garibaldi).[23] Pini stressed many times that cripples were clever, but remained illiterate, not being able to attend school. He used to quote the example of Giacomo Leopardi, the great Italian poet, who was a hunchback, to prove what a profound mind a deformed man could have. Pini challenged the traditional idea of a correspondence between physical imperfection and corruption of the soul.

Pini managed to raise money from rich and poor people, masons, liberal and Catholic, intellectuals, noblemen, shopkeepers and banks: the Milanese were known for their philanthropic attitude. The Institute directed by Pini opened in 1875 as a special school for crippled children aged 4-10, where they received both medical cures and educational instruction, following the state programme for primary schools. This school rapidly became a model and acquired international fame.

After Pini's death in 1877, the Board of the Institute appointed Pietro Panzeri (1849-1901) as the new director. Panzeri, who had also fought with Garibaldi, was a skilful surgeon. In 1884 he obtained the lectureship (*libera docenza*) on orthopaedics at the University of Pavia – the very first chair of orthopaedics in Italy. In 1884 he founded the first Italian review of orthopaedics, *Archivio di ortopedia*.

In 1896 the Orthopaedic Hospital of Bologna, the Rizzoli Institute, was opened, thanks to private investors, and Panzeri was appointed director. He died prematurely in 1901, and in 1903 Riccardo Galeazzi – after a competitive procedure – became director of the Pious Institute of Milan. Born in 1866 in Turin, in 1899 he had obtained the lectureship (*libera docenza*) in surgery.[24] He remained as director until his retirement in 1937.

In 1903 Galeazzi also became director of the review *Archivio di ortopedia*, an office he held for 35 years. Already in his first three years Galeazzi managed to restructure and renew the infirmaries and the surgical theatres and to build new wards. A big new ward, with an autonomous operating theatre, was dedicated to paying patients.

Thanks to the money coming from private patients the Institute eventually gained the desired economic viability.[25]

In this way, the Institute got bigger and reserved more space for adults, while still keeping its paediatric unit. The school for rachitic children became the *Asilo Mylius*, where only the youngest (2-5 years) and worst affected children were admitted. [26] Since rickets were now diagnosed early, rachitic children could integrate in normal schools, but for many others this was not the case. So Galeazzi in 1908 opened the home and school for lame, mutilated and paralysed children (*Scuola di lavoro per storpi, mutilati e paralitici Sofia Carmine Speroni*), and in doing so realised Pini's dream of a vocational school for young cripples and the mutilated. The young patients received prosthetic limbs, too. Since his arrival Galeazzi had opened a little workshop for prosthesis-making inside the Institute, thus putting into effect Panzeri's wish. Thanks to an agreement with the City Council, the Institute provided artificial limbs and orthopaedic aids for all the mutilated and crippled poor of Milan and the surrounding areas. The Pious Institute, together with the Rizzoli Institute, became a leading prosthesis centre. Galeazzi was particularly concerned with kinematic prostheses. Even if at the time that kind of prosthesis was still not very well developed and posed surgical, medical, training and rehabilitation problems, he was convinced it was the right solution and kept working on it.[27]

In 1906 the Institute gained the status of orthopaedic clinic in the recently founded post-graduate clinics in Milan.[28] In 1911 Galeazzi was appointed full professor of orthopaedics. The Institute and its director rapidly acquired international fame. In 1910 the Institute received the Grand Prix at the International Exhibition of Buenos Aires.[29]

Galeazzi's Educational Views on Cripples and the German Model

Galeazzi was a man of culture who had very up-to-date knowledge of the orthopaedic world, read the main foreign literature and attended international congresses. He knew of the German census carried out by Biesalski in 1906, which he had already quoted from extensively in his inaugural lecture for the academic year 1906-07.[30] In 1910 he took part in the first congress on the cure of cripples organised by the *Deutschen Vereinigung für Krüppelfürsorge*, representing Milan's Institute,[31] and when Biesalski died in 1930 he wrote a long and stirring obituary notice in his *Archivio di ortopedia*. He admired not only the brilliant orthopaedist, but – and perhaps even more – the socially engaged doctor and his invaluable work for cripples, saying that not only in Germany but in the entire world orthopaedists "shall always bow in reverence of his memory and shall always refer to his admirable example of scientific hard-working, of never ending charity and goodness in favour of so many forgotten by nature".[32] From Galeazzi's words it is clear that he knew Biesalski personally – he also remembered his dead colleague's human qualities, such as his courtesy, his patience with other people's mistakes and his great heart.

Galeazzi sometimes used language that echoed Darwinism and the *Krüppelpädagogik*; orthopaedics had a social aim, he said for instance in 1907, for not only did it cure bodily deficiencies, it also prevented diseases and deformities with the use of physical training and gymnastics, so that it managed to "uplift the level of the average body and increase the individual's vital energy, to make him stronger in the struggle for existence".[33] He too spoke of work as "regenerative" and of begging as "degrading", and defined the professional schools for the crippled as necessary for reasons of social order, morality, public security, as well as of charity and humanity.[34] However, Galeazzi's pedagogy did not consider the soul, the intellect and the heart of a cripple as the mirror of their deformed body. He rather indicated that a lack of education and moral misery were the causes of their way of thinking. In fact, Galeazzi, like Pini before him, stressed that crippled children could not attend public schools, since they often could not walk and, even if they could, they remained unemployed afterwards because of the revulsion at employing deformed persons. So they were condemned by society to begging and misery. True enough, cripples might be rancorous, liars and haters of other men, but not from birth: these behaviours were consequences of the environment.[35] The special school had not only to develop the intellectual faculties, it had also and above all to educate the character, with individual teaching, proper tools and prostheses, particularly the kinematic ones.

Galeazzi, like Pini, recognised the importance of parental links and therefore, whenever possible, of letting crippled children live at home, whereas the German approach claimed that it was necessary to provide homes for cripples, at which attendance was compulsory. Galeazzi used Darwinian language that echoed Biesalski and Würtz when he said that cripples should learn, through intense discipline and an individual technique, not to be overwhelmed by healthy persons, their paramount aim being to prove themselves to be equals. One can often catch the influence of Biesalski in Galeazzi's works: in the definition of the cripple as a sick man who needed a medical cure and social welfare; in the refusal to have a merely passive charity; in the pedagogical concept of work as a source of liberation. One can also trace Würtz's *Krüppelpsychologie* in Galeazzi's words, when he too defined the deformed man as one whose character had been hopelessly corrupted by society, which turned him in a morally despicable person, a selfish, nasty liar.

Yet, if he owed much to Biesalski and Würtz, Galeazzi seems less closed to a positivistic anthropology. For Galeazzi the key to cripples' redemption was indeed work, but he did not limit the meaning of work to the economic aspect. He aimed at giving cripples the cultural and social capacity of being independent. Nevertheless working did not simply coincide with earning a living. The worst affected cripples could not reach economic independence by their work and needed life-long assistance. Nonetheless, Galeazzi thought work was the means of giving them some dignity. By working (not necessarily by earning enough to be independent) a disabled person proved his own dignity: it was not the final product of work that counted (even if Galeazzi stressed that many times cripples managed to produce items by no means inferior to those made by normal workers), it was the sheer act of working, and the effort it implied, that gave people back human dignity. He clearly said it was not a question of the economic value of men, but a moral question that a civilised state could not refuse to face; "even if little or none were the product of the [cripple's] work", it would nonetheless be worthwhile and just to teach and provide him with an occupation, for that gave him "the moral satisfaction, which derives from having completed something useful. Consequently, from this point of view the question whether the economic value of the cripples' product compensates society for the expenditures it has to face to support them, is of secondary importance".[36]

Working without one or two limbs often meant constant fatigue, and required a "discipline" that through the years shaped the will. Galeazzi believed that "the re-generative influence of work" came from this acquired self-discipline, which proved that the disabled were not inferior to others.[37] He believed in a "defects-compensating pedagogy" and stressed that "incredible results could be obtained by developing the faculties of adaptation and compensation".[38] By describing this pedagogy as "compensatory", Galeazzi anticipated the work of the Russian psychiatrist Lev Vygotskji (1896-1934), but he may well have known it from Sante De Sanctis (1862-1935), the father of Italian child psychiatry (a friend of Montessori (1870-1952), who was developing it in the same period) or from Alfred Adler (1870-1937). The concept had also long been familiar in blind and deaf-mute education.[39]

Mutilated Soldiers: Re-education to Work and Prosthetics

Italy joined the war on 24 May 1915. Galeazzi, who was a true patriot, volunteered as a medical colonel, thus obtaining the officer status that would make it easier for him to deal with the army authorities. Between April and June 1915 he obtained from the Board of the Institute permission to transfer the *Casa di lavoro Ottolenghi* in Gorla (a little municipality outside Milan), originally planned for civilian invalids, to military sanitary authority.[40] The *Casa di lavoro Ottolenghi* was a villa with a vast garden, donated to the Pious Institute by the rich philanthropic countess Fanny Finzi Ottolenghi. Galeazzi agreed to be the unpaid director of the *Casa di lavoro Ottolenghi*, which was turned into a "retraining school" for war cripples, called the

Finzi Ottolenghi Refuge. Thanks to an agreement with the Ministry of War, a nearby military orthopaedic hospital was quickly opened, on 18 September 1915. Amputee soldiers came to the military orthopaedic hospital after having been operated on in other hospitals. Their stumps were seen to and artificial limbs were fitted. When the physical treatment was completed, the patient started occupational retraining in the nearby Ottolenghi Refuge.

Galeazzi's work for disabled veterans was tireless and his ideas were ahead of his time.[41] In 1915 he started organising conferences on maimed veterans' rehabilitation, in Milan and in other cities and published articles, booklets and brochures on the topic.[42] His model of assistance was the German one, and Biesalski remained a point of reference, despite the fact that Germany was now an enemy nation. Galeazzi in fact boasted that already in prewar Germany there were 54 industrial schools for the lame and cripples, with 221 workshops teaching 51 job skills. Six months after the outbreak of the war the number of these schools had already jumped to 138. They were modelled on the Industrial school of Münich.[43] Galeazzi already knew the German situation well, but obviously could not visit the enemy country during the war. Instead, he went to France and visited various institutes and retraining schools. He considered the Belgian school at Port-Villez to be the best for its scientific character.[44] Indeed in the Port-Villez Institute limbless veterans underwent a medical, pedagogical and technical examination to establish the inclination, strength and capabilities those men had.[45] He thought England and Russia had good models of welfare networks, which could be turned into centres for maimed veterans. He noticed that in France, where war disabled were free to decide whether or not to join a work rehabilitation programme, only 10% of them entered the retraining schools: thus, he thought this had to be made compulsory. Also Sir Robert Jones, whose work for mutilated British soldiers was immense, thought that discharging veterans into civil life without rehabilitation was wrong.[46] Actually, the Italian law of 1917 on disabled veterans prescribed only 15 days of compulsory stay in a school of re-education, and that only for indigent soldiers.[47] The official results confirmed Galeazzi's view: the disabled who had undergone re-education managed more easily to find a place in society, whereas those who had rejected that period tended to become passive.[48]

His ideas came from his conception of crippled people and his previous work for them, and were applied by him in the Ottolenghi retraining school for war cripples, which soon became a national model, as did that of Bologna. The Ottolenghi retraining school rehabilitated circa 500 men every year – totalling more than 2,500 men in the war years.[49] The war amputated had to stay until they were declared ready to go back to their families, when able to cope with their prostheses at the end of the training period. The school had 100 beds. It was run by the Board of the Pious Institute of Rickets Sufferers. Its discipline was military, with medical officers, but there were also nuns and civilian personnel. The Minister of War, the Milanese Committee for war needs and the Lombardy Committee for the Mutilated financially supported the Ottolenghi school.[50]

In the Ottolenghi school Galeazzi set up an experimental laboratory, where individual work and resistance coefficients (the capacity to carry on muscular activity for a determined length of time) of every mutilated soldier were empirically studied and improved, thanks to the rational training of the mutilated or weakened limb. Special training was provided for those who had lost their right arms and had to become left-handed (Fig. 1).

Eventually the veteran was trained to work with the artificial limb and began vocational training.[51] The loss of lower limbs was less problematic than amputation of arms: leg prostheses were in fact rather good and allowed walking and the climbing of stairs, whereas it was not possible to reproduce hands' complex functions.[52] In 1919 it was calculated that 12,289 Italians had lost upper limbs and 19,347 had suffered leg amputation.[53]

Galeazzi kept working at kinetic and functional prostheses for work, trying to reduce their functional inadequacies.[54] The orthopaedic workshop produced new prostheses for upper and lower limbs, also improving the Vanghetti Kineplasty hand (in 1898 Giuliano Vanghetti had constructed an artificial limb that moved using muscle contractions).

In 1916 the orthopaedic workshop of the Pious Institute could no longer cope with the increasing number of requests for prostheses. Utterly appalled by the potential danger of speculation on prosthesis, and knowing that their price in Italy was already higher than in other countries (industrial production did not exist), Galeazzi collected funds (60,000 lire) for the opening in Gorla of the National Prosthesis Workshop for mutilated soldiers, which was recognised by Royal Decree on 24 February 1916.[55] This National Workshop was industrial and scientific in character and was supervised by orthopaedists. It occupied a big area, of 2,200 square metres and produced leather, wood and fibre aids. In wartime it employed 200 workmen and was the leading Italian prosthesis workshop.[56] Artificial arms with special fittings to match types of industrial machinery were produced as well.

In the Ottolenghi school the illiterate were taught to read and write. When possible, the veterans were trained to go back to their previous workplaces, but that was only rarely possible. Often another type of work was suggested in accordance with the patient's remaining capacities and the results of the abovementioned experimental laboratory. Vocational teachers and officers helped the veterans to find the professions and the training most suitable for them.[57] There were four barracks with workshops for carpenters, tailors, clog and shoemakers, wicker basket makers, leather workers, sculptors in wood and saddlers (Fig. 2).

Farmers, too, were taught how to work with an artificial limb (the majority of soldiers were peasants: 60% of the amputees according to Galeazzi's experience, but

85% of disabled veterans according to official statistics of 1918).⁵⁸ The more cultivated invalids learned other professions in order to enter the post office or other state or private offices. This more advanced intellectual teaching was carried out in the Institute of the Marcelline Nuns. There was practical training in firms, too. Others had art lessons in the Academy of Fine Arts of Brera.⁵⁹

Fig 2. Shoemaker school for mutilated soldiers in the Finzi Ottolenghi Refuge. Riccardo Galeazzi, *L'Italia provvede ai suoi figli mutilati in guerra*, Milano: Tipografia del Corriere della sera, 1916, p.7

Galeazzi explained that six months were usually enough to complete the rehabilitation, which was carried on, as for young cripples, through the "regenerating" power of work (in fact in other Italian schools a year was the average period).⁶⁰ He stressed the importance of rapid intervention: straight after the mutilation, in fact, the disabled became very depressed. It was essential to fight the depression, and this was possible when they lived together with other mutilated soldiers, whose success could be seen. Residence in hospitals had to be reduced to the minimum, and crippled soldiers were rapidly (and compulsory) shifted to industrial schools, where the best teachers were veterans. Through work and thanks to the example of other veterans, it would be possible to overcome the horror of the mutilation. Sharing the same sorrow and efforts would make the maimed soldiers brothers in a deep sense: the retraining school was "a truly human school, because it respects the principle of social equality, that brings close the weak and the stout in a brotherly harmony [...] with the active cooperation of millions of citizens".⁶¹

Galeazzi advocated military discipline in the retraining schools, but he insisted on the necessity of opening many schools in order to let the mutilated be as close to their families as possible. He thought it would be desirable to reintegrate them into working society and to let them stay with sane people, whose gratitude would be a moral comfort. They also had to be free to leave the school to go to the cinema and to enjoy some entertainment. Amputees had to go out: no shame or pity for them, but pride.[62] Others feared that the impact of the sight of a mutilated soldier could produce revulsion against the war rather than encouragement to join the army. There was no fear of defeatism in Galeazzi, who was a patriot who kept insisting on society's moral duty to maimed soldiers. Indeed Italy followed this model in many schools for occupational re-education throughout the country, thanks to the involvement of citizens and local boards, institutions, local authorities and state finance. Galeazzi's system of "moral re-education" and his school, the very first to be scientifically organised in Italy, were put forward as models for all of Italy by medical captain Giovanni Selvi as early as in 1916.[63] Galeazzi also stressed the importance of female presence in the hospitals in the form of the nurse: women had a particularly well developed sense of mercy that could effuse a sense of peace in the highly distressed souls of men far from their families.[64]

As mentioned above, Galeazzi thought that work was necessary not just to give economic independence, but to restore human dignity. Indeed he immediately asked the state to provide mutilated veterans with an invalidity pension as soon as possible, before their prostheses were ready, and also to provide them with training for work and give them jobs in the state administration and offices. He often referred to the Industrial Home and School for Lame, Mutilated and Paralysed Children, which had opened in 1908, as an example because there the orthopaedist advised on what kind of jobs young cripples could be taught to do, on the basis both of the body's capabilities and problems and the children's character and psychology.

As for those invalids whose condition was so severe that independent living was impossible, occupational retraining was nonetheless to be done. Even if they could not earn enough to live on, they were not to be deprived of work and its moral value, as Galeazzi had already argued for the civilian disabled. All invalids had to be given both a pension and the chance to work. He advocated state welfare, as well as philanthropy: citizens too had to be involved. This position was similar to that proposed by Salvatore Galgano, professor of civil law at the University of Naples who, in 1919, stressed the importance of making the war disabled able to help themselves (with microcredit, cooperatives of the mutilated, payment facilities for buying wares or work tools, etc.). Their motto was to be "back to work" instead of perpetual welfare.[65] For Galeazzi and Galgano the state, civil society and the disabled themselves should work together.

In Italy local participation was high and committees for assistance to veterans spread everywhere in 1915-16 until, on 25 March 1917, Law n.481 unified them in the National Institution for War Disabled (ONIG) and on 29 April the disabled veterans themselves set up in Milan their own association (ANMIG, *Associazione Nazionale Mutilati e Invalidi di Guerra*), which in 1918 had 20,000 members, soon rising to

30,000.⁶⁶ The 1917 Law also gave the ONIG the task of facilitating the reintroduction of disabled veterans into the world of work, but only by Law n.1312 of 21 August 1920 were public services compelled to employ war invalids.⁶⁷ Invalid ex-servicemen were represented in the war propaganda and in the aftermath in school texts, posters and magazines as men worthy of respect and honour.⁶⁸

Galeazzi himself also set up the local committee for the assistance of mutilated soldiers and was made responsible for the occupational retraining schools; he published many scientific works on artificial limbs, prostheses and rehabilitation and held many meetings with military physicians about artificial limbs and rehabilitation; he worked with Lavinia Mondolfo, who in Milan looked after the blind veterans and their occupational retraining and advocated their rights.⁶⁹ In 1916 the Prime Minister appointed Galeazzi a member of the royal board which was set up to study assistance for and the re-education of mutilated, crippled and blinded soldiers. During the war he was member of the executive board of the ONIG.⁷⁰ Galeazzi was also often heard as expert in the special committee of the Chamber of Deputies in Rome.

The End of the War: Conclusions

After the war Galeazzi was appointed a member of the inter-allied conference on the aftercare of disabled men: he played an active part in the conferences in Paris and London and in 1920 chaired the conferences in Lisbon, Rome and Brussels. In Paris he was finally hailed as honorary chairman.⁷¹

In 1921 the Ottolenghi Refuge in Gorla ceased to function. In 1924 the *Casa di lavoro Ottolenghi* for civilian crippled was reactivated, as originally planned. The question of the war mutilated was now a social and political one, no longer a surgical and rehabilitative one. The Pious Institute in Milan, along with the Rizzoli Institute in Bologna, represented a leading source of experience in Italy and abroad, which had been strengthened during the Great War. In 1923 the prestigious American review, *The Journal of Bone and Joint Surgery*, pointed to the two as two of the best centres in Europe.⁷²

It has been noted that the success of a retraining school for mutilated veterans was strictly dependent on its director's personality, his attitudes, his teaching practice, his competence and his moral authority.⁷³ Galeazzi certainly had the right personality. He was as fervent a patriot as Pini and Panzeri, but politically conservative, whereas his predecessor had followed democratic left-wing trend. He shared with his two predecessors a strong belief in human dignity. He never distinguished between once healthy men who had suffered amputation and those who had been born crippled, defending the rights of both and stressing the importance of work as a means of respecting the dignity of men and women (it is worth noting that only in 1966 did the Italian state award pensions to people born with a severe physical disability). He admired Biesalski but surpassed his ideas of rehabilitation and work, conferring a moral value to them and not just an economic one. Therefore repairing a permanently injured body did not necessarily imply returning to the workforce and regaining economic independence (desirable but not always possible) but it always entailed the restoration of human dignity.

Notes

1. Jay M. Winter, *Sites of Memory, Sites of Mourning: The Great War in European Cultural History* (Cambridge: Cambridge University Press 1995).
2. See: Antoine Prost, *Les anciens combattants et la société française: 1914-1939* (Paris: Gallimard 1977; new edition 2014; English ed. 1992); Deborah Cohen, *The War come Home. Disabled Veterans in Britain and Germany, 1914-1939* (Berkely etc., CA: California University Press, 2001); Jeffrey S. Reznick, *Healing the Nation: Soldiers, Caregivers and British Identity During World War I* (Manchester: Manchester University Press, 2005); Julie Anderson, *War, Disability, and Rehabilitation in Britain: 'Soul of a Nation'* (Manchester: Manchester University Press, 2011). On men's identity and the war disabled in England, see: Joanna Bourke, *Dismembering the Male: Men's Bodies, Britains and the Great War* (London: Reaktion Books 1996).
3. On the causes of anti-Weimar feelings of war mutilated solders, see: Robert Weldon Whalen, *Bitter Wounds. German Victims of the Great War, 1914-1939* (Ithaca, NY, & London: Cornell University Press, 1984); Nils Löffelbein, "The Legacy of the Front: The Disabled Veterans of the First World War in Germany after 1918," in *New Political Ideas in the Aftermath of the Great War*, eds. Alessandro Salvador and Anders G. Kjøstvedt (New York: Palgrave Macmillan, 2017), 175-197; Cohen, *The War come Home;* and particularly Sabine Kienitz, *Beschädigte Helden. Kriegsinvalidität und Körperbilder 1914-1923* (Paderborn: Schöningh, 2008), which takes into account war invalids' identities and questions Cohen's interpretation.
4. In contemporary scholarship and writing about people with disabilities it is politically correct to use person-first terminology. Nevertheless it was decided to use the term "cripple" throughout this chapter. This choice is motivated by the wish to stay as close as possible to the original German word *Krüppel* which was commonly used during the interwar period to denote persons with physical disabilities in general and physically disabled soldiers in particular. While sticking to the original term, however, we by no means intend to linguistically discriminate persons living today with any kind of physical disability or reproduce any of the negative power-relations that came to be intimately connected to the term since the advent of the disability movement and the corresponding social-constructivist interpretations of disability.
5. Petra Fuchs, *"Körperbehinderte" Zwischen Selbstaufgabe und Emanzipation: Selbsthilfe-Integration-Aussonderung* (Neuwied-Berlin: Luchterhand, 2001), 28.
6. Hans Stadler, "Die Unterrichts- und Beschäftigungsanstalt für krüppelhafte Kinder des Edlen von Kurz in München," in *Pädagogik bei Körperbehinderung*, eds. Hans Stadler and Udo Wilken (Weinheim: Beltz, 2004), 46-81.
7. Philipp Osten, *Die Modellanstalt: über den Aufbau einer "modernen Krüppelfürsorge" 1905-1933* (Frankfurt a.M.: Mabuse Verlag, 2012); Heather Perry, *Recycling the Disabled: Army, Medicine and Modernity in WW1 Germany* (London: Oxford University Press, 2014), 25-26.
8. Fuchs, *"Körperbehinderte,"* 40-45.
9. Ibid., 20-65; Hans Stadler, "Überkonfessionelle und staatliche Krüppelfürsorge," in *Pädagogik bei Körperbehinderung*, eds. Stadler and Wilken,194-248; Philipp Osten, "Die Modellanstalt; a critical and documented approach to Würtz's pedagogy," in *Der Körperbehindertenpädagoge Hans Würtz (1875-1958). Eine kritische Würdigung des psychologischen und pädagogischen Konzepts vor dem Hintergrund seiner Biographie*, ed. Oliver Musenberg (Hamburg: Kovač, 2002).

10   Hans Würtz, *Das Seelenleben des Krüppels: krüppelseelenkundliche Erziehung und das Gesetz betr. öffentliche Krüppelfürsorge* (Leipzig: Voß, 1921), 4.
11   Fuchs, "*Körperbehinderte,*" 60; Stadler, Überkonfessionelle, 194-248.
12   Luise Merkens, *Fürsorge und Erziehung bei Körperbehinderten: eine historische Grundlegung zur Körperbehindertenpädagogik bis 1920* (Berlin [West]: Marhold, 1981), 114.
13   On the efforts of Biesalski to restore the capabilities of disabled soldiers, see: Perry, *Recycling the Disabled*, 36-37, 91, 94, 118-119, 124-126.
14   Fuchs, "*Körperbehinderte*", 36-37.
15   Osten, *Die Modellanstalt*.
16   Hans Würtz, "Der Wille siegt!," *Kriegsbeschädigten-Fürsorge in Niedersachsen*, 23 December 1916, 329-331; Cf. Perry, *Recycling the Disabled*, 128-129.
17   Kienitz, *Beschädigte Helden*, 47.
18   Würtz, *Das Seelenleben des Krüppels*, 62 and passim; Kienitz, *Beschädigte Helden*, 50-51.
19   Ibid., 113-120. On the spite and scorn shown to German cripples, see: Paul Heller, *Von der Ladeskrüppelanstalt zur Ortopädischen Universitätskilink: das "Elisabethheim" in Rostock* (Berlin, Munster: Lit, 2009), 24-25.
20   Gerald D. Feldman, *Army, Industry and Labor, 1914-1918* (Princeton, NJ: Princeton University Press, 1966), 93.
21   See above, note 3.
22   Löffelbein, "The Legacy of the Front", 184-186.
23   Simonetta Polenghi, "Gaetano Pini e l'Istituto dei Rachitici di Milano," *Archivio storico lombardo* (2005-06), 265-305; Simonetta Polenghi, *Educating the cripples. The Pious institute for rickets sufferers of Milan and its transformations (1874-1937)* (Macerata: EUM, 2009); Simonetta Polenghi, "Die Erziehung der Krüppelkinder in Italien zwischen Medizin und Pädagogik. Die Krüppelanstalt von Mailand: vom Positivismus bis zum Faschismus (1874-1937)," in *Normalität, Abnormalität und Devianz. Gesellschaftliche Konstruktionsprozesse und ihre Umwälzungen in der Moderne*, eds. Attila Nobik and Béla Pukánszky (Frankfurt a.M.: Peter Lang, 2010), 223-233.
24   On him see Simonetta Polenghi, "Raddrizzare gli arti, rieducare i mutilati. L'ortopedia di Riccardo Galeazzi all'Istituto dei Rachitici," in *Milano scientifica 1875-1924*, eds. Elena Canadelli and Paola Zocchi (Milan: Sironi editore, 2008), vol. II, *La rete del perfezionamento medico*, 217-235; Polenghi, *Educating the cripples*, 45-91; Anna Debè and Simonetta Polenghi, "Assistance and education of mutilated soldiers of World War I. The Italian case," *History of education & children's literature* 11, no. 2 (2016), 227-246.
25   The private patients' unit acquired 28,000 lire in 1905-1909 and more than 100,000 lire in 1910-1914. State Archives of Milan (ASM), *Prefettura di Milano, Archivio generale, Carteggio sino al 1937*, Serie I, file 7459, fasc. 184, Letter from Galeazzi to the Board [1916].
26   Riccardo Galeazzi, *L'Istituto dei Rachitici nel triennio 1903-1906* (Biella: Amosso, 1908).
27   Riccardo Galeazzi, *Sulla protesi cinematica* (Rome: Tip. Berterio, 1912).
28   On the Istituti clinici di perfezionamento, see: Canadelli and Zocchi, *Milano scientifica 1875-1924*.
29   Archives of the G. Pini Orthopaedics Institutes of Milan (AIOGP), *Minutes of the Board 1910-1912*, 29 November 1910.
30   Galeazzi, *I progressi dell'ortopedia moderna. Prolusione*.
31   Riccardo Galeazzi, *Die orthopädische Klinik in Mailand. Stenographischer Bericht über den 1. Deutschen Kongress für Krüppelfürsorge veranstaltet von der Deutschen*

Vereinigung für Krüppelfürsorge EV am 31 März 1910 zu Berlin (Hamburg, Leipzig: Leopold Voss, 1910), 146-155.
32 Riccardo Galeazzi, "Necrologio. Corrado Biesalski," *Archivio di ortopedia* XLVI, fasc. II (1930), 436.
33 Galeazzi, *I progressi dell'ortopedia moderna. Prolusione*, 15.
34 Galeazzi, *Relazione*, in *L'inaugurazione della scuola di Lavoro "Sofia Carmine Speroni,"* 20, 23.
35 Ibid., 19-21.
36 Ibid., 8.
37 Ibid., 19.
38 Ibid., 32-33.
39 Sante De Sanctis, "Autobiography," in *History of Psychology in Autobiography*, ed. C. Murchison (Worchester, MA: Clark University Press, 1936), 83-120; Giovanni P. Lombardo and Elisabetta Cicciola, "The Clinical Differential Approach of Sante De Sanctis in Italian 'Scientific' Psychology," *Physis* 43, no. 1-2 (2006): 443-457.
40 AIOGP, *Minutes of the Board 1913-1915*, 23 April, 5 June 1915.
41 Barbara Bracco, *La patria ferita. I corpi dei soldati italiani e la Grande Guerra* (Florence: Giunti, 2012), 86-96 points to Galeazzi's role and his ability to foresee issues concerning the rehabilitation of the war mutilated, their dignity and economic efficiency.
42 Riccardo Galeazzi, *Le moderne provvidenze sociali per i mutilati in guerra* (Milan: Rava & C., 1915); Id., *La rieducazione professionale dei lavoratori mutilati in guerra: relazione al Comitato lombardo per i soldati mutilati in guerra* (Biella: Amosso, 1916); Id., *L'Italia provvede ai suoi figli mutilati in guerra* (Milan: Tip. del Corriere della sera, 1916); Id., *Come si rieducano i soldati mutilati* (Florence: Bemporad, 1916). Galeazzi's speech to the Lombard Society of medical and biological sciences, held on 15 January 1915 in *Archivio di ortopedia* XXXIII (1916), attached to A. Galeazzi's report on "Professional re-education of war mutilated workers", which he read to the Lombardy Board for maimed soldiers on 24 October 1915 is attachment n.L.
43 Galeazzi, *Come si rieducano i soldati mutilati*, 4-5.
44 Galeazzi, *La rieducazione professionale*, XCIX. On French occupational retraining centres, see: Giovanni Chevalley, *Le scuole di rieducazione professionale dei mutilati e dei feriti in guerra in Francia* (Turin: Tip.Artigianelli, 1915), 11, who pointed out that articulated artificial limbs were not yet suitable for manual tasks, such that many mutilated people preferred to take them off when working.
45 On the Port-Villez Institute, see: Pieter Verstraete, "Disability, Rehabilitation and the Great War: Making Space for Silence in the History of Education," in *Educational Research: The Importance of Effects of Institutional Spaces*, eds. Paul Smeyers, Marc Depaepe, and Edwin Keiner (Amsterdam: Springer, 2013), 95-113.
46 David Le Vay, *The History of Orthopaedics* (Carnforth, etc.: Parthenon Publishing Group, 1990), 140.
47 Ettore Levi, "Technical Re-education in Italy, in its relation to the law for the assistance and protection of the disabled," in *Inter-allied Conference on the after care of disabled men, Second annual meeting* (London: His Majesty Stationery Office, 1918), 151. See also Giovanni Chevalley, "Technical Re-education in Italy," ibid., 138-150.
48 Levi, "Technical Re-education in Italy," 156.
49 Riccardo Galeazzi, *Curriculm vitae*, 1933, in Centro Apice – Historical archives of the University of Milan, *Archivio proprio, Ufficio personale, Fascicoli del personale cessato*, fasc. 1408.

50 See Giovanni Giachi, "Milano per i lavoratori mutilati in guerra," *Archivio di ortopedia* XXXIII (1916), III-CXIII.
51 Galeazzi, *L'Italia provvede*, 8.
52 Galeazzi, *Come si rieducano*, 13. The number of leg amputations was greater than that of arms, probably because of frostbite. Bracco, *La patria ferita*, 92.
53 Arturo Lancellotti, "La Terza Conferenza Interalleata per lo studio delle questioni inerenti gli invalidi di guerra," *Bollettino della federazione Nazionale dei Comitati di assistenza ai militari ciechi, storpi e mutilati*, (30 October 1919), 265. The number of war-crippled (not amputees) was higher: leg-crippled reached 30.304 units, arm-crippled 44.316. Ibid., 266.
54 See his report with the list of newly devised artificial limbs: Riccardo Galeazzi, "Mechanical Prothesis for Manual Work," in *Inter-allied Conference on the after care of disabled men, Second annual meeting* (London: His Majesty Stationery Office, 1918), 493-515, and Id., "Exact Constructive Drawings of the Prothesis and Orthopaedic Apparatus for the Lower Limbs," ibid., 516-519.
55 *Officina nazionale di protesi per mutilati in guerra in Gorla* (Milan, [1916/17]). A copy of this booklet is kept in ASM, *Prefettura di Milano, Gabinetto*, Serie I, fasc. 1036. See also Bracco, *La patria ferita*, 115-125; Antonio Gibelli, *L'officina della Guerra. La Grande Guerra e le trasformazioni del mondo mentale* (Turin: Bollati Boringhieri, 1991), 112-121.
56 Giachi, *Milano per i lavoratori mutilati in guerra*, and enclosed papers, III-CXIII.
57 See Riccardo Galeazzi, *L'Esposizione interalleata dei lavori degli invalidi di guerra (Gand, 14-22 aprile 1923) e la partecipazione italiana* (Rome, 1923).
58 Chevalley, *Technical Re-education in Italy*, 145.
59 ASM, *Prefettura di Milano, Gabinetto*, Serie I, b. 371. See also *Agli invalidi della guerra* (Rome: Opera nazionale per la protezione e l'assistenza degli invalidi della Guerra ed., 1918).
60 Galeazzi, *L'Italia provvede*, 9-11. Id., *La rieducazione professionale dei lavoratori mutilati in guerra*, 26.
61 Galeazzi, *L'Italia provvede*, 11.
62 Galeazzi, *La rieducazione professionale*, CII-CV.
63 Giovanni Selvi, *Il problema dei mutilati ed invalidi di guerra e le attuali provvidenza statali* (Rome, 1916), excerpt 5. This is useful for the pension system for the disabled before the passing of the law of 1917.
64 Galeazzi, *Come si rieducano i soldati mutilati*, 13.
65 Salvatore Galgano, *La protezione interalleata degli invalidi e dei mutilati di guerra e la legislazione internazionale del lavoro* (Rome: Nuova Antologia, 1919), 8.
66 Martina Salvante, "Italian Disabled Veterans between Experience and Representation," in *Men After War*, eds. Stephen McVeigh and Nicola Cooper (London: Routledge, 2013),111-129; Bracco, *La patria ferita*, 111-114, 138-181. See Opera Nazionale per la Protezione ed Assistenza degli Invalidi della Guerra, *L' opera svolta in Italia: 1915-1919* (Rome: Tipografia dell'Unione Editrice, 1919).
67 Gianpiero Fumi, "Politiche del lavoro e portatori di handicap: il collocamento obbligatorio (1917-1968)," in *Il lavoro come fattore produttivo e come risorsa nella storia economica italiana*, eds. Sergio Zaninelli and Mario Taccolini (Milan: Vita e pensiero, 2002), 73-77.
68 Salvante, "Italian Disabled Veterans"; Bracco, *La patria ferita*; Debè and Polenghi, "Assistance and education," 237-244.

69 Italy was advanced in the re-education of blind veterans, with the Colosimo School of Naples and the School of Milan, directed by Lavinia Mondolfo.
70 Unfortunately, the documents of the Milanese sections of ONIG 1917-1981 cannot be consulted by scholars, since all the 392 records have been deposited in ASM in 1995 but no inventory has yet been produced (http://www.lombardiabeniculturali.it/archivi/complessi-archivistici/MIBA002C7A/, last retrieved 20 September 2019).
71 These and many other official appointments are listed in Galeazzi, *Curriculum Vitae*.
72 Arthur Steindler, "A visit to some of the orthopaedic clinics of Europe," *Journal of Bone and Joint Surgery* 5, (1923), 127-134; Harry Platt, "Orthopaedics in continental Europe. 1900-1950. The changing pattern," *Journal of Bone and Joint Surgery*, 32-B(4) (1950), 576-579, considered Galeazzi and Putti the two leading orthopaedists of the time and the Milan and Bologna Institutes as among the best in Europe and in the world: 570. The same is said by Le Vay, *The History of Orthopaedics*, 286-292.
73 Chevalley, *Le scuole di rieducazione professionale*, 12.

Fig. 1. The Institute of Cancer of the University of Leuven, Belgium, was the first building of a new medical campus in the inner city. It was inaugurated in 1928. © University Archive KU Leuven.

Competition over Care
The Campaign for a New Medical Campus at the University of Leuven in the 1920s

Joris Vandendriessche

In June 1920 a special goods train arrived in Leuven. Its wagons were filled with matresses, bedding, reclining chairs, stretchers, pyjamas, soap, glasses, and even some religious objects such as a tabernacle and an altar piece. Their total value was estimated to be 150,000 Belgian francs, a considerable sum. They had belonged to Henriette of Belgium (1870-1948), the sister of King Albert I (1875-1934), who had furnished the Albert 1er Belgian military hospital in Cannes, a recovery centre for injured soldiers during the First World War. The Belgian royal family had invested heavily in this type of hospitals across France, especially in the south. When the hospital in Cannes was closed after the war, the Princess decided to donate its medical supplies to the Catholic University of Leuven.[1] She attached one important condition to the gift. The equipment was to be used for a new school for nursing. The gift clearly fit in with the politics of the royal family in supporting the profession of nursing in the immediate post-war years. Queen Elisabeth in particular cultivated the image of a caring "queen-nurse". While she had never practised nursing, she had regularly visited wounded soldiers in the L'Ocean war hospital in De Panne, in the unoccupied part of Belgium near the front line. In post-war Belgium, the Queen symbolised the newly gained prestige of nurses.[2]

Not everyone approved of the royal gift. The writer Léopold Courouble, whose son had died as a soldier in 1915, called for the reopening of the Albert 1er hospital. War victims, he argued, still needed care and room for recovery. He also suggested that religious motives were at play: the closing of the hospital, according to Courouble, was the result of patients not attending mass as frequently as the religious sisters, who ran the hospital, would have liked. The transfer of the equipment to the Catholic University of Leuven was, in his words, "incredible and truly sad".[3] The rector of the university, the priest Paulin Ladeuze (1870-1940), did not share that view. He rather regarded the royal gift as an opportunity in the post-war years to take off the shelf a project that been insisted on before the war by the professors of the Faculty of Medicine. In 1908 these medical men had argued for the construction of a new academic hospital to provide clinical training to the rising number of medical students.[4] Between 1904 and 1914 the total number of students at the Faculty of Medicine had grown from 391 to 647. In 1920, moreover, 382 students – all men – enrolled for the first year of medical studies.[5] These student figures necessitated a new medical infrastructure for the university, the financing of which, as Courouble's remarks indicate, became the subject of ideological strife.

This chapter focuses on the first efforts to establish a new medical campus at the Catholic University of Leuven in the context of post-war reconstruction.[6] When, in 1920 (just one month after Henriette of Belgium's gift), the Belgian bishops, who formed the board of directors of the university, decided to build a new hospital with a school for nursing, they envisaged a project for a city and a university that were still in ruins.[7] During the "Sack of Leuven", from 25 August to the first days of September 1914, the city was plundered by German troops who set fire to 1,100 buildings in the city centre and 1,000 more in the surrounding area. These included several university buildings such as the fourteenth-century Cloth Hall that also housed the university's precious library.[8] This devastation had resulted in an international imagery of martyrdom for the city during the war, which proved crucial to attracting (foreign) finance for reconstruction in the post-war era. As a symbol of academic renewal, a new university library was financed through American gifts.[9]

The campaign for a new medical campus, I will show, followed a different trajectory. While displaying features of post-war reconstruction, such as the extensive use of the media (for example, newspapers) in the promotion of philanthropy and a militaristic tone in the way the need to modernise healthcare was presented, the campaign also followed a logic that was peculiar to the medical field. The innovators of post-war medical education took up challenges that had already become clear in the pre-war period. These included the rising number of medical students and the need for more clinical instruction. In general, the function of the (academic) hospital as a professional learning space was becoming more important, not only for (lay) nurses but also for medical students whose education increasingly included specialist courses that made use of the technological infrastructure of hospitals for practical training. The interwar expansion of teaching hospitals was, to be clear, far from limited to Belgium alone. It was a much wider global phenomenon, which was moreover not only the product of a shift in medical education but also tied up with an ongoing process of medicalisation in the twentieth century and with the gradual expansion of welfare states.[10]

What seemed peculiar to the Belgian case was the central role of ideology. While post-war regeneration capitalised on strong national sentiments, I will show that ideological competition between Catholics and non-religious players constituted a determining factor in the reconstruction and expansion of Belgian medical infrastructure. To make this argument I will first look at the field of nursing education and the setting up of the St. Elisabeth School for Nursing in Leuven. Second, I will scrutinise the efforts to raise funds for a new academic hospital in Leuven and compare these to the efforts of the Free University of Brussels, its ideological counterpart. While the latter was more successful in attracting foreign funds (for example, from the American Rockefeller Foundation), the fundraising activities of the Catholic University of Leuven in their mediatised, militant and ideologically oriented form may be regarded just as much as typical of the post-war era.

Nursing Education and Catholic Health Care

The first nursing schools in Belgium were set up in Antwerp and Brussels in the first decade of the twentieth century. Three were of a liberal ideological bent, one – the St. Camille School for Nursing in Brussels – was Catholic. The introduction by the Belgian legislator in 1908 of an obligatory certificate to practise nursing was a response to these first educational initiatives. Such a certificate could be obtained after a year of theoretical study by taking an exam organised by the provincial medical commissions. It allowed religious sisters, many of whom possessed practical experience, to acquire formal degrees. During the First World War the existing Belgian nursing schools continued to train nurses in occupied Belgium. Temporary Belgian nursing schools were set up abroad, in Calais and London, to train nurses to assist in the military hospitals at the allied front. As Luc De Munck has shown, the wartime work of Belgian nurses contributed to the improvement of the profession's reputation in the immediate post-war years. In 1919, a professional organisation was also set up.[11]

The Law of 3 September 1921 on Nursing profoundly reorganised training. Boarding was made mandatory for female students and the duration of the training was extended to three years. The law stipulated three possible degrees: hospital nurse, psychiatric nurse and visiting (district) nurse. The last specialisation in particular had developed during and immediately after the war as care for mother and child – through home visits – became one of the spearheads of national health policy. During the war already, much attention had been paid to infant care (for example, through milk distribution). In 1919, the National Board for Child Welfare (NBCW) was established, with the support of Catholics, showing their willingness to support a certain professionalisation of the medical and social fields in the immediate post-war years.¹² Both the NBCW and the 1921 Law on Nursing may be interpreted as acknowledgements of the work of lay women during the war. New nursing schools were soon established in Ghent, Liège, Malines, Bruges, and indeed in Leuven.

What role did ideology play in these initiatives? Despite Catholics' willingness for political compromise in the establishment of the NBCW and the cooperation between Catholic representatives and their non-religious colleagues in the post-war professional organisation of nurses, ideological competition soon resurfaced. A look at the aggressive phrasing of a promotional booklet for the St. Elisabeth School for Nursing may serve as an illustration. Belgian archbishop Joseph-Désiré Mercier (1851-1926) addressed potential students in a preface: "We cannot let another year pass. The honor of the University of Leuven, the most sanctuary interests of our faith and love of our Catholic Works are at stake!".¹³ Referring to the new law of 1921, he wanted to safeguard the moral influence of religious sisters in healthcare and saw opportunities to extend this influence by training them as district nurses. At the same time, conflict arose over the religious convictions of the students. The nursing students received their practical training in the city's St. Pieters Hospital, which was a public hospital governed by the city's Commission for Hospitals. This Commission demanded that non-Catholic girls, too, be allowed to enrol in the school, making its case that the hospital was the only one in the city where nursing education was offered and no student should be excluded on the basis of religion. The University had no choice other than to agree, given its reliance on public infrastructure.¹⁴ The school itself, with its classrooms and student accommodation, was housed elsewhere, in a building in the Naamsestraat belonging to the Franciscan Sisters, a congregation which had downsized because of its German origins (several sisters had returned to Germany).

The case of nursing education may be regarded as typical of the increasing academic competition in the field of healthcare in the post-war years. Before the war the ideological struggles between universities had centred around the financing of laboratories. The Brussels *cité scientifique* had been met by equally impressive investments in pathological, physiological, chemical, electromechanical and bacteriological complexes in Leuven. These German-style research laboratories had been mostly funded through professors' personal means and private donations.¹⁵ After the war, providing one's students with access to patients and new technologies in the hospital (such as X-rays and radium therapy) became key. As medical care was professionalising rapidly – the 1921 Law on Nursing had shown this – the question, in the eyes of the Catholic leadership, was whether a dominant tradition of Christian care could be safeguarded. In the decade before 1914 the Leuven Faculty of Medicine had seen its influence rise considerably. In 1904, it had 391 students, compared to 276 at the Brussels Faculty of Medicine. By 1914, the divide between the two had further increased: the number of Leuven medical students had grown to 647, compared to 301 in Brussels.¹⁶ But times were changing for Belgian Catholics, so it seemed. In the national parliament, the Catholic party had lost the absolute majority it had held between 1884 and 1914. With the model of the socialist policlinic, a type of hospital that offered accessible and specialised care (such as X-rays) to the lower social classes, an important competitor for the institutions run by religious orders had come to the fore.[17] As a result, a sense of urgency pervaded the quest for Catholic medical infrastructure.

In the meantime, building projects that had been started before the war were taken up again. Both the Catholic University of Leuven and the Free University of Brussels set up new institutes in the urban periphery. Leuven created the psychiatric institute of Salve Mater in Lovenjoel, the land for which was donated to the university by Viscount Charles de Spoelbergh and leased to the Sisters of Love and Mary, who financed the construction of the asylum buildings. The asylum opened in 1926. It was built following typically Catholic neo-gothic architecture. Brussels established the Brugmann Hospital in Jette, named for benefactor and banker Georges Bruggman. It opened in 1923 and was designed by Victor Horta following his modernist (*art nouveau*) style. Its clean lines seemed more future-oriented and better fitted to the tradition of free-thinking and the grand medical ambitions of the University of Brussels.[18] But perhaps the strongest competition between the two universities centred around the medical campuses that were established in the city centre: the St. Rafaël Hospital in Leuven, of which a cancer institute was the first building, and the St. Pierre Hospital in Brussels, which also included a school for nursing. Both were post-war projects that capitalised on the widespread desire to assist with the regeneration of Belgium, but they did so in different ways.

Modernising Catholic Fundraising

Given Leuven's martyrdom during the war, the university stood a good chance when it came to raising funds among philanthropists, among whom there was a lot of sympathy for the university's cause. The medical field had also gained prestige because of the war. New technologies such as X-rays and new antiseptic methods had proven their use in war-time surgery. For Belgium, the military hospital of l'Océan had become known for its advancements in blood transfusion, its overall organisation and the treatment of wounds. The medical team under the leadership of the liberal physician and Brussels professor Antoine Depage (1862-1925) recruited from the different universities. For Leuven, the surgeon Georges Debaisieux (1882-1956) participated in the team. After the war, he continued to treat war victims and obtained great respect as a war hero.[19] The war circumstances seem to have ended – if only for a brief period – the ideological competition between medical academics.

If the school for nursing had been opened at relatively little cost, the construction of a new Catholic hospital required much greater finance. To acquire this the university looked eagerly to the newly available funds for reconstruction, including from international – mostly American – benefactors. The budget for reparation for the damage of war had paid for the reconstruction of the university's main building. The Belgian bishops in 1919 had organised a national collection to the benefit of the university, which had generated 2.5 million Belgian Francs. There was the University of Leuven's share of funds from the Commission for the Relief of Belgium, an international organisation founded by the later President of the United States, Herbert Hoover. An American committee financed the construction of a new library for the university.[20] In 1920 it was suggested to Ladeuze that the new hospital be financed in a similar way, for example by contacting Henry Bayard, an influential American lawyer and businessman in Philadelphia to assist in raising funds.[21] Yet, this effort proved a failure. Compared with the university's library project, the new hospital was less easily marketed as a project of reconstruction. There was no clear link with the war.

But that was not the only reason. The Leuven physicians enviously followed the efforts of the Brussels surgeon Antoine Depage who did succeed in raising funds from the Rockefeller Foundation. Depage presented the new St. Pierre Hospital in Brussels as a "medical model" for research and education in post-war Belgium, drawing on his achievement in L'Océan. This was something the Americans were willing to invest in. He succeeded in obtaining 30 million Belgian francs from the Rockefellers for the construction of a new clinic, which also included a school for nursing. A crucial moment in this effort was the visit of the president of the Rockefeller Foundation together with the medical reformer Abraham Flexner – famous for his report on American medical schools – to Brussels in January 1921. The hospital would serve as the teaching hospital of the Free University of Brussels.[22]

Other factors help to explain why Leuven failed where Brussels succeeded. First, religion played a role. The religious framing of the new hospital as a Catholic institution did not please foreign philanthropists. During the parallel construction of the new university library, American protestants had to be convinced to fund a "Catholic temple of learning". The University had to market itself as a free university, not in the ideological sense of "free-thinking" of course, but free from state control.[23] For healthcare this seemed even more difficult. At the end of his rectorate, Ladeuze did not hesitate to characterise the Rockefeller Foundation as an "anti-Catholic organisation".[24] Second, the relationship between the university and the city was important. The city of Brussels was willing to invest (15 million Belgian francs) alongside the Rockefeller Foundation (30 million Belgian francs) in the new hospital – this was an important prerequisite for Rockefeller investment. In Leuven this was not the case: the city did not have the financial means to invest in health care and, moreover, differences in political opinion between the liberal urban board and the Catholic university made collaboration even more difficult, as the dispute over the religious convictions of the nursing students has illustrated.

In such circumstances other means of financing were explored. Paulin Ladeuze decided to organise a major fundraiser among the Catholic population – the vast majority of the country's inhabitants being Catholic – calling for the help of the press, in the spring of 1924.[25] The focus of the campaign was the fight against cancer – one of the spearheads in interwar health policies – and the need to build a cancer institute. Strikingly, six years after the end of the war, references to reconstruction remained largely absent.

The campaign ran up against difficulties from the start. Potential benefactors questioned its very purpose. Paul Alexandre de Hemptinne, a professor at the Institute of Physics, pointed to the availability of state subsidies to the universities which – according to him – made private fundraising unnecessary.[26] Indeed, since 1922 the "free" universities of Brussels and Leuven had received one million Belgian francs annually from the Belgian state – an amount that was doubled from 1925 onwards.[27] Even Countess Jeanne de Mérode, one of the later leaders of the campaign, initially had to be convinced of its necessity. She suggested the example of France, where the state financed and coordinated the fight against cancer through a centralised institute and regional centres. It took some effort to convince de Mérode that the French system could not work in Belgium because, as she was told, "we [in Belgium] have two free, competing universities" and that "from a religious point of view" it was necessary to act.[28]

The timing of the campaign was another obstacle. In the spring of 1924 the University of Leuven faced negative attention from the press because of its slow progress in offering courses in Dutch – the majority of courses up to that point had been taught in French, while the number of Flemish (Dutch-speaking) students was rising. The latter students and the Flemish Movement protested in order to improve the situation – protests that were reported upon in the newspapers. The St. Elisabeth School for Nursing, for that matter, offered courses in both French and Dutch. But the timing of the fundraising campaign was also poor for another reason. A certain weariness had emerged when it came to collecting. An alumnus from the university, in a letter to the rector, explained, "The timing is unfavourable, there has been much donating lately […] people will say: another one for Leuven".[29] Perhaps parishioners remembered the major collection of 1919 in favour of the University. But also annually, all churches in the country made a collection for the country's only Catholic university. Others pointed to the collections for the fight against tuberculosis, for war victims, for the widely celebrated 50th anniversary as a priest of archbishop Mercier in 1924 etc. In the midst of a country in full reconstruction there had been no lack of good causes to donate money to.

Such competition for funds aside, the war experience also strengthened the campaign. As Susan Sontag has highlighted, the First World War was also an occasion for mass ideological mobilisation and showed how the notion of war could be turned into a useful metaphor for all sorts of public health campaigns in the early twentieth century. Of course, such health discourse built on pre-war experiences. In the second half of the nineteenth century, physicians specialising in public health cast alcoholism, venereal diseases and tuberculosis as national "plagues". This discourse took a militaristic form. The pathogens that were identified by bacteriologists as the causes of disease were cast as "enemies" and the politics against those diseases were more generally depicted as a "fight" or "struggle".[30] After the First World War, military metaphors continued to infuse the rhetoric of health politics. The goals of preventive campaigns, which became the responsibility of society and not just of the physician, were the defeat of an "enemy".[31] The fundraiser for a cancer institute in Leuven fits in with this frame. In a brochure from 1924 cancer was presented as "the illness that today 'spreads terror'". It was further added, "Since the war in particular, its ravages are constantly increasing. […] It is urgent to conduct the same fight against cancer [as against tuberculosis]. This battle will be, similarly, victorious, if it is fought well".[32]

At the same time, post-war health politics found new ground. The moralistic ambitions that had underpinned much of pre-war health provision were now felt to be naïve. The spread of venereal diseases among Belgian soldiers during wartime, for example, was perceived as a threat to the health of the nation as a whole (of which the army was seen as a reflection). The nineteenth-century "moral conferences" in which abstention had been preached no longer seemed effective. Instead, soldiers were shown medical films containing images of different venereal diseases, and were provided with prophylactic soaps and ointments, to be used after sexual intercourse in specific rooms allocated for that purpose in the military barracks. This was a controversial measure as it promoted rather than discouraged, according to some, extramarital sex. Preventive politics for the Belgian civil population comprised the foundation of dispensaries, free drugs and intensive information campaigns. As Liesbet Nys has shown, Belgium became regarded as a successful international example in the prevention of venereal diseases in the interwar years.[33]

A final element, typical of post-war reconstruction, was the relationship between the university and its financial donors. By actively approaching members of the nobility and industrialists, who could become "founding members" of the institute by donating large sums, considerable funds were raised. Two rich industrialists – August De Becker and Fernand Van der Straeten – donated respectively 300,000 and 150,000 francs.[34] To accommodate them a machinery of recognition was put into play which consisted of personal letters of gratitude from the rector, having their names printed in the newspapers, commemorative placards with their names on being hung on the walls of the institute, rooms being named after them, etc. Some patients thus received radiation treatment in the Salle Comtesse de Mérode. These signs of recognition of major financial donors reveal that the campaign for the cancer institute, even if it was a national and not an international project and had no clear link with the war, bears a clear resemblance to the parallel campaign for the construction of a new university library. In the latter campaign a similar public machinery of philanthropy with visual signs of gratitude was set in motion. The project of (re)building a new Belgium required planning and organisation, better use of media and fundraising on a larger and more diversified scale.

Such diversification was also present in Ladeuze's cancer campaign of the 1920s. Its success may be attributed, at least partly, to reaching different audiences. Provincial committees steered the work of local committees, which motivated workers and everyday parishioners to "buy a brick" for the cancer institute. They could do this very cheaply for just one, two or five Belgian francs. It was a form of contributing that was accessible to every parishioner. In the margins of the registers we find some additional information on these modest benefactors: "a grateful typographer, 5 F", "a religious sister cured by prof. Maisin [Leuven's cancer specialist], 100 F".[35] Donating to a hospital – which was in fact a traditional way of financing medical care in the nineteenth century – was now "democratised".[36] In total, 2.5 million Belgian francs were raised. The cancer institute, which was inaugurated in 1928, became the first building of a new hospital complex in Leuven's inner city.

Fig. 2. The entrance hall of the Institute of Cancer contained engravings with the names of major benefactors whose donations had allowed the university to build the institute. © University Archive KU Leuven.

Conclusion

The First World War led to an increase in the speed with which Belgium's free universities constructed a new medical infrastructure. The idea of these hospitals dated from before the war, but was now connected to an idea of (re)constructing a new Belgium in which the medical field – the prestige of which, certainly for nursing, had grown – would play an important role. Their realisation achieved a new sense of urgency. Ideological competition proved a major driving force of hospital construction in the 1920s. Here as well, the context of the reconstruction and the financial means that became available for all sorts of building projects – among others from American philanthropists – reinforced this competition. The result was a struggle for means and sympathy. When it came to medical infrastructure, the Free University of Brussels conducted this fight more successfully, presenting its new hospital as a necessary component and model institution for the future of Belgium. As a result, American philanthropists heavily funded its clinic.

The University of Leuven, of course, had its own successes. On the medical level it was more successful in raising funds among royalty, nobility and the Catholic population than among foreign philanthropists. For this latter group, funding a "Catholic" hospital was a bridge too far, while for the former the religious nature of the new hospital and, more generally, of the Catholic healthcare sector, of which care by religious sisters was an established component, was a key selling point. It was indicative of the firm ideological grounding of healthcare in the interwar years. Yet, at the same time the campaign for the St. Elisabeth School for Nursing and the cancer institute, too, was typical of the post-war era. It engaged in the contemporary competition for financial means, used modern fundraising strategies and employed a militaristic rhetoric.

Notes

1 University Archive of Leuven (UAL), Archive of rector Paulin Ladeuze (AL), Letter of 18 June 1920 from sister Marie-Xavier to P. Ladeuze, including an inventory of the goods donated by Henriette of Belgium. On the Albert 1er war hospital, see: François Olier and Jean-Luc Quénec'hdu, *Hôpitaux militaires dans la guerre 1914-1918. Tome IV France sud-est* (Louviers: Ysec, 2014), 242.
2 UAL, AL, XXIX, Letter of 4 October 1920 from sister Marie-Xavier to P. Ladeuze. On the role of Queen Elisabeth in the L'Océan hospital, see: Luc De Munck and Luc Vandeweyer, *Het hospitaal van de koningin. Rode Kruis, L'Océan en De Panne, 1914-1918* (De Panne: Gemeentebestuur De Panne, 2012), 112.
3 Léopold Courouble, "Pour nos défenseurs," *La Gazette*, 22 May 1922 (press clipping preserved in: UAL, AL, XXIX).
4 Archiepiscopal Archive of Malines (AAM), *Inventaris Archief Kardinaal Mercier*, Bisschoppenconferenties, Order of business for 20 April 1912.
5 Renaud Bardez, "La Faculté de médecine de l'Université Libre de Bruxelles: entre création, circulation et enseignement des savoirs (1795-1914)" (PhD Thesis, Free University of Brussels, 2016), 389.
6 This chapter draws on the first chapter of my book on the twentieth-century history of the Leuven academic hospitals: Joris Vandendriessche, *Zorg en wetenschap. Een geschiedenis van de Leuvense academische ziekenhuizen in de twintigste eeuw* (Leuven: Universitaire Pers Leuven, 2019), 19-45.
7 UAL, AL, XX, 58, Report on the Catholic University of Leuven, July 1919; AAM, *Acta episcopalia Cameracensia, Leodiensia, Mechliniensia et provincialia*, 22.
8 Mark Derez, "The Flames of Louvain: The War Experiences of an Academic Community," in *Facing Armageddon. The First World War Experienced*, eds. Hugh Cecil and Peter H. Liddle (London: Leo Cooper, 1996), 617-629.
9 See: Mark Derez and Axel Tixhon, *Martelaarssteden: Visé, Aarschot, Tamines, Dinant, Leuven, Dendermonde. Belgie, augustus-september 1914* (Namur: Presses Universitaires de Namur, 2014); Chris Coppens, *Universiteitsbibliotheek Leuven 1425-2000: Sapientia aedificavit sibi domum* (Leuven: Leuven University Press, 2005).
10 For an overview, see: Guenter Risse, *Mending Bodies, Saving Souls: A History of Hospitals* (New York: Oxford University Press, 1999). For an example of a well-developed case study, see: Anne Digby, Howard Phillips, Harriet Deacon, and Kirsten Thomson, *At the Heart of Healing: Groote Schuur Hospital 1938-2008* (Cape Town: Jacana, 2008).
11 Luc De Munck, *Altijd troosten. Belgische verpleegsters tijdens de Eerste Wereldoorlog* (Amsterdam: Amsterdam University Press, 2018).
12 Claudine Marissal, *Protéger le jeune enfant: enjeux sociaux, politiques et sexués (Belgique, 1890-1940)* (Brussels: Editions de l'Université de Bruxelles, 2014); Pieter Dhondt, "Social Education or Medical Care? Divergent Views on Visiting Nurses in Belgium in the Interwar Years," *History of Education & Children's Literature* 7, no. 1 (2012): 505-522.
13 UAL, AL, XXIX, *Hoogeschool van Leuven. School voor Ziekenverpleegsters Sint-Elisabeth*, 19 November 1921. On this nursing school, see also: Annelies Cousserier, *In goede handen: 75 jaar onderwijs verpleeg- en vroedkunde Leuven* (Leuven: KADOC, 2004).
14 Archive of the Social Service of Leuven, Register of the Committee of Hospitals, Board Meeting of 22 January 1922.
15 Nathalie Poot, Geert Vanpaemel, and Siska Waelkens, *Een walvis in de stad. De collecties van de Leuvense Faculteit Wetenschappen* (Leuven: Leuven University Press, 2014);

Geert Vanpaemel, *Wetenschap als roeping. Een geschiedenis van de Leuvense faculteit voor wetenschappen* (Leuven: Leuven University Press, 2017), 69-134. An edited photo album of the Catholic University of Leuven gives an excellent overview of the scientific infrastructure of the university on the eve of the First World War: Mark Derez, Jo Tollebeek, and G. Vanpaemel, eds., *Album van een wetenschappelijke wereld: de Leuvense universiteit omstreeks 1900/ Album of a scientific world : the University of Louvain around 1900* (Leuven: Leuven University Press, 2012). For an overview of the building efforts of the Free University of Brussels, see: Kenneth Bertrams, *Universités et entreprises: milieux académiques et industriels en Belgique, 1880-1970* (Brussels: Le Cri, 2006).

16 Bardez, "La Faculté," 389.
17 On the model of the socialist polyclinic, see: Paule Verbruggen, "De volkskliniek: een socialistische polikliniek in Gent," in *Er is leven voor de dood. Tweehonderd jaar gezondheidszorg in Vlaanderen*, eds. Jan De Maeyer, Lieve Dhaene, Gert Hertecant, and Karel Velle (Kapellen: Pelckmans, 1998), 233-241.
18 Anne Meiresonne, "Brussel, Brugmannziekenhuis in Laken," in *Architectuur van Belgische hospitalen*, eds. Patrick Allegaert and Jean-Marc Basyn (Brussels: Ministerie van de Vlaamse Gemeenschap, Afdeling Monumenten en Landschappen, 2005), 116-121. On modernist hospital architecture in Belgium, see: Johan Wambacq, *Het paleis op de heide: architect Maxime Brunfaut en het sanatorium van Tombeek* (Brussels: ASP, 2009).
19 J. Morelle, "M. George Debaisieux, professeur-émérité à la Faculté de Médecine, 1882-1956," *Annuaire de l'Université catholique de Louvain* (1954-1956): 149-156; UAL, AL, XXIX, Letter of 27 November 1920 from sister Marie-Xavier to the Belgian cardinal and archbishop Joseph-Desiré Mercier.
20 Emiel Lamberts and Jan Roegiers, *De universiteit te Leuven, 1425-1985* (Leuven: Universitaire Pers Leuven, 1986), 223-228.
21 UAL, AL, XXIX, Letter of 26 April 1920 from sister Marie-Xavier to P. Ladeuze.
22 Julie Mortier, "Entre médicalisation et modernité: l'étude des structures hospitalières. Le cas de l'hôpital Saint-Piere de Bruxelles (1890-1935)" (Master's Diss., Free University of Brussels, 2017); David Guilardian, "Saint-Pierre and Bordet: de l'art déco au modernisme," in *Du monumental au fonctionnel: l'architecture des hôpitaux publics bruxellois (XIXè-XXè siècles)*, eds. Astrid Lelarge, Claire Dickstein-Bernard, David Guilardian, and Judith Le Maire (Brussels: CIVA, 2005), 65-115.
23 Coppens, *Universiteitsbibliotheek*.
24 UAL, AL, XX, Report on the Catholic University of Leuven, July 1938.
25 UAL, Archive of the Central Administration (ACA), 1047, Letter 1 December 1924 from P. Ladeuze to the editors of Belgian newspapers.
26 UAL, ACA, 1046/4, Letter of 12 April 1924 from Alexandre de Hemptinne to P. Ladeuze
27 Lamberts and Roegiers, *De universiteit*, 192.
28 UAL, ACA, 1048, Undated letter from Ms. Morelle to Countess J. de Mérode. In France, the state took the lead in the organization of the "fight" against cancer: Patrice Pinell, *The Fight Against Cancer: France, 1890-1940* (London: Routledge, 2002).
29 UAL, ACA, 1046/4, Letter of 19 March 1924 from F. Van Ongeval to P. Ladeuze.
30 For Belgium see, Liesbet Nys, "Nationale plagen. Hygiënisten over het maatschappelijk lichaam," in *De zieke natie. Over de medicalisering van de samenleving*, eds. Jo Tollebeek, Liesbet Nys, Henk De Smaele, and Kaat Wils (Groningen: Historische Uitgeverij, 2002), 220-241; Hans Neefs, *Between Sin and Disease. The Social Fight Against Syphilis and AIDS in Belgium (1880-2000)* (Saarbrücken: Lambert, 2010).

31 Susan Sontag, *Aids and its metaphors* (New York: Farrar, Straus and Giroux, 1989), 9-11.
32 UAL, ACA, 1047, *Pour la creation d'un Institut du Cancer à l'Université de Louvain* (Leuven: Van Linthout, 1924), 4.
33 Liesbet Nys, "De grote school van de natie. Legerartsen over drankmisbruik en geslachtsziekten in het Belgisch leger (circa 1850-1950)," *BMGN – The Low Countries Historical Review* 115, no. 3 (2000): 392-425.
34 UAL, ACA, 1049, List of "dons particuliers, 1919-1929".
35 UAL, ACA, 1049, List of donations to the local committees of the campaign for the Leuven Institute of Cancer.
36 Barry Doyle, "Healthcare before Welfare States: Hospitals in Early Twentieth Century England and France," *Canadian Bulletin of the History of Medicine* 33, no. 1 (2016): 174-204.

PART FOUR
REFORM

Post-war picture postcard of the rebuilt
city centre of Leuven (Belgium).

© City Archive Leuven

But in our lives there was no repetition;
nothing of the past survived, nothing came back.
It was reserved for us to participate to the full in that which history
formerly distributed, sparingly and from time to time,
to a single country, to a single century.
At most, one generation had gone through a revolution,
another experienced a putsch, the third a war, the fourth a famine,
the fifth national bankruptcy: and many blessed countries,
blessed generations, bore none of these.
But we, who are sixty today and who, *de jure* still have a space of
time before us, what have we *not* seen, *not* suffered,
not lived through? We have ploughed through the catalogue
of every conceivable catastrophe back and forth
(and we have not yet come to the last page).

Stefan Zweig, *The World of Yesterday* (1941)

Fig. 1. Roberto J. Payró's residence at
327 Brugmann Avenue, Brussels.
A plaque on the façade indicates that the
writer lived here between 1909 and 1922.
Picture taken by the author in May 2018.

An Argentine Witness of the Occupation and Reconstruction of Belgium
The Writings of Roberto J. Payró (1918-1922)

María Inés Tato

In 1909 the renowned Argentine writer and journalist Roberto J. Payró (1867-1928) settled down in Brussels to work as a correspondent for the Buenos Aires newspaper *La Nación*. He was the author of notable accounts of manners and a pioneer of travel chronicles. His contributions covered different issues from culture to politics, and showed the insightful and ironic nature that characterised his work. When the First World War broke out, he decided to remain in Belgium with his family to provide his readers with first-hand information on the conflict, despite the risks and discomfort involved in that choice.

After the German invasion, he admitted that his observations about the war encountered serious difficulties because of the restrictions imposed by censorship and in the growing informational isolation. However, he offered a priceless testimony of daily life in Brussels during the invasion and occupation and carried out a thorough enquiry about the German incursion in Dinant, where the honorary vice-consul of the Argentine Republic – Rémy Himmer – was executed.[1] Payró also investigated the death of Julio Lemaire, vice-consul and ambassador of the General Argentine Consulate in Antwerp during the bombardment of that city in October 1914.[2] These cases were analysed by the Argentine government, which accepted the explanations given by the German authorities and considered the diplomatic incidents closed.[3] Nevertheless, Payró's reports had a great impact on public opinion, being reproduced not only in Argentina but also in the European press.[4] As a result, the occupation authorities decided to silence him. On 22 September 1915 his home was raided, many of his writings were requisitioned, and the writer was put under strict surveillance during the rest of the conflict.[5] Therefore, his journalistic contributions were interrupted until February 1919, when he was able to restart them. He continued as correspondent for *La Nación* until 1922, when he returned to Argentina.

This chapter will deal with the chronicles written immediately after the war (1918-1922). Some of these chronicles recalled Payró's experience of the occupation – such as those concerning the deportation of Belgian workers to Germany, the local impact of the German revolution of November 1918, and the sudden armistice. The memory of the war also resurfaced in some public scandals related to war profiteering and collaboration. However, the vast majority of his new articles were dedicated to the future of Belgium and Europe. Unlike those referring to the war, these abandoned the intimate and emotional tenor to adopt instead a more neutral and informative tone.

The importance of these chronicles lies, in the first place, in their character as external testimonies of the European post-war reconstruction and reform endeavours. In the second place, they show how Europe continued serving as a benchmark for Latin America, despite the negative impact of the war on her image as a beacon of civilisation.[6]

An Eyewitness to Post-War Material and Political Reconstruction in Belgium

Shortly after the German invasion, Payró had travelled around cities and small villages devastated by the German army, an itinerary that he had called "a pilgrimage to the ruins".[7] After the war, he repeated the experience, going down to the principal theatres of war: Nieuwpoort, Diksmuide, Ypres, and their surroundings, "razed to the ground [...] regions that currently are sterile swamps, fields of devastation [...] a bald lunar landscape".[8]

The Great War had bequeathed extremely high levels of material destruction, a huge burden for Belgium's recovery and reconstruction.[9] As our chronicler pointed out, the economic rebirth was

> the most arduous task of this heroic, martyr country, tortured first, overexploited later, and which, without equipment and tools, with its industrial buildings razed, without building materials, will need years to return to the condition previous to the war, and it will only accomplish that with superhuman efforts, no matter how much it gets as compensation for damages.[10]

In June 1919, the Argentine writer stated that "we live very harshly here – almost as in wartime – because urgent material needs do not disappear or diminish with the illusion of the future".[11] He reported that one quarter of the Belgian population was unemployed, surviving through government aid, in a context of high inflation and salary depreciation, which led employed workers to demand "salaries apparently huge, but in fact hardly enough". These demands complicated the recovery of the industry, also shaken by lack of equipment, capital, raw materials and markets.[12] The housing crisis was extremely serious[13] and – like unemployment – particularly hit the war veterans, who found the compensation and pensions insufficient due to the high cost of living. As Payró asserted, official aid through endowments for veterans "does not improve the sad situation of those who – compulsory or voluntarily – spilled their blood and risked their lives for the common will".[14] Despite the depth of the crisis and the high public debt to cover social emergencies – channelled through an advanced social legislation[15] – Payró reported the incipient rebirth of some industries and foreign trade. As a result, he predicted the recovery to prewar economic levels.[16]

The success of the economic recovery resided in what he considered an original and praiseworthy system adopted during the war: the "government of reconstruction",[17] the continuity in peacetime of the 1914-18 "sacred union":

> The cooperation of the main political parties in the Executive Power of a country, with a participation and responsibility proportional to their strength, is an event [...] exemplary and new [...] Such a sharing out of influences and obligations was usual in the parliaments, but not in the governments.[18]

The collaboration – embodied in a coalition government led by Prime Ministers León Delacroix first (1918-1920) and Henry Carton de Wiart later (1920-1921) – implied the balancing of different ideological tendencies and provided a necessary political stability, which favoured economic reconstruction.[19]

In addition to the government of national unity, the Belgian rebirth rested on another pillar: the establishment of universal suffrage, as a direct result of the war. In other words, the right to vote was compensation for the blood tax paid by the male population through army service in wartime and, to a lesser extent, by women, a consequence of "equality in suffering and resistance".[20] Electoral reform granted suffrage to all men over 21 years old and also to some categories of women: former political prisoners, widows (not remarried) and widowed mothers of dead soldiers and executed civilians.[21] In this sense, the Great War had meant the crisis of the old systems and had led to a "republic without the name": "[f]or the first time in History, the war will have cooperated – direct, immediate and effectively – to the progress of mankind, not as war but in its character of revolution". A revolution rooted in the principles of 1789, with universal effects, including Germany and even Russia.[22]

Payró considered that Belgian political exceptionality was based on the moderation of its socialism – represented by the Belgian Labour Party – which contrasted with the post-war ideological extremisms: "although [the party] names itself revolutionary, it is evolutionist, and bolshevikism does not prey on it".[23]

> [it] distinguishes itself for the moderation of its methods and for the realism of its propaganda [...] it could be easily confused with French radicalism or the American advanced democracy.[24]

Socialist temperance would precisely explain that "the reconstruction of Belgium works with less slowness than the one of other countries devastated by the war".[25]

Payró and the Peace Conference

The Argentine writer recorded in his contributions to *La Nación* widespread bewilderment and uncertainty in post-war Europe:

> Europe – and, with her, the entire world [...] – revolves nowadays in the darkness and the vagueness of chaos. She is fully in a revolutionary epoch; its upheavals have diverse intensity but appear everywhere without exception.[26]

Payró's expectations were set against the background of the Peace Conference. He hoped that it would contribute "to establish the union of the nations and to create a new method to solve the border issues, as otherwise the terrifying experiment we have just witnessed will be useless".[27] A crucial point that the peace conference had to solve was the German question, which was how to punish the defeated and to avoid it becoming a new threat to peace. The Allied nations gave opposing answers to this pressing dilemma, from the United States' conciliatory proposals to the demands of the recalcitrant French and Belgians – whose reconstruction, at least in theory, was dependent on indemnities for the German occupation.

The Belgian socialists intervened in those debates with a proposal that, according to our writer, indicated "equity and serenity", stating:

that only a peace of justice can avoid future wars; that the right of peoples to self-determination is violated in Poland, seriously compromising peace, when German communities are incorporated to that country; that they cannot admit that the strongest powers seize the German colonies invoking the rights of the victors; that depriving Germany or any other nation of raw materials and colonial markets creates a dangerous and unsustainable situation; that they do not accept neither that Germany is forced to sign a blank check under the pretext of reparation, nor making the balance of the damages caused by her without her intervention, thus depriving her of defense, nor that she is reduced to a kind of economic slavery.[28]

On the other hand, the socialists demanded guarantees that neither Belgium nor France would again be attacked by Germany. To prevent that risk, they proposed disarmament instead of a new arms race or the military occupation of German territory.[29]

In the peace conference, the sternest position towards Germany prevailed. The Treaty of Versailles, signed on 28 June 1919, included many harsh provisions designed to compensate France and Belgium for the damage inflicted by the occupation, and to reduce German military power.[30] For its part, Belgium received much less of the expected amount of reparations, since the Allies considered that the damage and military losses suffered were less than those of other countries.[31] Although the Belgian coalition parties were overall dissatisfied with the provisions of the Treaty of Versailles, considering them an insufficient reward for Belgium's sacrifice in wartime, the socialists took a slightly more positive view. They considered that at least the Treaty had put an end to the nightmare of the war, and offered some promising prospects, such as the liberation of Poland and the League of Nations.[32] However, the socialist leaders continued to criticise the spirit of the Treaty and to warn about the risks it involved for long-term peace. In the words of Louis De Brouckère, socialist delegate to the League of Nations in the 1920s, quoted by Payró:

> Nowadays, Germany is defeated. The Allies subject her at will, impose on her a rough and hard treaty that, from a certain point of view, is unfair, and the Germans are told: "These are the legal rules of punishment". And, because we are fairly outraged due to Germany's disloyalty, we tell her: "You will be squashed in Europe, without even the opportunity to invoke the same warranties that we have created for you and for us" […] I took part in the fight and I keep my sorrows. But, not because I have contributed to the triumph of law, I have to despise now the very idea of justice in front of the beaten enemy![33]

Émile Vandervelde, socialist Minister of Justice and delegate to the peace conference, also condemned the terms of the Treaty imposed on Germany:

> Reactionaries have declared that Germany had to pay everything, that is to say the hundreds of thousands of millions that the war has costed, when they perfectly know that the German people will never be able to produce enough to pay such a sum.[34]

Payró sided with the socialist leader and with his gloomy prognosis for the post-war period:

> The picture that the future presents [...] is in fact frightening, and it would be desirable that the Briands,[35] the Lloyd Georges,[36] the Clemenceaus,[37] see it in that way, as the Caillaux[38] and other excommunicated persons for excess of perspicacity saw it in advance.[39]

An Observer and Mediator between Europe and Latin America

Payró was undoubtedly a subtle observer of the social and political realities of his time and acted as a mediator between the events in European and his Argentine readers. In his chronicles he always tried to make the experiences understandable to his audience, translating them into a shared cultural code and establishing parallels with Argentine culture. During the post-war period, Payró's aims as a journalist were not only to keep his readers well informed about the dramatic events of this time of turmoil, but also to extract from the European experience lessons that could be useful to his native country. Despite the crisis of civilisation produced by the Great War, the Old Continent continued to provide tools and examples to the young Latin American nations, where economic and political modernisation had started late, in the second half of the nineteenth century. Generally, Payró drew attention to some developments that could apply to Argentina to solve specific problems, but without going more deeply into their concrete adaptation.

He paid particular attention to some innovative changes in Belgium that could serve as a model for other countries, including Argentina. In the first place, Payró considered "that knowledge of the conquests of modern law [is] useful to our country", mainly Belgian social security legislation. He especially emphasised the protection of the old by means of a progressive pension system, based on the principles of assistance and sharing.[40]

In second place he addressed a pressing and global social problem: a critical housing shortage:

> The entire world currently encounters [...] the same difficulty that in some countries has serious proportions: the shortage of houses for rent, and above all, of housing for workers. This problem, which deeply concerns Buenos Aires, all the more reason interests the Belgians and the French, who have seen many of their villages and towns destroyed or razed by the war. But the lack and shortage of housing are also observed in Italy, England, the United States, as well as in Buenos Aires… It can be said that the problem is universal.[41]

Post-war Belgium witnessed the emergence of a national organisation, sponsored by the government, devoted to promoting the construction and/or leasing of dwellings which supported local initiatives. Among its projects, Payró praised the design of neighbourhood gardens as part of a renewed and hygienic urban model, and the central role attributed to the communes.[42] He considered that if Belgium was able to accomplish this new urban initiative, his own country should adopt it without excuses.

Finally, the last Belgian development proposed by Payró as a model to consider in Argentina was the political coalition system.[43] Since 1912, Argentina had gone through a political democratisation process based on universal suffrage, which had led to the traditional conservative elite's loss of office and the ascent of the principal opposition organisation, the Radical Party. However, unlike in Belgium, political parties did not have a well defined ideological profile, and the ruling party and the opposition were engaged in constant and irreconcilable disputes.[44] The Belgian political parties' experience of coexistence and conciliation during the war was unusual for the Argentine, who certainly considered it as a precious model for his country's turbulent political system.

To conclude, during his stay in Belgium, between 1909 and 1922, Roberto J. Payró witnessed the dramatic hours that would herald the "short twentieth century".[45] From his outpost as correspondent of the Argentine newspaper *La Nación* he observed the outbreak of the First World War, the invasion and occupation of Belgium by German troops and the first years of a disrupted post-war period. His columns transmitted his impressions and emotions, based on direct experience of the events.

The Great War unleashed a profound crisis, which led to the questioning of the main pillars of the social and political order prevailing until 1914. Demands for reform spread across the continent and even globally. After the armistice, Payró paid close attention to the developments in Europe, always through the prism of Belgium. He tried to extract lessons to apply in his native country, such as those related to the social question and the political system. He observed both areas as promising fields to implement reforms in Argentina, following the Belgian example.

Moreover, in the post-war scene two main issues captured his interest and were the axis of his reflections: the reconstruction of Belgium and the reconfiguration of the European geopolitical map. Concerning the first point, he sketched a discouraging prospect of the war's legacy of destruction and of the economic and social situation in the immediate post-war period. However, he also perceived that the formidable task of the reconstruction of Belgium was starting to produce positive results. In that assessment Payró attributed an important role to the attitude of the political parties: in pursuit of the country's recovery they postponed some of their programmatical demands. In particular, he granted a vital role to socialism, whose moderation in times of widespread ideological radicalisation would act as a guarantee of the social and political stability necessary for reconstruction.

Regarding the new international order designed by the peace conference, he sided again with the criticisms of the Belgian socialists. He advocated for equitable treatment towards Germany, which contemplated both the need to take moral and material responsibility for its acts during the war and its effective capacity to pay. Like the Belgian socialists, Payró warned that excessively harsh treatment of the defeated power could lead to renewed militarism and to a new global catastrophe. His diagnosis would prove to be accurate, although he would not live to witness its tragic development

Notes

1. For a description of Payró's war chronicles, see: Martha Vanbiesem de Burbridge, "Un Argentin témoin de la guerre: la Belgique occupée vue par Roberto Payró", *Textyles* 32-33 (2007). For an analysis of these sources from the perspective of the history of emotions, see: María Inés Tato, "Trapped in occupied Brussels: Roberto J. Payró's war experience, 1914-1915," in *The Great War in Belgium and the Netherlands. Beyond Flanders Fields*, ed. Felicity Rash and Christophe Declercq (Basingstoke: Palgrave MacMillan, 2018).
   Payrós' chronicles were compiled by Martha Vanbiesem de Burbridge in the book *Roberto J. Payró, Corresponsal de guerra. Cartas, diarios, relatos (1907-1922)* (Buenos Aires: Biblos, 2009). Bernard Goorden has translated the articles referring to Belgium into French and Dutch, available online at his site www.idesetautres.be/?p=ides, which also gathers together many valuable materials on Payró and wartime Belgium.
2. Payró, "Diario de un testigo. Dos representantes argentinos muertos en la guerra", article dated 20 October 1914 and published in *La Nación* on 17 November 1914, in Payró, *Corresponsal de guerra*, 631-642.
3. Argentine, Buenos Aires, Archivo del Ministerio de Relaciones Exteriores y Culto (AMREC), Fondo Primera Guerra Mundial (FPGM), AH/00044/1, "Fusilamiento del vicecónsul argentino en Dinant Sr. Himmer", and AH/00044/2, "Muerte del canciller del Consulado Gral. en Amberes, Sr. Lemaire, a consecuencia del bombardeo de esa plaza".
4. For instance, the Parisian *Le Figaro* translated Payró's chronicles on this event, later published by the Belgian *Le XXe siècle* ("Pires que des sauvages. Les massacres de Dinant. Le Consul Argentin, M. Himmer, fusillé", 17 December 1914) and *L'Echo Belge* ("A Dinant", 26 December 1914).
5. The Argentine government tried to arrange for his repatriation, but the German authorities refused and demanded that Payró stay in Germany for several months before his return to Buenos Aires; this proposal was rejected by the writer (AMREC-FPGM, AH/00056/1, "Bélgica. Detención del ciudadano argentino Roberto J. Payró por autoridades alemanas en Bruselas").
6. On the impact of the First World War in Latin America, see: Olivier Compagnon, *L'adieu à l'Europe. L'Amérique latine et la Grande Guerre* (Paris: Fayard, 2013); Stefan Rinke, *Latin America and the First World War* (Cambridge: Cambridge University Press, 2017); María Inés Tato, *La trinchera austral. La sociedad argentina ante la Primera Guerra Mundial* (Rosario: Prohistoria, 2017); Olivier Compagnon, Camille Foulard, Guillemette Martin, and María Inés Tato, eds., *La Gran Guerra en América Latina. Una historia conectada* (Mexico City: Centro de Estudios Mexicanos y Centroamericanos/Institut des Hautes Études de l'Amérique Latine – Centre de Recherche et de Documentation des Ameriques, 2018).
7. Payró, "Pilgrimage to the ruins" (published between 4 and 12 December 1914), in Payró, *Corresponsal de Guerra*, 711-744.
8. Roberto J. Payró, "El campo de batalla de Bélgica" (dated 18 December 1918 and published on 1 March 1919), in Roberto J. Payró, *Corresponsal de guerra*, 1053-1054.
9. On the economic and social difficulties faced by Belgium after the liberation, see: Sophie de Schaepdrijver, *La Belgique et la Première Guerre mondiale* (Brussels: Peter Lang, 2006), 292-294.
10. Payró, "A guisa de prólogo" (published on 27 December 1919), in Payró, *Corresponsal de guerra*, 1120-1121.

11	Payró, "Episodios y eventualidades. Danza de millones" (dated 8 June 1919 and published on 18 August 1919), in Payró, *Corresponsal de guerra*, 1096.
12	Payró, "Episodios y eventualidades. Más millones" (dated 12 June 1919 and published on 9 September 1919), in Payró, *Corresponsal de guerra*, 1107.
13	Payró, "El problema de la habitación" (dated May 1920 and published on 12 July 1920), in Payró, *Corresponsa de guerral*, 1139-1142.
14	Payró, "Reliquias de la guerra" (dated May 1920 and published on 29 June 1920), in Payró, *Corresponsal de guerra*, 1136.
15	Payró, "Las pensiones a la vejez en Bélgica" (dated December 1920 and published on 6 February 1921), in Payró, *Corresponsal de guerra*, 1183-1184; Sophie de Schaepdrijver, *La Belgique et la Première Guerre mondiale*, 297-298.
16	Payró, "Hacia la normalidad" (dated May 1920 and published on 27 July 1920), in Payró, *Corresponsal de guerra*, 1142-1146.
17	Payró, "A guisa de prólogo" (dated 9 December 1918 and published on 27 February 1919), in Payró, *Corresponsal de guerra*, 1046.
18	Payró, "La unión hace la fuerza" (dated 20 November 1920 and published on 10 January 1921), in Payró, *Corresponsal de guerra*, 1170. The coalition gathered together Catholics, socialists and liberals.
19	Payró, "Política positivista" (dated May 1920 and published on 29 July 1920), in Payró, *Corresponsal de guerra*, 1149.
20	Payró, "El discurso del trono y el programa de gobierno, 1" (dated 12 December 1918 and published on 27 February 1919), in Payró, *Corresponsal de guerra*, 1048.
21	Sophie de Schaepdrijver, "Belgium," in *A Companion to World War I*, ed. John Horne (Oxford: Blackwell Publishing, 2010), 396.
22	Payró, "El discurso del trono y el programa de gobierno, 1", in Payró, *Corresponsal de guerra*, 1047.
23	Payró, "Un ultimátum socialista" (published on 16 June 1920), in Payró, *Corresponsal de guerra*, 1133.
24	Payró, "El socialismo se define en Bélgica" (published on 12 June 1921), in Payró, *Corresponsal de guerra*, 1215.
25	Payró, "Un ultimátum socialista", in Payró, *Corresponsal de guerra*, 1133.
26	Payró, "El sufragio universal en Bélgica" (dated April 1919 and published on 6 July 1919), in Payró, *Corresponsal de guerra*, 1088.
27	Payró, "Cartas informativas 4" (published on 5 March 1919), in Payró, *Corresponsal de guerra*, 1068.
28	"Cartas informativas 4", in Payró, *Corresponsal de guerra*, 1094.
29	Ibid., 1094.
30	Michael Neiberg, *The Treaty of Versailles. A concise history* (New York: Oxford University Press, 2017), 57-65.
31	Sally Marks, *Innocent Abroad: Belgium at the Paris Peace Conference of 1919* (Chapel Hill, NC: The University of North Carolina Press, 2011).
32	Payró, "Bélgica y el tratado de paz" (dated September 1919 and published on 7 December 1919), in Payró, *Corresponsal de guerra*, 1118-1119.
33	Quoted in Payró, "Bélgica y las naciones. Un discurso notable" (dated April 1921 and published on 27 May 1921), in Payró, *Corresponsal de guerra*, 1214-1215.
34	Quoted in Payró, "El socialismo se define en Bélgica", in Payró, *Corresponsal de guerra*, 1218.
35	Aristide Briand, Prime Minister of France.
36	David Lloyd George, British Prime Minister.

37 Georges Clemenceau, Former Prime Minister of France.
38 Joseph Caillaux, leader of the French Radical Party, pacifist and in favour of a peace without annexations or compensation.
39 Payró, "El socialismo se define en Bélgica", in Payró, *Corresponsal de guerra*, 1219.
40 Payró, "Las pensiones a la vejez en Bélgica", in Payró, *Corresponsal de guerra*, 1183.
41 Payró, "El problema de la habitación", in Payró, *Corresponsal de guerra*, 1139.
42 "El problema de la habitación", in Payró, *Corresponsal de guerra*, 1139-1140.
43 Payró, "A guisa de prólogo" (published on 27 December 1919), in Payró, *Corresponsal de guerra*, 1120.
44 About Argentine political life in this period and its main conflicts, see: María Inés Tato, *Viento de Fronda. Liberalismo, conservadurismo y democracia en la Argentina, 1911-1932* (Buenos Aires: Siglo Veintiuno Editores, 2004).
45 Eric J. Hobsbawm, *Age of extremes: the short twentieth century, 1914-1991* (London: Michael Joseph, 1994).

Fig 1. The Spanish war correspondent, Carmen de Burgos, and her sister, visiting the Hebrew neighbourhood of Melilla in 1909. Photo: Francisco Goñi (1909), © Diario ABC.

The New Post-war Order from the Perspective of the Spanish Struggle for Regeneration (1918-1923)

Carolina García Sanz

War Abandons Europe and "Regeneration" Reaches the Spanish Government

The beginning of the twentieth century triggered a heated debate on national identity in Spain. The loss of the last remaining colonies in the Caribbean and the Pacific, military powerlessness in Morocco and domestic political crisis portrayed Spain as a country poles apart from the positivist ideal of a healthy and robust society to which the Spanish regenerationists aspired.[1] One of the principal manifestations of this debate was the general outcry against an oligarchic, exclusionary and, at the same time, inoperative political system in the context of a world in deep and fast transformation. Only a few months before the Great War broke out, conspicuous philosopher José Ortega y Gasset would reiterate the national need for profound change in the lecture that he gave on "Old and New Politics" at Madrid's Theatre of Comedy on 23 March 1914.

The four-year war in Europe would later kindle a yearning for change and national reconstruction fostered by a minority of Spanish intellectuals, interiorised by society at large. The debate on the government policy of neutrality favouring the Entente Cordiale led to a social rift that would place the country – in the words of the socialist and fervent Anglophile Luis Araquistain – "between war and revolution". The international circumstances were generally seen as an opportunity for national regeneration from the "outside in" from two opposing perspectives. On the one hand, for those sectors closest to republicanism and socialism the ultimate Allied victory would contribute to the establishment of a democratic regime in Spain. In this regards, the magazine *España*, a pro-Allied mouthpiece since January 1915, would survive the war as a so-called "organ of neo-regenerationism".[2] And, on the other, for the most traditionalist sectors a German victory would have the same effect by curbing the influence of France and Great Britain on Spanish politics, thus anticipating a long-awaited Iberian reconstruction. For its part, the New Right, represented by the young followers of conservative Antonio Maura, would take centre stage with an interpretation of change in terms of counter-revolution.

However, the revolutionary events in Russia and Spain in 1917 paved the way for Maura's return to power at the head of a government of national unity coinciding with the last months of war. The old Majorcan establishment politician, who had maintained an ambivalent attitude towards the system after the national schism over the "Maura, yes", "Maura, no" conundrum in 1909,[3] would become committed to the "moral superiority of an authoritarian government of elites" in view of the Red Scare and the system's collapse. The end of the war coincided, therefore, with the accession to power of conservative regenerationism. The so-called Maurists, the followers of Juan de la Cierva (alienated conservatives of the moment) and the supporters of the Catalonian autonomist party *Lliga Regionalista*, such as its co-founder and conservative leader Francesc Cambó, would join Spanish governments between 1919 and 1923.

Once in power, the internal flaws of that nationalist, regenerationist and conservative cross-class project were soon evinced amid defiance provoked by the spirit of the "People's Spring" capitalised on President Wilson's idealism, which led to the campaign for the Statute and the *Mancomunitat de Catalunya* (a fusion of Catalonia's four provincial entities).[4] Furthermore, within the Spanish right, tensions between those who were committed to an increasingly more authoritarian nationalism and those who refused to renounce democratic liberalism bubbled to the surface. Of the new conservative ideas suggested, expectations of the changes brought about by the Great War attracted social attention, facilitating "the departure from former mental habits, from the old liberal formulary", thanks to the establishment in Europe of "regimes for which freedom is a subordinated common good".[5] Antonio Goicoechea was one of the most relevant figures of this political current and *La Acción*, a self-proclaimed "newspaper, unrelated to the political establishment, whose sole mission is to tell the truth" was its mouthpiece. During the war, Goicoechea had written about "the war of ideas", according to the "dictates of reason and ethics". Similarly, he had reflected on "the European war and the new approaches to public law" in a conference speech given in February 1916 at the Royal Academy of Jurisprudence and Legislation, of which he would become vice-president. Later on, in May 1921, he would deliver an address on "[t]he legal and economic tradition and social reform programme".[6]

Yet, between 1919 and 1922, the vigorous regenerationist right failed to articulate a unitary political project with stable governments. The maintenance of law and order in light of the conflict between workers and their employers and its vulnerability with respect to the Military Defence Councils (*Juntas Militares de Defensa*) insubordination to civil power were the right wing's Achilles heel. By then Spanish domestic politics did not fit plausible alternative scenarios. In the spring of 1922, nor would the liberal reformers led by Santiago Alba manage to breathe life into the political programme that left-wing groups also demanded (the supremacy of civil over military authority, the setting up of a civilian protectorate in Morocco, progressive tax reforms, land legislation, a public works plan, taxes on war profits, legalising workers' organisations, etc.).[7]

Against this convoluted political backdrop coinciding with the European post-war period, the aim of this chapter is to draw connections between Spanish old and new politics before regenerationism "by lawful means" was replaced by the authoritarianism of General Primo de Rivera in 1923. I will bring in here some examples of Spanish discourses on reform matching different views of the momentous European reconstruction. Spanish society also had to elaborate a national and dichotomous interpretation of repair and reform in the aftermath of war. On the one hand, Spanish citizens had been collateral victims of economic and naval war, suffering high inflation rates and internal shortages.[8] On the other hand, they would have to face a post-war world and make sense of it. Despite its pro-allied neutrality throughout the conflict, Spain was a mere spectator at the peace negotiations in Versailles. Spanish cabinets felt deeply affected by the national weaknesses and military insecurities behind their wartime policies. However, despite wartime disappointments for Spanish diplomacy whose agency had been linked to Alfonso XIII's peace initiatives, clear commitment to the multilateralism of the League of Nations would also exhibit the political-establishment parties' aspirations for reform in the international arena.[9]

Rebuilding the National Army: Same Old

Notwithstanding the fact that the Spanish army did not participate in the Great War, the war fuelled decisive battles in the country's internal struggles. A hypertrophic military fed by the promotion of war merits in Morocco became the centrepiece of the discussion about the condition of the Spanish army. The military problem was only a symptom of a wider national disease. Geopolitical calculations integrated collective conflicting emotions and the possibility of war in Europe inevitably fuelled the social controversies over "national essences" after the horrendous nightmare of 1898. On those bases, the pressing need for military reform had been repeatedly highlighted by different Spanish cabinets. Conservative Maura's naval reform in 1907, liberal José Canalejas' military bill in 1912 and, already during the European war, General Luque's draft were political responses to social disaffection in 1916. In 1917 the *Juntistas* under Coronel Benito Márquez used the newspaper *La Correspondencia Militar* to denounce the petty corruption stemming from the connivance between the *Compañía Española de Colonización* (Spanish Colonisation Company) in the eastern region of Spanish Morocco and High Commissioner Francisco Gómez Jordana. Therefore, the *Juntistas'* insubordination to the generals assumed a regenerationist rhetoric, airing the republicans' and socialists' lack of enthusiasm for colonialism and public opposition to the arbitrary quota-based recruitment system. But the challenges arising in the summer of 1917, above all the General Strike in the August, laid bare the Government's dependence on the army to guarantee law and order. Furthermore, the rift between the insubordinate Military Defence Councils and the Africanist sector not only precipitated the fall of the liberal government of Manuel García Prieto, but also called attention to the conservatives' policy of granting concessions to the army.

It was in this context that a new military reform should be to reduce the surplus of officers and increase spending on training and equipment: "from whatever angle we approach this problem, we will see that the first task should and must be to cut back; and this requires energy rather than science".[10] The most noteworthy aspects of the Law passed by the conservatives in June 1918 had to do with the regulation of promotions and postings, which were granted on a seniority basis, and the investments for modernising military equipment with the doubling of the Ministry of War's budget.[11] That proposal for a closed promotion system was strongly opposed by the army in Morocco. Moreover, the pressure brought to bear on the Government by the Military Defence Councils became a subject of political debate.[12]

In 1920, the Count of Romanones reflected on both issues in *El ejército y la política* (*The Army and Politics*). His criticism of the 1918 Outline Law and the alternatives that he suggested were strongly inspired by the European scenario. Due to its military weakness neutrality was imposed on Spain and "in face of the different phenomena that have occurred in the post-war period we, neutralists at all costs, continue to be inhibited, letting the minutes, during which the fate of mankind is being decided, pass by".[13] Nonetheless, in Romanones' view, not all the neutral countries had chosen this path because of the weakness of their armed forces, as demonstrated by Switzerland whose lessons in the field of military organisation even the warring nations found useful:

> I am not saying that we should take the Swiss army as an example; I, of course, declare that it is incompatible with our social milieu; but I do be-

lieve that much of what is done there contains very useful lessons. Currently, France itself regarding the military reform, is turning its eyes towards Switzerland; the example set by its last mobilisations has impressed the military world.[14]

Belgium embodied quite the opposite. The Belgians had paid the price of not observing the teachings of Hobbes: "if only Belgium had thus considered it! Events have taught that treaties are of little use".[15] Between January and March of 1919 that same idea was echoed in the Spanish press closest to the regime. Specifically, attention was drawn to the absence of Belgium in laying out the groundwork for the Paris Peace Conference:

> Heroic Belgium, that little big nation, a martyr of the struggle, has not been able to attend that assembly [...].There is no doubt that the moral effect would have been more gratifying for the world if, with an elegant gesture, the powerful nations had included in their deliberations those who, at the time of sacrifice, did not stop to gauge the magnitude of what was being imposed on them. The pain of Belgium made it worthy of that [...][16]

Romanones claimed that building a strong army would put an end to Spain's isolation, facilitating new international alliances.[17] Despite the hopes placed in the League of Nations, the post-war world was still one that needed alliances. He illustrated this by referring to the Franco-Belgian move in April 1920, which he interpreted as an "military agreement" rather than a political tool for managing the occupied territories.[18] The army reforms in Italy, France and Great Britain aimed at adapting their armed forces to peace provided lessons for Spain too. Examples given were the decree amending the Italian Recruitment Act, presented in the spring of that same year by the socialist Ivanoe Bonomi, and French and British recourse to the Reserve Officers' Training Corps (ROTC). The latter – in his opinion – could be a way of resolving the severe problem of the surplus of officers in the Spanish army:

> Everyone knows the very important and decisive role that those non-professional officers have played in France, and it must be confessed that the same can be said of the English and American armies, 90 percent of whose officers were not full-time professionals.
> In this regard, we have made the grave mistake of believing that only professional officers have the necessary skills to command on the battlefield.[19]

In reality, the old statesman instrumentalised the national debate on the army to insist on the policy of rapprochement with France and Great Britain. So, much to his regret, action had not been taken according to traditional "foreign policy as defined by the conservatives and liberals in many diplomatic addresses and documents" for decades.[20] The post-war period offered, however, an opportunity to rectify this. Romanones reaffirmed his commitment to the dream of returning Spain to its rightful place among the major powers capitalising on European reconstruction:

> There is no reason why Spain should not harbour such an aspiration; the simple fact of proclaiming its ambition would make it worthy of it; and now is the time to do so, in which a great anaemia, the fatal result of war, is enervating all the peoples of Europe to the same degree.[21]

But the count's opportunism and his lack of legitimacy as an advocate of "old politics" explain the scant power of seduction, beyond his immediate circle, of his invocation of Spain's role as a modern and "European" power, committed to France and Great Britain, in the post-war world. In the autumn of 1920, Romanones – who was interested in Spanish businesses in Morocco – pretended to win over the Africanist officers and, at the same time, as Manuel Azaña would comment in *España*, proposed "not what he is going to do in the Government, but what he believes is convenient to say and offer to return to the Government".[22]

European Reconstruction and National Economy

In August 1914, the uncertainty in the international markets had a very negative impact on the Madrid Stock Exchange. Simultaneously, the Government placed an export ban on basic commodities to stave off the spectre of domestic shortages.[23] Months afterwards, the passing of the British Order in Council of 11 March 1915, allowing the detention of non-contraband goods forwarded, presumably, to belligerent countries, unsuccessfully prompted organisations such as *Fomento del Trabajo Nacional* (Promotion of National Labour), the *Liga de Defensa Industrial y Comercial* (Industrial and Trade Defence League) and the *Cámara Industrial de Barcelona* (Barcelona Chamber of Industry) to ask Eduardo Dato's government for protection.[24]

However, despite the initial concern about the country's economy, war would ultimately be "a fabulous period" for some companies and sectors, giving rise to "an authentic orgy of profits".[25] Spain was the main European producer of copper, lead and sulphur and, moreover, Great Britain and France controlled production through major corporations like *Rio Tinto Co. Ltd.* and *Peñarroya* (Société minière et métallurgique). From the spring of 1917, the negotiation of trade and financial agreements with Great Britain, France, Italy and the USA turned the country into the

Entente's exclusive supplier. Consequently, the Spanish Central Bank would become the fourth largest in the world as regards the volume of its reserves.

Nonetheless, the war was also a lost opportunity for the Spanish state and the modernisation of its economy. In 1916, the liberal Santiago Alba tried to introduce a tax on profits. This initiative met with opposition from the Catalan and Biscay MPs who defended their respective shipping and mining interests in Parliament. Alba's tax programme included a "project of national reconstitution", an idea that the conservative Augusto González Besada would unsuccessfully revive in 1918.[26] So the failure of all these redistributive measures, the tough post-war adjustment plan, galloping inflation that in some cases had doubled prices, would widen the gap between the two "Spains".[27] Events such as the *La Canadiense* strike and the lockouts in Barcelona, in addition to the outbreak of the "Bolshevik Triennium" in Andalusia, underscored yet again the sensation of economic derailment and social unrest prevailing in the country.

Strikingly, European reconstruction would again allow those who longed for a different and better country to give free rein to their political imaginations. In 1919, the picture of European destruction contrasted with that of a country like Spain in which the rich had become enormously wealthy. Spanish papers would resort to irony to illustrate this stark reality. An example of this can be found in the caricature *Un rico presente del futuro* (A rich gift of the future), published in *La Acción* in the spring of the same year. It depicted an upper class salon in which a gentlemen is approaching an elegant lady (*Condesita*) with an onion. In a cruel show of frivolity, she replies, "An onion? You are terrible, Carlos, quite terrible. I accept it because it is most 'fashionable' in the great world".[28]

The war had ended but the "Conquest of Markets. The trade war in Europe and America" continued, thanks to the reconstruction work in those countries that had been hardest hit by it.[29] In particular, the homage paid to the humanitarian work of the Marquis of Villalobar inevitably focused attention on "the provisioning of shattered Belgium".[30] A report of the Consul General of Spain in Antwerp provided food for thought on "the means of fostering and developing Spain's trade relations".[31] It gave an account of the reconstruction of land and sea communications, the thwarted project of a *comptoir d'achat*, the system of trade licences granted by the Ministries of Work and Industry and Financial Affairs, and the role played by the Commission for Relief in Belgium. The consul's proposals were based on the notion that the imposition of trade penalties on the Central Powers, because of "an animosity that, even though it will not last forever, will indeed prevail for some time", could open up markets for Spanish goods. The needs of the Belgians and the procurement requirements of the occupation forces opened up a market for "fabrics, hosiery, leather goods, footwear, hats, umbrellas, buckles, buttons, broaches, haberdashery products in general, horn and bone articles, ordinary perfumes, cars, fortified wines".[32] Peace might also offer

Spain identical opportunities in the markets of Romania, Syria, Bohemia and Poland. The national economy was not only capable of exporting food products (oils and preserves) – as it had done hitherto – but would also discover markets for its industrial and consumer goods.

Moreover, press releases dealing with the devastating effects of the war were not only considered to be of interest to the Spanish public in relation to repairing the material damage versus the "destructive spirit of Leuven". Addressing social and labour issues amidst such frenetic activity was also important. In the spring of 1919, the press covered the reconstruction of Leuven's courthouse.[33] On 13 June, coinciding with the concern about the workers' conflict in Andalusia, the front page of *El Liberal* included a story about the Paris strikes and a brief note on "the reconstruction of Belgium and a major metal industry trade union".[34] The words of unity and heroism were continually paraphrased in reports on Belgium, a country that could set an example of national economic reconstruction. Spanish workers and their unions should also follow it, putting aside class demands and labour for the superior cause.

A New Society of New Spanish Women

"New women" in Madrid had stood out among those who championed pacifism wholeheartedly in Spain between 1914 and 1918.[35] Moreover, the conflict had served to highlight the contribution of women to the war effort in a neutral country such as Spain, thanks to the activism of the women residing in the colonies of the warring nations. For instance, the *Junta de Damas Aliadas* (Junta of Allied Ladies) had been very active in Andalusia with the involvement of the British archaeologist Ellen Whishaw in fundraising at children's parties for peace for the child welfare institutions *Gota de Leche* and the war wounded and POWs.[36]

The end of the war coincided with an especially intense period of feminist activity. On the one hand, the role played by the young educator María de Maeztu by linking the *Instituto Internacional* of Madrid (and its American curriculum) to the *La Residencia de Señoritas* under the aegis of the Free Institution of Education was noteworthy. On the other, it was the success of the new Anglo-Saxon pedagogical ideals among women coming from families who were socially and culturally very influential (Lucila Posada, the daughter of Adolfo Posada, María Teresa García, the niece of the painter Sorolla, Consuelo Vaca, the granddaughters of Concepción Arenal, etc.).[37] In October 1918, the National Association of Spanish Women was founded by the entrepreneur María Espinosa de los Monteros, the sales manager of the *Yost Writing Machine Company*. That same year, the more left-wing Spanish Women's Union was also founded by the Marchioness of Ter and María Lejárraga, whose members included the war correspondent Carmen de Burgos (Fig. 1). In particular, versus the dominant stance in the Spanish intellectual debate, amplified by hyperbolic masculinities in which the war experience was coded as an opportunity for national regeneration, either through strict neutrality or a closer alliance with France and Great Britain, women like Carmen de Burgos genuinely embodied the values of pacifism and anti-war sentiment. In the pro-Allied field, she managed to convey a belligerent message against war understood as an instrument of abuse wielded by the rich and powerful. After the Barranco del Lobo fiasco in the summer of 1909, her reports would reveal her famous pacifism in "War on War":

> And I have seen war, I have witnessed the sorrow of the struggle; I have contemplated the pain of the wounded in cold hospital wards, and I have seen the dead on the battlefield.... But more than anything else, I have been horrified by the cruelty of war, how it stirs up the quagmire of violence in our souls, how we get used to the suffering of others practically to the point of indifference... and above all how hatred invades hearts! Indeed, with the barbarity of war bestial atavisms erased from the history re-emerge.[38]

In an article about the dramatic work, *War Brides,* by an American authoress, published in the *Heraldo de Madrid* in December 1915, de Burgos insisted on the responsibility of women not only as housewives but as educators of men: "all modern women abominate and should rebel against the infamy of bearing sons in order to continue to fuel barbarity and destruction. But this cannot be remedied by refusing to have them. It is remedied by educating them".[39] Her vigorous pacifism would continue after the war, when she became wary of a peace imposed by the victors. Women should have a place in the public sphere because it was not only their right, but also their moral duty or ethical commitment to a new society in construction. This idea was vividly present in her post-war writings.

The proliferation of articles in the conservative press – in the immediate post-war period – in favour of women returning to "their place" after assuming masculine roles in the rearguard, would give greater impetus to activism in pursuit of civil and political equality in Spain. Throughout 1919, the Spanish right-wing press frequently questioned British electoral reform, while keeping a close eye on the women's suffrage movement in France:[40] "Will universal suffrage, which has not yet managed to make men happy, make women happy?" In a nutshell, Spanish women should not let themselves be seduced by the siren calls of foreign doctrines, based on the deforming experiences of women during the war. And, at any rate, universal suffrage should mark the final frontier of women's participation in politics:

> [...] that if women can and should participate in politics contributing with their will, which means their vote to the election of legislators who are believed to be honest, this is where their participation should end, contenting themselves with this and without intending to occupy political posts for which they are not and cannot be qualified. This is at least how the vast majority of Spanish women feel.[41]

In 1921, Carmen de Burgos created the *Cruzada de las mujeres españolas* (Crusade of Spanish Women) inspired by the progressive ideals and regenerationist activities of its Portuguese namesake, with which she had had ties. On 31 May of that same year, she organised the first demonstration for effective equality between men and women, presenting her manifesto before Parliament. Its main points were as follows: full equality as regards political rights (voters and candidates); freedom to pursue a trade or profession; jury service; equality in the criminal justice system; paternity investigation and equal legal rights for legitimate and illegitimate offspring; women's education; and the persecution of prostitution.[42] The political transformations anticipated in the old warring nations of Europe also opened the door to women in order that they might change and improve Spanish society.

Final Remarks

The period between 1914 and 1923 constitutes one of the richest in twentieth-century Spanish historiography. Since the 1970s there has been a prolific line of research that has allowed us to discover such transcendental aspects – for development in Spain – as the collapse of the constitutional system of the Restoration, a crisis that was triggered by the economic effects of the First World War and in which political and social insubordination "from below" and "from above" would prove to be the deathblow of the establishment in 1917. This is why the regenerationist antagonism characterised by the opposition between the "real Spain" and the "official Spain" in the context of the Great War has conditioned the approach of studies of the period for decades. However, there is a need for further research that draws parallels between the Spanish and European war and post-war imagologies. Therefore, the intention here has been to approach the issue of reform in a necessarily partial and incomplete manner, using particular examples to explore connections between discursive strategies of "old-school politicians", "mainstream papers" and "new women" alike on the changes that took place in Spain during the process of European post-war reconstruction.

Notes

1 A vivid depiction of this intellectual and regenerationist climate is provided by Josua Goode, *Defining Race in Spain, 1870-1930* (Baton Rouge, LA: LSU Press, 2009), 76-96, 143-181.
2 Manuel Tuñón de Lara, *España. Semanario de la Vida Nacional* (Madrid: Turner 1982), vii-xvii.
3 The military mobilisation of reservists in Barcelona to reinforce the troops already in Morocco, in July 1909, had been the trigger for an intense wave of social violence, which ended with the resignation of the conservative Antonio Maura as prime minister after the anarchist Francisco Ferrer i Guardia's execution.
4 Those campaigns led to tensions within the autonomist movement itself. José María Capdevila, "En Cataluña. Ruptura entre la Inteligencia y la Política," *España*, 31 January 1920, 7.
5 Juan Gil Pecharromán, *Conservadores subversivos. La derecha autoritaria Alfonsina (1913-1936)* (Madrid: Eudema, 1994), 31.
6 Regarding Antonio Goicoechea and his ideological evolution within the Spanish right, see: Pedro Antonio González Cuevas, "Antonio Goicoechea. Político y doctrinario monárquico," *Historia y Política* 6 (2001): 161-189.
7 Eduardo González Calleja, *La España de Primo de Rivera. La modernización autoritaria 1923-1930* (Madrid: Alianza, 2005), 29.
8 There is a comprehensive collection of essays on Spanish neutrality in a transnational perspective in Jose Leonardo Ruiz Sánchez, Inmaculada Cordero, and Carolina García Sanz, eds., *Shaping Neutrality throughout the First World War* (Seville: Universidad de Sevilla, 2015); See also a recent collection focused on the domestic view: Carlos Sanz Díaz and Zorann Petrovici, eds., *La Gran Guerra en la España de Alfonso XIII* (Madrid: Sílex, 2019).
9 On Spain and the League of Nations, see: José Luis Neila Hernández, *La Sociedad de Naciones* (Madrid: Arco Libros, 1997).
10 Comandante Beta, "Apuntes para historiar tres años de reformas militares (1915-1917)," in *La política pretoriana en el reinado de Alfonso XIII*, ed. Carolyn P. Boyd (Madrid: Alianza Universidad, 1990), 44.
11 The Royal Decree of March foresaw an outlay of approximately 1,300 million pesetas. Fundamental principles for the reorganisation of the army, envisaged in the Royal Decree of 7 March 1918. In *Gaceta de Madrid*, 30 June 1918, 823-841.
12 The issue, which would be debated in Parliament, overlapped with the discussions on the military and political responsibilities for the disaster at Annual on 22 July 1921 at the hands of Berber combatants of the Rif region, with between 12,000 and 14,000 Spanish casualties.
13 Romanones Conde and Álvaro Figueroa, *El ejército y la Política. Apuntes sobre la organización militar y el Presupuesto de la Guerra* (Madrid: Renacimiento, 1920), 21.
14 Romanones, *El ejército y la Política*, 41.
15 Ibid., 40.
16 "El ocaso del Imperialismo. La gran obra del congreso de la Paz," *El Imparcial*, 15 January 1919, 1.
17 Romanones, *El ejército y la Política*, 238.
18 Ibid., 240.
19 Ibid., 104.

20	Romanones Conde and Álvaro Figueroa *Notas de una vida* (Madrid: Marcial Pons, 1999).
21	Romanones, *El ejército y la Política*, 242.
22	Boyd, *La política pretoriana en el reinado de Alfonso XIII*, 188.
23	*Gaceta de Madrid*, 7 August 1914, 219.
24	*Gaceta de Madrid*, 25 April 1915. Royal Order amending the list of goods banned for export. Goods banned for export cannot be re-dispatched abroad under the form of transit or transhipment when there is full knowledge that they have arrived at a Spanish port and the certificate of origin indicates that their country of destination is Spain or when the destination is unclear.
25	This is how the Catalan textile manufacturer Pedro Gual Villalbí saw the situation in Miguel Martorell Linares: "It was not only a war, it was a revolution". ("España y la Primera Guerra Mundial," *Historia y Política*, 26 (2011): 24.)
26	Francisco Comín, "El período de entreguerras (1914-1936)," in *Historia económica de España, siglos XIX-XX*, ed. Francisco Comín (Barcelona: Critica, 2002), 285-329.
27	Miguel Martorell Linares, "No fue aquello", 31.
28	*La Acción*, 9 March 1919, 1.
29	"Conquista de Mercados. La lucha comercial en Europa y América", *La Ilustración Española y Americana*, 28 February 1919, 125.
30	"Recorriendo los campos de ruinas", *La época*, 5 January 1919, 3-4.
31	Ibid.
32	"Conquista de Mercados. La lucha comercial en Europa y América".
33	*La época*, 24 April 1919, 1.
34	*El Liberal*, 13 June 1919, 1.
35	There were others like Rosario de Acuña that followed the Alliadophile belligerent speech.
36	Whishaw would raise 200,000 pesetas, "La Caridad de Las Damas Aliadas," *Mundo Gráfico*, 3 April 1918, 21.
37	Monserrat Huguet Santos, "Desembarco en 'tierras papales': educadoras estadounidenses en España en el tránsito entre siglos (1877-1931)," in *Regeneracionismo autoritario. Desafíos y bloqueos de una sociedad en transformación: España, 1923-1930*, ed. Francisco Villacorta Baños and María Luisa Rico Gómez (Madrid: Biblioteca Nueva, 2013), 192-193.
38	Concepción Núñez Rey, *Carmen de Burgos, Colombine (1867-1932). Biografía y Obra Literaria* (PhD Thesis., Universidad Complutense de Madrid, 1992), 46.
39	Colombine, Femeninas, "Las novias de la guerra," *Heraldo de Madrid*, 29 December 1915, 4.
40	"Impresiones de la victoria. Las mujeres después de la Guerra," *La época*, 9 January 1919, 1.
41	"Consideraciones generales acerca del feminismo. Las Consecuencias de la Guerra en el estado de la mujer" (Condesa de la Junquera), *La Ilustración Española y Americana*, 28 February 1919, 126-127.
42	Concepción Núñez Rey, *Carmen de Burgos*, 77.

Fig. 1. Ambulance of the Cruz Vermelha Portuguesa (1924).
© Portuguese Red Cross Historical Archive

The Act of Giving

Political Instability and the Reform(ation) of Humanitarian Responses to Violence in Portugal in the Aftermath of the First World War

Ana Paula Pires

"Do you realize what it means to have half a continent in ashes and starving?", asked the Portuguese-American, and still unknown writer John dos Passos to his friend, Ramsey Marvin, on 11 November 1918.[1] The relationship between war and humanitarian action has frequently stimulated a debate in arts, law and political sciences, but it has become a subject that historians have only recently begun to investigate systematically.[2] The global society in which we all live placed human suffering at the centre of its concerns, but it was the First World War that marked a watershed in the professional development of humanitarian action;[3] in 1914 when the war broke out the International Committee of the Red Cross had no strategic plan, reacting to humanitarian need on an ad hoc basis.[4]

A hundred years ago 15 million people were displaced from their homes, 10,057,600 soldiers were killed, 20,235,907 were wounded, and 1,500,000 civilians died from famine or malnourishment. Even between 1918 and 1923, in the aftermath of the armistice of November 1918, Europe was the most violent place on the planet, with four million deaths resulting from revolutions, counter-revolutions and civil wars.[5] The end of the First World War diversified the scope and variety of victims affected not only by the conflict, but by its consequences, providing Red Cross National Societies with a new field of intervention: to provide help for the victims of political violence, as this chapter will show.

Traditionally First World War historiography associates post-war reconstruction with the financial rebuilding of a country and does not immediately note the importance of humanitarian aid in a turbulent post-war period marked by revolutions and counter-revolutions. In the Portuguese case this "reconstruction" contributed to a drastic change in the nature of its political regime, incubating the fascist movement which led to António de Oliveira Salazar's "Estado Novo" in 1933.

From 1916, the year the country entered the war, until the establishment of a military dictatorship in 1926, violence and political instability were a feature of the country's daily life. From the assassination of the President of the Republic in 1918 to confrontations during strikes or a failed attempt to restore the monarchy, in 1919 Portugal entered the post-war phase in political and social turmoil. The Portuguese case fits, therefore, into the greater pattern of political instability and the cycle of European and global violence that Robert Gerwarth[6] has analysed for northern Europe. These "vectors of violence", which in the Portuguese case occurred in the political void left by the assassination of the President of the Republic days before the signing of the Armistice, erupted in association with social protests related to food scarcity and the rising of prices, and were stimulated by revolutionary syndicalism. Portugal therefore constitutes a good observatory to analyse violence not as a culture of defeated First World War countries, but as a feature of the daily life of states victorious and almost untouched by the material destruction caused by war. The uniqueness of the Portuguese case rests, however, not on clashes between communist and anti-communist forces or the consequences of the collapse of its empire – the country entered the post-war period as still the fourth largest empire in the world – but on the divisions that had characterised the country since October 1910 when the republicans victoriously took power.

The Portuguese case shows us that upheaval was not only a feature of defeated countries but a visible characteristic of those disillusioned by the war. In the beginning of the 1920s, a mood of disillusion with the country's involvement in the war took hold in many sectors of Portuguese society, targeting the lack of results obtained by the Portuguese delegation to the Paris Peace Conference and the poor performance of the Portuguese army on the battlefield, both in Europe and in Africa. For these republicans the regime emerged defeated from the war. Despite fully obtaining the right to sit at the negotiation table at the Peace Conference, Portugal would end up staying out of the League of Nations Executive Council where, ironically, neutral Spain would end up taking a seat. The young Republic emerged from the war unable to reach out to the great mass of the population to secure allies against a mounting conservative backlash. The problems faced by the country were summed up by the former Portuguese ambassador to Paris, João Chagas: "Politically we lost our prestige". From this perspective, "the revolutionary coup of December 5 1917 was a blow at the head of the nation. The place whose right we secured at the peace conference will not make us any bigger, after this amazing disaster".[7]

Humanitarian organisations, namely the Red Cross, responded to this "brutalization of violence" by providing aid – medical assistance – to the local populations caught in almost daily confrontations, and to mutilated, gassed and crippled soldiers returning home from Angola, Mozambique and Flanders. Post-war reconstruction, as this paper will show, has many different meanings and must include an entire range of tasks such as those related to assisting the victims of post-war political violence.

This chapter aims to analyse Portugal's entry into the post-war period. It proposes a different approach to this period and actors – very often analysed within the frame of the rise of authoritarian regimes in Europe – by tackling different languages and focusing on the role and importance of humanitarian aid in times of political instability and economic crisis.[8]

The First World War and its aftermath were big events whose consequences affected everyday life, impacting on the lives of ordinary Portuguese men and women. In 2009 Richard Wilson and Richard Brown studied how individuals' and societies' support for the humanitarian project was prompted by empathy[9], that same feeling that 100 years ago prompted Dos Passos to sail from the United States to France and help millions in need.[10]

Turbulent Transition

Portugal's experience of the First World War was unique; a latecomer to the conflict, entering the war was not entirely in Portugal's power, depending instead on approval by Great Britain. Between 1914 and March 1916 Portuguese political life would be played out against the increasingly pressing question of whether to enter the conflict. The interventionist current, although not necessarily large, was politically and culturally influential, and sought entry into the war as essential to safeguard Portugal's colonial empire and prevent a Spanish invasion of the country.[11] On the other side of the Republican political spectrum the Unionist party was reluctant to take to the battlefield without an unambiguous invitation from London.

Once it was decided that the Portuguese Expeditionary Corps would fight alongside the British and the terms under which it would do so were hammered out in a Convention, another setback arose: naval officer Machado Santos led a coup against the government on 13 December 1916, claiming that the time had come to restore the Republic's lost purity, supposedly sullied by party strife.[12]

Theatre of war	Troops		Totals
	European	African	
France[a]	56,411		56,411
Angola	12,430	6,000	18,430
Mozambique	20,423	10,278	30,701
TOTAL	**89,264**	**16,278**	**105,542**

[a] These numbers include the CEP (55 083) and CAPI (1328) contingents (CAPI – Independent Heavy Artillery Corps
Table based on: Luís Alves de Fraga, *Portugal e a Grande Guerra: balanço estatístico*; Aniceto Afonso, Carlos de Matos Gomes, eds. *Portugal: Grande Guerra 1914-1918*, (Lisbon: Quidnovi, 2010).

Table 1: Total troops mobilised by Portugal in the three theatres of war (1914-1918)

As Michael Barnett has pointed out, violence has been the path to benevolence; it is one of the conditions that has made and remade humanitarianism,[13] and here Portugal is no exception. It was the high commissioner for the Red Cross who addressed the leader of the insurgents and asked him to "trust the Red Cross with the guard of military and civilian prisoners",[14] a request that was denied by Machado Santos. José d'Abreu then asked permission "for the Red Cross to act as liaison between the insurgents and the governmental forces",[15] a request that was agreed to. The Portuguese Red Cross acted as an ally to the state, and started to devise a new role for itself: that of assisting and protecting civilians affected by violence in regions that were not directly touched by the destruction that the conflict provoked. Red Cross members used their reputation and diplomatic contacts to respond to this civilian distress.[16] Violence and political instability have therefore acted as turning points in the history of individual humanitarian intervention, and the Red Cross was no exception.

The harsh legal measures adopted to deal with the *coup* resulted in a split within the Evolutionist Party, which in April 1916 left the government because of a sudden parliamentary crisis. Since the beginning of the war the Portuguese political power had devoted much attention to solving the problems caused by the shortage of essential supplies and food. Throughout the country there were numerous protests against the dramatic crisis and hunger during the war. The first protests regarding food shortages surfaced in Oporto on 18 September 1914, culminating in attacks on several food establishments. The movement was spontaneous and the government did not know how to react to it. In the months of April, May and June 1917 workers' conferences were held in the cities of Lisbon and Oporto. They brought together 176 unions, four industry federations, two confederations of unions, several workers' newspapers and a number of cooperatives. On 13 May 1917 bakeries in Lisbon closed and the people, suspecting that they might be hoarding bread, sacked them. In the absence of bread, everything that could replace it was used; the price of potatoes went up from six cents a kilo to 12, then 14 cents, strengthening the momentum of the workers' protests and the feeling of discontent and revolt. Six days later the first attacks against bakeries were carried out, and after that against grocery shops, food shops, taverns and restaurants. In a movement known as the "potato revolt", 186 bakeries were looted from 13 to 20 May 1917; similar action had occurred in Brownsville, New York, in the months of February and March, when the female population took a stand against the rising prices of onions and potatoes, starting a riot which quickly spread to several East coast cities.[17] On 20 May, the President of the Republic declared a state of emergency and handed over the command of Lisbon to the military.[18] The combined effects of unemployment, food shortages and high prices gained a momentum of their own, inevitably producing significant disruptions of public order in several districts of the country; 88 people were wounded and 12 died. All victims were assisted by the Portuguese Red Cross.

During the summer of 1917 several strikes occurred in Lisbon, in a clear demonstration by the population against the shortage of essential goods, hunger, speculation and hoarding, but, first and foremost, against what it considered to be the absence of immediate answers by the government, but also of the global reach of the February Revolution that occurred in Russia. From 12 to 17 July the Portuguese Red Cross provided aid to 22 people wounded by a bomb, resulting from a construction workers' strike, leading to a new wave of violence.[19] On 27 May 1918 in a conference in Rio de Janeiro, João Paulo Freire, head of the propaganda services of the Portuguese Red Cross, declared that the political upheavals that had taken place in Portugal from 1915 onwards represented a new path in the activities of the Red Cross.[20] The organisation was placed under military authority and provided ambulances and first-aid posts to help the wounded. José d'Abreu noted that its action was authorised only because the insurgents did not think of organising or providing any health service of their own.[21] On the other hand Abreu emphasised that the "[…] purposes of the Red Cross personnel were purely humanitarian […]",[22] identifying them straightforwardly as life-savers, who provided "neutral" care to the injured.[23].

Public order was breaking down thus, and several strikes were organised, culminating in the general strike of September 1917. The war ended up paving the way to the rise of ideas which were clearly anti-parliamentary and anti-liberal. Weeks after the Bolshevik Revolution, Portugal was seeing its war effort compromised by a violent uprising;[24] on 5 December 1917, Sidónio Pais, former minister at Berlin, overthrew the government with the aid of a small military force. The Prime Minister was detained when returning from an official visit to France, the Minister of War was also arrested and sent into exile, being joined there by the President of the Republic, whom Sidónio quickly deposed.

Once again, the Portuguese Red Cross acted as intermediary between the insubordinates and the government,[25] reporting their demands to the President of the Republic. In the three days that the revolution lasted the Red Cross treated – in the country's three main cities Lisbon, Oporto and Coimbra – 1,202 wounded and planned for the funerals of 55 dead. According to the Red Cross' report this was the bloodiest revolution that had occurred in the country.[26] The coup had serious consequences; it weakened political power, interventionist officers were exposed to the criticism of their peers and political tensions rose.[27] Pais did not have a powerful political party behind him, and in Flanders the Portuguese Expeditionary Corps was close to breaking point.

Sidónio Pais ended up by being killed at the Rossio railway station in Lisbon on 14 December 1918 and the country was left in chaos with different groups trying to seize power, only one month after the signing of the armistice. From 19 January to 13 February 1919 Paiva Couceiro, the monarchist leader, launched an insurrection in the north of Portugal (Oporto) that became known as the "Northern Monarchy", its main objective being to overthrow the Republican regime, and despite republicans speedily joining hands to overcome this threat, the movement reached Lisbon quickly and the council of ministers determined the need for the Red Cross to intervene. Five campaign hospitals were built, 1,079 wounded were treated, and for the first time a Red Cross ambulance volunteer was wounded; a male nurse injured in the leg by shrapnel fragments.[28] During the confrontations, when the monarchist positions were stormed at Monsanto Hills in Lisbon, 43 people were killed. Advertisements concerning personal insurance against damage caused by revolution and strikes were published in the press.

There were reasons that raised contradictory feelings, justifying the concerns felt by some deputies, like Brito Camacho, who gave vent to his doubts during the June 1919 session of the Chamber of Deputies:

> If it is true, as was said here, that the preliminary Peace agreements have already been signed, the final Peace Treaty has not yet been signed […]. And if wartime politics have determined the formation of the Sacred Union, this union cannot be considered definitively ended as long as the specific terms of the peace conditions are not known […].[29]

Hence the words with which the President of the Republic, António José de Almeida, gave vent to his emotions, admitting the country was in danger "common to all peoples that do not understand the meaning of the last terrible events that bloodied the world, and remained immobile, their inertia both imbecile and criminal".[30]

At the end of 1919 the cost of the Portuguese participation in the war was estimated at around 1,400,000 *contos* (thousands of *réis*). Looking beyond the numbers, we see that the marks left by the world conflict were not confined to the budget deficit and the increase in foreign debt. The financial situation became worse. Without any programme or structured policy, the Republic ran budgetary deficits, issued bonds and printed money using inflation as its main instrument. A third of Portugal's military spending was financed by Great Britain, and totalled £22 million sterling.

	1914	1917	1918	1919
Cost of living index	100	162	292	317
Agricultural prices index	100	192	300	400
Industrial salaries index	100	225	270	317
Wheat production	1916=256	260	335	286

Source: Ana Paula Pires, *Portugal e a I Guerra Mundial. A República e a Economia de Guerra* (Casal de Cambra, Caleidoscópio, 2011), 150.

Table 2. The economic situation in Portugal (1914-1919)

The creation of a fitting development plan that would give greater importance to the improvements to be carried out in the post-war era was strongly recommended by the law professor Fernando Emídio da Silva: "[t]he immense viabilities that are always presented to influence our common-sense, the sadness and sickness caused by all these years of distress, the qualities of race and soil, must quickly bring the first and exuberant examples of what might constitute a rigorous exploration of our wealth […]".[31] Nevertheless, during the post-war years, little would happen; there was no political will to foster a self-sustained development dynamic in the country. The President of the Republic, Canto e Castro, insisted on the need of the Portuguese delegates to the Peace Conference to have the contours and characteristics of the national economy well defined in order to avoid violent crises:

> It should not be forgotten that our exportation is fed almost exclusively of metropolitan and colonial products and that our industries, although modest, guarantee the lives of a considerable working class population […], that our trade still struggles with professional education, organization and expansion method, lack of capitals, etc., and that our tariff policy is not only protective but most of all fiscal.[32]

The War at Home

Portugal's wartime casualties totalled 8,000 killed and 13,000 wounded, including all battlefields (with the majority of deaths occurring in Africa). They were not sufficiently high to create a sense of a "lost generation" in the post-war years, and the Republic would find it difficult to generate a consensus on the war's meaning.[33] Of the 13,000 wounded only 1,500 would be considered war-disabled. The battle between interventionists and their opponents thus continued in the post-war period, as different sides looked at with each other to establish a dominant narrative over the war effort and its achievements.

	France[a)]	Angola	Mozambique	Navy	Totals
Dead	1,997	810	4,811	142	7,760
Wounded	5,359	683	1,600	30	7,672
Missing in action	199	200	5,500		5,899
Unfit for duty	7,280	372	1,283		8,935
Prisoners	7,000[b)]	68	678		7,746
TOTALS	21,835	2,133	13,872	172	38,012

a) These numbers include the CEP (7,346) and CAPI (10) troops.
b) Of whom 6,767 were returned by Germany and 233 died in captivity.
Table based on: Luís Alves de Fraga, *Portugal e a Grande Guerra: balanço estatístico*; Aniceto Afonso and Carlos de Matos Gomes, eds. *Portugal: Grande Guerra 1914-1918* (Lisbon, Quidnovi, 2010).

Table 3. Casualties at the theatres of war (Army and Navy) (1914-1918)

Once peace was signed on 11 November 1918 the Portuguese who participated in the First World War acquired a multiplicity of new identities: veterans, mutilated, gassed, crippled. The last were the most visible victims of the conflict, the men who brought home the horrors of the war. Humanitarian organisations, namely the Red Cross, responded to this "brutalization of violence" providing aid to the local population caught between almost daily confrontations, and to mutilated, gassed and crippled soldiers returning home from Angola, Mozambique and Flanders. The first troops arrived in Portugal during the first half of 1919, a period marked by violence and political instability. On 8 April 1920, the public subscription that had been opened four years previously by the Red Cross in favour of war victims made a total of 1,056,562$25 *escudos*,[34] leading to a mushrooming of activity with several communities across Brazil establishing funds too.

Although the African empire was part of the national imaginary and Portugal defined itself as a colonial power, from January 1917 onwards the Portuguese military intervention on the African battlefield always played second fiddle to the sending of troops to Flanders.[35] This reality was described by some combatants, like António de Cértima, who voiced his discontent in a small work published in 1925: "Look at what's going on outside! It's the '9 April', the apotheosis of your brothers who died in Flanders, richer and nobler than you, covered with honors, medals, and glorious citations, serving, no doubt, a better Fatherland than you [...] Soldier of Africa! How many medals were pinned to your chest?"[36]

What was the nature of the state's obligations to these men, the victims of war? Would the payment of a pension be enough to compensate for their suffering? The medical doctor Tovar de Lemos mentions in his memoirs that the first mutilated man who returned home came "willing to beg". The reintegration into society of these men was carried out by the philanthropic action of institutions such as the Red Cross, the Portuguese Women's Crusade and the Veterans League. The Red Cross and the Woman's Crusade continued the activities they had begun during the war in a clear demonstration that the "[...] ethos and practice of voluntarism remained important far longer than generally acknowledged".[37]

The Republic responded very late to the need for support, assistance and social integration of many of these men, especially those whom the war left unable to work. Here we should stress the publication of a decree, in March 1921, that guaranteed the employment in the public services of all war mutilated. A Commission for the Study of Reform and Pensions was set up by the Ministry of War only on 21 October 1919. The status of "war invalid" was established on 17 September 1924, but it was not until 1927, during the military dictatorship and nine years after the signing of the armistice, that a War Invalid Code was approved, a true guide to the evaluation and treatment of invalids and dependents. General Ferreira Martins describes the sacrifices that they faced throughout the years:

> they have been bleeding from the offer of their lives in Flanders fields [...] and the rest, besides those who became useless [...] constituting today the tragic legion of tuberculosis and crazy that the State doesn't know, living almost exclusively from the meagre budget of the League of Combatants [....].[38]

The post-war setting represented a moment of transition for the Red Cross. Although the Geneva Conventions did not designate assistance to non-combatants as a responsibility of the Red Cross Societies, the Portuguese Red Cross made them a priority. This perspective will allow us to incorporate solidarity as an asset in the transmission chain of memories in turbulent periods, bringing important lessons for today's challenges.

Conclusions

The uncomfortable situation Portugal was left in after the First World War was quite evident, not only as far as its internal politics – perhaps the more visible aspect – were concerned, but, particularly, considering its position within the international context. If it is true that few doubts remained that Portugal, having fought in Africa and Flanders' trenches on the Allied side, had fully earned the right to sit at the negotiation table, proclaiming its wishes and aspirations, when the Peace Conference was assembled[39] to regulate the international post-war society, the truth was that, despite having won some victories on the diplomatic field, namely keeping the integrity of its colonial territories in Africa, Portugal would end up staying out of the League of Nations Executive Council where, ironically, neutral Spain would end up taking a seat. As a matter of fact, this had been foreseen by Portugal's minister in Paris, João Chagas, who noted in his diary that the Portuguese government had almost vanished "amidst general congratulations",[40] once the war ended. The Portuguese case seems to fit in the "continuum of violence that characterized the transition from war to peace well into 1920s", as Robert Gerwarth recently analysed.[41] In 1921 the Portuguese Communist Party was created and the General Labour Confederation, founded by anarcho-syndicalist workers, was formed, accompanied by a wave of strikes that swept the country. In the same year, in October, several conservative politicians were assassinated during a republican radical coup known as the "Bloody Night".

During the wave of political violence that swept Portugal immediately after the First World War all civilian and military wounded were treated by the Red Cross, the several governments in power never requested the interference of the army's health services. In the report presented by the High Commissioner for the Portuguese Red Cross, José d'Abreu, to the President of the Executive Commission of the 10th Red Cross Conference, Paul des Gouttes, Abreu concludes that "[t]he long experience gained in so many public order disturbances […] leads us to the conclusion that it is necessary to stop the abuse of several voluntary services – health and the fire-brigades – that also provide assistance in the above mentioned cases, adopt as their badge a cross similar to that of the Geneva Convention, but of a different colour".[42] Red Crossers therefore represented a distinctive type of humanitarians, a powerful factor in motivating individuals to engage in the movement.

Notes

1   James McGrath Morris, *The Ambulance Drivers: Hemingway, Dos Passos, and a Friendship Made and Lost in War* (Philadelphia, PA: Da Capo Press, 2017).
2   Branden Little, "An Explosion of New Endeavours: Global Humanitarian Responses to Industrialized Warfare in the First World War Era," *First World War Studies* 5, no.1 (2014): 1.
3   Heather Jones, "International or transnational? Humanitarian action during the First World War," *European Review of History* 16, no. 5 (2009): 697.
4   David P. Forsythe, *The Humanitarians. The International Committee of the Red Cross* (Cambridge: Cambridge University Press, 2005), 32.
5   Robert Gerwarth, *The Vanquished. Why the First World War Failed to End, 1917-1923* (London: Penguin Books, 2016), 7.
6   Gerwarth, *The Vanquished*; Robert Gerwarth and John Horne, "Vectors of Violence: Paramilitarism in Europe after the Great War, 1917-1923," *The Journal of Modern History* 83, no. 3 (2011): 493.
7   Cf. João Chagas, *Diário IV – 1918-1921* (Lisbon: Edições Rolim, November 1986), 152.
8   Neville Wylie, Melanie Oppenheimer, and James Crossland, *The Red Cross Movement. Myths, practices and turning points* (Manchester: Manchester University Press, 2020).
9   Richard Ashby Wilson and Richard D. Brown, ed., *Humanitarianism and Suffering: The Mobilization of Empathy* (Cambridge: Cambridge University Press, 2009), 2.
10 McGrath Morris, *The Ambulance Drivers*.
11 Maria Fernanda Rollo, Ana Paula Pires, and Filipe Ribeiro de Meneses, "Portugal," *1914-1918-online. International Encyclopedia of the First World War*, ed. Ute Daniel et al. (Berlin: Freie Universität, 2017).
12 Rollo et al. Cf. Aniceto Afonso and Marília Guerreiro, "A Revolta de Tomar (13 de Dezembro de 1916)," *Boletim do Arquivo Histórico Militar*, no. 51, (1981): 67-196.
13 Michael Barnett, *Empire of Humanity. A History of Humanitarianism* (Ithaca, NY: Cornell University Press, 2011), 65.
14 *Cruz Vermelha Portuguesa 1865-1925* (Lisbon: Centro Tipográfico Colonial, 1926), 159.
15 Ibid.
16 Little, "An explosion of new endeavours"; and David P. Forsythe, "The International Red Cross: Decentralization and its Effects," *Human Rights Quarterly* 40, no. 1 (February 2018): 61.
17 Frank Trentmann and Just Flemming, ed., *Food and Conflict in the Age of the Two World Wars* (London: Palgrave Macmillan, 2004).
18 Arquivo Histórico Militar, 1/35/box 1281, announcement of 20 May 1917.
19 Red Cross Archive, *Boletim Oficial da Sociedade Portugusa da Cruz Vermelha* 1, III Série (July 1917): 193.
20 Cf. João Paulo Freire, *Em Serviço da Cruz Vermelha. Notas d'um Comissário* (Lisbon: Edição da Sociedade Portuguesa da Cruz Vermelha, 1919), 74-75.
21 *Cruz Vermelha Portuguesa*, 153.
22 Ibid.
23 Craig Calhoun, "The Imperative to Reduce Suffering. Charity, Progress, and Emergencies in the Field of Humanitarian Action," in *Humanitarianism in Question. Politics, Power, Ethics*, ed. Michael Barnett and Thomas G. Weiss (Ithaca, NY: Cornell University Press, 2008), 75.

24	Filipe Ribeiro de Meneses, "Revolutions (Portugal)," in *1914-1918-online. International Encyclopedia of the First World War,* eds. Ute Daniel et al. (Berlin: Freie Universität, 2017).
25	*Cruz Vermelha Portuguesa,* 157.
26	Ibid, 159.
27	Cf. Rollo et al., "Portugal".
28	*Cruz Vermelha Portuguesa,* 164.
29	*Diário da Câmara dos Deputados,* session no. 16, 30 June 1919, 34.
30	Ibid., 63.
31	Fernando Emídio da Silva, *Cousas de Portugal* (Coimbra: França & Arménio, 1919), 4.
32	The Peace Conference began on 18 January 1919. The instructions given by the President of the Republic, Canto e Castro, to the Portuguese delegates are reproduced in José Medeiros Ferreira, *Portugal na Conferência da Paz* (Lisbon: Quetzal, 1992), 20.
33	Rollo et al., "Portugal".
34	Cf. *Cruz Vermelha Portuguesa.*
35	Ana Paula Pires, "The First World War in Portuguese East Africa: Civilian and Military Encounters in the Indian Ocean," *E-Journal of Portuguese History* 15, no. 1 (2017): 101.
36	António de Cértima, *Legenda Dolorosa do Soldado Desconhecido de África* (Lisbon: NP., 1925), xi.
37	Deborah Cohen, *The War Come Home. Disabled Veterans in Britain and Germany, 1914-1939* (Berkeley, CA: University of California Press, 2001), 28.
38	Luís Augusto Ferreira Martins, *As Virtudes Militares na Tradição Histórica de Portugal* (Lisbon: Tipografia da Liga dos combatentes da Grande guerra, 1953), 337.
39	It should be noted that, earlier, Portugal had also not been invited to take part in the meeting of the inter-allied committee, held in Paris, in the first days of November. NAUK, FO 371/3369, official letter dated 6 November 1918, 1-2.
40	See specifically the entries of 13 and 16 November in João Chagas' diary. João Chagas, *Diário IV – 1918-1921* (Lisbon: Edições Rolim, 1986), 91 and 98.
41	Cf. Horne and Gerwarth, "Paramilitarism in Europe after the Great War an introduction," 1.
42	*Cruz Vermelha Portuguesa,* 166.

Fig. 1. Aerial view of Salonika before the fire (taken by a French military photographer). La Contemporaine, Paris (album VAL GF07), by permission.

Reconstruction, Reform and Peace in Europe after the First World War

John Horne

Between 1918 and 1933 reconstruction in Europe meant repairing the material damage on the former fronts. But it meant more, extending to political, social and cultural reconstruction. For the war had revealed multiple meanings of the fatherland and state for which the sacrifice had been made.[1] As dynastic empires fell in the east (Ottoman Turkey, Austria-Hungary, Tsarist Russia), nation-states replaced them. In western and central Europe nations underwent political change, sometimes radical. This was clearest with the Weimar Republic in defeated Germany. But in Belgium, too, universal male suffrage (the great pre-war cause) was conceded even if language equality was not. The nation, usually in the form of a parliamentary state, became the European norm in an era of political experiment.

The war also created obligations. Returned soldiers carried their combat experience (and trauma) into civilian life. Veterans' organisations (especially the disabled) demanded rights and reforms in recognition of the debt contracted to their members by society. War widows added to the moral and fiscal burden. Everywhere, the military dead posed the issue of how to remember and commemorate. The fact that civilians had also suffered hugely in the war (including the hungry and millions of refugees) meant that this was the era that invented international humanitarianism.[2]

In other ways, too, the world faced demands for social change. The Russian Revolution and the new Bolshevik state dramatised these in their most radical form. Yet because the war required the mobilisation of all resources, it had drawn on workers and farmers as well as soldiers and women across the board. These groups made their own sacrifice and consequently advanced their own post-war demands for a better future, whether in vanquished or victor states. Women's suffrage, land reform, better housing, public health, child-care and a shorter working day were among the principal demands. The war fostered competing visions of social reform.

The Paris peace conference (from which the defeated were excluded until asked to sign their treaties) fashioned the politics of the post-war settlement. This included the novelty of reparation, a legal and financial principle that made Germany in particular guilty, and so liable for the costs of the war, material and economic. Yet the peace conference innovated in creating the League of Nations as the basis of a new world order founded on the principle of sovereignty, international law and collective security.[3] The defeated were not initially members of the League but the logic of peacemaking meant that in time they would be. Reconstructing the post-war world entailed a choice – to sustain wartime enmity or create peace via reconciliation. It was an era of diplomatic experiment, too.

For all its significance, physical reconstruction was less important to reconstruction overall than it would be after the Second World War, when material devastation was far more extensive. Had the Cold War turned hot, it is safe to say that physical reconstruction would have been the overriding concern of a post-war period that thankfully never happened. Yet since the built (and re-built) environment always relates to larger social, cultural, political and even diplomatic developments (shaping them and shaped by them), I propose to look at how four specific cases of physical reconstruction illuminate this larger process after the Great War: the city of Salonika, the universities of Leuven and Paris, the Parisian suburb of Suresnes and the Palace of the Nations in Geneva.

Salonika: Rebuilding the Nation

The first case concerns the role of both empire and nationality (so central to the Great War) in the largest urban renewal to arise from the conflict, and which began while the war was still taking place: Salonika (today Thessaloniki) in Greece. In 1912, it was the largest city in Ottoman Europe. Religiously and ethnically mixed, 39% of its 160,000 people were Sephardim Jews, the rest Turks, Bulgarians and Greeks.[4] After the Balkan Wars (1912-13), Greece gained southern Macedonia and western Thrace in the biggest expansion of the new nation-state since independence in 1830. Salonika was its regional capital.

In 1915, a Franco-British force arrived in Macedonia, with the permission of neutral Greece, intending to help Serbia, which had been invaded by Austria-Hungary, Germany and Bulgaria. It failed, but established defences along the border against Bulgaria which now occupied Serb Macedonia. This turned into a major front of the Great War, with Salonika as the allied base-camp and military capital. The nationalist premier, Eleftherios Venizelos, had tried to bring Greece into the war so as to enlarge the country further by the *idea megali*, the dream of a new Byzantium including north-western Anatolia and Constantinople. King Constantine, who favoured neutrality, dismissed him, so Greece entered the conflict only in June 1917, when the king was forced to abdicate. But prior to that, Venizelos also made Salonika the headquarters of his alternative government.

While pre-war Salonika had stood for a kind of Ottoman modernity (it was the birth place of the Young Turk movement), its western-style buildings coexisted with a tangle of wooden-built neighbourhoods abounding in domes and minarets. To British and French soldiers, it seemed distinctly "Turkish" or "oriental" (meaning the opposite of modern). In fact, the French and British behaved very much in the tradition of nineteenth-century colonial expeditions. Arriving in a land where they had not expected to stay, they found themselves occupying a city and region about which they knew little. In this, however, they were not so different from the new Greek administration. Both allies and Greeks saw the region as alien (its Turkish and Bulgarian minorities a possible internal enemy) though they also held cultural expectations derived from classical Greek antiquity (this was, after all, the homeland of Philip of Macedon and Alexander the Great) or of Byzantium. In the manner of western military expeditions since Napoleon's invasion of Egypt in 1798, the allied armies also embarked on an imperial "civilising mission" – modernising transport, attacking malaria, carrying out ethnic censuses, listing the artistic patrimony and conducting archaeological digs.[5]

Then in August 1917 a terrible (but accidental) fire occurred that destroyed some 40% of the city, especially the wooden-built Jewish quarter, rendering 70,000 people homeless (Figs. 1-2). In a city already crammed with refugees it was a numbing calamity. The allies did what they could to control the fire and help the victims in its immediate aftermath, using all the resources of a modern army.[6] However, for that same reason, the fire gave them a unique opportunity to collaborate with Venizelos (now premier) and the mayor of Salonika in rebuilding the city. Within a week of the blaze, Venizelos had set up an international committee composed of a small number of international experts, including the British town planner, Thomas Mawson, and the French architect and archaeologist, Ernest Hébrard, as well as two Greek architects.

Hébrard rapidly emerged as the key figure. In fact, as an officer in the French army he had already been conducting archaeological digs in the city. He was also a member of the influential Société Française des Architectes et Urbanistes whose 1915 booklet defined the principles of modern "urbanisation" (wide streets, squares and zones of different usage) that were to be used in reconstructing the towns and villages of the western front.[7] The key in Salonika was collective expropriation with compensation, despite Jewish protests. The effect was to allow a single master plan for the city, which Hébrard, backed by the French army's engineering and technical services, was mainly responsible for delivering before the war's end, in June 1918.[8]

Fig. 2. Salonika after the fire. Musée de l'Armée, Paris: photograph album of Captain Schaller, commander of the 17th Division artillery, by permission.

Given the circumstances, the allies enjoyed an almost colonial-style freedom in this work (Hébrard went on to become one of the architects rebuilding Hanoi as the capital of French Indochina). Yet this was not independent of the Greek state. On the contrary, Hébrard helped to turn Ottoman Salonika into the capital of the new Greek territories by an architecture that consciously reinvented both its classical and Byzantine past. For Hébrard replaced the city centre with a grid plan and hierarchy of streets that pivoted on two squares connected by a boulevard on a north-south axis so as to frame the distant view of Mount Olympus, south across the harbour. The square at the northern end of this boulevard incorporated the find of the original *agora*, while Hébrard aligned other axes on Byzantine monuments (Figs. 3-4).

The French thus provided the architect who designed modern Thessaloniki in tune with the Hellenisation sought by the Venizelos government. By an irony of history, this cultural vision was fulfilled socially in the 1920s when Venizelos' failure to achieve the *idea megali* and create a "Greater Greece" in Anatolia after defeat at the hands of Turkey in the latter's war of independence resulted in the first ever legal ethnic cleansing under the Treaty of Lausanne. As Greek Muslims left for Turkey, Greeks expelled from Anatolia (especially Smyrna) flooded into Salonika, while many Jews went to France or Palestine. The city itself became more "Greek".

Reconstruction, Reform and Peace in Europe after the First World War 301

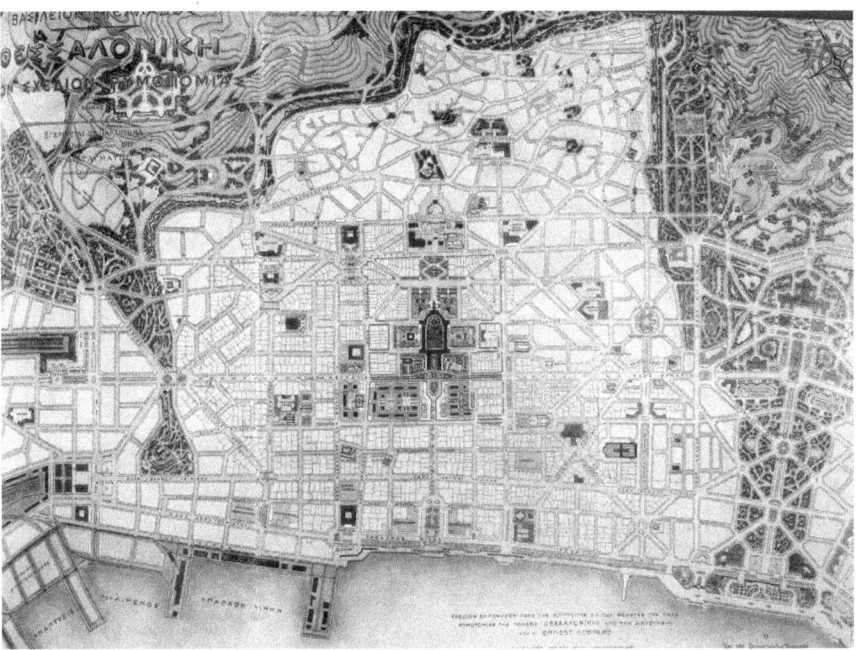

Fig. 3. Reconstruction of the (now lost) original plan for Salonika drafted by Ernest Hébrard (1919). Alexandra Yerolympos, *Urban Transformations in the Balkans (1820-1920): Aspects of Balkan Town Planning and the Remaking of Thessaloniki* (Thessaloniki: 1996), by permission of the author.

Fig. 4. Aristotelous Square, with Byzantine-influenced colonnades, looking north to the *agora*. The statue is of Eleftherios Venizelos. Photograph by John Horne.

Salonika remained exceptional owing to the degree of destruction and because reconstruction dovetailed with the nationalist aspirations of the Venizelos government. Nonetheless, nationality assumed architectural form more widely after the Great War. It did this most clearly in symbolic ways, through myriad war memorials and battlefront monuments. The war dead, in other words, became part of the reconstruction of the fighting zones. But it might be instructive to look for it also in architecture and town planning, especially in the capitals of the new nation-states in Eastern Europe and Turkey, from Warsaw to Ankara, or in the independent settler dominions of the British Empire, such as Canada and Australia.

Inter-allied or International? The Universities of Leuven and Paris

However, post-war recovery was not a purely national affair. It entailed collaboration between countries, as shown by the work of foreign civic bodies and philanthropists, such as the Rockefeller and Carnegie foundations, in rebuilding destroyed towns in Belgium and France. But there were two modes in which such collaboration might occur – inter-allied and international. The former meant prolonging the collaboration of the western allies beyond the war and also hoping that Germany would pay. The latter implied at some point establishing connections with the former enemy states and accepting German entry into the League of Nations.

Recent research has shown us just how extensive wartime inter-allied collaboration really was. As the USA entered the war in 1917 and Bolshevik Russia left, the allied effort became a kind of democratic crusade. For all the divergence of national interests and the failure of the USA to ratify the Treaty of Versailles, this collaboration continued after the peace conference against what was still seen as the enemy (even if defeated), especially Germany. We need to remind ourselves of just how powerful those wartime cultures were that hinged on total repudiation of the "barbaric" enemy and of how emotions like hatred persisted long afterwards.

Nowhere was inter-allied cooperation more evident than in the world of academics and universities. While the war had ruptured the collaboration on which international scientific communities had been based, it did not only drive academics back into their national shells because inter-allied collaboration was an alternative. Ideas, individuals and funding circulated especially between British, French and American institutions.[9] However, both international scientific bodies and universities faced the issue after the war of whether it was better to maintain the taboo on the enemy or to re-engage with him. This brings me to my second case, that of Leuven.

The story of how this university and its library were rebuilt in the 1920s after their destruction by the Germans in August 1914 is well known. What I wish to focus on is the notorious balcony with its inscription: "furore teutonico diruta, donato americano restituta" (Destroyed by German fury, restored by American gift). The library had indeed been rebuilt by American generosity in a civic effort across the USA led first by Nicholas Murray Butler, president of Columbia University, and then by Herbert Hoover, founder of the Commission for Relief in Belgium. Since the Germans wrongly claimed the town had resisted in 1914, justifying the massacre or deportation of many of its inhabitants and the destruction of the library, the spirit of this project was resolutely anti-German. By the Treaty of Versailles, German reparations included restoring the library's contents while the New York architect responsible for its neo-Renaissance design, Whitney Warren, had been outraged at German behaviour in the war, including shelling Rheims cathedral. Rebuilding the library was a personal mission for him in the spirit of wartime inter-allied solidarity. He added the motto for the balcony on the suggestion of Cardinal Mercier[10] (Fig. 5).

Fig. 5. The new library, University of Leuven. Sketch by the New York architecture firm, Warren and Wetmore (1922), incorporating the balustrade with the inscription (in Latin): 'Destroyed by German fury, restored by American gift.' Warren & Wetmore architectural drawings and photographs, 1889-1938, Avery Architectural & Fine Arts Library, Columbia University.

However, in the climate of growing reconciliation in the mid-1920s, and above all faced with the need to restore scientific links with German scholars, the Rector of Leuven University, Monsignor Paulin Ladeuze, wanted to remove the offending motto although he himself had witnessed the German destruction in 1914. Butler (now president of the Carnegie Endowment for International Peace) agreed, as did Hoover, who wrote that it was "time to eliminate war bitterness".[11] In fact, the American backers of the project had now firmly switched from inter-allied solidarity to international reconciliation. The *New York Times* wrote of the affair that "if the people are to go on indefinitely fighting the war, lasting peace will be an empty phrase".[12]

That was to reckon without Whitney Warren and anger in both Leuven and Belgium. After a fierce dispute between Ladeuze and the architect, the inauguration of the library took place in July 1928 without the offending inscription, though it was marred by an aeroplane that dropped thousands of leaflets inscribed: "Furore teutonico diruta". Felix Morren, a foreman on the library building, then smashed the empty balcony with his mason's hammer, declaring: "We aren't all *Boches* in Louvain yet". In the end, Warren gave the inscription to Dinant where it was mounted on the memorial to that town's martyrs of 1914 – before being blown into the Meuse by German tanks in 1940 just as Leuven library was destroyed a second time[13] (Fig. 6).

The tensions involved in moving from the inter-allied to the international in reconstructing the academic world can be shown in another project. Right after the

Fig. 6. Part of the Leuven balustrade 'Furore Teutonico', incorporated in the 1936 'national monument' erected in Dinant to the German sack of the town in 1914, and destroyed by the German army in 1940. Contemporary postcard. (collection John Horne)

war, the French planned a new international residential campus for the Sorbonne in southern Paris on the site of the demolished nineteenth-century fortifications. The aim was two-fold: socially, the Cité Internationale Universitaire de Paris (CIUP), as it is still known, was to solve the problem of slum lodgings and tuberculosis in the Latin Quarter by a garden city for students; academically, it was to use German defeat to make the Sorbonne the academic Mecca of Europe. It was to be a place of international reconciliation but one firmly under the aura of inter-allied victory. As the dedication stone on the first residence to go up in 1923 put it, students from all countries would have "books, fresh air and sunshine" so as to "work together harmoniously to improve their minds and bodies, the progress of science and understanding between their nations"[14] (Fig. 7).

Initially, the emphasis was indeed on recruiting from friendly nations, which funded more residences. By 1927, however, reconciliation with the former enemy seemed possible as liberal circles in Germany proposed a Maison de l'Allemagne, welcomed by the French. But a suspicious German Foreign Ministry refused to back the idea, fearing that Germany would simply be paying for France to propagandise its best students at its own expense. Ten years later when a newly confident Nazi Germany raised the question again, the French refused, fearing infiltration by the ideological avant-garde of a new enemy. Only in 1956 did a thoroughly modernist Maison Heinrich Heine open its doors in a very different post-war period.

Fig. 7. The Deutsch de la Meurthe Foundation – the first student residence at the Cité Internationale Universitaire de Paris (1923-1925). Architect's aerial view. Fonds Lucien Bechmann. SIAF/Cité de l'architecture et du patrimoine/Archives d'architecture du XXe siècle.

Social Reconstruction and International Peace: Henri Sellier's Suresnes

As the Cité Internationale shows, the antagonisms of the war persisted throughout the 1920s, only to grow stronger in the 1930s, and were manifest in other buildings and monuments. Among them was the memorial to the German victory over Russia at Tannenberg in 1914. This took the form of a neo-crusader castle inaugurated in 1927 by Field Marshal Hindenburg, victor of the battle and German president.

Nonetheless, it was the opposite mood of reconciliation between enemies (especially in the west) that prevailed from 1925 to 1933. By the Locarno treaties of 1925, Germany recognised its new western frontiers and the former enemies agreed to resolve disputes by arbitration. Germany entered the League of Nations in 1926. Above all, the French and German foreign ministers, Aristide Briand and Gustav Stresemann, led what amounted to the real peace process in Europe after the Great War. Both men believed the war had been a catastrophe, both were criticised within their own country, and both proposed a European Federation, the distant forerunner of the European Union. They were jointly awarded the Nobel Peace Prize in 1927.

Such diplomatic reconstruction might seem far removed from other varieties of the process. Yet the League of Nations (a predominantly European institution with its headquarters in Geneva) was central to the whole endeavour and was deeply involved in all manner of social reforms. These involved women, labour, intellectuals and veterans among others. Such activity reflected the belief of many who supported the League (from social Catholics to social democrats including a broad progressive centre) that peace and social reform were two sides of the same coin: without peace, no lasting social improvement; without social improvement, war would return.

This conviction found remarkable expression in a housing project built in the Paris suburb of Suresnes in the 1920s by Henri Sellier, socialist mayor and later Minister of Health in the Popular Front government of 1936. While large-scale social housing (drawing on Le Corbusier's "city in the sky" principle) occurred in France only after the Second World War, municipalities undertook smaller experiments between the wars, often linked to slum clearance and inspired by the garden-city movement. This was the case with Suresnes, whose population had mushroomed during the war as Paris became the centre of French munitions production. Sellier was driven by the usual concerns with alcoholism and tuberculosis attendant on squalid living conditions and their impact on children. But a world free from war was equally part of his vision for what was a miniature town, with model dwellings of various kinds and also schools, retirement home, *maison du peuple* (or community centre) and church.

In 1932, Sellier declared the garden city a *"quartier de la paix"* in homage to Briand, who had just died. He was, as he put it, honouring the man "who proclaimed the need to smash the cannon and machine-guns" and his friend, Stresemann, who had "laid the foundations of a Franco-German union [...] vital for world peace".[15]

Reconstruction, Reform and Peace in Europe after the First World War 307

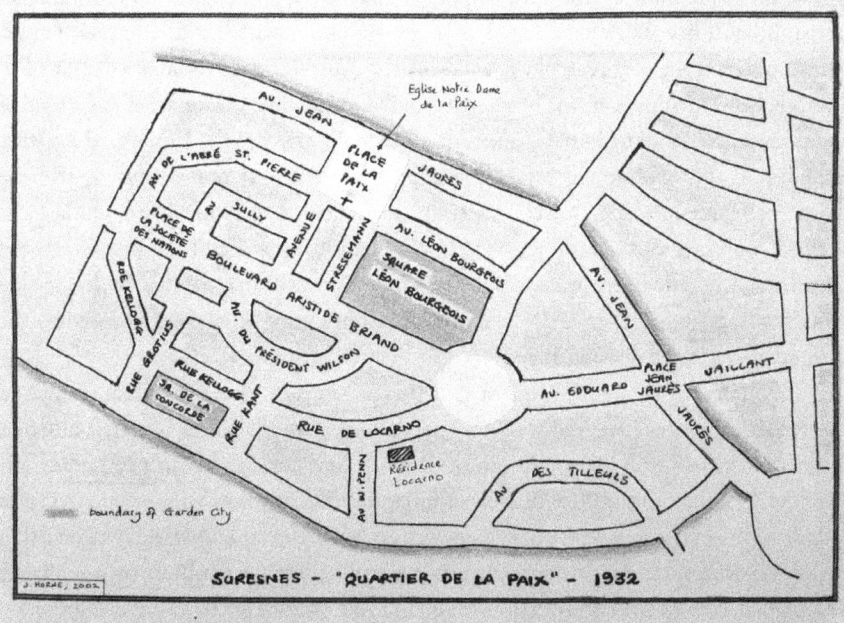

Fig. 8. Map of the Garden City of Suresnes (built later 1920s) dedicated as a 'Peace District' (1932). Reconstruction based on sources in the Archives Municipales, Suresnes. © John Horne.

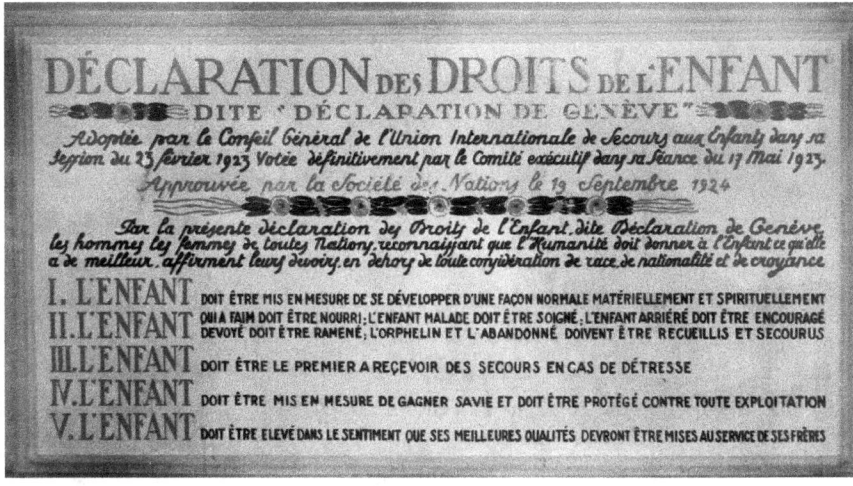

Fig. 9. Declaration of the Rights of Children, League of Nations, 1924 (mosaic mural, Paul Langevin school, Suresnes). Photograph, John Horne.

The streets were named after philosophers of peace (Grotius, Kant) and Republican anti-militarist heroes (Victor Hugo, Romain Rolland), with a statue to Jean Jaurès, assassinated on the outbreak of war in 1914. The central square was named after Léon Bourgeois, French progenitor of a League of Nations, while others were dedicated to the League itself and to Peace. To this day, the main axes are the Boulevard Aristide Briand and the Avenue Gustav Stresemann and the old people's home is still the Locarno Residence. The church, naturally, is dedicated to Notre Dame de la Paix. Should you enter the school, you will find a beautiful mosaic of the first charter of Children's Rights (forerunner of the 1989 UN Convention), drafted by Eglantyne Jebb, the English founder of the Save the Children Fund, which was adopted by the League of Nations in 1924 (Figs. 8-9).

Of course, my contention is not that every European social housing project of the 1920s expressed this vision. Tackling the accommodation crises that afflicted many countries resulted in numerous schemes that combined with different political beliefs, including those of Fascist Italy. Rather, Suresnes was an architectural tribute to the belief that peace and social progress were inseparable. But because that belief was widespread, Suresnes was not the only scheme to embody it (one thinks of Villeurbanne in the suburbs of Lyon or the Karl Marx Hof in socialist Vienna).

Geneva – the Palace of the Nations

If there is one place one would expect to find the Geneva vision expressed in stone and mortar (or at least concrete), it is Geneva itself. The League of Nations provided the institutional framework for post-war reconciliation in a process that I have described elsewhere as "cultural demobilisation".[16] This means dismantling wartime enmity and replacing it by collaboration. It requires a shift in language, behaviour and above all perception. After the Great War, it meant that former enemies reconciled enough to enable them to think of war as the real enemy. The politics of peace (arbitration, collective security, disarmament) were used to mobilise against war, not for it. Bodies working with the League, such as trade unions and political groups, caught this shift (Fig. 10). Briand expressed it as he welcomed the Germans into the League in a speech that echoed around the world.

> Is it not a moving spectacle […] that barely a few years after the most frightful war that has ever convulsed the world, when the battlefields are still almost damp with blood […] the same peoples which clashed so roughly meet in this peaceful assembly and affirm mutually their common desire to collaborate in the work of universal peace? […]

Messieurs, peace for France and Germany means that the series of painful and bloody encounters that has stained every page of history is over; over too, are the long veils of mourning for sufferings which will never ease. No more wars, no more brutal and bloody solutions to our differences! […] Away with rifles, machine-guns, cannon! Make way for conciliation, for arbitration, for peace![17]

Fig. 10. Cultural demobilisation: 'War against war': poster of the International Trades Union Federation, c.1924. Poster collection, La Contemporaine, Paris, by permission.

By the mid-1920s, when the Germans entered it, the autumn meeting of the League had become a fixture of the European diplomatic scene and its headquarters the focus of European reconciliation. Nothing illustrates this more clearly than the competition held among member states in 1927 for a Palace of the Nations to replace the old church hall where the League had met up to that point. According to the rules, this was to house all the League's functions and "symbolize by the purity of its style [and] the harmony of its lines [...] the peaceful glory of the twentieth century".[18] The competition turned to controversy when a stunning design by Le Corbusier (floating on pillars, with walls of glass and concrete) was rejected. Yet the final plan, in a clean neo-classical style with a wealth of internal decoration, was deemed by many to be the best expression of the League. Built on the shores of Lake Geneva next to the International Labour Organisation, it was nothing less than a palace of democratic internationalism and a theatre for cultural demobilisation (Figs. 11-12).

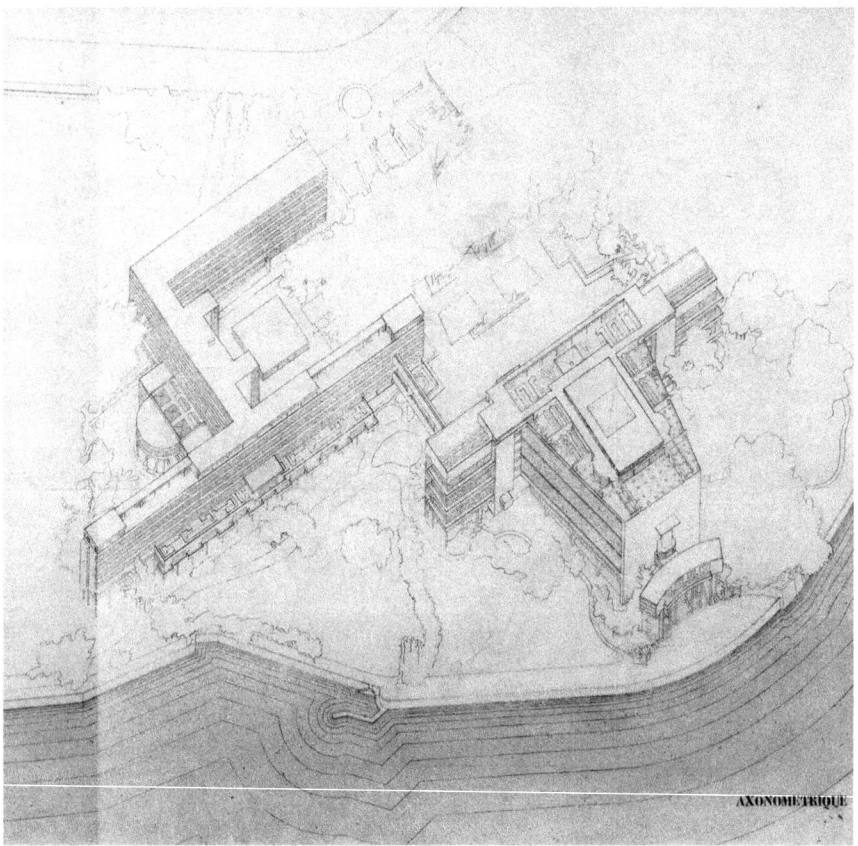

Fig. 11. Plan by Le Corbusier for the competiton to build the Palace of the Nations, Geneva, 1927. United Nations Archives at Geneva.

Fig. 12. The Palace of the Nations under construction, 3 October 1933. United Nations Archives at Geneva.

The League's vision is seen above all in the murals created for the Council chamber by the Catalan artist, José Maria Sert. Wall panels show the building of peace. First comes "Hope" represented as military demobilisation. It is followed by social and scientific progress, the prerequisite of peace. The murals culminate in the ceiling, "The Lesson of Salamanca", in which scholars of that famous university lay the basis of international law during the Renaissance and show how Humankind can live in peace (Fig. 13). The Spanish Republic (itself on the brink of civil war) donated Sert's murals in 1935-36. The Palace of the Nations was completed in 1938 – a bad year for Europe. Sert himself fled into exile and cultural demobilisation was over before its temple was even finished. Today, the building remains largely forgotten as the European headquarters of the United Nations. But in fact it is the culminating architectural expression of the hopes vested in reconstruction after the Great War.

Fig. 13: Mural of 'The Lesson of Salamanca' on the ceiling of the Council Chamber in the Palace of the Nations by José Maria Sert, Catalan artist. Donated by the Spanish Republic, 1935. United Nations Archives at Geneva.

Coda

The kinds of reconstruction discussed elsewhere in this volume were physical and material but also political, social, economic and cultural, as they would be in different proportions after the Second World War. Their architectural expression was less inclined to internationalism and modernism than would be the case 30 years later, perhaps reflecting how important a traditionalist sense of the national or regional had proved to be in response to the Great War, as shown by Hébrard's plan for Salonika and Whitney Warren's for the library in Leuven, though as both of these also show, tradition was quite compatible with modern planning and infrastructure.

However, what I have wanted to suggest is that when we focus away from the rebuilding of the devastated fighting zones, we also find architectural expressions of reconstruction in its broader sense. These were more diverse than I have been able to suggest here. Recovery from the Great War entailed radical ideological visions – proposals to re-enchant a disillusioned world – and both Soviet Russia and Fascist Italy, and later Nazi Germany, translated their visions into architecture and monuments. One thinks of Vladimir Tatlin's model in 1919-20 for an unbuildable tower, his monument to the Third International, or Mussolini's complex for the never-to-be-held Rome World Fair of 1942, with its physical articulation of a corporatist Fascist state.

But we can find traces of other ways of rebuilding the world after the war, both within the new nations (as at Salonika) and in the British and French empires (not only Hanoi but also Delhi was being rebuilt as an imperial capital between the wars). We can find them, too, in projects that defied the enemy (as in Leuven) or reconciled with him (Suresnes and Geneva). In many of these projects, social reform and future peace were integral to the building (or rebuilding) that they involved. I have given a few examples. But I am convinced that if we take all of Europe as our canvas, we will find more physical expressions of this democratic reconstruction after the Great War (with all its inner tensions). It is a question of knowing how to see and where to look.

Notes

1. John Horne, "Patriotism and the Enemy: Political Identity as a Weapon in World War One," in *Nations, Identities and the First World War: Shifting Loyalties to the Fatherland*, eds. Nico Wouters and Laurence Van Ypersele (London: Bloomsbury, 2018), 17-39.
2. Bruno Cabanes, *The Great War and the Origins of Humanitarianism 1918-1924* (Cambridge: Cambridge University Press, 2014).
3. Leonard V. Smith, *Sovereignty at the Paris Peace Conference of 1919* (Oxford: Oxford University Press, 2018), 222-262.
4. Alexandra Yerolympus, "La Part du feu," in *Salonique 1850-1918: la "ville des Juifs" et le réveil des Balkans*, ed. Gilles Veinstein (Paris: Editions Autrement, 1993), 262. See also: Mark Mazower, *Salonica: City of Ghosts: Christians, Muslims and Jews, 1430-1950* (London: Harper Collins, 2004), 305-331.
5. John Horne, "'A Civilizing Work?': The French Army in Macedonia, 1915-1918," in *Militarized Cultural Encounters in the Long Nineteenth Century: Making War, Mapping Europe*, eds. Joseph Clarke and John Horne (London: Palgrave Macmillan, 2018), 319-341.
6. Alexandra Yerolympos, "L'Incendie de Salonique en août 1917: fait divers ou 'dégât collateral'?" in *The Salonica Theatre of Operations and the Outcome of the Great War*, ed. Danai Kaplanidou et al. (Thessaloniki: Institute for Balkan Studies, 2005), 252.
7. Alfred Agache, Marcel Auburtin, and Edouard Redont, *Comment reconstruire nos cités détruites* (Paris: Colin, 1915); Yerolympos, "L'Incendie de Salonique," 258.
8. Charalambos Papastathis, "The Fire of Salonica and the Allies," in *The Salonica Theatre of Operations*, 258-259.
9. Tomás Irish, *The University at War, 1914-25: Britain, France and the United States* (Basingstoke: Palgrave Macmillan, 2015), 83-106.
10. Chris Coppens, Mark Derez, and Jan Roegiers, *Leuven University Library, 1425-2000* (Leuven: Leuven University Press, 2005), 243-247; John Horne and Alan Kramer, *German Atrocities 1914: A History of Denial* (New Haven, CT: Yale University Press, 2001), 387-390.
11. *Nation Wide Review*, July 1928, 8.
12. *New York Times*, 8 October 1928.
13. Horne and Kramer, *German Atrocities, 1914*, 390-400.
14. For this and what follows on the CIUP, see: John Horne, "Locarno et la politique de démobilisation culturelle: 1925-1930," in *Démobilisations culturelles après la Grande Guerre*, 14-18 Aujourd'hui. Today. Heute 5, ed. John Horne (Paris: Editions Noesis, 2002), 82-83.
15. Archives Municipales, Suresnes, conseil municipal, registre de délibérations, D53, 22 March 1932, 2.
16. Horne, "Locarno," 72-87; John Horne, "Demobilizing the Mind: France and the Legacy of the Great War, 1919-1939," *French History & Civilization* 2 (2009): 101-119.
17. Achille Elisha, ed., *Aristide Briand. Discours et écrits de politique étrangère* (Paris: Plon, 1965), 178.
18. Jean-Claude Pallas, *Histoire et architecture du Palais des Nations, 1924-2001* (Geneva: United Nations, 2001), 49.

Bibliography

Adam, H. Pearl. *Paris Sees it Through. A Diary, 1914-1919*. London: Hodder and Stoughton, 1919.
Adriaenssens, Werner. "Belgian Art During the First World War: Exhibitions and Salons in Brussels." In *14/18 Rupture or Continuity. Belgian Art around World War I*, edited by Inga Rossi-Schrimpf and Laura Kollwelter, 143-159. Leuven: Leuven University Press, 2018.
Afonso, Aniceto, and Marília Guerreiro. "A Revolta de Tomar (13 de Dezembro de 1916)." *Boletim do Arquivo Histórico Militar*, no. 51 (1981): 67-196.
Agache, Alfred, Marcel Auburtin, and Edouard Redont. *Comment reconstruire nos cités détruites*. Paris: Colin, 1915.
Agli invalidi della guerra. Rome: Opera nazionale per la protezione e l'assistenza degli invalidi della Guerra, 1918.
Albrechts, Louis. "Changing aspects of Belgian public planning." In *Perspectives on planning and urban development in Belgium*, edited by Ashok Dutt and Frank J. Costa, 27-42. Dordrecht: Kluwer, 1992.
"Algemeene politie verordening op de bouwwerken ten behoeve der aangenomen gemeenten." *Beknopte bekendmaking nopens den Dienst der Verwoeste Gewesten* 1, no. 3 (1919): 159-171.
Alleman. "Port-Villez. Technisch Onderwijs II." *De Belgische Verminkte*, April 15, [1918], 1.
Anderson, Julie. *War, Disability, and Rehabilitation in Britain: 'Soul of a Nation'*. Manchester: Manchester University Press, 2011.
———. and Neil Pemberton. "Walking Alone: Aiding the War and Civilian Blind in the Inter-war Period." *European Review of History – Revue européene d'Histoire* 14, no. 4 (2007): 459-479.
Assmann, Aleida "Re-framing Memory. Between Individual and Collective Forms of Constructing the Past." In *Performing the Past. Memory, History, and Identity in Modern Europe*, edited by Karin Tilmans, Frank van Vree, and Jay Winter, 35-50. Amsterdam: Amsterdam University Press, 2010.
Audoin-Rouzeau, Stéphane, Jean-Jacques Becker, Gerd Krumeich, and Jay M. Winter, eds. *Guerres et cultures, 1914-1918*. Paris: A. Colin, 1994.
———. and Annette Becker. *14-18, retrouver la Guerre*. Paris: Éditions Gallimard, 2000.
———. and Annette Becker. *14-18: Understanding the Great War*. Translated by Catherine Temerson. New York: Hill and Wang, 2002.
———. and Christophe Prochasson. *Sortir de la Grande Guerre: Le monde et l'après-1918*. Paris: Tallandier, 2008.
Baert, Koen. *Ieper: De herrezen stad. De wederopbouw van Ieper na 14-18*. Ypres: In Flanders Field Museum, 1999.
Baillieul, Jean-Marie. "Recht op herstel? De Belgische regering staat op de rem bij het vergoeden van de geteisterden." In *Ieper, de herrezen stad*, edited by Koen Baert, 21-62. Koksijde: De Klaproos, 1999.

Bairoch, Paul, and Gary Goertz. "Factors of Urbanisation in the Nineteenth Century Developed Countries: A Descriptive and Econometric Analysis." *Urban Studies* 23, no. 4 (1986): 285-305.

Balck, William. *Entwickelung der Taktik im Weltkriege* (2nd edition). Berlin: R. Eisenschmidt, 1922.

Bardez, Renaud. "La Faculté de médecine de l'Université Libre de Bruxelles: entre création, circulation et enseignement des savoirs (1795-1914)." PhD Thesis, Free University of Brussels, 2016.

Barnett, Michael. *Empire of Humanity: A History of Humanitarianism.* Ithaca, NY: Cornell University Press, 2011.

Bauman, Zygmunt. *Liquid Times: Living in an Age of Uncertainty.* Cambridge: Polity Press, 2007.

Béchet, Cristophe. "La révision pacifiste des manuels scolaires: Les enjeux de la mémoire de la guerre 14-18 dans l'enseignement belge de l'entre-deux-guerres." *Cahiers d'Histoire du Temps Présent*, no. 20 (2008): 49-101.

Becker, Annette. "Monuments aux morts après la Guerre de Sécession et la Guerre de 1870-1871: Un legs de la guerre nationale?". *Guerres mondiales et conflits contemporains*, no. 167 (1992): 23-40.

———. *Oubliés de la Grande Guerre. Humanitaire et culture de guerre, 1914-1918: populations occupées, déportés civils, prisonniers de guerre.* Paris: Noesis, 1998.

Bekaert, Geert. "Wederopbouw of het uur van de waarheid." In *Resurgam: De Belgische wederopbouw na 1914*, edited by Marcel Smets, 18-32. Brussels: Gemeentekrediet, 1985.

Bendall, Ernest A. Lord Chamberlain's Plays, British Library, Add MS 66198 HH, in *Great War Theatre*, https://www.greatwartheatre.org.uk/db/script/2805/

Benjamin, Walter. "Experience and Poverty." In *Walter Benjamin. Selected Writings.* Vol. 2: *1927-1934*, edited by Michael W. Jennings, Howard Eiland, and Gary Smith, 731-737. Translated by Rodney Livingstone et al. Cambridge, MA: Harvard University Press, 1999.

Bentley, Phyllis E. *O Dreams, O Destinations: An Autobiography.* New York: Macmillan Company, 1962.

Bertrams, Kenneth. *Universités et entreprises: milieux académiques et industriels en Belgique, 1880-1970.* Brussels: Le Cri, 2006.

Bessel, Richard. *Germany after the First World War.* Oxford: Clarendon Press, 2003.

"Bestuur van den Bouwdienst – Standaarddeuren en vensters." *Beknopte bekendmaking nopens den Dienst der Verwoeste Gewesten* 2, no. 3 (1920): 162-166.

Bevan, Robert. *The Destruction of Memory. Architecture at War.* second expanded ed. London: Reaktion Books, 2016.

Beyen, Marnix. "Art and Architectural History as Substitutes for Preservation. German Heritage Policy in Belgium During and After the First World War." In *Living with History, 1914-1964: Rebuilding Europe after the First and Second World Wars and the Role of Heritage Preservation*, edited by Nicholas Bullock and Luc Verpoest, 32-43. Leuven: Leuven University Press, 2011.

Biernoff, Suzannah. "The Rhetoric of Disfigurement in First World War Britain." *Social History of Medicine* 24, no. 3 (2011): 666-685.

"Bij onze blinden soldaten." *De Belgische Verminkte*, May 15, [1918], 3.

BIM [Brussels Institute for Conservation]. 'The Parmentier Park', Infofiches over de Groene Ruimten in het Brussels Hoofstedelijk Gewest. 4 January 2011.
Biraghi, Giuseppe. *La fondazione dell'Università di Milano*. Milan: Associazione per lo sviluppo dell'alta cultura, 1929.
Blom, Philipp. *Fracture: Life and Culture in the West, 1918-1938*. London: Atlantic Books, 2015.
Blomme, Jan. *The Economic Development of Belgian Agriculture: 1880-1980: A Quantitative and Qualitative Analysis*. Brussels: Royal Academy of Belgium for Science and the Arts, 1992.
Blücher, Evelyn. *An English Wife in Berlin*. New York: E. P. Dutton & Co., 1920.
Boerenbond. *Bouwen en heropbouwen van huis en stal*. Leuven: Smeesters, 1915.
Bond, Brian. *Survivors of a Kind: Memoirs of the Western Front*. London: Continuum, 2008.
Booth, Michael R. *English Melodrama*. London: H. Jenkins, 1965.
Borg, Alan. *War Memorials from Antiquity to the Present*. Londen: Cooper, 1991.
Bourke, Joanna. *Dismembering the Male: Men's Bodies, Britain and the Great War*. London: Reaktion Books 1996.
———. "Love and Limblessness: Male Heterosexuality, Disability, and the Great War." *Journal of War & Culture Studies* 9, no. 1 (2016): 3-19.
Bourne, John, Peter Liddle, and Ian Whitehead, eds. *The Great World War, 1914-1945*. New York: Harper & Collins, 2000.
Boyd, Carolyn O. *La política pretoriana en el reinado de Alfonso XIII*. Madrid: Alianza, 1990.
Bracco, Barbara. *La patria ferita. I corpi dei soldati italiani e la Grande Guerra*. Florence: Giunti, 2012.
Braeken, Jo. "The Remains of War and the Heritage of Post-War Reconstruction in Flanders Today." In *Living with History 1914-1964: Rebuilding Europe after the First and Second World War and the Role of Heritage Preservation*, edited by Nicholas Bullock and Luc Verpoest, 322-333. Leuven: Leuven University Press, 2011.
Brandt, Susanne. "Le voyage aux champs de bataille." *Vingtième Siècle. Revue d'Histoire*, no. 41 (1994), 18-22.
Brittain, Vera. *Testament of Youth*. New York: Penguin, 1989.
Brock, Arthur J. "Evolving Edinburgh." *The Hydra*, n.s., no. 7, May 1918, 4-7; no. 8, June 1918, 10-12; and no. 9, July 1918, 4-7.
———. "The Re-Education of the Adult. I. The Neurasthenic in War and Peace." *The Sociological Review* 10, no. 1 [1918]: 25-40. Reprinted in *Papers for the Present issued by the Cities Committee of the Sociological Society*: 1-19. London: Headly Bros. Publishers, [1918]: 1-19.
———. *Health and Conduct*. London: Williams and Norgate, 1923. Brooks, Helen E. M. *Great War Theatre Project* (www.greatwartheatre.org.uk).
Brown, Richard D., and Richard Ashby Wilson. *Humanitarianism and Suffering: The Mobilization of Empathy*. Cambridge: Cambridge University Press, 2009.
Bruant, Catherine. "L'École d'art public du Collège Libre des Sciences Sociales: une formation à l'urbanisme comme 'sociologie appliquée'." *Le Télémaque* 33, no. 1 (2008): 83.
Buijs, Joke, Marika Ceunen, Rebecca Gysen, Herman Van de Vijver, Luc Verpoest, and Rudi Vranckx. *Herleven. Leuven na 1918*. Leuven: Stadsbestuur Leuven, 2018.

Bullock, Nicholas, and Luc Verpoest, eds. *Living with History 1914-1964: Rebuilding Europe after the First and Second World Wars and the Role of Heritage Preservation.* Leuven: Leuven University Press, 2011.
Buls, Charles. *Esthétique des villes.* Brussels: Bruylant-Christophe, 1893.
Burchhardt, Jeremy. *Paradise Lost: Rural Idyll and Social Change since 1800.* London: Taurus, 2002.
Buttlar, Adrian von, Gabi Dolff-Bonekämper, Michael S. Falser, Johannes Habich, Achim Hubel, and Georg Mörsch, eds. *Denkmalpflege statt Attrappenkult: gegen die Rekonstruktion von Baudenkmälern - eine Anthologie.* Gütersloh: Bauverlag, 2013.
Buyst, Erik. *An Economic History of Residential Building in Belgium between 1890 and 1961.* Brussels: Royal Academy of Belgium for Science and the Art, 1992.
Cabanes, Bruno. *The Great War and the Origins of Humanitarianism, 1918-1924.* Cambridge: Cambridge University Press, 2014.
Calleja, Eduardo González. *La España de Primo de Rivera. La modernización autoritaria, 1923-1930.* Madrid: Alianza, 2005.
Calhoun, Craig. "The Imperative to Reduce Suffering: Charity, Progress, and Emergencies in the Field of Humanitarian Action." In *Humanitarianism in Question: Politics, Power, Ethics,* edited by Michael Barnett and Thomas G. Weiss, 73-97. Ithaca, NY: Cornell University Press, 2008.
Canadelli, Elena, and Paola Zocchi. *Milano scientifica, 1875-1924.* 2 vols. Milan: Sironi, 2008.
Cantor, David. "Between Galen, Geddes, and the Gal: Arthur Brock, Modernity and Medical Humanism in Early-Twentieth-Century Scotland." *Journal of the History of Medicine and Allied Sciences* 60, no. 1 (2005): 1-41.
Cappronnier, Jean-Charles, and Franck Delorme. "La reconstruction des fermes dans le département de l'Aisne après 1918." *In Situ,* no. 21 (2013): 1-46.
Catalogue des ouvrages classiques dont le Gouvernement a autorisé ou recommandé l'emploi dans les établissements d'enseignement moyen soumis au régime des lois organiques sur la proposition du conseil de perfectionnement de l'instruction moyenne et des moyens matériels d'enseignement et d'ornementation des classes. Brussels, 1920.
Ceunen, Marika, and Piet Veldeman, eds. *Aan onze helden en martelaren...: Beelden van de brand van Leuven (augustus 1914).* Leuven: Peeters, 2004.
Ceunen, Marika. "Wat een monument lijden kan... Oprichting, lotgevallen en restauratie van het oorlogsmonument op het Martelarenplein." In *Aan onze helden en martelaren... Beelden van de brand van Leuven (augustus 1914),* edited by Marika Ceunen and Piet Veldeman, 305-338. Leuven: Peeters, 2004.
Chagas, João. *Diário IV – 1918-1921.* Lisbon: Edições Rolim, 1986.
Chambers, Emma, ed. *Aftermath: Art in the Wake of World War One.* London: Tate Publishing, 2018.
Chevalley, Giovanni. *Le scuole di rieducazione professionale dei mutilati e dei feriti in guerra in Francia.* Turin: Tipografia Collegio degli Artigianelli, 1915.
———. "Technical Re-education in Italy." In *Inter-allied Conference on the after care of disabled men, Second annual meeting,* 138-150. London: His Majesty Stationery Office, 1918.
Chickering, Roger, and Marcus Funck, eds. *Endangered Cities: Military Power and Urban Societies in the Era of the World Wars.* Boston, MA: Brill, 2004.

Claeys, Dries. "World War I and the Reconstruction of the Countryside in Belgium and France: A Historiographical Essay." *British Agricultural History Society* 65, No. 1 (2017): 108-129.
Claeys, Dries. "Land, staat en bevolking: De wederopbouw van het Belgische platteland na de Eerste Wereldoorlog." PhD Thesis, KU Leuven, 2019.
Claisse, Stéphanie."Les monuments aux morts." In *De la guerre de l'ombre aux ombres de la guerre*, edited by Laurence Van Ypersele and Emmanuel Debruyne, 134-146. Brussels: Éditions Labor, 2004.
———. "Pouvoir(s) et mémoire(e). L'État belge et les monuments aux morts de la Grande Guerre." In *Une guerre totale? La Belgique dans la Première Guerre Mondiale. Nouvelles tendances de la recherche historique*, edited by Serge Jaumain, Michaël Amare, Benoît Majerus, and Antoon Vrints, 545-560. Brussels: Algemeen Rijksarchief, 2005.
———. "Visages de la Patrie belge à travers les monuments aux morts de 14-18." In *Comment (se) sortir de la Grande Guerre? Regards sur quelques pays 'vainqueurs': la Belgique, la France et la Grande Bretagne*, edited by Stéphanie Claisse and Thierry Lemoine, 37-58. Paris: Harmattan, 2005.
———. *Du soldat inconnu aux monuments commémoratifs Belges de la Guerre 14-18*. Brussels: Académie Royale de Belgique, 2013.
Clark, Peter, ed. *The Oxford Handbook of Cities in World History*. Oxford: Oxford University Press, 2013.
Clavin, Patricia. "Defining Transnationalism." *Contemporary European History* 14, no. 4 (2005): 421-439.
Clement, Piet. "De Belgische overheidsfinanciën en het ontstaan van een sociale welvaartsstaat 1830-1940: Drie benaderingen." PhD Thesis, KU Leuven, 1995.
Clout, Hugh. *After the Ruins: Restoring the Countryside of Northern France after the Great War*. Exeter: University of Exeter Press, 1996.
———. "The Great Reconstruction of Towns and Cities in France 1918-1935." *Planning Perspectives : An International Journal of History, Planning and the Environment*. 20, no. 1 (2005): 1-34.
Cohen, Deborah. *The War Come Home. Disabled Veterans in Britain and Germany, 1914-1939*. Berkeley, CA: California University Press, 2001.
Colombine. "Femeninas. Las novias de la guerra," *Heraldo de Madrid*, December 29, 1915, 4.
Comín, Francisco. "El período de entreguerras (1914-1936)." In *Historia económica de España, siglos XIX-XX*, edited by Francisco Comín, Mauro L. Hernandez, and Enrique Llopis, 285-329. Barcelona: Critica, 2002.
Committee on Alleged German Outrages. *Report of the Committee on Alleged German Outrages Presented to Parliament by Command of His Majesty*. London: Her Majesty's Stationery Office, Eyre and Spottiswoode, 1915.
Compagnon, Olivier. *L'adieu à l'Europe. L'Amérique Latine et la Grande Guerre*. Paris: Fayard, 2013.
———, Camille Foulard, Guillemette Martin, and María Inés Tato, eds. *La Gran Guerra en América Latina. Una historia conectada*. Mexico City: Centro de Estudios Mexicanos y Centroamericanos / Institut des Hautes Études de l'Amérique Latine – Centre de Recherche et de Documentation des Ameriques, 2018.
Connelly, Mark. *The Great War, Memory and Ritual: Commemoration in the City and East London, 1916-1939*. London: Boydell & Brewer, 2015.

———. *Celluloid War Memorials: The British Instructional Films Company and the Memory of the Great War*. Exeter: University of Exeter Press, 2016.

"Conquista de Mercados. La lucha comercial en Europa y América." *La Ilustración Española y Americana*, February 28, 1919, 125.

"Consideraciones generales acerca del feminismo. Las Consecuencias de la Guerra en el estado de la mujer (Condesa de la Junquera)." *La Ilustración Española y Americana*, February 28, 1919, 126-127.

Constandt, Marc. "We reizen om te leren: schoolreizen in het interbellum." *Brood & Rozen. Tijdschrift voor de Geschiedenis van Sociale Bewegingen* 14, no. 2 (2009): 54-67.

Coppens, Chris, ed. *Leuven in Books, Books in Leuven: the Oldest University of the Low Countries and its Library*. Translated by Ardis Dreisbach. Leuven: Leuven University Press, 1999.

———., Mark Derez, and Jan Roegiers. *Universiteitsbibliotheek Leuven 1425-2000: Sapientia aedificavit sibi domum*. Leuven: Leuven University Press, 2005.

———., Mark Derez, and Jan Roegiers. *Leuven University Library, 1425-2000*. Leuven: Leuven University Press, 2005.

Cornilly, Jeroen. "Gevraagd: architecten. Kiezen tussen alternatieven." In *Bouwen aan wederopbouw 1914/2050. Architectuur in de Westhoek*, edited by Jeroen Cornilly, Sofie De Caigny, Dominiek Dendooven, Caroline Goossens, and Katrien Vandermarliere, 117-141. Ypres: Erfgoedcel CO7, 2009.

———. Sofie De Caigny, Dominiek Dendooven, Caroline Goossens, and Katrien Vandermarliere, eds. *Bouwen aan wederopbouw 1914/2050. Architectuur in de Westhoek*. Ypres: Erfgoedcel CO7, 2009.

Cortjaens, Wolfgang. "'The German Way of Making Better Cities.' German Reconstruction Plans for Belgium during First World War." In *Living with History, 1914-1964: Rebuilding Europe after the First and Second World Wars and the Role of Heritage Preservation*, edited by Nicholas Bullock and Luc Verpoest, 44-59. Leuven: Leuven University Press, 2011.

Cotting, Francis J. "Industrial School for Crippled and Deformed Children." *Journal of Bone and Joint Surgery* S2-6, no. 4 (1909): 734-750.

Cousserier, Annelies. *In goede handen: 75 jaar onderwijs verpleeg- en vroedkunde Leuven*. Leuven: KADOC, 2004.

Cozzolino, Robert, Anne Classen Knutson, and David M. Lubin, eds. *World War I and American Art*. Philadelphia, PA: Pennsylvania Academy of the Fine Arts, 2016.

Crossman, A.M. "The Hydra. Captain, A.J. Brock and the Treatment of Shell-Shock in Edinburgh." *Journal of the Royal College of Physicians* 33, no. 2 (2003): 119-123.

Crouthamel, Jason. *An Intimate History of the Front: Masculinity, Sexuality, and German Soldiers in the First World War*. New York: Palgrave MacMillan, 2014.

Cruz Vermelha Portuguesa 1865-1925. Lisbon: Centro Tipográfico Colonial, 1926.

Cuevas, Pedro Antonio González. "Antonio Goicoechea. Político y doctrinario monárquico." *Historia y Política*, no. 6 (2001): 161-189.

Curl, James Steven. *Oxford Dictionary of Architecture*. Oxford: Oxford University Press, 2000.

Dalisson, Rémi, and Elise Julien. "Bereavement and Mourning, Commemoration and Cult of the Fallen (France)." In *1914-1918-online. International Encyclopedia of the First World War*, edited by Ute Daniel, Peter Gatrell, Oliver Janz, Heather Jones, Jennifer Keene, Alan Kramer, and Bill Nasson. Translated by: Jocelyne Serveau, issued by Freie Universität Berlin, Berlin, 2014-10-08. DOI: 10.15463/ie1418.10378.

Damen, Mario. "The Town, the Duke, His Courtiers and Their Tournament: A Spectacle in Brussels, 4-7 May 1439." *Studies in Medieval and Early Renaissance Art History* 69 (2013): 85-95.

Damousi, Joy. *The Labour of Loss: Mourning, Memory, and Wartime Bereavement in Australia*. Cambridge: Cambridge University Press, 1999.

da Silva, Fernando Emídio. *Cousas de Portugal*. Coimbra: França & Arménio, 1919.

Debè, Anna, and Simonetta Polenghi. "Assistance and education of mutilated soldiers of World War I. The Italian case." *History of Education & Children's Literature* 11, no. 2 (2016): 227-246.

DeBord, Guy. *The Society of the Spectacle*. Translated by Donald Nicholson-Smith. New York: Zone Books, 1995.

Debruyne, Emmanuel. *"Femmes à Boches": Occupation du corps féminin, dans la France et la Belgique de la Grande Guerre*. Paris: Les belles lettres, 2018.

De Caigny, Sofie. *Bouwen aan een nieuwe thuis: Wooncultuur in Vlaanderen tijdens het interbellum*. Leuven: Leuven University Press, 2010.

———. and Wouter Vanderstede. "Spiegel van het hemelhuis: De wisselwerking tussen woonideaal en sociale rollen bij de Belgische Boerinnenbond (1907-1940)." *Tijdschrift voor sociale en economische geschiedenis* 2, no. 1 (2005): 3-29.

de Cértima, António. *Legenda Dolorosa do Soldado Desconhecido de África*. Lisbon, 1925.

Deschanel, Paul. "Le Grand Devoir." *Le Journal des Régions Dévastées*, 18 May 1919.

Dehaisnes, Chrétien. *Fêtes et marches historiques en Belgique et dans le Nord de la France*. Lille: L. Danet, 1893.

Demasure, Brecht. *Boter bij de vis: Landbouw en voeding tijdens de Eerste Wereldoorlog*. Leuven: Davidsfonds, 2014.

de Meneses, Filipe Ribeiro. "Revolutions (Portugal)." In *1914-1918-online. International Encyclopedia of the First World War*, edited by Ute Daniel, Peter Gatrell, Oliver Janz, Heather Jones, Jennifer Keen, Alan Kramer, and Bill Nasson, issued by Freie Universität Berlin, Berlin, 2014-12-08. DOI: 10.15463/ie1418.10438.

De Meulder, Bruno. "Galerijwoningen te Brussel. Proeve van een historisch-typologische analyse van de sociale meergezinswoningbouw in de Brusselse agglomeratie. 1870-1914." MA Diss., KU Leuven, 1983.

———. "Reformisme thuis en overzee: Geschiedenis van de Belgische planning in een kolonie (1880-1960)." PhD Thesis, KU Leuven, 1994.

De Munck, Luc. *Altijd troosten: Belgische verpleegsters tijdens de Eerste Wereldoorlog*. Amsterdam: Amsterdam University Press, 2018.

———. and Luc Vandeweyer. *Het hospitaal van de koningin. Rode Kruis, L'Océan en De Panne, 1914-1918*. De Panne: Gemeentebestuur De Panne, 2012.

Dendooven, Dominiek. "Asia in Flanders Fields. A Transnational History of Indians and Chinese on the Western Front, 1914-1920." PhD Thesis, University of Antwerp and University of Kent, 2018.

———. *De vergeten soldaten van de Eerste Wereldoorlog*. Berchem: EPO, 2019.

De Paeuw, Léon. *La rééducation professionnelle des grands blessés de guerre et l'institut militaire belge de rééducation professionnelle de Port-Villez-les-Vernon (Eure)*. Port-Villez: Institut militaire belge de rééducation professionnelle des grands blessés de guerre, 1916.

Deplechin, Davy. "De ontwerper als redacteur van een nationale geschiedenis: Het concept van de Gentse cortège historique des comtes de Flandre (1849)." *Tijdschrift voor Interieurgeschiedenis en Design*, no. 40 (2018): 47-67.

Derez, Mark. "The Flames of Louvain: The War Experience of an Academic Community." In *Facing Armageddon: The First World War Experienced*, edited by Hugh Cecil and Peter H. Liddle, 617-629. London: Leo Cooper, 1996.

———. and Axel Tixhon, *Martelaarssteden: Visé, Aarschot, Tamines, Dinant, Leuven, Dendermonde. België, augustus-september 1914*. Namur: Presses Universitaires de Namur, 2014.

———. Jo Tollebeek, and G. Vanpaemel, eds. *Album van een wetenschappelijke wereld: De Leuvense universiteit omstreeks 1900/Album of a Scientific World: The University of Louvain around 1900*. Leuven: Leuven University Press, 2012.

De Sanctis, Sante. "Autobiography." In *History of Psychology in Autobiography*, edited by Carl Murchison, 83-120. Worcester, MA: Clark University Press, 1936.

de Schaepdrijver, Sophie. *La Belgique et la Première Guerre Mondiale*. Brussels: Peter Lang, 2004.

———. "Gemartelde steden en verwoeste gewesten: Twee legaten van 1914-1918." In *België. Een parcours van herinnering*, vol. 2, *Plaatsen van tweedracht, crisis en nostalgie*, edited by Johan Tollebeek, Geert Buelens, Gita Deneckere, Chantal Kesteloot, and Sophie De Schaepdrijver, 195-207. Amsterdam: Bakker, 2008.

———. "Belgium." In *A companion to World War I*, edited by John Horne, 386-402. Oxford: Blackwell Publishing, 2010.

———. *Gabrielle Petit: The Death and Life of a Female Spy in the First World War*. London: Bloomsbury, 2015.

———. and Tammy M. Proctor. *An English Governess in the Great War: The Secret Diary of Mary Thorp*. New York: Oxford University Press, 2017.

Deschanel, Paul. "Le grand devoir." *Le Journal des Régions Dévastées*, May 18, 1919, 1.

"Desert House Richard Neutra Architect." *Arts and Architecture* 66, no. 7 (1949): 30-33.

De Smaele, Henk, Kaat Wils, and Tine Van Osselaer, eds. *Sign or Symptom? Exceptional Corporeal Phenomena in Religion and Medicine, 19th and 20th Century*. Leuven: Leuven University Press, 2017.

Devlieger, Patrick, Ian Grosvenor, Frank Simon, Geert Vanhove, and Bruno Vanobbergen. "Visualising Disability in the Past." *Paedogogica Historica* 44, no. 6 (2008): 747-760.

De Volder, Jan. *Cardinal Mercier in the First World War: Belgium, Germany and the Catholic Church*. Leuven: Leuven University Press, 2018.

De Vriendt, Samuel. *Aveugles de la guerre: croquis/Oorlogsblinden: schetsen/The Blind of the War: Sketches*. Boitsfort: Institut des Aveugles de Guerre, 1919.

De Vuyst, Paul. *Le village moderne à l'Exposition universelle et internationale de Gand 1913: Notes, comptes rendus, vues et plans*. Brussels: Goemaere, 1913.

Dhondt, Pieter. "Social Education or Medical Care? Divergent Views on Visiting Nurses in Belgium in the Interwar Years." *History of Education & Children's Literature* 7, no. 1 (2012): 505-522.

Dhuicque, Eugène. «Un monument commémoratif de la défense nationale à eriger à Liège.» *L'Émulation* 41, no. 12 (1921): 177-183.

Dickinson, Frederick. "Toward a Global Perspective of the Great War: Japan and the Foundations of a Twentieth-Century World." *American Historical Review* 119, no. 4 (2014): 1154-1183.

Diers, Michael. "Nagelmänner. Propaganda mit Ephemeren Denkmälern im Ersten Weltkrieg." In *Mo(nu)mente: Formen und Funktionen Ephemerer Denkmäler*, edited by Michael Diers, 113-135. Berlin: Akademie Verlag, 1993.

Digby, Anne, Howard Phillips, Harriet Deacon, and Kirsten Thomson. *At the Heart of Healing: Groote Schuur Hospital 1938-2008*. Cape Town: Jacana, 2008.

Dirkx, H. *Jusqu'à la chute d'Anvers*. Brussels: Touring-Club de Belgique, 1920.

D'Monte, Rebecca. *British Theatre and Performance 1900-1950*. London and New York: Bloomsbury, 2015.

Donato, Maria Pia, ed. *Médecine et religion: Compétitions, collaborations, conflits (XIIe-XXe siècles)*. Collection de l'École française de Rome 476. Rome: École française de Rome, 2013.

Dorgelès, Roland. *Le réveil des morts*. Paris: Albin Michel, 1923.

Douglas Wilson, Johnson. *Topography and Strategy in the War*. New York: Henry Holt, 1917.

———. *Battlefields of the World War. Western and Southern Fronts. A Study in Military Geography*. New York: Oxford University Press, 1921.

Dowdall, Alex. *Communities under fire: urban life at the western front, 1914-1918*. Oxford: Oxford University Press, 2020.

Doyle, Barry. "Healthcare before Welfare States: Hospitals in Early Twentieth Century England and France." *Canadian Bulletin of the History of Medicine* 33, no. 1 (2016): 174-204.

Drew Gilpin Faust, Catharine. *This Republic of Suffering: Death and the American Civil War*. New York: Random House, 2008.

Dubos, René, and Jean Dubos. *The White Plague. Tuberculosis, Man and Society*. Boston, MA: Little, Brown, 1952.

Dutry, Albert. *De kunst op het platteland (Schets eener landelijke schoonheidsleer)*. Ghent: De Scheemaecker, 1915.

Eichenberg, Julia. *Kämpfen für Frieden und Fürsorge : polnische Veteranen des Ersten Weltkriegs und ihre internationalen Kontakte, 1918-1939*. Studien zur Internationalen Geschichte 27. Munich: Oldenbourg, 2011.

Elisha, Achille, ed. *Aristide Briand. Discours et écrits de politique étrangère*. Paris: Plon, 1965.

Engelen, Cor, and Mieke Marx. *Compagnie des bronzes de Bruxelles: Archief in beeld*. Brussels: Algemeen Rijksarchief, 2002.

Engelen, Leen, and Marjan Sterckx, "Herinneringen in steen en op papier. Monumenten en prentbriefkaarten voor twee heldinnen van de Eerste Wereldoorlog: Gabrielle Petit en Edith Cavell." *Volkskunde* 111, no. 4 (2010): 379-403.

———. and Marjan Sterckx. "Remembering Edith and Gabrielle. Picture postcards of monuments as portable *Lieux de mémoire*." In *Imaging History. Photography after the Fact*, edited by Bruno Vandermeulen and Danny Veys, 87-103. Brussels: ASP Publishers, 2011.

———. and Marjan Sterckx. "An Ephemeral Open-Air Sculpture Museum: Ten Temporary Monuments for the Festive Return of the Belgian Royal Family to Brussels, November 1918." *Sculpture Journal* 26, no. 3 (2017): 321-348.

———, Erik Martens, and Bénédicte Rochet, eds. *14'18. De grote oorlog in de Belgische film*. 2 DVD's and booklet. Brussels: Cinematek, 2014.

English, John A. *A Perspective on Infantry*. New York: Praeger, 1981.

——. and Bruce I. Gudmundsson. *On Infantry*. Revised Edition. Westport, CT: Praeger, 1994.
Enwezor, Okwul, ed. *The Short Century. Independence and Liberation Movements on Africa, 1945-1994*. Munich: Prestel, 2001.
Federico, Giovanni. *Feeding the World: An Economic History of Agriculture, 1800-2000*. Princeton, NJ: Princeton University Press, 2009.
Feldman, Gerald D. *Army, Industry and Labor, 1914-1918*. Princeton, NJ: Princeton University Press, 1966.
Fell, Alison. *Women as Veterans in Britain and France after the First World War*. Cambridge: Cambridge University Press, 2018.
Ferreira Martins, Luís Augusto. *As virtudes militares na tradição histórica de Portugal*. Lisbon: Tipografia da Liga dos Combatentes da Grande Guerra, 1953.
Finckh, Gerhard, ed. *Das Menschenschlachthaus: Der Erste Weltkrieg in der französischen und deutschen Kunst*. Wuppertal: Von der Heydt-Museum, 2014.
Frateur, Leopold. *De nieuwe methode tot verbetering van het vee*. Leuven: Ceuterick, 1922.
Floré, Fredie. "Lessen in modern wonen: Een architectuurhistorisch onderzoek naar de communicatie van modellen voor 'goed wonen' in België, 1945-1958." PhD Thesis, University of Ghent, 2006.
Foner, Eric. *Reconstruction: America's Unfinished Revolution, 1863-1877*. New York: Harper & Row, 1988.
Ford, George (Geo) B. "Rebuilding France for Posterity. How the Renaissance des Cités is helping the people in devastated areas to plan a new life." *La France* 5, No. 5 (1921): 202-223.
Forment, Bruno. "In kleur en op ware grootte. De operadecors van Albert Dubosq." In *Opera: Achter de schermen van de emotie*, edited by Francis Maes and Piet De Volder, 228-249. Tielt: Lannoo, 2011.
Forsythe, David P. *The Humanitarians. The International Committee of the Red Cross*. Cambridge: Cambridge University Press, 2005.
——. "The International Red Cross: Decentralization and its Effects." *Human Rights Quarterly* 40, no. 1 (2018): 61-90.
Fraga, Luís Alves de. "Portugal e grande guerra. Balançestatístico." In *Portugal e a Grande Guerra*, edited by Afonso Aniceto and Carlos Matos de Gomes. Lisboa: Matosinhos QuidNovi, 2010
Frateur, Joseph-Léopold. *De nieuwe methode tot verbetering van het vee*. Leuven: Ceuterick, 1922.
Freire, João Paulo. *Em serviço da Cruz Vermelha. Notas d'um Comissário*. Lisbon: Edição da Sociedade Portuguesa da Cruz Vermelha, 1919.
Fuchs, Petra. *"Körperbehinderte" zwischen Selbstaufgabe und Emanzipation: SelbsthilfeIntegration-Aussonderung*. Neuwied-Berlin: Luchterhand, 2001.
Fuglister, Albert. *Louvain, ville martyre*. Paris: Éditions Delandre, 1916.
Fumi, Gianpiero. "Politiche del lavoro e portatori di handicap: il collocamento obbligatorio (1917-1968)." In *Il lavoro come fattore produttivo e come risorsa nella storia economica italiana*, edited by Sergio Zaninelli and Mario Taccolini, 73-110. Milan: Vita e pensiero, 2002.
Fussell, Paul. *The Great War and Modern Memory*. Oxford: Oxford University Press, 2000.

Gagen, Wendy Jane. "Remastering the Body, Renegotiating Gender: Physical Disability and Masculinity During the First World War, the Case of J. B. Middlebrook." *European Review of History/Revue européenne d'Histoire* 14, no. 4 (2007): 525-541. DOI: 10.1080/13507480701752169.
Gale, Maggie. "The London Stage, 1918-1945." In *The Cambridge History of British Theatre*, Vol. 3, *Since 1895*, edited by Baz Kershaw, 143-166. Cambridge: Cambridge University Press, 2015.
Galgano, Salvatore. *La protezione interalleata degli invalidi e dei mutilati di guerra e la legislazione internazionale del lavoro*. Rome: Nuova Antologia, 1919.
Galeazzi, Riccardo. *Le Case di lavoro per gli storpi, paralitici e mutilati. Rapporto presentato al VI Congresso internazionale d'assistenza pubblica e privata, Milano 23-27 maggio 1906*. Milan: Tip. Operai, 1906.
———. *I progressi dell'ortopedia moderna. Prolusione al corso di clinica ortopedica negli ICP 1906-07*. Biella: Amosso, 1907.
———. *L'Istituto dei Rachitici nel triennio 1903-1906*. Biella: Amosso, 1908.
———. *Die orthopädische Klinik in Mailand Hamburg. Stenographischer Bericht über den Deutschen Kongress für Krüppelfürsorge veranstaltet von der Deutschen Vereinigung für Krüppelfürsorge E. V. am 31 März 1910 zu Berlin*. Leipzig: Leopold Voss, 1910.
———. *Sulla protesi cinematica*. Rome: Tip. Berterio, 1912.
———. *L'inaugurazione della scuola di Lavoro "Sofia Carmine Speroni", maggio 1913*. Biella: Amosso, 1913.
———. *Le moderne provvidenze sociali per i mutilati in guerra*. Milan: Rava & C., 1915.
———. *Come si rieducano i soldati mutilati*. Florence: Bemporad, 1916.
———. "La rieducazione professionale dei lavoratori mutilati di Guerra." *Archivio di ortopedia* 33 (1916): attachment n.L.
———. "Discorso alla Società lombarda di scienze mediche e biologiche." *Archivio di ortopedia* 33 (1916): attachment n.A.
———. *L'Italia provvede ai suoi figli mutilati in guerra*. Milan: Tip. del Corriere della sera: 1916.
———. *La rieducazione professionale dei lavoratori mutilati in guerra: relazione al Comitato lombardo per i soldati mutilati in guerra*. Biella: Amosso, [1916].
———. "Exact Constructive Drawings of the Prothesis and Orthopaedic Apparatus for the Lower Limbs." In *Inter-allied Conference on the after care of disabled men, Second annual meeting*, 516-519. London: His Majesty's Stationery Office, 1918.
———. "Mechanical Prothesis for Manual Work." In *Inter-allied Conference on the after care of disabled men, Second annual meeting*, 493-515. London: His Majesty's Stationery Office, 1918.
———. *L'Esposizione interalleata dei lavori degli invalidi di guerra (Gand, 14-22 Aprile 1923) e la partecipazione italiana*. Rome, 1923.
———. "Necrologio: Corrado Biesalski." *Archivio di ortopedia* 46, fasc. 2 (1930): 436.
Galtier-Boissière, Emile. *Larousse médical illustré de guerre*. Paris: Librairie Larousse, 1917.
Geddes, Patrick, and Gilbert Slater. *Ideas at War*. London: Williams and Norgate, 1917.
Geeraert, Pieter. "After the War. Het herstel van boerderijen in Oostduinkerke na de Eerste Wereldoorlog (1918-1925)." MA Diss., KU Leuven, 2017.
Gerber, David. "Disabled Veterans and Public Welfare Policy: Comparative and Transnational Perspectives on Western States in the Twentieth Century." *Transnational & Contemporary Problems* 11, no. 1 (Spring 2001): 77-106.

Geroulanos, Stefanos, and Todd Meyers. *The Human Body in the Age of Catastrophe. Brittleness, Integration, Science, and the Great War.* Chicago, IL: The University of Chicago Press, 2018.

Gerwarth, Robert. *The Vanquished: Why the First World War Failed to End, 1917-1923.* New York: Farrar, Straus and Giroux, 2016.

———, ed. *Twisted Paths. Europe 1914-1945.* Oxford: Oxford University Press, 2007.

———. and John Horne. *War in Peace. Paramilitary Violence in Europe after the Great War.* Oxford: Oxford University Press, 2012.

Geurst, Jeroen. *Cemeteries of the Great War by Sir Edwin Lutyens.* Rotterdam: 010 Publishers, 2010.

Giachi, Giovanni. "Milano per i lavoratori mutilati in guerra." *Archivio di ortopedia* 33 (1916): 3-113.

Gibelli, Antonio. *L'officina della guerra. La Grande Guerra e le trasformazioni del mondo mentale.* Turin: Bollati Boringhieri, 1991.

Giblin, John. "Critical Approaches to Post-Colonial (Post-Conflict) Heritage." In *The Palgrave Handbook of Contemporary Heritage Research*, edited by Emma Waterton and Steve Watson, 313-328. Basingstoke: Palgrave Macmillan, 2015.

Giele, Jacques. "Hygiène des constructions rurales." In *Cinq leçons d'embellissement de la vie rurale données pendant les travaux du jury de perfectionnement* (Études de reconstructions rurales). Brussels: Goossens, 1916.

———. *Nationaal komiteit voor de verfraaiïng van het landleven: zijn doel en zijne werking.* Leuven: Ceuterick, 1925.

Gille, Louis, Alphonse Ooms, and Paul Delandsheere. *Cinquante mois d'occupation allemande.* Brussels: Librairie Albert Dewit, 1919.

Gillette, Arthur J. "Editorial." *Journal of Bone and Joint Surgery* S2-6, no. 4 (1909): 723-726.

Glendinning, Miles. *The Conservation Movement: A History of Architectural Preservation: Antiquity to Modernity.* New York: Routledge, 2013.

Goebel, Stefan, and Derek Keene, eds. *Cities into Battlefields: Metropolitan Scenarios, Experiences and Commemorations of Total War.* Historical Urban Studies Series. Farnham: Ashgate, 2011.

Goode, Josua. *Defining Race in Spain, 1870-1930.* Baton Rouge, LA: LSU Press, 2009.

Goossens, Paul. "Belgium: The End Started in 1968." In *1968: Memories and Legacies of a Global Revolt*, edited by Philipp Gassert and Martin Klimke, 191-194. Washington, DC: German Historical Institute, 2009.

Graftiau, Firmin. "Notice sur la commission nationale pour l'embellissement de la vie rurale." In *Congrès national de la restauration agricole et de l'embellissement de la vie rurale, Bruxelles, 28 septembre - 1 octobre 1919: Compte rendu des travaux du congrès*, 5-8. Leuven: Ceuterick, 1919.

Gras, Léon. *Enkele practische gegevens nopens het bouwen van hoeven.* Brussels: Ministry of Economic Affairs, 1921.

Grima, Joseph. "Adhocracy." *M+ Matters* 1, no. 1 (2012): 1-10. https://www.mplusmatters.hk/asiandesign/#/en/topic3intro.

Grixti, Joseph. *Terrors of Uncertainty: The Cultural Contexts of Horror Fiction.* London: Routledge, 1989.

Guilardian, David. "Saint-Pierre & Bordet: de l'Art Déco au Modernisme." In *Du monumental au fonctionnel: l'architecture des hôpitaux publics bruxellois (XIXè-XXè siècles)*, edited by Astrid Lelarge, Claire Dickstein-Bernard, David Guilardian, and

Judith Le Maire, 65-115. Brussels: CIVA, 2005.
Guillemain, Hervé, ed. *Diriger les consciences, guérir les âmes: une histoire comparée des pratiques thérapeutiques et religieuses (1830-1939)*. Paris: La Découverte, 2016.
Haffner, Jeanne. *The View from Above. The Science of Social Space*. Cambridge, MA: MIT Press, 2013.
Hanna, Emma. "Contemporary Britain and the Memory of the First World War." *Matériaux pour l'histoire de notre temps* 113-114, no. 1 (2014): 110-117.
Hanotaux, Gabriel. *Les villes martyres. Les Falaises de l'Aisne*. Paris: Plon, 1915.
Harding Davis, Richard. *With the Allies*. New York: C. Scribner's Sons, 1914.
Harris, Garrard. *The Redemption of the Disabled. A Study of Programmes of Rehabilitation for the Disabled of War and of Industry*. New York: D. Appleton & Company, 1919.
Heller, Paul. *Von der Landeskrüppelanstalt zur Orthopädischen Universitätsklinik: das "Elisabethheim" in Rostock*. Berlin: Lit, 2009.
Hens, Tine, Saartje Vandenborre, and Kaat Wils. "De oorlog maakt school: Herinneringspraktijken in het Belgische onderwijs na de Eerste Wereldoorlog." *Volkskunde* 115, no. 1 (2014): 5-25.
———, Saartje Vanden Borre, and Kaat Wils, *Oorlog in tijden van vrede. De Eerste Wereldoorlog in de klas (1919-1940)*. Kalmthout: Pelckmans, 2015.
Hibberd, Dominic. "A Sociological Cure for Shellshock: Dr. Brock and Wilfred Owen." *The Sociological Review* 25, no. 2 (1977): 377-386.
Hobsbawm, Eric J. *Age of Extremes: The Short Twentieth Century, 1914-1991*. London: Michael Joseph, 1994.
Hoegaerts, Josephine. "'Op 't bloedig oorlogsveld, is ied're man een held': Hoe kinderen het slagveld verbeeldden en beleefden aan het eind van de negentiende eeuw." *Volkskunde* 113, no. 3 (2012): 306-324.
Hölscher, Lucian. "The First World War as a 'Rupture' in the European History of the Twentieth Century: A Contribution to the Hermeneutics of Not-Understanding." *German Historical Institute London Bulletin* 35, no. 2 (2013): 73-87.
Horne, John. *Labour at War. France and Britain 1914-1918*. Oxford: Clarendon Press, 1991.
———, ed. *State, Society, and Mobilization in Europe during the First World War*. Cambridge: Cambridge University Press, 1997.
———, ed. *Démobilisations culturelles après la Grande Guerre*. 14-18. Aujourd'hui. Today. Heute 5. Paris: Noesis, 2002.
———. "Locarno et la politique de démobilisation culturelle: 1925-1930." In *Démobilisations culturelles après la Grande Guerre*, 14-18 Aujourd'hui. Today. Heute 5, edited by John Horne, 72-88. Paris: Noesis, 2002.
———. "Demobilizing the Mind: France and the Legacy of the Great War, 1919-1939." *French History & Civilization* 2 (2009):101-119.
———. "The living." In *The Cambridge History of the First World War*, Vol. 3, *Civil Society*, edited by Jay Winter, 592-601. Cambridge: Cambridge University Press, 2014.
———. "Patriotism and the Enemy: Political Identity as a Weapon in World War One." In *Nations, Identities and the First World War: Shifting Loyalties to the Fatherland*, edited by. Nico Wouters and Laurence Van Ypersele, 17-39. London: Bloomsbury, 2018.
———. "'A Civilizing Work?': The French Army in Macedonia, 1915-1918." In *Militarized Cultural Encounters in the Long Nineteenth Century: Making War, Mapping Europe*, edited by Joseph Clarke and John Horne, 319-341. London: Palgrave Macmillan, 2018.

———. and Robert Gerwarth, eds. *War in Peace. Paramilitary Violence in Europe after the Great War*. Oxford: Oxford University Press, 2012.

———. and Robert Gerwarth. "Paramilitarism in Europe after the Great War: an introduction." In *War in Peace. Paramilitary Violence in Europe after the Great War*, edited by Robert Gerwarth and John Horne, 1-20. Oxford: Oxford University Press, 2012.

———. and Alan Kramer. *German Atrocities, 1914: A History of Denial*. New Haven, CT: Yale University Press, 2001.

Horwitz, A. E. "Seventh Congress of the German Association for Orthopaedic Surgery." *The Journal of Bone and Joint Surgery* S2-6, no. 1 (1908): 137-142.

Houben, Claudia. "De wederopbouw van hoeves in de Westhoek na de Eerste Wereldoorlog." MA Diss., KU Leuven, 2017.

Howard, Ebenezer. *To-Morrow: A Peaceful Path to Real Reform*. London: Swan Sonnenschein & Co, 1898.

Hubert, Lucien. *La renaissance d'un département dévasté*. Paris: Boivin & Cie, 1923.

Hughes, Gordon, and Philipp Blom, eds. *Nothing but the Clouds Unchanged: Artists in World War I*. Los Angeles, CA: Getty Research Institute, 2014.

Huguet Santos, Monserrat. "Desembarco en 'tierras papales': educadoras estadounidenses en España en el tránsito entre siglos (1877-1931)." In *Regeneracionismo autoritario. Desafíos y bloqueos de una sociedad en transformación: España, 1923-1930*, edited by Francisco Villacorta Baños and María Luisa Rico Gómez, 179-200. Madrid: Biblioteca Nueva, 2013.

Hunt, Edward Eyre. *War Bread: A Personal Narrative of the War and Relief in Belgium*. New York: Henry Holt and Company, 1916.

Huygebaert, Stefan. "The Quest for the Decisive Constitutional Moment (Dcm)." In *Sensing the Nation's Law. Historical Inquiries into the Aesthetics of Democratic Legitimacy*, edited by Stefan Huygebaert, Condello Angela, and Marusek Sarah, 45-84. Cham: Springer, 2018.

Huyse, Luc. *Alles gaat voorbij behalve het verleden*. Leuven: Uitgeverij Van Halewyck, 2006.

Hymans, L. *XXVe anniversaire de l'inauguration du roi. Les fêtes de juillet, compte rendu des solennités et cérémonies publiques célébrées à Bruxelles les 21, 22 et 23 juillet*. Brussels: Alexandre Jamar, 1856.

Hynes, Samuel. *A War Imagined. The First World War and English Culture*. London: Pimlico, 1992.

"Inlichtingen nopens de gemeentemagazijnen." *Beknopte bekendmaking nopens den Dienst der Verwoeste Gewesten* 2, no. 4 (1920): 271-273.

Irish, Tomás. *The University at War, 1914-25: Britain, France and the United States*. Basingstoke: Palgrave Macmillan, 2015.

Irwin, Julia. *Making the World Safe: The American Red Cross and a Nation's Humanitarian Awakening*. Oxford: Oxford University Press, 2013.

Jalland, Pat. *Death in War and Peace: Loss and Grief in England, 1914-1970*. Oxford: Oxford University Press, 2010.

Janssens, Jeroen. *De Belgische natie viert: De Belgische nationale feesten, 1830-1914*. Leuven: Leuven University Press, 2001.

Jarry, Paul. *Le passé qui saigne: Les Villes Martyres, hier et aujourd'hui*. Paris: E. Champion, 1916.

Jasanoff, Sheila. "Reconstructing the Past, Constructing the Present: Can Science Studies and the History of Science Live Happily Ever After?" *Social Studies of Science* 30, no. 4 (2000): 621-631.
Jaspers, Patrick. "Huib Hoste and the Reconstruction of Zonnebeke, 1919-1924." In *Living with History, 1914-1964: Rebuilding Europe after the First and Second World Wars and the Role of Heritage Preservation*, edited by Nicholas Bullock and Luc Verpoest, 218-222. Leuven: Leuven University Press, 2011.
Jencks, Charles, and Nathan Silver. *Adhocism: The Case for Improvisation*. New York: Doubleday/Anchor Books, 1973.
Jones, Heather. "International or Transnational? Humanitarian Action During the First World War." *European Review of History* 16, no. 5 (2009): 697-713.
———. "Romantic Ireland's Dead and Gone? How Centenary Publications are Reshaping Ireland's Divided Understanding of Its Decade of War and Revolution, 1912-1923." *First World War Studies* 9, no. 3 (2018): 344-361.
Kauffman, Duane S. ed. *"Your son and brother Sol": Letters from Solomon E. Yoder while serving with the American Friends Service Committee in post-World War I Europe*. Morgantown, WV: Masthof Press, 2011.
Kent, Susan Kingsley. *Making Peace: The Reconstruction of Gender in Interwar Britain*. Princeton, NJ: Princeton University Press, 1993.
Kervyn de Lettenhove, Henri. *La guerre et les œuvres d'art en Belgique: 1914-1916*. Paris: Van Oest, 1917.
Kesteloot, Chantal. "Une nouvelle joyeuse entrée dans Bruxelles libérée". in *Albert & Elisabeth. Le film de la vie d'un couple royal*, edited by Chantal Kesteloot, 86-97. Brussels: Mardaga, 2014.
Kienitz, Sabine. *Beschädigte Helden. Kriegsinvalidität und Körperbilder 1914-1923*. Padeborn: Schöningh, 2008.
King, Alex. *Memorials of the Great War in Britain: The Symbolism and Politics of Remembrance*. London: Berg Publishers, 1998.
Kosseleck, Reinhart. *Futures Past: On the Semantics of Historical Time*. Cambridge, MA: MIT Press, 1985.
Kramer, Alan. *Dynamic of Destruction: Culture and Mass Killing in the First World War*. Oxford: Oxford University Press, 2007.
Kuhlman, Erika. *Of Little Comfort: War Widows, Fallen Soldiers, and the Remembering of the Nation after the Great War*. New York: New York University Press, 2012.
Kuhr, Piete. *There We'll Meet Again: A Young German Girl's Diary of the First World War*. Translated by Walter Wright. Gloucester: Walter Wright, 1998.
Kurth, Godefroid. *La patrie belge, y a-t-il une nationalité belge? La Belgique dans la Grande Guerre*. Brussels: De Wit, 1922.
Küster, Bernd. *Der erste Weltkrieg und die Kunst: Von der Propaganda zum Widerstand*. Oldenburg: Merlin Verlag, 2008.
Lagae, Johan. "Kongo zoals het is: Drie architectuurverhalen uit de Belgische kolonisatiegeschiedenis (1920-1960)." PhD Thesis, Ghent University, 2002.
Lagasse de Locht, Charles, and Paul Saintenoy. "La reconstruction des villes et villages détruits par la guerre de 1914. Rapport sur les devoirs administratifs incombant aux Pouvoirs publics." *Bulletin des Commissions Royales d'Art et d'Archéologie* 54 (1914): 253-264.

Lamberts, Emiel, and Jan Roegiers, eds. *De universiteit te Leuven, 1425-1985*. Leuven: Leuven University Press, 1986.

Lancellotti, Arturo. "La Terza Conferenza Interalleata per lo studio delle questioni inerenti gli invalidi di guerra." *Bollettino della federazione Nazionale dei Comitati di assistenza ai militari ciechi, storpi e mutilati*, (1919): 261-266.

Lawrence, Jon. "Forging a peaceable kingdom. War, Violence, and Fear of Brutalization in post-First World War Britain." *The Journal of Modern History* 75, no. 3 (2003): 557-589.

Lebas, Elizabeth, Susanna Magri, and Christian Topalov. "Reconstruction and Popular Housing after the First World War: A Comparative Study of France, Great Britain, Italy and the United States." *Planning Perspectives* 6, no. 3 (1991): 249-267.

Leclercq, Cathérine. "Standbeelden en monumenten van Brussel Na 1914." In *De beelden van Brussel*, edited by Patrick Derom, 181-273. Brussels: Patrick Derom Gallery - Pandora, 2000.

Leclère, Léon. *La Grande Guerre, 1914-1919*. Brussels: Vanderlinden, 1919.

Le Corbusier, *Urbanisme*. Paris: G. Crès & cie., 1924.

———. *The City of To-morrow and its Planning*, translated from the 8th French edition of *Urbanisme*, with an introduction by Frederick Etchells. New York: Payson & Clarke, 1929.

———. *Précisions sur un état présent de l'architecture et de l'urbanisme*. Paris: G. Crès et cie., 1930.

———. *La ville radieuse, éléments d'une doctrine d'urbanisme pour l'équipement de la civilisation machiniste. Paris, Genève, Rio de Janeiro, Sao Paolo, Montevideo, Buenos Aires, Alger, Moscou, Anvers, Barcelone, Stockholm, Nemours, Piacé*. Boulogne: Éditions de L'Architecture d'aujourd'hui, 1935.

———. *Les plans de Paris*. Paris: Les Éditions de Minuit, 1956.

———. Preface, in *Architecture of Truth: The Cistercian Abbey of Le Thoronet* edited by François Cali and illustrated by Lucien Hervé. New York: Phaidon Press, 2001.

Lefèvre, Marguerite. *L'habitat rural en Belgique. Etude de géographie humaine*. Liège: Vaillan-Carmanne, 1926.

Le Goff, Jacques. "Documento/monumento." In *Enciclopedia Einaudi*, edited by Ruggiero Romano and Alfredo Salsano, 38-48. Turin: Einaudi, 1977.

Leonard, Edward. *Land en dorp: Aanteekeningen en wenken ter overweging bij het bouwen en heropbouwen op het land*. Antwerp: 't Kersouwken, 1916.

———. *Voor 's Lands Wederopbouw: korte opstellen over bouwkunst*. Amsterdam: Maatschappij voor Goede en Goedkope Literatuur, 1920.

Leplae, Edmond. *La restauration agricole des régions dévastées*. Brussels: Imprimerie Van Buggenhoudt, 1920.

Le Vay, David. *The History of Orthopaedics*. Carnfoth: Parthenon, 1990.

Levi, Ettore. "Technical Re-education in Italy, in its relation to the law for the assistance and protection of the disabled." In *Inter-allied Conference on the after care of disabled men, Second annual meeting*. London: His Majesty's Stationery Office, 1918, 150-156.

Levine, Philippa. "'Walking the Streets in a Way No Decent Woman Should': Women Police in World War I." *The Journal of Modern History* 66, no. 1 (1994): 34-78.

Lewin, Kurt. "The Landscape of War" [1917], translated by Jonathan Blower, introduced by Volker M. Welter, in *Art in Translation* 1, no. 2 (2009): 199-209.

L'istituto ortopedico Rizzoli a S. Michele in Bosco in Bologna. Bergamo: Ist. Italiano d'Arti Grafiche, 1910.
Little, Branden. "An explosion of new endeavours: global humanitarian responses to industrialized warfare in the First World War era." *First World War Studies* 5, no. 1 (2014): 1-16.
Lobbes, Tessa. "Het Belgische geschiedenisonderwijs en de uitdaging van de eigentijdse geschiedenis (1945-1961)." *Tijdschrift voor Geschiedenis* 126, no.1 (2013): 76-91.
———. *Verleden zonder stof: Strijd om het geschiedenisonderwijs in België (1945-1989)*. Ghent: Academia press, 2017.
Löffelbein, Nils. "The Legacy of the Front: The Disabled Veterans of the First World War in Germany after 1918." In *New Political Ideas in the Aftermath of the Great War*, edited by Alessandro Salvador and Anders G. Kjøstvedt, 175-197. New York: Palgrave Macmillan, 2017.
Lombardo, Giovanni P., and Elisabetta Cicciola. "The Clinical Differential Approach of Sante De Sanctis in Italian 'Scientific' Psychology.'" *Physis* 43, no. 1-2 (2006): 443-457.
Looyenga, Arjen. "Recreating an Urban Atmosphere. The Rebuilding of Three Dutch Towns: Middelburg, Rhenen and Wageningen." In *Living with History, 1914-1964: Rebuilding Europe after the First and Second World Wars and the Role of Heritage Preservation*, edited by Nicholas Bullock and Luc Verpoest, 188-199. Leuven: Leuven University Press, 2011.
Löschnigg, Martin, and Marzena Sokolowska-Paryz, *The Great War in Post-Memory Literature and Film*. Berlin: De Gruyter, 2014.
L'Œuvre d'aide et apprentissage aux invalides de guerre durant l'Occupation. Brussels: Laurent, 1918.
"L'Œuvre nationale des invalides de la guerre." *L'invalide belge*, 1 June (1920).
Mackaman, Douglas, and Michael Mays, eds. *World War I and the Cultures of Modernism*. Jackson, MI: University of Mississippi Press, 2000.
Maeterlinck, Maurice. *The Burgomaster of Stilemonde*. New York: Dodd, Mead and Company, 1919.
Maier, Charles S. *Recasting Bourgeois Europe. Stabilization in France, Germany, and Italy in the Decade after World War I*. Princeton, NJ: Princeton University Press, 1975.
Mak, Geert. *In Europa. Reizen door de twintigste eeuw*. Amsterdam: Atlas, 2017.
Marissal, Claudine. *Protéger le jeune enfant: Enjeux sociaux, politiques et sexués (Belgique, 1890-1940)*. Brussels: Éditions de l'Université de Bruxelles, 2014.
Marks, Sally. *Innocent Abroad: Belgium at the Paris Peace Conference of 1919*. Chapel Hill, NC: The University of North Carolina Press, 2011.
Martin, John Rupert. *The Decorations for the Pompa Introitus Ferdinandi*. Corpus Rubenianum Ludwig Burchard. Vol. XVI, London: Phaidon, 1972.
Martorell Linares, Miguel. "'No fue aquello solamente una guerra, fue una revolución': España y la Primera Guerra Mundial." *Historia y Política*, 26 (2011): 17-45.
Massart, Jean. *Le Front de Flandre*. Brussels: Société anonyme belge d'imprimerie, 1919.
Matless, David. *Landscape and Englishness*. London: Reaktion Books, 1998.
Mayer, Arno. *The Persistence of the Old Regime: Europe to the Great War*. New York: Pantheon, 1981.
McCoy, Esther. *Richard Neutra*. New York: George Braziller, 1960.
McDonald, Robert I., Peter J. Marcotullio, and Burak Güneralp. "Urban Governance of Biodiversity and Ecosystem Services." In *Urbanization, Biodiversity and Ecosystem*

Services: Challenges and Opportunities, edited by Cathy Wilkinson, Marte Sendstad, Susan Parnell, and Maria Schewenius, 539-587. Dordrecht: Springer, 2013.

McMurtrie, Douglas C. "The Care of Crippled Children in the United States." *Journal of Bone and Joint Surgery* S2-9, no. 4 (1912): 527-556.

Medeiros Ferreira, José. *Portugal na Conferência da Paz*. Lisbon: Quetzal, 1992.

Meganck, Leen. "Domi or Dom-Ino? The Role of Genius Loci in Post-War Reconstruction and Interwar Urbanism." In *Living with History, 1914-1964: Rebuilding Europe after the First and Second World Wars and the Role of Heritage Preservation*, edited by Nicholas Bullock and Luc Verpoest, 230-243. Leuven: Leuven University Press, 2011.

———. "Patriotism, Genius Loci, Authentic Buildings and Imitation Farmsteads: Regionalism in Interwar Belgium." In *Regionalism and Modernity: Architecture in Western Europe 1914-1940*, edited by Leen Meganck, Linda Van Santvoort, and Jan De Maeyer, 73-93. Leuven: Leuven University Press, 2013.

———, Linda Van Santvoort, Jan De Maeyer, eds. *Regionalism and modernity: Architecture in Western Europe 1914-1940*. Leuven: Leuven University Press, 2013.

———, Linda Van Santvoort, and Jan De Maeyer, "Introduction." In *Regionalism and Modernity: Architecture in Western Europe 1914-1940*, edited by Leen Meganck, Linda Van Santvoort, and Jan De Maeyer, 7-13. Leuven: Leuven University Press, 2013.

Meire, Johan. *De stilte van de Salient: De herinnering aan de Eerste Wereldoorlog rond Ieper*. Tielt: Lannoo, 2003.

Meiresonne, Anne. "Brussel, Brugmannziekenhuis in Laken." In *Architectuur van Belgische hospitalen*, edited by Patrick Allegaert and Jean-Marc Basyn, 116-121. Brussels: Ministerie van de Vlaamse Gemeenschap, Afdeling Monumenten en Landschappen, 2005.

Merkens, Luise. *Fürsorge und Erziehung bei Körperbehinderten: Eine historische Grundlegung zur Körperbehindertenpädagogik bis 1920*. Berlin: Marhold, 1981.

Meyer, Jessica. *Men of War: Masculinity and the First World War in Britain*. Basingstoke: Palgrave Macmillan, 2011.

Mihaïl, Benoit. "Traditionalist Architecture in Belgium between the Wars. The Obsession with National Culture and the French Influence." In *Regionalism and Modernity: Architecture in Western Europe 1914-1940*, edited by Leen Meganck, Linda Van Santvoort, and Jan De Maeyer, 95-110. Leuven: Leuven University Press, 2013.

Ministère de la guerre. *Aperçu général des opérations de l'armée belges d'août 1914 au 11 novembre 1918*. Brussels: Imprimerie H. Mommens, 1919.

Moignet-Gaultier, Anne. "Alignements urbains et reconstructions après-guerre à Louvain et Saint-Malo." In *Living with History, 1914-1964: Rebuilding Europe after the First and Second World Wars and the Role of Heritage Preservation*, edited by Nicholas Bullock and Luc Verpoest, 134-153. Leuven: Leuven University Press, 2011.

Morandini, Maria Cristina. "Tra educazione e assistenza: la scuola speciale per ragazzi rachitici di Torino." *History of Education & Children's Literature* 7, no. 2 (2012): 241-257.

Morelle, J. "M. George Debaisieux, professeur-émérité à la Faculté de Médecine, 1882-1956." *Annuaire de l'Université catholique de Louvain (1954-1956)*: 149-156.

Morris, James McGrath. *The Ambulance Drivers: Hemingway, Dos Passos, and a Friendship made and lost in war*. Philadelphia, PA: Da Capo Press, 2017.

Mortier, Julie. "Entre médicalisation et modernité: l'étude des structures hospitalières. Le cas de l'hôpital Saint-Pierre de Bruxelles (1890-1935)." MA Diss., Free University of Brussels, 2017.

Moss, Walter G. *An Age of Progress? Clashing Twentieth-Century Global Forces.* London: Anthem Press, 2008.
Mosse, George L. *Fallen Soldiers: Reshaping the Memory of the World Wars.* Oxford: Oxford University Press, 1990.
Mouton, Michelle. *From Nurturing the Nation to Purifying the Volk: Weimar and Nazi Family Policy, 1918-1945.* Cambridge: Cambridge University Press, 2007.
Mulligan, William. *The Great War for Peace.* New Haven, CT: Yale University Press, 2014.
Munzel-Everling, Dietlinde. *Kriegsnagelungen, Wehrmann in Eisen, Nagel-Roland, Eisernes Kreuz.* Wiesbaden: Munzel-Everling, 2008.
———. "Kriegsnagelungen." http://www.munzel-everling.de/pr_nag.htm (last updated 8 August 2012).
Narmon, François. "Woord vooraf." In *Resurgam: De Belgische wederopbouw na 1914*, edited by Marcel Smets, 7. Brussels: Gemeentekrediet van België, 1985.
Nasr, Joe, and Mercedes Volait, eds. *Urbanism: Imported or Exported? Native Aspirations and Foreign Plans.* Chichester: Academy Editions, 2003.
Nationaal instituut voor de statistiek. *Landbouw: Telling op 31 december 1910.* Brussels: NIS, 1910.
Neefs, Hans. *Between sin and disease. The social fight against syphilis and AIDS in Belgium (1880-2000).* Saarbrücken: Lambert, 2010.
Neiberg, Michael. *The Treaty of Versailles. A concise history.* New York: Oxford University Press, 2017.
Nerdinger, Winfried. *Geschichte der Rekonstruktion - Konstruktion der Geschichte.* Munich: Prestel, 2010.
Neumann, Christel. "De dienst der verwoeste gewesten en zijn historisch kader." In *Inventaris van het archief van de Dienst der verwoeste gewesten*, edited by Alexandre Notebaert, Christel Neumann, and Willem Vanden Eynde, 37-53. Brussels: State Archives of Belgium, 1986.
Neumeyer, Fritz. *The Artless Word: Mies van der Rohe on the Building Art.* Translated by Mark Jarzombek. Cambridge, MA: MIT Press, 1991.
Neutra, Richard. *Survival Through Design.* Oxford: Oxford University Press, 1954.
———. *Life and Shape.* New York: Appleton-Century-Crofts, 1962. Reprint, Los Angeles, CA: Atara Press, 2009.
Newman, John Paul. *Yugoslavia in the Shadow of War: Veterans and the Limits of State Building, 1903-1945.* Cambridge: Cambridge University Press, 2015.
Noël, Léon. *Louvain, 891-1914.* Oxford: Clarendon Press,1915.
Nothomb, Pierre. *Les barbares en Belgique.* Paris: Perrin et cie, 1915.
Notteboom, Bruno. "De verborgen ideologie van Jean Massart. Vertogen over landschap en (anti-) stedelijkheid in België in het begin van de twintigste eeuw." *Stadsgeschiedenis* 1, no. 1 (2006): 51-68.
———. "'Ouvrons les yeux!': Stedenbouw en beeldvorming van het landschap in België 1890-1940." PhD Thesis, Ghent University, 2009.
———."Boeren op de wereldtentoonstelling. Het Moderne Dorp." In *Gent 1913. Op het breukvlak van de moderniteit*, edited by Wouter Van Acker and Christophe Verbruggen, 126-139. Ghent: Snoek Uitgevers, 2013.
Núñez Rey, Concepción. "Carmen de Burgos, Colombine (1867-1932). Biografía y obra literaria." PhD Thesis, Universidad Complutense de Madrid, 1992.

Nys, Liesbet. "De grote school van de natie. Legerartsen over drankmisbruik en geslachtsziekten in het Belgisch leger (circa 1850-1950)." *BMGN – The Low Countries Historical Review* 115, no. 3 (2000): 392-425.

Nys, Liesbet. "Nationale plagen: hygiënisten over de ziekten van het maatschappelijk lichaam." In *De zieke natie: over de medicalisering van de samenleving 1860-1914*, edited by Liesbet Nys, Henk de Smaele, Jo Tollebeek, and Kaat Wils, 220-241. Groningen: Historische Uitgeverij, 2002.

Œuvre Nationale des Invalides de la Guerre. *25 ans d'activité 1919-1945.* Liège: Impr. nationale des militaires mutilés et invalides de la guerre, [1948].

Officina nazionale di protesi per mutilati in guerra in Gorla. Milan, [1916].

Olier, François, and Jean-Luc Quénec'hdu, *Hôpitaux militaires dans la guerre 1914-1918*, Tome IV *France sud-est.* Louviers: Ysec, 2014.

Opera nazionale per la protezione ed assistenza degli invalidi della Guerra. *L'opera svolta in Italia: 1915-1919.* Rome: Tipografia dell'Unione Editrice, 1919.

Orde, Anne. *British Policy and European Reconstruction after the First World War.* Cambridge: Cambridge University Press, 2002.

Osten, Philipp. "Die Modellanstalt: A Critical and Documented Approach to Würtz's Pedagogy." In *Der Körperbehindertenpädagoge Hans Würtz (1875-1958): Eine kritische Würdigung des psychologischen und pädagogischen Konzepts vor dem Hintergrund seiner Biographie*, edited by Oliver Musenberg. Hamburg: Kovač, 2002.

———. *Die Modellanstalt: über den Aufbau einer "modernen Krüppelfürsorge" 1905-1933*, 2nd edition. Frankfurt am Main: Mabuse Verlag, 2012.

Otero-Pailos, Jorge, Erik Langdalen, and Thordis Arrhenius, eds. *Experimental Preservation.* Zürich: Lars Müller Publishers, 2016.

Pallas Jean-Claude. *Histoire et architecture du Palais des Nations, 1924-2001.* Geneva: United Nations, 2001.

Papastathis, Charalambos. "The Fire of Salonica and the Allies." In *The Salonica Theatre of Operations and the Outcome of the Great War*, edited by Hidryma Meletōn Chersonēsou tou Haimo. Thessaloniki: Institute for Balkan Studies, 2005.

Payne, Michael, and Jessica Ray Barbera. *A Dictionary of Cultural and Critical Theory.* Chichester: Wiley-Blackwell, 2013.

Payró, Roberto J. *Corresponsal de guerra. Cartas, diarios, relatos (1907-1922).* Buenos Aires: Biblos, 2009.

Pecharromán, Juan Gil. *Conservadores subversivos. La derecha autoritaria Alfonsina (1913-1936).* Madrid: Eudema, 1994.

Pedersen, Susan. *Family, Dependence, and the Origins of the Welfare State: Britain and France, 1914-1945.* Cambridge: Cambridge University Press, 1993.

———. "From National Crisis to 'National Crisis': British Politics, 1914-1931." *Journal of British Studies* 33, no. 3 (July 1994): 322-335.

———. *The Guardians. The League of Nations and the Crisis of Empire.* Oxford: Oxford University Press, 2015.

Perlès, C. *Histoire de la Grande Guerre racontée aux enfants belges: Causeries.* Brussels: Lebègue, 1919.

Perry, Heather. *Recycling the Disabled: Army, Medicine and Modernity in WWI Germany.* London: Oxford University Press, 2014.

Pirenne, Henri. *La Belgique et la Guerre Mondiale.* Paris: Presses Universitaires de France, 1928.

Pires, Ana Paula. "The First World War in Portuguese East Africa: Civilian and Military Encounters in the Indian Ocean." *E-Journal of Portuguese History* 15, no. 1 (2017): 82-104.
Pinell, Patrice. *The Fight Against Cancer: France, 1890-1940*. London: Routledge, 2002.
Pinero, Arthur Wing. *The Enchanted Cottage*. London: William Heinemann, 1922.
Platt, Harry. "Orthopaedics in continental Europe. 1900-1950. The changing pattern." *The Journal of Bone and Joint Journal* 32-B, no. 4 (1950): 570-586.
Pleij, Herman. *De Sneeuwpoppen van 1511. Literatuur en stadscultuur tussen middeleeuwen en moderne tijd*. Amsterdam: Meulenhoff, 1988.
Plunz, Richard, and Michael Sheridan. "Deadlock Plus 50. On Public Housing in New York." *Harvard Design Magazine* no. 8 (1999): 4-9; republished in William S. Saunders ed., *Urban Planning Today* (Minneapolis, MN: University of Minnesota Press, 2006), 14-23.
Polenghi, Simonetta. "Gaetano Pini e l'Istituto dei Rachitici di Milano." In *Archivio storico lombardo*, no. 6 (2005): 265-305.
———. "Raddrizzare gli arti, rieducare i mutilati. L'ortopedia di Riccardo Galeazzi all'Istituto dei Rachitici." In *Milano scientifica 1875-1924*, vol. 2, *La rete del perfezionamento medico*, edited by Elena Canadelli and Paola Zocchi, 217-235. Milan: Sironi editore, 2008.
———. *Educating the cripples. The Pious Institute for rickets sufferers of Milan and its transformations (1874-1937)*. Macerata: EUM, 2009.
———. "Die Erziehung der Krüppelkinder in Italien zwischen Medizin und Pädagogik. Die Krüppelanstalt von Mailand: vom Positivismus bis zum Faschismus (1874-1937)." In *Normalität, Abnormalität und Devianz. Gesellschaftliche Konstruktionsprozesse und ihre Umwälzungen in der Moderne*, edited by Attila Nobik and Béla Pukánszky, 223-233. Frankfurt am Main: Peter Lang, 2010.
Poot, Nathalie, Geert Vanpaemel, and Siska Waelkens. *Een walvis in de stad: De collecties van de Leuvense Faculteit Wetenschappen*. Leuven: Leuven University Press, 2014.
Poppe, August. *Hoe moet men op den buiten bouwen?* Ghent: Scheerder, 1916.
Proctor, Tammy M. *On my Honour: Guides and Scouts in Interwar Britain*. Philadelphia: American Philosophical Society, 2002.
———. "An American Enterprise: British Participation in U.S. Food Relief Programmes (1914-1923)." *First World War Studies* 5, no. 1 (2014): 29-42.
———. "Repairing the Spirit: The Society of Friends, Total War and the Limits of Reconciliation." *Peace & Change: A Journal of Peace Research* 45, no. 2 (2020): 198-224.
Prost, Antoine. *Les anciens combattants et la société française: 1914-1939*. Paris: Gallimard 1977.
———. *Les monuments aux morts: Culte républicain? Culte civique? Culte patriotique?* In *Les lieux de mémoire*, edited by Pierre Nora, 195-225. Paris: Gallimard, 1984.
———. "Mémoires locales et mémoires nationales: Les monuments de 1914-1918 en France." *Guerres mondiales et conflits contemporains*, no. 167 (1992): 41-50.
———. "Les limites de la brutalisation. Tuer sur le front occidental, 1914-1918", *Vingtième Siècle* 81, no. 1 (2004): 5-20.
———. and Jay Winter. *Penser la Grande Guerre: Un essai d'historiographie*. Paris: Éditions du Seuil, 2004.
Raemdonck, Liesje, and Ingeborg Scheiris. *Ongehoord Verleden. Dove frontvorming in België aan het begin van de 20ste eeuw*. Ghent: Fevlado-Diversus, 2007.

Rapport spécial sur le fonctionnement et les opérations de la section agricole du Comité national de secours et d'alimentation: section agricole 1914-1919. Brussels: Vromant, 1920.

'Recorriendo los campos de ruinas', *La época*, January 5, 1919, 3-4.

Report of the Committee on Alleged German Outrages Presented to Parliament by Command of His Majesty. London: His Majesty's Stationery Office, Eyre and Spottiswoode, 1915.

Reznick, Jeffrey S. *Healing the Nation: Soldiers, Caregivers and British Identity During World War I*. Manchester: Manchester University Press, 2004.

Riegl, Alois. "Der moderne Denkmalkultus. Sein Wesen, seine Entstehung (1903)." In *Denkmalpflege: Deutsche Texte aus drei Jahrhunderten*, edited by Norbert Huse, 131-39. Munich: C.H. Beck, 2006.

Rinke, Stefan. *Latin America and the First World War*. Cambridge: Cambridge University Press, 2017.

———. and Karina Kriegesmann. "Latin America." In *1914-1918-online. International Encyclopedia of the First World War*, edited by Ute Daniel, Peter Gatrell, Oliver Janz, Heather Jones, Jennifer Keene, Alan Kramer, and Bill Nasson, issued by Freie Universität Berlin, Berlin, 2015-11-05. DOI:10.15463/ie1418.10760.

Risse, Guenter. *Mending Bodies, Saving Souls: A History of Hospitals*. New York: Oxford University Press, 199.

Rollo, Maria Fernanda, Ana Paula Pires, and Filipe Ribeiro de Meneses. "Portugal" In *1914-1918-online. International Encyclopedia of the First World War*, ed. Ute Daniel, Peter Gatrell, Oliver Janz, Heather Jones, Jennifer Keen, Alan Kramer, and Bill Nasson, issued by Freie Universität Berlin, Berlin, 2017-08-30. DOI: 10.15463/ie1418.11152.

Romanones, Conde de (Figueroa, Álvaro). *El ejército y la Política. Apuntes sobre la organización militar y el Presupuesto de la Guerra*. Madrid: Renacimiento, 1920.

———. *Notas de una vida*. Madrid: Marcial Pons, 1999.

Ronse, Alfred, and Theo Raison. *Fermes-types et constructions rurales en West-Flandre*, 2 vol. Bruges: Beyaert, 1918.

Ronsyn, X. *Commerce and the Countryside. The Role of Weekly Markets in Flemish Rural Society, 1751-1900*. Ghent: Academia Press, 2011.

Rose, Sarah. *No right to be idle: The Invention of Disability, 1840s–1930s*. Chapel Hill, NC: University of North Carolina Press, 2017.

Rousseaux, Xavier, and Laurence Van Ypersele. "Leaving the War: Popular Violence and Judicial Repression of 'Unpatriotic' Behaviour in Belgium (1918-1921)." *European Review of History* 12, no. 1 (2005): 3-22.

———. and Laurence Van Ypersele. *La Patrie crie vengeance! La Répression des 'inciviques' belges au sortir de la guerre 1914-1918*. Brussels: Le Cri, 2008.

Rutten, J. *Voor Vrijheid en Recht. Verslag gegeven op de plechtige prijsuitreiking van het Onze-Lieve-Vrouwcollege den 31sten juli 1919*. Antwerp, 1919.

Saey, Silke. "De 'Groote Oorlog' in het onderwijs: Herinneringseducatie over de Eerste Wereldoorlog in het Vlaams secundair onderwijs (1970-heden)." MA Diss., KU Leuven, 2012.

Saintenoy, Paul. "Rebâtissons en beauté!" *Le Home*, no.1 (1915): 9.

Salvante, Martina. "Italian Disabled Veterans between Experience and Representation." In *Men After War*, edited by Stephen McVeigh and Nicola Cooper, 111-129. London: Routledge, 2013.

Schmidt, Jan. *Nach dem Krieg ist vorn der Krieg. Mediatisierte Erfahrungen des Ersten*

Weltkrieges und Nachkriegsdiskurse in Japan (1914-1919). Frankfurt a.M.: Campus Verlag GmbH, 2018.
———. and Katja Schmidtpott, ed. *The East Asian Dimension of the First World War. Global Entanglements and Japan, China and Korea, 1914-1919*. Frankfurt a.M.: Campus Verlag GmbH, 2020.
Schmitz, David, Maarten Liefooghe, Tine Bulckaen, and Pieter Uyttenhove. *Omgaan met wederopbouwarchitectuur in de Frontstreek van 1914-1918: Ieper en Heuvelland*. Ghent: Labo S - Department of Architecture and Urban Planning, 2008.
Schneider, Gerhard. *In Eiserner Zeit. Kriegswahrzeichen im Ersten Weltkrieg*. Schwalbach am Taunus: BD-Edition, 2013.
Scholten, Frits. "Malleable Marble: The Antwerp Snow Sculptures of 1772." *Netherlands Yearbook for History of Art/Nederlands Kunsthistorisch Jaarboek* 62, no. 1 (2012): 266-295.
Schoonbrodt, René. *Sociologie de l'habitat social: comportement des habitants et architecture des cités*. Brussels: Éditions des Archives d'architecture moderne, 1979.
Schütze, Karl-Robert. *Der Eiserne Hindenburg. Bildergeschichte in Postkarten: Chronologie Der Ereignisse Und Berichte*. Berlin: Schütze, 2007.
Seberechts, Frank. "Slechts de graven maken een land tot vaderland. Van Heldenhulde tot IJzertoren: een stenen hulde aan de Vlaamse IJzersoldaten." In *Duurzamer dan graniet. Over monumenten en Vlaamse Beweging*, edited by Frank Seberechts, 123-154. Tielt: Lanno, 2003; Antwerp: Perspectief, 2003.
Sedgwick, S.N. "At the Menin Gate: a melodrama." London: Sheldon Press, 1929.
Segers, Gustaaf. *De Belgische volksschool en de heropbeuring van ons vaderland*. Ghent: Erasmus, 1921.
Segers, Yves, Leen Van Molle, and Geert Vanpaemel. "In de greep van de vooruitgang, 1880-1950." In *Leven van het land. Boeren in België, 1750-2000*, edited by Yves Segers and Leen Van Molle, 49-109. Leuven: Davidsfonds, 2004.
Seignobos, Charles, ed. *La réorganisation de La France: Conférences faites à l'école des hautes études sociales (Novembre 1915 à Janvier 1916)*. Paris: F. Alcan, 1917.
Sellier, Henri, and A. Bruggeman. *Le Problème du logement. Son influence sur les conditions de l'habitation et l'aménagement des villes*. Histoire Économique et Sociale de La Guerre Mondiale. Paris - New Haven, CT: Dotation Carnegie - PUF - Yale UP, 1927.
Selvi, Giovanni. *Il problema dei mutilati ed invalidi di guerra e le attuali provvidenza statali*. Rome: Cassa Nazionale d'Assicurazione per Gli Infortuni Degli Operai sul Lavoro, 1916.
Shelby, Karen. *Flemish Nationalism and the Great War: The Politics of Memory, Visual Culture and Commemoration*. Basingstoke: Palgrave MacMillan, 2014.
———. *Belgian Museums of the Great War: Politics, Memory, and Commerce*. New York: Routledge, 2018.
Sherman, D. J. "Bodies and Names. The Emergence of Commemoration in Interwar France." *American Historical Review* 103, no. 2 (1998): 443-466.
Siegel, Mona, and Kirsten Harjes. "Disarming Hatred: History Education, National Memories, and Franco-German Reconciliation from World War I to the Cold War." *History of Education Quarterly* 52, no. 3 (2012): 370-402.
Smets, Georges. "Les régions dévastées et la réparation des dommages de guerre." In *La Belgique restaurée: étude sociologique*, edited by Ernest Mahaim, 71-139. Brussels: Lamertin, 1926.

Smets, Marcel. *L'avènement de la cité-jardin en Belgique: Histoire de l'habitat social en Belgique de 1830 à 1930*. Brussels: Mardaga, 1977.

———. "De Belgische wederopbouw op de overgang tussen stadsbouwkunst en stedebouw." In *Resurgam: De Belgische wederopbouw na 1914*, edited by Marcel Smets, 70-97. Brussels: Gemeentekrediet van België, 1985.

———, ed. *Resurgam: De Belgische wederopbouw na 1914*. Brussels: Gemeentekrediet van België, 1985.

———, ed. *Resurgam: la reconstruction en Belgique après 1914*. Brussels: Crédit communal, 1985.

Smith, F. B. *The Retreat of Tuberculosis, 1850-1950*. New York: Croom Helm, 1988.

Smith, Leonard. *Sovereignty at the Paris Peace Conference of 1919*. Oxford: Oxford University Press, 2018.

Sontag, Susan. *Aids and its metaphors*. New York: Farrar, Straus and Giroux, 1989.

Sosset, F. *La Guerre de 14-18 en Belgique et l'occupation allemande*. Brussels: De Boeck, 1921.

Spencer, Jones. "Ypres, Battles of." In *1914-1918-online. International Encyclopedia of the First World War*, edited by Ute Daniel, Peter Gatrell, Oliver Janz, Heather Jones, Jennifer Keene, Alan Kramer, and Bill Nasson, issued by Freie Universität Berlin, Berlin, 2015-02-13. DOI: 10.15463/ie1418.10552.

Stadler, Hans. "Die Unterrichts- und Beschäftigungsanstalt für krüppelhafte Kinder des Edlen von Kurz in München." In *Pädagogik bei Körperbehinderung*, edited by Hans Stadler and Udo Wilken, 46-81. Weinheim: Beltz, 2004.

———. "Überkonfessionelle und staatliche Krüppelfürsorge." In *Pädagogik bei Körperbehinderung*, edited by Hans Stadler and Udo Wilken, 194-248. Weinheim: Beltz, 2004.

Stalpaert, Christel. "The Entry of Charles-Alexandre De Lorraine into Brussels: Monarchical Discourse in Public Ceremonies and Theatrical Performances." *Eighteenth-Century Life* 26, no. 2 (2002): 69-82.

Stassen. "Ontwerp voor inrichting in België van een Nationalen Dienst voor Verminkten en Gebrekkelijken van den Oorlog." *De Belgische Verminkte*, 10 May 1919, 2.

———. and Delvaux, "La rééducation agricole à l'institut militaire belge des Invalides et Orphelins de la Guerre à Port-Villez (Armée Belge)." *Revue interalliée pour l'étude des questions intéressant les mutilés de la guerre*, no. 4 (1918): 375-386.

Statistical Abstract for the United Kingdom: No. 72 (1913-1927). London: HMSO, 1929.

Steindler, Arthur. "A Visit to some of the Orthopaedic Clinics of Europe." *Journal of Bone and Joint Surgery* 5, no. 1 (1923): 127-134.

Steiner, Zara. *The Lights that Failed: European International History, 1919-1933*. Oxford: Oxford University Press, 2005.

Strauven, Francis. *René Braem: Les aventures dialectiques d'un moderniste flamand*. Brussels: Archives d'Architecture Moderne, 1985.

Streuvels, Stijn. *Land en leven in Vlaanderen*. Amsterdam: Veen, 1923.

Stumm, Alexander. *Architektonische Konzepte der Rekonstruktion*. Basel: Birkhäuser, 2017.

Stynen, Herman. "De rol van de instellingen." In *Resurgam: De Belgische wederopbouw na 1914*, edited by Marcel Smets, 99-130. Brussels: Gemeentekrediet van België, 1985.

———. *De onvoltooid verleden tijd: een geschiedenis van de monumenten- en landschapszorg in België 1835-1940*. Brussels: Stichting Vlaams erfgoed, 1998.

———, Georges Charlier, and An Beullens. *15-18, het verwoeste gewest: Mission Dhuicque / 15-18, the Devastated Region: Mission Dhuicque*. Bruges: M. Van de Wiele, 1985.

Stynen, Ludo, and Sylvia van Peteghem, eds. *In oorlogsnood: Virginie Lovelings dagboek 1914-1918*. Ghent: Koninklijke Academie voor Nederlandse Taal-en-Letterkunde, 1999.

Syllabus and Time Table of Summer Meeting at King's College, Strand, July 12-31, 1915, on The War: Its Social Tasks & Problems. London: Co-operative Printing Society, 1915.

Tallier, Pierre-Alain, and Sofie Ongenae. *Cents ans – et plus – d'ouvrages historiques sur la Première Guerre Mondiale / Honder jaar – en meer – geschiedschrijving over de Eerste Wereldoorlog in België*, 2 vols. Brussels: Rijksarchief, 2019.

Tanielian, Melanie S. *The Charity of War: Famine, Humanitarian Aid, and World War I in the Middle East*. Stanford, CA: Stanford University Press, 2017.

Tato, María Inés. *Viento de Fronda. Liberalismo, conservadurismo y democracia en la Argentina, 1911-1932*. Buenos Aires: Siglo Veintiuno Editores, 2004.

———. *La trinchera austral. La sociedad argentina ante la Primera Guerra Mundial*. Rosario: Prohistoria, 2017.

———. "Trapped in Occupied Brussels: Roberto J. Payró's War Experience, 1914-1915." In *The Great War in Belgium and the Netherlands. Beyond Flanders Fields*, edited by Felicity Rash and Christophe Declercq, 143-161. Basingstoke: Palgrave MacMillan, 2018.

Terret, Thierry. "Prologue: Making Men, Destroying Bodies: Sport, Masculinity and the Great War Experience." *The International Journal of the History of Sport* 28, no. 3-4 (2011): 323-328.

The Rapid Cure, 1916, Lord Chamberlain's Plays, British Library, Add MS 66128 G, in Great War Theatre, https://www.greatwartheatre.org.uk/db/script/1182/

Thiébaut, F. *La Reeducation professionnelle des invalides de la Guerre à l'Institut Militaire belge de Port-Villez*. Port-Villez: impr. de l'institut, 1918.

Thomas, Edward, and Edna Longley, eds. *The Annotated Collected Poems*. Hexham: Bloodaxe Books, 2008.

Tixhon, Axel, and Laurence Van Ypersele, "Du sang et des pierres. Les monuments de la guerre 1914-1918 en Wallonie." *Cahiers d'Histoire du Temps Présent*, no. 7 (2000): 83-126.

Todd, Lisa M. *Sexual Treason in Germany during the First World War*. Cham: Palgrave Macmillan, 2017.

Touring Club de Belgique. *Ce qu'il faut voir sur les champs de bataille et dans les villes détruites de Belgique*, 2 vol. Brussels: Touring club de Belgique, 1919-1920.

Troyansky, David G. "Monumental Politics: National History and Local Memory in French 'Monuments Aux Morts' in the Department of the Aisne since 1870." *French Historical Studies* 15, no. 1 (1987): 121-142.

Tunbridge, John E., and Gregory John Ashworth. *Dissonant Heritage: the Management of the Past as a Resource in Conflict*. Chichester: Wiley Blackwell, 1996.

Tuñón de Lara, Manuel. *España. Semanario de la Vida Nacional*. Madrid: Turner, 1982.

Uyttenhove, Pieter. "Internationale inspanningen voor een modern België." In *Resurgam: De Belgische wederopbouw na 1914*, edited by Marcel Smets, 33-68. Brussels: Gemeentekrediet, 1985.

———. "Continuities in Belgian Wartime Planning." In *Rebuilding Europe's Bombed Cities*, edited by Jeffry Diefendorf, 48-63. Basingstoke: Macmillan, 1990.

——. and Jo Celis. *De wederopbouw van Leuven na 1914*. Leuven: Leuven University Press, 1991.
Vachon, Marius. *Les villes martyres de France et de Belgique: Statistique des villes et villages détruits par les Allemands dans les deux pays*. Paris: Payot et Cie 1915.
Vaes, Henri. "Le sens du regionalisme." *La Cité* 1, no. 6 (1919), 103-105.
Van Avermaet. "Jongens! Leert goed uw vak." *De Belgische Gebrekkelijke*, October 1, 1917.
Vanbiesem de Burbridge, Martha. "Un Argentin témoin de la guerre: la Belgique occupée vue par Roberto Payró." *Textyles*, no. 32-33 (2007): 197-223.
Van de Grift, Liesbeth. "On new land a new society: internal colonization in the Netherlands, 1918-1940." *Contemporary European History* 22, no. 4 (2013): 609-626.
——, and Amalia Ribi Forclaz, eds., *Governing the Rural in interwar Europe* (London: Routledge, 2018).
Vandendriessche, Joris. "Ophthalmia Crossing Borders: Belgian Army Doctors between the Military and Civilian Society, 1830-1860." *Belgisch Tijdschrift voor Nieuwste Geschiedenis/Journal of Belgian History* 46, no. 2 (2016): 48-71.
——. *Zorg en wetenschap: Een geschiedenis van de Leuvense academische ziekenhuizen in de twintigste eeuw*. Leuven: Leuven University Press, 2019.
Van den Mooter, Johan. "German Reconstruction in Belgium during World War I: A Regional Experiment." In *Regionalism and Modernity: Architecture in Western Europe, 1914-1940*, edited by Leen Meganck, Linda Van Santvoort, and Jan De Maeyer, 49-71. Leuven: Leuven University Press, 2013.
Vandevelde, Honoré. *Het heropbouwen van hoeven*. Antwerp: Land-en tuinbouwcomiteit, 1917.
Van Dorpe, Helena. "Landelijke esthetica: De woning." In *Handboek van landelijke maatschappijleer*, 205-224. Leuven: Belgische nationale commissie voor de verfraaiing van het landelijk leven, [1931].
Van Espen, J. "De gezondheid op den buiten." In *Handboek van landelijke maatschappijleer*, 147-158. Leuven: Belgische nationale commissie voor de verfraaiing van het landelijk leven, 1931.
Vanhaute, Eric, and Guy Dejongh. "Arable Productivity in Belgian Agriculture, c. 1800-c. 1950." In *Land Productivity and Agro-Systems in the North Sea Area (Middle Ages-Twentieth Century): Elements for Comparison*, edited by Erik Thoen and Bas Van Bavel, 65-84. Turnhout: Brepols, 1999.
Van Molle, Leen. "De Belgische Katholieke landbouwpolitiek voor de eerste wereldoorlog." *Belgisch Tijdschrift Voor Nieuwste Geschiedenis* 10, no. 3 (1979): 417-456.
——. *Katholieken en landbouw: Landbouwpolitiek in België, 1884-1914*. Leuven: Leuven University Press, 1989.
Vanpaemel, Geert. *Wetenschap als roeping: Een geschiedenis van de Leuvense faculteit voor wetenschappen*. Leuven: Leuven University Press, 2017.
Vanraepenbusch, Karla, and Matthias Meirlaen, "Van trauma sites naar herinneringsplekken: De integratie van de executies en de gefusilleerden in de stedelijke ruimte van Antwerpen, Luik en Rijsel (1914-1940)." *Stadsgeschiedenis* 11, no. 2 (2017): 146-164.
Van Santvoort, Linda. "Wederopbouwarchitectuur in de fusiegemeente Zemst." *M&L: Monumenten, Landschappen en Archeologie* 33, no. 3 (2014): 6-29.
Van Ypersele, Laurence. "Héros, Martyrs et Traîtres: Les fractures de La Belgique libérée." In *Sortir de La Grande Guerre. Le monde et l'après-1918*, edited by Stéphane Audoin-Rouzeau and Christophe Prochasson, 213-236. Paris: Tallandier, 2008.

———. "Commemoration, Cult of the Fallen (Belgium)." In *1914-1918 online. International Encyclopedia of the First World War*, edited by Ute Daniel, Peter Gatrell, Oliver Janz, Heather Jones, Jennifer Keene, Alan Kramer, and Bill Nasson Berlin: Freie Universität Berlin, 2014-10-08. DOI: 10.15463/ie1418.10313.

———. "Bereavement and Mourning (Belgium)." In *1914-1918-online. International Encyclopedia of the First World War*, edited by Ute Daniel, Peter Gatrell, Oliver Janz, Heather Jones, Jennifer Keene, Alan Kramer, and Bill Nasson, issued by Freie Universität Berlin, Berlin, 2014-10-08. DOI: 10.15463/ie1418.10176.

———, Emmanuel Debruyne, and Chantal Kesteloot. *Brussel: De oorlog herdacht (1914-2014)*. Waterloo: Renaissance du Livre, 2014.

Verbeek, Gerard. *Virga Jesse: Schat van de Hasselaar*. Hasselt: Comité Zevenjaarlijkse Virga-Jessefeesten, 1988.

Verboven, Hilde, and Dries Claeys, "Kolonisten en de Westhoek: Het verhaal van de wederopbouw van het landschap na 1918." *M&L: Monumenten, Landschappen en Archeologie* 39, no. 3 (2020): 54-55.

Verbruggen, Paule. "De volkskliniek: een socialistische polikliniek in Gent." In *Er is leven voor de dood. Tweehonderd jaar gezondheidszorg in Vlaanderen*, edited by Jan De Maeyer, Lieve Dhaene, Gert Hertecant, and Karel Velle, 233-241. Kapellen: Pelckmans, 1998.

Verstraete, Pieter. "Disability, Rehabilitation and the Great War: Making Space for Silence in the History of Education." In *Educational Research: The Importance and Effects of Institutional Spaces*, edited by Paul Smeyers, Marc Depaepe, and Edwin Keiner, 95-113. Amsterdam: Springer, 2013.

———. "Remastering Independence: The Re-education of Belgian Blinded Soldiers of the Great War, 1914-1940." *Educació i Història: revista d'història de l'educació*, no. 32 (2018): 257-277.

———, and Christine Van Everbroeck. *Verminkte stilte: De Belgische invalide soldaten van de Groote Oorlog*. Namur: Presses Universitaires de Namur, 2014.

———, Martina Salvante and Julie Anderson. "Commemorating the Disabled Soldier, 1914-1940." *First World War Studies* 6, no. 1 (2015) (Special issue: Commemorating the Disabled Soldier, 1914-1940): 1-7.

Veyne, Paul. *Did the Greeks Believe in Their Myths? An Essay on the Constitutive Imagination*. Chicago, IL: University of Chicago Press, 1988.

———. "The Final Foucault and His Ethics." In *Foucault and his Interlocutors*, edited by Arnold I. Davidson, 146-182. Chicago, IL: University of Chicago Press, 1997.

———. *Palmyra: An Irreplaceable Treasure*. Chicago, IL: The University of Chicago Press, 2017.

Vigato, Jean-Claude. *L'architecture régionaliste: France 1890-1950*. Paris: Norma, 1994.

———. "Between Progress and Tradition: The Regionalist Debate in France." In *Regionalism and Modernity: Architecture in Western Europe 1914-1940*, edited by Leen Meganck, Linda Van Santvoort, and Jan De Maeyer, 15-37. Leuven: Leuven University Press, 2013.

Vrielinck, Sven. *De territoriale indeling van België (1795-1963): Bestuursgeografisch en statistisch repertorium van de gemeenten en de supracommunale eenheden (administratief en gerechtelijk), met de officiële uitslagen van de volkstellingen*, 3 vols. Leuven: Leuven University Press, 2000.

Wambacq, Johan. *Het paleis op de heide: Architect Maxime Brunfaut en het sanatorium van Tombeek*. Brussels: ASP, 2009.

Warland, Geneviève, ed. *Experience and Memory of the First World War in Belgium. Comparative and Interdisciplinary Insights*, Historische Belgienforschung. Münster: Waxmann Verlag, 2018.

Warnke, Martin. "Schneedenkmäler." In *Mo(nu)mente: Formen Und Funktionen Ephemerer Denkmäler*, edited by Michael Diers, 51-59. Berlin: Akademie Verlag, 1993.

Watson, Janet S. K. *Fighting Different Wars: Experience, Memory, and the First World War in Britain*. Cambridge: Cambridge University Press, 2004.

Webb, Thomas E.F. "'Dottyville'. Craylockhart War Hospital and Shell-Shock Treatment in the First World War." *Journal of the Royal Society of Medicine* 99, no. 7 (2006): 342-346.

Weber, Eugen. *Peasants into Frenchmen, The modernization of rural France 1870-1914*. Stanford, CA: Stanford University Press, 1976).

Wellings, Ben, and Shanti Sumartojo, eds. *Commemorating Race and Empire in the First World War Centenary*. Oxford: Liverpool University Press, 2018.

Welter, Volker M. "Arcades for Lucknow: Patrick Geddes, Charles Rennie Mackintosh and the Reconstruction of the City." *Architectural History* 42 (1999): 316-332.

———. *Biopolis: Patrick Geddes and the City of Life*. Cambridge, MA: MIT Press, 2002.

———. "From the Landscape of War to the Open Order of the Kaufmann House: Richard Neutra and the Experience of the Great War." In *The Good Gardener? Nature, Humanity, and the Garden*, edited by Annette Giesecke and Naomi Jacobs, 216-233. London: Artifice Books on Architecture, 2014.

Weygand, Zina. *Vivre sans voir: Les aveugles dans la société française du Moyen Age au siècle de Louis Braille*. Paris: Creaphis Editions, 2003.

Whalen, Robert Weldon. *Bitter Wounds. German Victims of the Great War, 1914-1939*. Ithaca, NY: Cornell University Press, 1984.

Wheeler-Bennett, John W. *Wooden Titan. Hindenburg in Twenty Years of German History (1914-1934)*. New York: William Morrow, 1936.

Wijnsouw, Jana, and Marjan Sterckx. "'Een machtige veropenbaring der jeugdige Gentsche kunst': Publieke kunst in het kader van de Gentse wereldtentoonstelling van 1913." *Handelingen der Maatschappij voor Geschiedenis en Oudheidkunde te Gent*, no. 66 (2012): 205-229.

Williams, David. *Media, Memory and the First World War*. Montreal: McGill-Queen's University Press, 2009.

Wils, Kaat. "The Evaporated Canon and the Overvalued Source: History Education in Belgium: An Historical Perspective." In *National history standards: the problem of the canon and the future of teaching history*, edited by Linda Symcox and Arie Wilschut, 15-31. Charlotte, NC: Information Age Publishing, 2009.

———. "Commemorating War 100 Years after the First World War." *Low Countries Historical Review* 131, no. 3 (2016): 74-75.

Wilson, Richard Ashby, and Richard D. Brown, eds. *Humanitarianism and Suffering: The Mobilization of Empathy*. Cambridge: Cambridge University Press, 2009.

Winter, Jay. *Sites of Memory, Sites of Mourning: The Great War in European Cultural History*. Cambridge: Cambridge University Press, 1995.

———. *Remembering the War*. Cambridge: Yale University Press, 2006.

———. "Historiography 1918-Today." In *1914-1918-online. International Encyclopedia of the First World War*, edited by Ute Daniel, Peter Gatrell, Oliver Janz, Heather Jones, Jennifer Keene, Alan Kramer, and Bill Nasson, issued by Freie Universität Berlin, Berlin, 2014-11-11. DOI: 10.15463/ie1418.10498.

———. "Commemorating Catastrophe: 100 years On." *War & Society* 36, no. 4 (2017): 239-255.

———, Karin Tielmans, and Frank van Vree, eds. *Performing the Past: Memory, History, and Identity in Modern Europe*. Amsterdam: Amsterdam University Press, 2010.

Woolfe, Michael. "Theatre: Roots of the New." In *Literature and Culture in Modern Britain*, vol. 1, *1900-1929*, edited by Clive Bloom, 100-119. London: Longman, 1993.

Woollacott, Angela. *On Her Their Lives Depend: Munitions Workers in the Great War*. Berkeley, CA: University of California Press, 1994.

Würtz, Hans. "Der Wille siegt!" *Kriegsbeschädigten-Fürsorge in Niedersachsen*, December 23, 1916, 329-331.

———. *Das Seelenleben der Krüppels: krüppelseelenkundliche Erziehung und das Gesetz betr. öffentliche Krüppelfürsorge*. Leipzig: Voß, 1921.

Young, James E. "Écrire le monument: Site, mémoire, critique." *Annales: Économies, Sociétés, Civilisations* 48, no. 3 (1993): 729-743.

Yerolympus, Alexandra. "La Part du feu." In *Salonique 1850-1918: la "ville des Juifs" et le réveil des Balkans*, edited by. Gilles Veinstein, 261-269. Paris: Éditions Autrement, 1992.

———. "L'Incendie de Salonique en août 1917: fait divers ou 'dégât collateral'?" In *The Salonica Theatre of Operations and the Outcome of the Great War*, edited by Hidryma Meletōn Chersonēsou tou Haimo. Thessaloniki: Institute for Balkan Studies, 2005.

Zuckerman, Larry. *The Rape of Belgium: The Untold Story of World War I*. New York: New York University Press, 2003.

Zweig, Stefan. *Die Welt von Gestern. Erinnerungen eines Europäers*. Berlin: Fischer Taschenbuch Verlag, 1975.

List of Contributors

Helen Brooks is Reader in Theatre and Cultural History at the University of Kent. She is the primary investigator on the AHRC community-research "Great War Theatre" project and co-investigator on the AHRC projects "Performing Centenaries" and "Gateways to the First World War". Prior to working on First World War theatre she published widely on eighteenth-century theatre and her book *Actresses, Gender, and the Eighteenth-Century Stage: Playing Women* was published with Palgrave in 2014.

Dries Claeys obtained his doctoral degree in history at the Interfaculty Centre for Agrarian History (ICAG, KU Leuven) with a thesis on the reconstruction of the Belgian countryside after the First World War (2019). He is co-curator of the temporary exhibition *Feniks: Reconstructing Flanders Fields* (2020-2021) that is hosted by the In Flanders Fields Museum in cooperation with the Centre for Agrarian History (CAG).

Marisa De Picker is a PhD Student at the Centre for the History of Education of KU Leuven (Belgium). She received a Master's degree in History at the University of Antwerp (Belgium). During her studies she participated in the Robert Schuman traineeship programme of the European Parliament in Brussels, where she worked on a research project about robotics and assistive technologies for people with disabilities. At the moment Marisa is preparing a dissertation on re-education and employment assistance for people with physical disabilities in Belgium between 1908 and 1958.

Leen Engelen is a senior researcher at LUCA School of Arts (KU Leuven) and at the Visual Poetics research group of the University of Antwerp. She conducts research in the field of film and media history and the history of visual culture. She has published on a diversity of topics – such as media, film, sculpture and visual culture during the First World War; cultures of spectacle; the magic lantern; panoramas and ephemera such as film posters and postcards – in several academic books and journals. Leen is president of the International Association for Media and History (www.iamhist.net), an association bringing together scholars and media practitioners with an interest in media (and) history.

Rajesh Heynickx is Professor in Architectural Theory and Intellectual History at the KU Leuven. He has published in *Modern Intellectual History, Modernist Cultures, Environment and History* and *Architectural Theory Review*, among many others. In 2018, together with Stéphane Symons, he acted as co-editor of *So What's New About Scholasticism? How Neo-Thomism Helped Shape the Twentieth Century* (De Gruyter, Berlin). In 2020 he edited, together with Hilde Heynen and Sebastiaan Loosen, the volume *The Figure of Knowledge. Conditioning Architectural Theory, 1960s-1990s.* (Leuven University Press). In the same year, he also co-edited *Architecture Thinking Across Boundaries: Knowledge Transfers since the 1960s* (Bloomsbury, London). At the KU Leuven Department of Architecture, he is spokesman of the FWO-Scientific Research Network "Texts ≈ Buildings: Dissecting Transpositions in Architectural Knowledge (1880-1980)".

John Horne is an historian. He is emeritus Fellow and former Professor of Modern European History at Trinity College Dublin. A Member of the Royal Irish Academy, he is also Vice-President of the International Research Centre at the Historial de la Grande Guerre, Péronne (France). In 2016-17 he was Leverhulme Visiting Professor at Oxford University and in 2019 Paterno visiting fellow at Pennsylvania State University, College Park. He is the author and editor of a number of books and over a hundred chapters and articles, many relating to the Great War. http://johnhorne.ie

Maarten Liefooghe is Assistant Professor in Architecture Theory at Ghent University. His research revolves around intersections of architecture, heritage, and curatorial practice. His doctoral research engaged with single-artist museums and the clichés and tensions in their discursive and architectural make-up. More recently he has been studying experiments with showing architecture 1:1 and in situ, and their relevance for historic preservation. In 2019 he co-curated 'Open Call. 20 Years of Public Architecture'. He writes reviews about architecture and about art exhibitions and is a member of the editorial board of OASE, Journal for Architecture.

Ana Paula Pires holds a PhD in History from NOVA University of Lisbon. She is a researcher at NOVA School of Social Sciences and Humanities at NOVA University of Lisbon. Pires was a post-doctoral student at Stanford University (2016-2019) and a Remarque Fellow at the University of New York (2019). Her main topics of research are the economic and social history of the First World War, particularly its impact on Portugal and on Africa. She is currently working on humanitarian mobilisation in Portugal during the war. She is the author of *A Grande Guerra no Parlamento* (2018), *Portugal e a I Guerra Mundial. A República e a Economia de Guerra* (2011), and co-editor of *Guerras del siglo XX. Experiencias y representaciones en perspectiva* *global* (2019) and *There come a time... Essays on the Great War in Africa* (2018). She is Section Editor for Portugal of *1914-1918 Online International Encyclopaedia of the First World War*.

Richard Plunz is an architect and urbanist based in New York City. He is Professor of Architecture and Earth Institute Professor at Columbia University, where he has served as Acting Chair of the Division of Architecture and as Director of the post-graduate Urban Design Program. He is founding Director of the Urban Design Lab at the Columbia University Earth Institute and is on the faculty of the Data Science Institute. On numerous occasions he has been Visiting Professor at the Katholieke Universiteit Leuven. Recent books include a revised edition of *A History of Housing in New York City* (2016) and *City Riffs: Urbanism, Ecology Place* (2017). He has been named Centennial Historian of the City of New York and is a member of the New York Academy of History.

Simonetta Polenghi is full Professor of History of Education at the Catholic University of the Sacred Heart in Milan, where she has been Head of the Department of Education since 2010. She is President of the Italian Society of Education (SIPed) (2017-20) and a member of the EC of ISCHE (2016-21). Her research focuses on history of university; history of childhood; history of schooling and pedagogy; history of special education. She is co-editor of two series of history of education and has published several works, including *Educating the cripples. The Pious Institute for rickets sufferers of Milan and its transformations (1874-1937)*, (Macerata: EUM, 2009); with A.F.co Canales (eds), Classifying children: a historical perspective on testing and measurement, Special issue of *Paedagogica Historica*, 2019, 55:3, 343-352; with A.Debè, Agostino Gemelli (1878-1959) and mental disability: science, faith and education in the view of an Italian scientist and friar, *Paedagogica Historica*, 55:3, 429-450.

Tammy M. Proctor is Distinguished Professor of History and Department Head at Utah State University. Proctor is a specialist in modern European and gender history with a special emphasis on the history of youth, gender and conflict. In addition to studies of the Boy Scouts and Girl Guides, women in espionage and civilians, she has more recently published *World War I: A Short History, Gender and the Great War* (with Susan Grayzel), and *An English Governess in the Great War: The Secret Brussels Diary of Mary Thorp* (with Sophie de Schaepdrijver). She is presently completing a book, *Saving Europe: Food, War, and American Intervention*, on the history of US relief in Europe during and after the First World War.

Pierre Purseigle, FRHistS is Associate Professor of Modern European History at the University of Warwick. A co-founder and past president of the International Society for First World War Studies, he has published on the comparative social and urban history of the Great War. Among other publications, he is the author of *Mobilisation, Sacrifice, Citoyenneté. Angleterre-France. 1900-1918* (Les Belles Lettres, 2013). He is now completing a book on the comparative and transnational history of urban reconstruction in Belgium and France.

Carolina Garcia Sanz is Associated Professor in Modern and Contemporary History at the University of Seville. Her main field is International History. She is an expert on the history of World War I, Spanish section editor of the Free University of Berlin collaborative project, International Encyclopedia of the First World War 1914-1918 online, and coordinator of the Transnational Cultural Studies Network on Conflicts and Identities. She also joined the HERA Project "Beyond Stereotypes: Cultural Exchanges and the Romani Contribution to European Public Spaces". Recent publications include: (ed.) *Shaping Neutrality throughout the First World War* (2016); (co-author) "Neutralist crossroads: Spain and Argentina facing the Great War," *First World War Studies* (2017); "'Disciplinando al Gitano' en el siglo XX: Regulación y parapenalidad en España desde una perspectiva Europea," *Historia y Politica* 40 (2018) and "Presuntos culpables: Un estudio de casos sobre el estigma racial del 'gitano' en juzgados franquistas de Vagos y Maleantes," *Historia social* 93(2019).

Jan Schmidt is Associate Professor of Modern History of Japan in the Faculty of Arts at KU Leuven. He has worked on the impact of the First World War on Japan within the research project "A Trans-Disciplinary Study of the First World War" (2007-2015) at the Institute for Research in Humanities at Kyoto University. In 2020 the volume *The East Asian Dimension of the First World War. Global Entanglements and Japan, China and Korea, 1914-1919* co-edited with Katja Schmidtpott was published. Currently he is preparing a major exhibition in the Central Library of KU Leuven on *Japan's Book Donation to the University of Louvain: Japanese Cultural Identity and Modernity in the 1920s* and an accompanying publication with Leuven University Press. Further projects are focusing on future visions throughout modern East Asian History and on a political-cultural history of the Japanese Chambers of Commerce in transition from Empire to Post-war Japan.

Yves Segers is head of the Centre for Agrarian History (CAG) and associate professor at KU Leuven. He teaches rural history at the Interfaculty Centre for Agrarian History (ICAG) and economic history at the Faculty of Economy and Management in Brussels. His research focuses on the social and economic history of the nineteenth and twentieth century, mainly on agriculture, rural landscapes, the development of the food chain and gastronomy in Belgium.

Marjan Sterckx is Associate Professor of Art History at Ghent University, where she is Programme Chair and lectures on the histories of nineteenth-century art and of interior design. She heads the research group *The Inside Story: Art, Interior and Architecture 1750-1950* (ThIS). Sterckx is co-editor of Brepols publishers' series *XIX. Studies in Nineteenth-Century Art and Visual Culture* and the scholarly journal *Tijdschrift voor Interieurgeschiedenis en Design*. Her own research has so far focused on nineteenth- and early twentieth-century art, especially sculpture, in relation to gender and space.

María Inés Tato. PhD in History from the University of Buenos Aires (UBA). Researcher of the National Scientific and Technical Research Council – Argentina (CONICET) at the Institute of Argentine and American History "Dr Emilio Ravignani", UBA/CONICET. Founder and coordinator of the Group of Historical War Studies at that Institute. Professor at the Faculty of Social Sciences - UBA, and the Master in War History – Superior War College – Army Faculty – National Defense University (UNDEF). Her current research area is the social and cultural history of war in twentieth-century Argentina, particularly the impact of the First World War and the Falklands/Malvinas War. Among her books it is worth mentioning: *La trinchera austral. La sociedad argentina ante la Primera Guerra Mundial* (2017) and *La cuestión Malvinas en la Argentina del siglo XX. Una historia social y cultural* (coeditor, 2020).

Pieter Uyttenhove is full professor in Theory and History of Urbanism and was Head of the Department of Architecture and Urbanism at Ghent University. He studied urban planning at the Institut d'urbanisme de Paris (IUP, Paris XII) and engineer-architecture at Leuven University, and received his doctorate at the École des Hautes Études en Sciences Sociales (EHESS) in Paris. He is doing research and supervising doctoral research on nineteenth- and twentieth-century theory and history of urbanism and landscape. He was recently visiting professor as the P.P. Rubens Chair on History and Culture of the Low Countries at the University of California, Berkeley. His most recent books are *Beaudouin et Lods* (2012), *Stadland België* (2009), *Recollecting Landscapes* (2018, with co-editor B. Notteboom) and *Information and Space* (2013, with co-editor Wouter Van Acker).

Joris Vandendriessche is a Postdoctoral Fellow of the Research Foundation – Flanders (FWO) and member of the research group Cultural History since 1750 at KU Leuven. After studying cultural history and history of science at the universities of Leuven and Minnesota (USA), he conducted (post)doctoral research in Leuven with research stays in Utrecht, Manchester and Leiden. He is author of *Medical Societies and Scientific Culture in Nineteenth-Century Belgium* (Manchester University Press, 2018) and *Zorg en wetenschap. Een geschiedenis van de Leuvense academische ziekenhuizen* (Leuven University Press, 2019). His research focuses on the history of science and medicine in the nineteenth and twentieth centuries, with particular attention to the construction of scientific knowledge, scientific sociability and publishing, medicine and religion, and the history of care. He also a member of the Flemish Young Academy.

Luc Verpoest (Vosselare, 1945) Civil engineer-architect (KU Leuven, 1969). He obtained his doctorate in engineering (KU Leuven 1984) with a thesis on the history of architectural education in Belgium in the nineteenth century. He has taught nineteenth- and twentieth-century architectural history and history and theory of historic preservation at KU Leuven (Department of Art Science, Archeology and Musicology, Faculty of Arts, and Department of Architecture, Faculty of Engineering). He has done research and published on the Catholic neo-Gothic movement, history and theory of monument preservation and twentieth-century Modern Architecture. For research on the Gohtic Revival he collaborated with KADOC, KU Leuven. He is a founding member of DOCOMOMO International, DOCOMOMO Belgium and the *Fonds Henry van de Velde* (La Cambre, Brussels). He is emeritus Professor at the Raymond Lemaire International Centre for Conservation/RLICC (KU Leuven) and a member of the editorial board of *M&L. Monumenten, Landschappen en Archeologie*. In 2018 he curated, with Joke Buijs (City of Leuven), the exhibition *Herleven. Leuven na 2018* (Revival. Leuven after 1918).

Pieter Verstraete is an associate professor of history of education at the Research Unit for Culture, Education and Society (KU Leuven/Belgium). He is (vice-)president of the Belgian-Dutch Society for the History of Education. He has published widely on the history of education for people with disabilities and is now working on a book manuscript that will look into the history of silence from an educational point of view. He was awarded several prizes for both his research and his education like the KU Leuven Educational Council Prize and the Disability History Association best Book award and was visiting scholar at the University of British Columbia (Canada) and the University of Paris-Descartes (France). Since 2011 he has curated the annual Leuven DisABILITY filmfestival and became involved in several heritage projects related to the history of disability in Belgium.

Volker M. Welter is professor of history of architecture at the Department of the History of Art and Architecture, University of California at Santa Barbara. Among his books are *Biopolis: Patrick Geddes and the City of Life* (Cambridge, MA, 2002), *Ernst L. Freud, Architect: The Case of the Modern Bourgeois Home* (Oxford, 2012), *Walter S. White: Inventions in Mid-century Architecture* (Santa Barbara, 2015) and *Tremaine Houses: Private Patronage of Domestic Architecture in Mid-Century America, 1936-1977* (Los Angeles, 2019). His current research and book projects focus on revival styles in Southern California and on gay domesticity in Southern California.

Kaat Wils is Full Professor of Contemporary European Cultural History at the University of Leuven. Her research deals with the modern history of the humanities and the biomedical sciences, gender history and the history of education. In 2015, she co-authored a book on the memory of the First World War in interwar education in Belgium (Tine Hens, in collaboration with Saartje Vanden Borre and Kaat Wils, *Oorlog in tijden van vrede. De Eerste Wereldoorlog in de klas, 1914-1919*).

CPSIA information can be obtained
at www.ICGtesting.com
Printed in the USA
LVHW082152260321
682588LV00015B/450